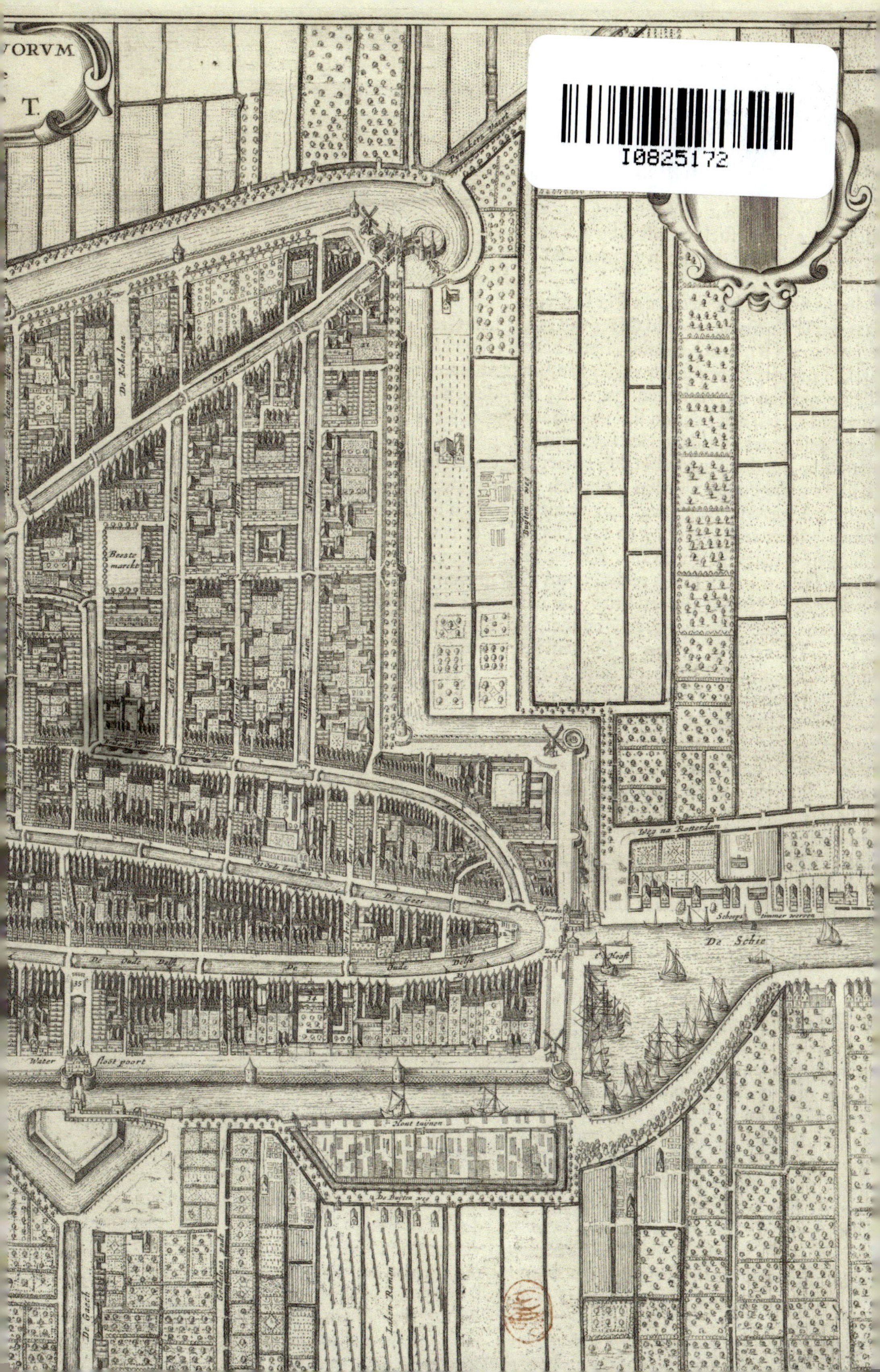

VORUM
T.
Beeste marckt
Weg na Rotterdam
De Schie
De Geer
De Oude Delft
Water sloot poort
Hout tuynen

Beyond Blue and White

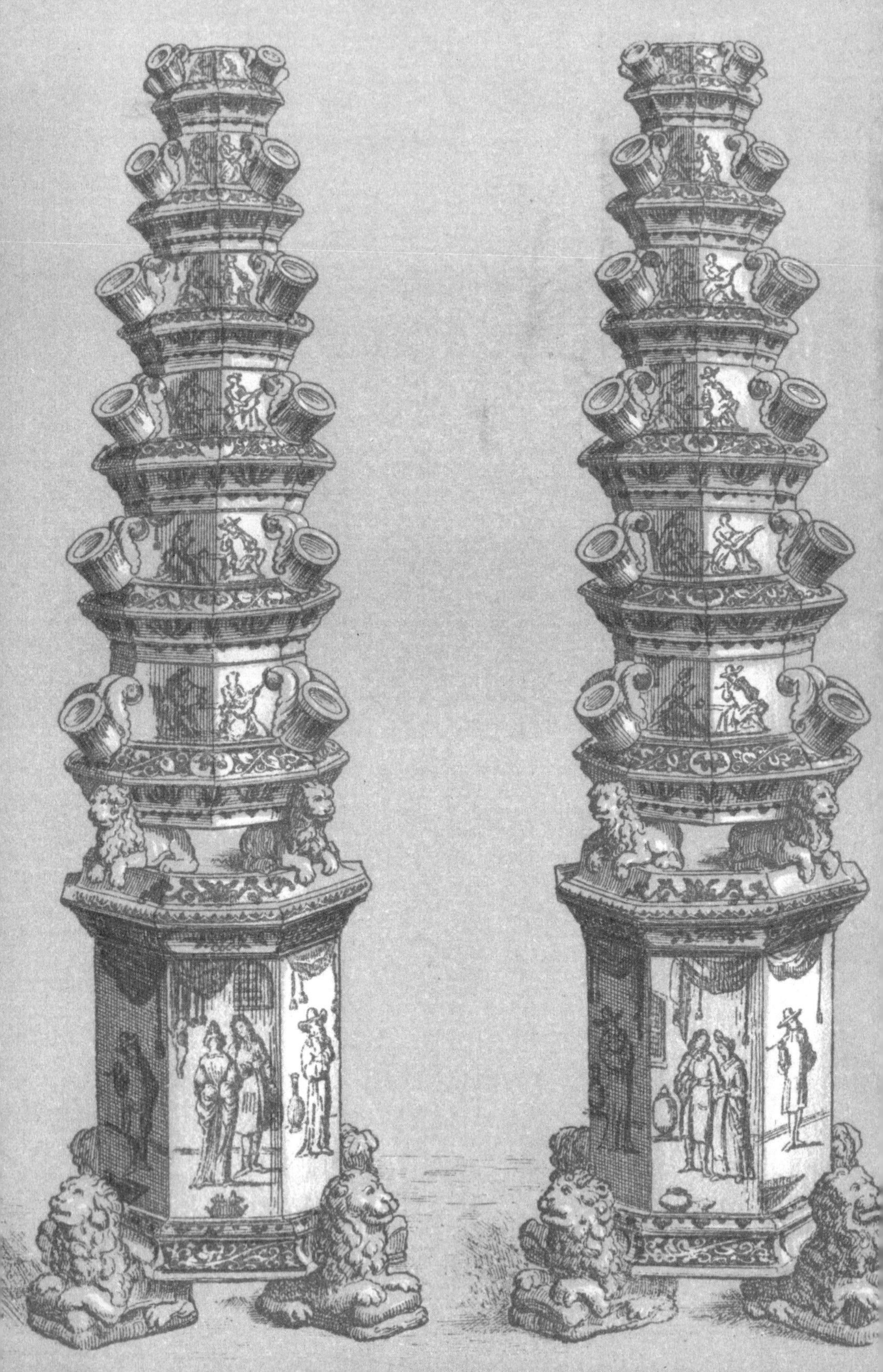

Beyond Blue and White

The Hidden History of Delftware and the Women Behind the Iconic Ceramic

Genevieve Wheeler Brown

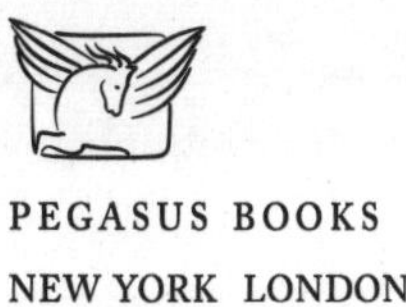

PEGASUS BOOKS
NEW YORK LONDON

BEYOND BLUE AND WHITE

Pegasus Books, Ltd.
148 West 37th Street, 13th Floor
New York, NY 10018

First Pegasus Books cloth edition August 2025

Interior design by Maria Fernandez

FRONT ENDPAPERS: A 1652 map offers a detailed bird's-eye view of Delft, illustrating meticulously rendered homes, parterre gardens, canals, and surrounding polders, together with the coats of arms of Holland and Delft. Rijksmuseum, Amsterdam.

BACK ENDPAPERS: *Historical Sketch Map of Kings Bridge, 1645–1783*, 1887, offers a layered view of early Bronx life, featuring the "Van der Donck's Planting Field," a nod to one of the region's earliest settlers, and "Van Cortlandt 1748." Lionel Pincus and Princess Firyal Map Division, The New York Public Library.

FRONTISPIECE: Charles Antoine Goutzwiller's 1878 lithograph of Dutch Delft blue and white flower vases, known over the centuries by various names, from *tulipières* to *bloemenpiramides* (flower pyramids), from Henry Havard's *Histoire de la Faïence de Delft*. Author's collection.

Library of Congress Cataloging-in-Publication Data is available.

ISBN: 978-1-63936-891-4

10 9 8 7 6 5 4 3 2 1

Printed in the United States of America
Distributed by Simon & Schuster
www.pegasusbooks.com

For

Amenaide and Catherine

&

Frances, in beauty

Contents

A blue-and-white *woordenlijst*

"It will be necessary as we proceed to make use of certain terms, the meaning of which should be defined with as much exactness as possible. It may be premised that considerable confusion exists in the nomenclature of the art. This has arisen partly from the want of precision in the language employed by writers, and partly from diversity of usage."

—Jennie J. Young, *The Ceramic Art: A Compendium of the History and Manufacture of Pottery and Porcelain*, 1878

Call it **Dutch Delftware**, **Delftware**, or just **Delft**, this tin-glazed earthenware was made in the town of Delft from approximately 1620 to 1850. Potters around the world had made tin-glazed earthenware for millennia, but the artisans of this small Dutch community in Holland took the medium to new heights and created multitudes of forms, from everyday dishes and bowls to ornamental garnitures and monumental "vases with spouts" unlike anything seen before. Delftware's glazed surfaces could be decorated with an infinite variety of styles and motifs inspired by everything from Chinese imported goods to European engravings and often—though not always—in shades of blue and white.

Dutch tiles (sometimes called Delft tiles) are frequently associated with Delftware but were actually produced in factories throughout Holland. These squares of tin-glazed earthenware were used by the Dutch for practical as well as decorative purposes—around fireplaces, along baseboards, covering sections of walls—in areas prone to smoke, dirt, and dampness. Dutch tiles were also decorated with a myriad of motifs, from blooming roses or instructive religious scenes to children at play.

As Europeans and Americans began to fall under the spell of collecting blue-and-white, from masses of dishes, bowls, and vases to tiles—a Chinamania—in the nineteenth century, a new term was permeating the English lexicon: **ceramics**. First used by erudite collectors and enthusiasts beginning around 1850, the word is an adaptation of the French *céramique* and derived from the Greek *keramos* (pottery). Ceramics refer to objects made of clay that have been permanently hardened by heat. Generally grouped by their material composition and firing temperature, most ceramics fall into three basic types: porcelain, stoneware, and earthenware.

Earthenware, formed from natural clay in warm shades from sandy buff to terracotta red, is the oldest form of ceramics. Dating to at least the tenth millennium B.C.E. in Japan, Jomon potters—mostly women—are believed to have crafted some of the first vessels. Fired at relatively low temperatures (800–1100°C), it stays porous unless glazed, and its softer, less dense structure often requires thicker forms for stability. While more prone to chipping than other ceramics, its accessibility and versatility have made it a staple in cultures worldwide for thousands of years.

Tough and dense, **stoneware** is prized for its hardness, as its name suggests. Its clay varies in tones from red and brown to slate gray and black, depending on mineral content. Fired at higher temperatures (1100–1300°C), it becomes vitrified, forming a smooth, nonporous body that can hold liquids without the need for glazing. Strong and adaptable, stoneware became a preferred material for everything from tableware to durable storage vessels.

Porcelain stands apart with its luminous white clay and mysterious balance of delicacy and strength. Fired at the highest temperatures (1200–1450°C), it develops a smooth, nonporous, translucent quality that is both refined and hard, producing a bell-like resonance when tapped. Made of *kaolin*, a fine white clay, and *petunse*, a feldspathic rock, porcelain was perfected in sixth-century China. For centuries, its production remained a closely guarded secret, fueling Europe's obsession and relentless attempts to replicate this prized ceramic.

Yet, despite the clear distinctions between ceramic types, the potters of Delft pushed the boundaries of tradition, developing earthenware so exquisitely delicate and refined that it was often mistaken for porcelain—and earning the seventeenth-century moniker ***Delft porcelyne***.

Between 1602–1682, at least 3.2 million pieces of Chinese and Japanese porcelain were imported by the **Dutch East India Company** (Vereenigde Oostindische Compagnie). By 1730–1789 that number had exploded to 42 million. When its ships returned from East Asia to the cities of the Dutch Republic, their cargo was packed with wooden crates marked with the company's distinctive interlocking initials: **VOC**. These containers carried riches from the East including spices, silk, exotic plants, and animals, as well as blue-and-white porcelain for sale throughout the world. Established in 1602, the VOC was the uncontested leader in international trade in the seventeenth century, making many Dutch very, very wealthy.

Homes of burghers, prosperous Dutch citizens in the seventeenth and eighteenth centuries, prominently featured ***kasten***, tall and broad cabinets with deeply molded cornices. Often made of rich exotic woods, kasten served as storage for valuable household items such as silverware and linens. But a *kast* was also a vehicle for the proud display of prized objects, denoting power, wealth, and influence. Chinese porcelain and sparkling Delftware were prominently placed across the top of the kast as well as symmetrically arranged on mantels and above doorways.

But only the truly wealthiest and most powerful owned the grandest form of Delftware, a pyramidal flower vase often called today a ***tulipière*** or tulip vase. These towering multilevel vases, some almost five feet in height, were characterized by their profusion of spouts for individual flowers. The name was born in the nineteenth century during the resurgent interest in Tulipmania, though the objects themselves were developed in the late seventeenth century, well after the Dutch vogue for tulips in the 1630s had passed. These vases were, in fact, not only for tulips but a breadth of flowering botanical beauties, including jonquils, hyacinth, narcissi, peonies, roses, and irises.

No Delftware, from the grandest flower vase to the smallest butter dish, could be produced without the sanction of the **Guild of St. Luke**. Regulating the commerce and production of artists and artisans in Delft, it oversaw its members—from painters and art dealers to glassmakers and Delftware potters. The Guild's fixed and numerous rules and regulations were attentively followed by its members, including compulsory Master's tests and annual dues. Potters working in Delft who were nonmembers would be fined. Any Delftware produced by nonmembers of the Guild of St. Luke could be seized and destroyed.

Delftware potters and painters, ***plateelschilders***, were required to pass the rigorous master tests of the Guild of St. Luke in order to produce their works of art. To prepare for this role they apprenticed for six years honing their craft. The potters of Delft produced millions of pieces of Delftware from their wheels and benches, and each year sold not just in the Dutch market but around the globe, from Indonesia to Massachusetts, fueling the world's insatiable appetite for blue-and-white.

From the Dutch *winkel* (shop) and *houster* (keeper), the ***winkelhouder*** was an owner-manager of a Delftware pottery, overseeing its global business. Each pottery was required to have a single owner-manager, who had to be either a master craftsman or a winkelhouder. The winkelhouder, like the Delftware potter, was required to join the Guild of St. Luke and followed its lengthy list of strict laws. But there was no rule of the venerable Guild of St. Luke that said the winkelhouder couldn't be a woman.

Introduction

The pottery hums with activity. Braying horses strain their harnesses as they pull the gears of the mill, mixing heavy quantities of clay. Potters gently shape bowls while rhythmically kicking pottery wheels and the crackling fire spits and roars as plates and bowls continue their firing in the kiln. Painters sit side by side at long tables quickly applying cobalt decorations as assistants with baskets bring a constant stream of even more plates and chargers. It is 1769 in Delft, the heart of Holland's flourishing worldwide trade of Dutch Delftware—the eponymous blue-and-white tin-glazed ceramic that has entranced collectors since the 1600s.

In the center of this pottery is its owner, a woman.

Wearing a long wool petticoat, apron, and linen hood, she orchestrates the movements of her staff as they quietly attend to their numerous tasks, from dipping pieces in vats of thick white glaze to gently placing prepared plates and bowls on shelves for drying. Out of the corner of her eye, she notices two young boys in her workshop lingering and chatting when they should be shuttling bunches of small kindling to the awaiting kiln. She stops briefly to admire her newly finished works, recently cooled from the kiln, which sit on the broad open wood shelves lining the pottery walls. She lifts one piece of Delftware in particular to inspect—it was a specially commissioned work made for a patron under her direction. It is indeed beautiful and, with its final glazing complete with no cracks, meets with her approval and is ready for delivery.

Now, centuries later, the piece rests in an urban aerie high above the streets of Manhattan. Locked in bronze cases behind thick glass panels, it lies on faded ivory velvet padding within a cache of blue-and-white Dutch Delftware. With its gently curved handle, protruding spouts, and a body adorned with cobalt flowers framing stylized rocaille panels of river landscapes, this uniquely shaped Delftware is nestled among a myriad of chargers, figurines, bowls, and vases. The afternoon light dances across its shimmering glaze. Unaffected by time, its cobalt painting remains as vibrant as the day it emerged from the kiln over 250 years ago.

Dutch Delftware was born in the 1600s, an age of piracy, when Dutch fleets audaciously commandeered galleons returning from the East laden with spices, silks, and porcelain. By the 1690s, Delftware had risen to international fame, becoming a symbol of royal favor in European courts. Nearly two centuries later, it captivated collectors once again as Gilded Age Americans, swept up in the craze of Chinamania and the enthusiasm of Holland Mania, voraciously sought blue-and-white ceramics as prized trophies.

But fashions shifted again, and for the last fifty years, the once-coveted Delftware in these cases has sat untouched. Now, the blue-and-white waits patiently, a silent testament to its enduring allure and the cycles of human desire.

Beyond Blue and White tells the story of a particular collection of Dutch Delftware. Its rediscovery in New York City opens the door to a ceramic journey from potter's wheels in the workshops of seventeenth-century Delft to museum shelves.

But it also tells the story of another rediscovery—that of the singular women behind this collection of blue-and-white who were as impactful, dynamic, and colorful as the Delftware itself.

Glimpses of their lives were gleaned from many separate spheres across a myriad of contexts and sources. While some were hidden in plain sight in reference books on ceramics, others were found deep in seldom-accessed files of museums, archives, and libraries. From combing overflowing closets of private archives in New York to sifting through the digital files of the modernist

Stadsarchief Delft (Delft City Archives), four years of research—digging through town records, newspaper articles, early travel writing, seventeenth-century guild ledgers, notarial records, and eighteenth-century court proceedings—uncovered its own treasure: the stories of these women's lives. I had set out to learn about this collection but along the way I found not a few, but many women who were also a part of this story.

Some of these women are well-known, having lived their lives in the public eye since birth, including Queen Mary II, who changed the course of British history and many say usurped her father's crown to become a reigning queen of England, or Alice Claypoole Vanderbilt, otherwise known as Mrs. Cornelius Vanderbilt II, a fearless self-made leader of New York society who raised the art of opulent living to new zeniths during America's Gilded Age. In revisiting their stories through the lens of Delftware, I hope they will be viewed with a fresh perspective, revealing new angles, nuances, and truths.

Others, although prominent in their time, are now largely forgotten, like Alice Morse Earle, the American historian who wrote sixteen bestselling books, fueling popular interest in collecting and early American history, or Elizabeth Colt, the indefatigable industrialist who not only maintained control of the Colt's Patent Arms Manufacturing Company through the Civil War and beyond but, as an art collector, was the first woman to have a museum wing named in her honor. By reintroducing these women and situating them within previously unexplored contexts—alongside the equally dynamic women they lived, worked, and collaborated with—I hope to illuminate the breadth of their influence, both individually and collectively, in shaping industries, culture, and historical narratives.

But most numerous were the women whose lives have been obscured in the shadow of blue-and-white's mythos. These are the countless daughters, sisters, mothers, wives, and widows from the seventeenth and eighteenth centuries who served as everything from supporting household members to unnamed partners in business with their spouses in Delftware potteries. Some of them defy our notions of who an entrepreneur was in the seventeenth and eighteenth centuries—many were Delftware pottery owners themselves. Their stories are perhaps the most inspiring of all.

Following the brick-paved streets along the canals of Delft, the gravel garden paths of Hampton Court Palace and the Het Loo Palace, the Dutch royal summer residence in Apeldoorn, and the yellow pine floorboards of the oldest surviving building in the upper Bronx, I retraced their footsteps, hoping to understand their inspirations and motivations. *Beyond Blue and White* tells the forgotten story of these women's ambitions.

There is a myth that follows women and art, whether in painting, sculpture, furniture, glass, or ceramics.

The long-held tale goes that women were not able to produce works of art for any number of reasons, because they were not strong enough, weren't a member of an artist's guild, lacked the training, the financial resources, business acumen, or simply the wherewithal. Museum labels, auction catalogues, and art histories seem to support this vision, rarely presenting the broader picture beyond the name of what may be the artist, head of workshop, or name of a maker or firm. The mythos seeps into the historic perception of artistic patronage, collecting, and the histories of museums themselves, casting a shadow over women's participation in the arts as the exceptions or oddities, instead of part of the fabric.

But with each piece of Dutch Delftware and every document I held, more and more women emerged from history. I began to imagine their presence—along the canals of seventeenth-century Delft, in the bustling shops of eighteenth-century London, within the opulent salons of the nineteenth century, and later in the twentieth-century museum galleries of New York. Connecting the dots across four centuries revealed a richer, more complete picture of inspiring female contributions.

These women appeared across the full spectrum of artistic life—acknowledged and integral participants—whether as artists, patrons, dealers, collectors, historians, pioneering preservationists, museum founders, or shop-girls selling blue-and-white pottery in the bustling salesrooms of seventeenth-century Delft.

The words Dutch Delftware may evoke the image of a monumental seventeenth-century blue-and-white pyramidal vase, or *tulipière*, with its numerous spouts brimming with spring flowers. These magnificent sculptures, icons of Dutch culture, reflect the artistic and technical mastery of an era when the Netherlands ascended to global prominence in commerce, art, philosophy, and science.

Over time, the Dutch Delftware aesthetic seeped into the international consciousness, influencing design across interiors, fashion, and beyond—a legacy that endures to this day. It has been widely imitated but rarely rivaled, and the term itself became so ubiquitous that it is often mistakenly used to describe all blue-and-white pottery, regardless of its origin.

Yet, as we admire the intricate spouts and masterful painting of Delftware, perhaps we should look beyond the surface and ask: Who shaped its creation, its very existence, and its enduring appeal?

Who was this woman?

"Every cup, every jar in our china ingatherings, has the charm of fantasy, visions of past life and beauty, though only imagined. I like to think that the china I love has been warmly loved before—has been made a cherished companion, been tenderly handled ere I took it to be my companion and to care for it. It is much the same friendly affection that I feel for an old well-read, halfworn book; the unknown hands through which it has passed, the unseen eyes that have gazed on it, have endeared it to me.

"This imagined charm exists in china if it be old, though we know not a word of its past, save that it has a past and is not fresh from the potter's wheel and the kiln. The very haze of uncertainty is favorable to the fancies of a dreamer; I summon past owners from that shadowy hiding-place; weave romances out of that cloud . . ."

—Alice Morse Earle,
China Collecting in America,
New York, 1892

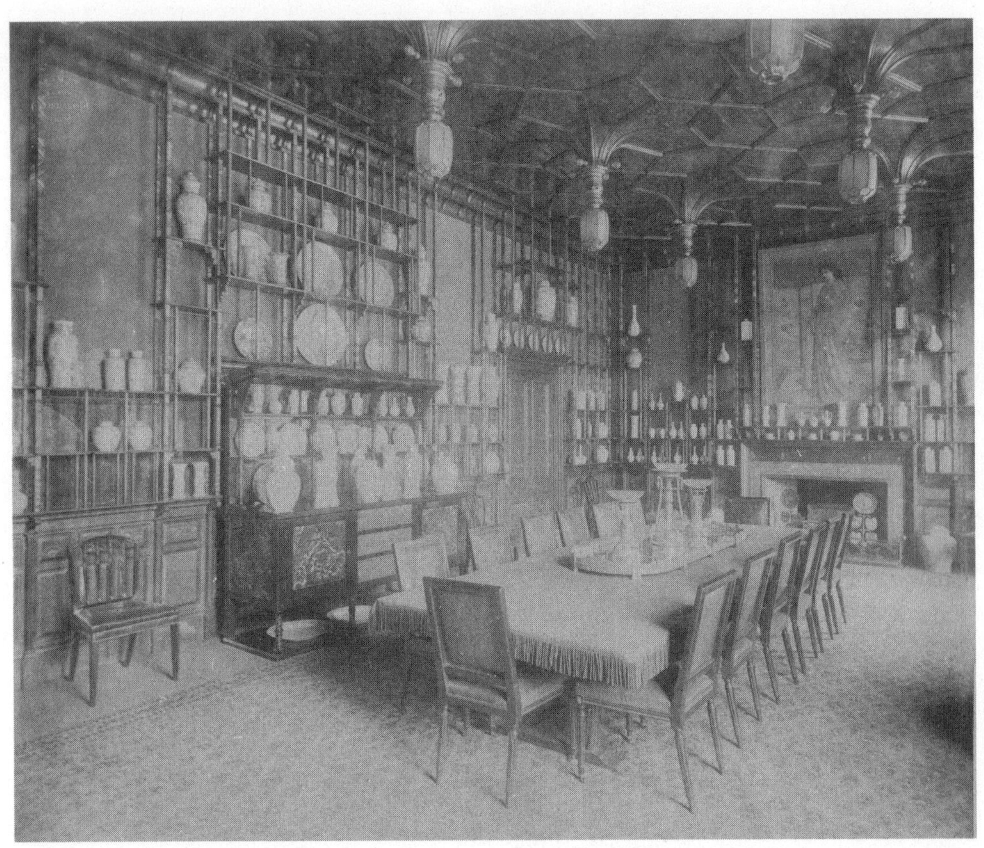

ABOVE: An 1892 view of the legendary *Peacock Room* at 49 Princes Gate, London, showcasing its opulent fusion of art and porcelain, with shelves of blue-and-white ceramics and Whistler's *La Princesse du Pays de Porcelaine* (1863–64) above the fireplace. Victoria and Albert Museum, London. OPPOSITE: George Hayward's 1856 lithograph, *New York & City Banks and the McEvers Mansion, Wall Street in 1800*, features the neo-classical facade of the McEvers residence, built ca. 1750. The Miriam and Ira D. Wallach Division of Art, Prints and Photographs: Picture Collection, The New York Public Library.

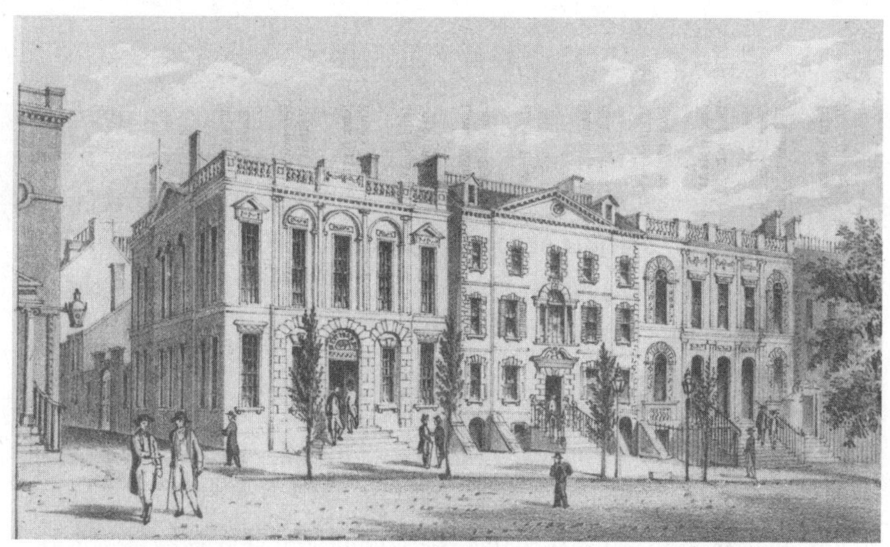

1

Delven

delven (del-ven), verb (trans., intr., st., sw.)
1. To dig.
2. To stop or store underground; to bury.
3. Bringing up by digging; dig up; excavate.
4. Dig through; digging search.
5. To separate (from) by digging; to hide.

—Woordenboek der Nederlandsche Taal
(*WNT, Dictionary of the Dutch Language*), 1500–1976

There was no need to turn on the switch. Brilliant sunlight streamed through the multipaned windows, flooding the white-painted gallery and illuminating the twelve bronze-mounted glass display cases. The vitrines stood elegantly, with narrow frames and slender, tapering legs. The soft brown hue of the metal bore a depth of patina, a testament to their age—over a century old.

Behind the glass panels of each cabinet, seemingly floating on translucent shelves, were more than seventy-five pieces of Dutch Delftware in blues and whites of every hue, saturation, and brightness. Delicately painted on the white tin-glazed bodies were the bold shades of cobalt, indigo, and cerulean, magnetic tones of ultramarine, sapphire, turquoise, and the powdery tints of soft violet and grayish blue. My eyes darted from piece to piece, excited by the proliferation of shapes and colors that elicited a visceral response. A single piece of Dutch Delftware can be entrancing, but blue-and-white in profusion like this was exhilarating, saturating the space with visual complexity. It was uncontrollable. I craved more.

I'm an art advisor, but a type that is less commonly found in New York.

While most art advisors are consumed with canvases, works on paper, photographs, sculptures, or now the digital arts of NFTs, I am absorbed with the essentially tangible—the decorative arts. Whether garnitures of delicate porcelain, canteens of lustrous silver, suites of furniture, or finely woven textiles, decorative arts are defined by their functionality, works that were created for a purpose not solely as artistic achievement. Although populated with many an opulent *objet de vertu*, it is a field equally inhabited by more simple, everyday objects—a chair, a table, a cup, a bowl.

And while fine art, such as paintings, was traditionally found in the homes of the smallest portion of society, often only the wealthiest, the decorative arts, on the other hand, have long inhabited even the most modest households. By nature of the broad availability of decorative arts, the variety of narratives that can be told, extending across the socioeconomic spectrum, provide a wide exploration of social, political, and cultural contexts of the past. Decorative arts are not only works of art, but history you can hold in your hands.

Or at least try to get *my* hands on, as was often the case when I was growing up in Washington, D.C. in the 1970s and '80s. Wandering through the museum doorways of the Smithsonian in a time with few entry lines and no security checks, I could freely meander and experience works on my own, including one in particular that would draw me to return again and again—*Harmony in Blue and Gold: The Peacock Room*, located at the Freer Gallery of Art. More than a decorative interior originally made for a home in London, this former dining room is an intoxicating immersive masterpiece by James McNeill Whistler created in 1876 and 1877. Blurring the lines between fine and decorative arts, it was a fusion of architecture, ceramics, and painting. Its walls of seventeenth-century Dutch gilt leather, shutters, and even the ceiling had been covered with shades of Prussian blue, green, and gold, featuring panels depicting peacocks with wings lifted, feathers poised.

As a girl standing before its staggered lattice of carved giltwood shelving, I imagined reaching out to rearrange the blue and white Chinese vases interspersed with Syrian pottery and Japanese and Korean porcelain, juxtaposing colors, textures, and forms to create patterns in infinite variations in search of the perfect balanced composition.

There was no shortage of great collections to explore in Washington at the time, much of which was defined by dynamic women, including the not-so-distant legacies of Marjorie Acker Phillips, cofounder of The Phillips Collection, Marjorie Merriweather Post, founder of the Hillwood Estate, Museum & Gardens, and Mildred Barnes Bliss, cofounder of Dumbarton Oaks. The women of my family were also entwined in this vibrant confluence of female collectors and philanthropists. Where my great-aunt, cofounder of the Washington Antiques Show in 1955, was drawn to porcelain, both Chinese export and eighteenth-century Meissen, my grandmother was a modernist, commissioning works by artists including the American Abstract Expressionist Franz Kline. In the summers she concocted plans with Rebekah "Betty" Harkness, founder of the Harkness Ballet, including an exhibition of the works of the young painter Sam Francis and the sculptor George Sugarman in 1959 in a former fire station by the water's edge in Watch Hill, Rhode Island.

I was a witness as a child to her purchasing and research, following her throughout the aisles of "antique shows" to meet with dealers, brought to galleries and auctions, and traveling to see collections, museums, or artists' studios. But there were parameters in my early art education to be followed.

Playing with the towering Victorian-style doll house in my third-floor bedroom of our N Street townhouse was discouraged as, according to my grandmother, playing with miniatures "makes a girl think small."

Decorative arts brought me to my work as an adult in the auction rooms of London and New York where the opportunity to hold endless numbers of objects, including everything from Fabergé eggs to violins by Antonio Stradivari, was not only fulfilled but a vital part of the job. At Christie's the estimation of authenticity or value was not based solely on the visual; it was also sensorial. To understand a work of decorative art is to feel its weight, gauge the temperature of the material against skin, discern the texture of its surfaces, and manipulate its parts in every direction to reveal the nuances of its construction.

After more than a decade at Christie's, I opened my own office, starting in a gallery space on Madison Avenue. I worked with collectors, their families, and attorneys, discreetly facilitating the sale or appraisal of single objects or entire estates. One inquiry, however, stood out.

A woman contacted me with an unusual request: would I come and review a collection of Dutch Delftware? Not just a few pieces, but an entire room's worth. Intrigued, I agreed to meet Sue on a November afternoon in the ceramic galleries of the Metropolitan Museum of Art to discuss her proposal.

Side by side before the cases on the quiet balcony at the top of the Great Hall steps, we considered the Chinese, Japanese, and Dutch vases, teapots, and dishes on display, mounted on panels and staggered on cream linen-covered risers. A dish with flowers and birds painted with cobalt-blue pigment was juxtaposed next to its Chinese precedent. A stylistic comparison but also a game. Casting a cursory glance through the heavy glass, it might be difficult to determine which was the porcelain thrown by potters in the hills of Jingdezhen and which was the earthenware made by the canals in the small town of Delft.

Sue was tall and elegant, in her mid-eighties, with a presence that hinted at her earlier career as a prominent New York interior designer, though now she appeared more delicate. As chair of the art committee for a private women's organization founded during New York's Gilded Age, Sue sought assistance with a unique problem: a large collection of Dutch Delftware stored at the organization's headquarters. According to her, it hadn't been addressed—or even touched—in many years.

I had many questions. Where had this Delftware come from? Why was it there? Sue could provide little insight beyond a copy of an old insurance appraisal and a curious anecdote: years ago, members of the United Nations had reportedly visited the collection. Beyond that, its story remained forgotten.

She explained the Delftware was located in a secure room, tucked away in the upper floors of the headquarters, a townhouse just blocks away on Manhattan's Upper East Side. I was instructed to call the office to set up a time for keys to be located and the cabinet locks to be opened. I said I would consider it. Sue was determined in a persistent way that made it impossible to say no. But with so many unanswered questions about this Dutch Delftware, I was curious, too.

I arrived on a quiet side street, a secluded pocket in a city otherwise filled with the sounds of bus brakes and car horns punctuating the constant rumble of speeding traffic. Nestled in the shade of modern apartment towers stood what appeared to be an eighteenth-century Georgian mansion. Its three-story red brick facade was embellished with eleven white-painted double-hung windows, each framed by keyed brick surrounds and some boasting as many as sixteen-over-sixteen windowpanes. Flanking the broad front door was not only a pair of brick gate posts with monumental carved stone finials of pineapples but black tole lanterns, each with their lamps gently flickering. If not for the tightly parked cars at the curb and groups of students lingering near the front steps, it wouldn't have been hard to imagine the approach of a horse-drawn carriage rather than a yellow New York taxi.

This stately townhouse, however, is an architectural illusion. Built in the early twentieth century, it is an idealized recreation of a distinguished home that once graced Wall Street in the 1750s. Its design evokes an era when the city—founded by ambitious Dutch traders around 1624 and claimed by the British in 1664—was a patchwork of churchyards, a synagogue, a prominent fort, bustling markets, neatly fenced gardens, windmills, tree-lined paved streets, and a variety of brick and stone homes. More than just a building, it stands as a meticulously crafted tribute to a vanished chapter of New York's architectural history—its last traces occasionally unearthed as chipped bricks, fragments of Dutch tiles, or nails embedded in the layers beneath modern steel and concrete skyscrapers.

When the Dutch first arrived on the island of Manhattan, the land beneath this house was the hunting grounds of the Lenape. Pigeons, spotted turtles, wild turkeys, and eastern gray squirrels thrived here, while summers brought gatherings of sweet honeysuckle, wild grapes, and scarlet hawthorn berries.

By the eighteenth century, the area became known as Jones Wood, a remnant of untamed wilderness that persisted well into the nineteenth century. At one point, it was considered as a potential site for a public park for New Yorkers. However, the proposal was ultimately abandoned in favor of a centrally located parcel of land—now known as Central Park—deemed more accessible than the eastern location of Jones Wood.

Over time, the old growth forests of hickory, chestnut, tulip poplar, and elm were felled, rock outcroppings were removed, and development rapidly followed. The relentless spread of new construction reshaped the island, eventually creating the street, a new urban landscape, where I now stood.

I was buzzed in and found myself alone in the silent wood-paneled foyer with black-and-white marble-tiled floor. But I knew where to go. I had been given my directions.

I passed the century-old Otis elevator with its brass accordion gate to take the staircase. With broad proportions and treads of a certain shallow height, modeled after an eighteenth-century design that would have allowed a well-dressed female guest in a gown with even the widest panniers to elegantly ascend unobstructed with fluidity and grace. With intermediate landings between the floors, it invited the opportunity to pause and consider the works of art arranged on the walls, not so unlike the twentieth-century nautilus-shaped center of the Guggenheim Museum just a few blocks away.

But I didn't slow. Reaching the top, I arrived at a simple area with bare walls and clean wood baseboards. The uppermost floor of this townhouse consisted of rooms with more perfunctory purposes: an archive, an office, an oak-paneled boardroom. Through a separate doorway across the landing, a room of Dutch Delftware awaited.

Once I had stepped into the long white-painted gallery with its series of bronze display cases lining the walls, I stood entranced before what seemed to be countless pieces of Dutch Delftware. Sunlight reflected off the surfaces decorated with the nuances of vibrant cobalt on milky white. A spell had been cast, I was drawn in. Shades of blue and white invited me to pause and linger, to let my eyes wander as its hues covered faces of chargers, wrapped bodies of bowls, and enveloped lidded vases from their bases to their finial tips.

Of all the myriad color combinations, why does blue-and-white elicit such enduring fascination? Why do we love it so?

According to the nineteenth-century polymath Johann Wolfgang von Goethe, regarding the color blue, we have little choice. Blue exerts an inherent hold on us; few can resist its pull. "We love to contemplate blue, not because it advances to us, but because it draws us after it," he wrote in his *Zur Farbenlehre* (*Theory of Colors*, 1810), the first systematic study of color's physiological effects. Goethe explored how colors influence our moods and thoughts. Unlike Sir Isaac Newton, who viewed color through a scientific lens in the 1660s, Goethe argued that color was a deeply subjective experience, unique to each viewer.

Blue embodies peace and calm, even melancholy. Historically, it has also been described as magical, heavenly, and ethereal, its allure captivating humanity for millennia.

In ancient Egypt, blue symbolized life-giving power, reflecting the fertile Nile River. Amulets carved from expensive lapis lazuli—imported from more

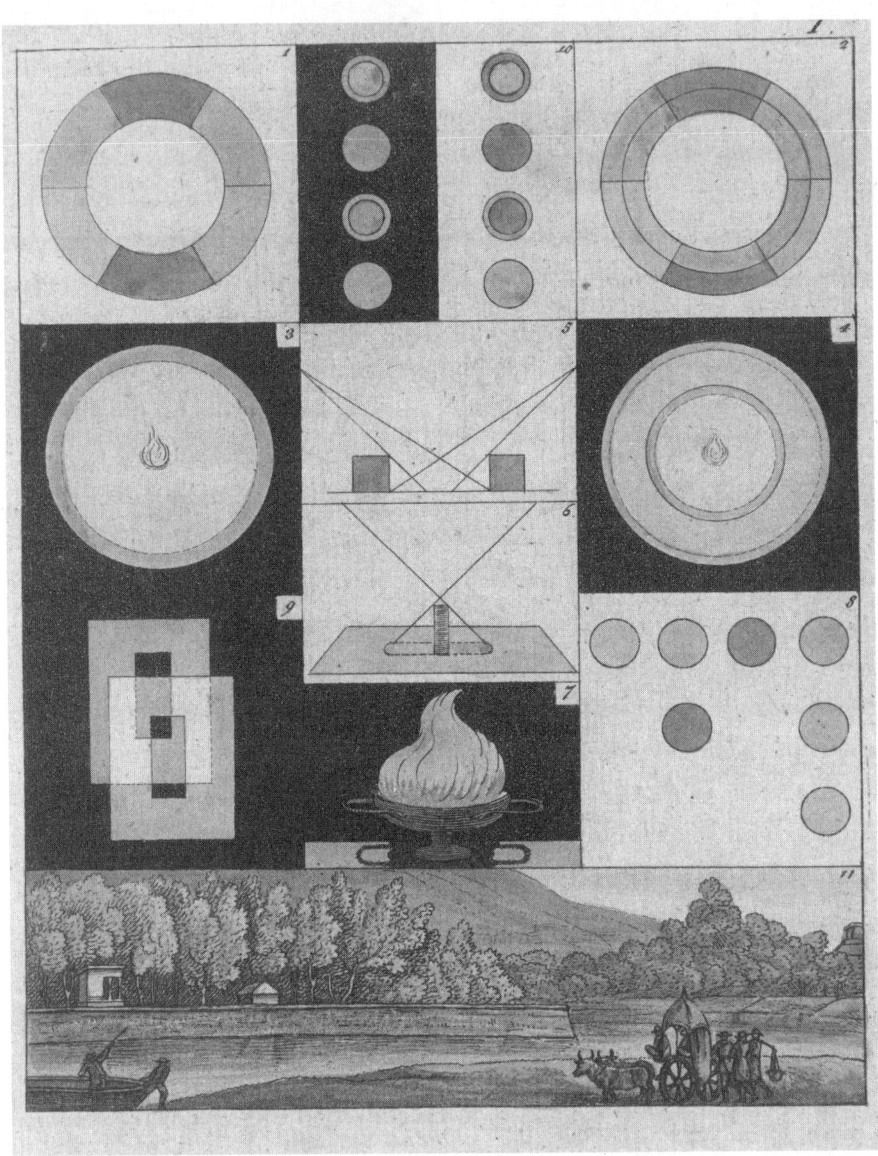

A plate from *Zur Farbenlehre* (*Theory of Colors*) by Johann Wolfgang von Goethe, 1810, featuring a color wheel alongside diagrams illustrating theories of distorted color perception. British Library Board.

than two thousand miles away in present-day Afghanistan—were placed in tombs to bestow life upon the deceased. This vibrant stone, often the most valuable material in the Egyptian economy, carried deep religious and symbolic significance. Gods, depicted with blue locks of hair, were believed to have tresses made from lapis lazuli itself.

During the Medieval and Renaissance periods, European artists revered one blue above all: ultramarine, derived from finely ground lapis lazuli. This vivid blue, as bright as an ultraviolet sky, was described in the late 1300s by the artist Cennino Cennini in his treatise *Il libro dell'Arte* (*The Book of the Art*) as "a colour noble, beautiful, and perfect beyond all other colours." For masters like Giotto, Titian, Michelangelo, and Leonardo da Vinci, ultramarine was reserved for sacred subjects, from the celestial heavens to the Virgin Mary's robes. Johannes Vermeer used it sparingly, choosing ultramarine to adorn the headdress of his *Girl with a Pearl Earring* (1665).

For pottery, however, cobalt was the preferred blue for centuries. This metallic chemical element, atomic number 27 on the periodic table, held its own mystique. The word cobalt derives from the German *kobold*, meaning "goblin" or "evil spirit." Miners in medieval Germany often found cobalt intermingled with silver ores, believing it harmed valuable silver deposits—and possibly their health.

Cobalt's appeal for ceramics lay in its vibrancy and ability to withstand the intense heat of a kiln. But its beauty came at a cost. In powdered form, cobalt is indeed toxic. Mill workers inhaled its hazardous dust during grinding, and ceramic painters risked poisoning themselves by licking brushes to achieve fine points. Prolonged exposure caused symptoms ranging from vision and hearing loss to heart ailments. Like alchemy, the dangerous cobalt transformed when fired in a kiln, shifting from a flat, dull gray paint to a saturated, intoxicating blue. The purer the cobalt, the more radiant that tone of blue.

White, too, captivates with its glowing energy. The Old English word *hwit* means "bright" or "shining." Romans differentiated between two types of white: *albus*, a plain matte white, and *candidus*, a luminous white associated with light. The Latin *candere* (to shine) gave rise to words like candle and

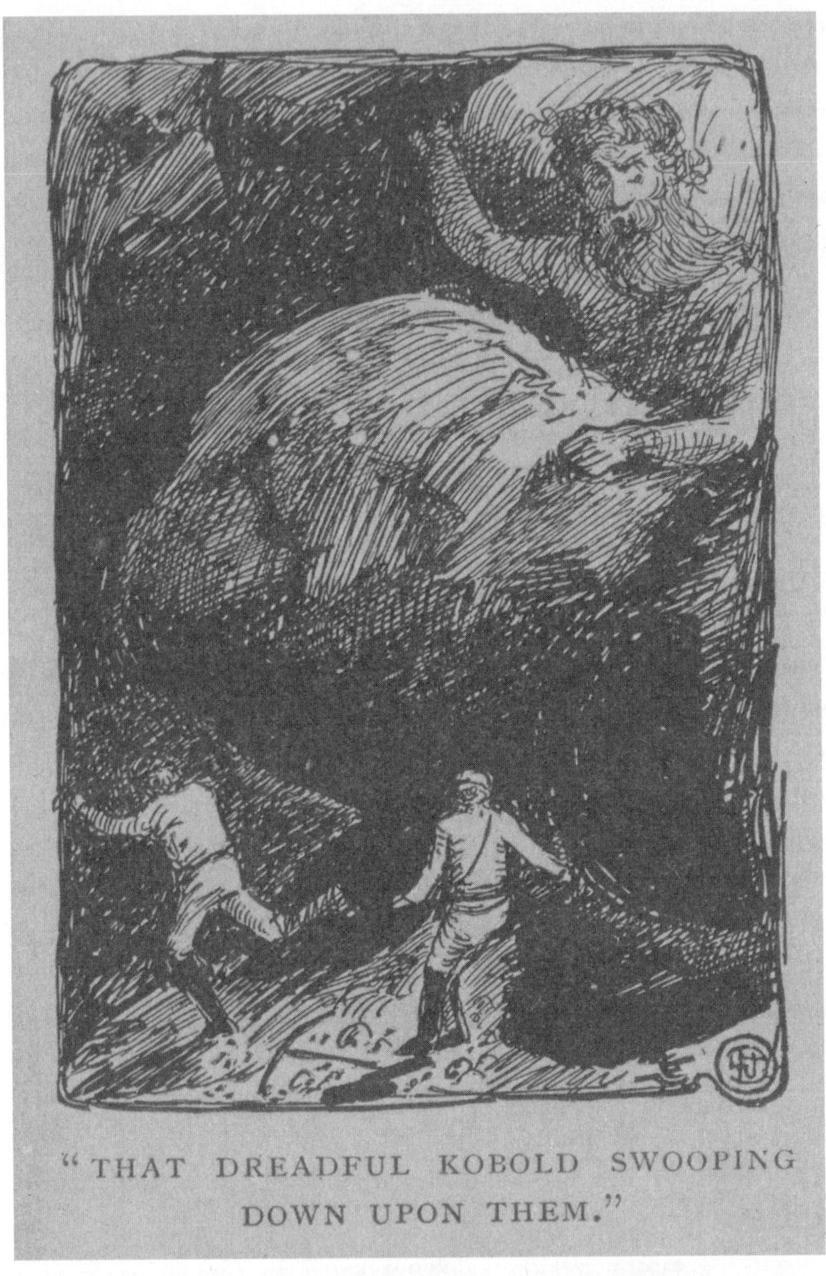

An 1887 illustration from chemist and author Lucy Rider Meyer's *Real Fairy Folks, or Fairy Land of Chemistry* introducing young readers to cobalt and other atomic wonders. Courtesy of the Science History Institute.

candid. Though white was not part of his visual spectrum, Sir Isaac Newton noted in 1672 that "whiteness is the usual color of light."

For artists, white has long been the perfect ground—a foundation with the power to amplify other colors. Leonardo da Vinci, in his *Trattato della Pittura* (*Treatise on Painting*), noted, "For those colours which you mean should appear beautiful, prepare a ground of pure white."

Potters, too, sought pristine white surfaces as their canvas, though the methods for achieving them varied across traditions. In China and Japan, artisans working in porcelain had the advantage of naturally white clay, composed of native kaolin and petunse, which provided a luminous surface for their intricate blue designs.

Elsewhere, from Mexico to Persia, ceramicists without access to these rare white clays had to innovate to replicate porcelain's delicate appearance. To achieve a similar effect, they turned to tin oxide, developing an opaque white glaze that concealed the natural hues of earthenware, which ranged from deep red to pale buff.

Tin, sourced across Europe and Asia, was burned to create tin ash, then blended with mastic—a mixture of sand, salt, and soda—and other materials. When fired, this combination produced a smooth, glossy white surface, ideal for the rich cobalt-blue decorations that transformed simple earthenware into objects of striking beauty.

Together, blue and white create a pairing of unparalleled vibrancy. Each color is individually attractive, but together their tones harmonize—the depth of blue magnified by the contrasting lightness of white. Whether in nature, with a clear sky dotted by cumulus clouds, or crafted by human hands in a potter's studio using cobalt and tin extracted from beneath the earth's surface, this duo's power is undeniably mesmerizing.

Why are we so drawn to blue-and-white? Does its magnetism stem from the materials' exotic origins, the mystique of distant lands, or something deeper—an optic or emotional resonance hardwired in our brains?

The reason may be elusive, but the combination of blue and white remains timelessly and universally appealing. It is a pairing with the power to launch ships, shape industries, and inspire artists across generations. Dutch Delftware exemplifies this chromatic union, its luminous blue and white surfaces standing as a testament to the world's enduring fascination.

I remained entranced by the sight of the Delftware in this third-floor gallery. Slowly, my focus shifted from the vivid interplay of colors to the objects themselves—their forms and striking silhouettes. This display of Dutch Delftware was not merely a study in color but also an exploration of shape, a celebration of the sculptural.

Circular, ovoid, or undulating in baluster form, much of the Delftware showcased here was formed on the potter's wheel, the product of hands skillfully shaping clay against its spinning force. Glass shelves held row upon row of chargers, bowls, covered vases, tobacco jars, posset pots, salts, sugar casters, ewers, teapots, and vases.

Yet amid these familiar shapes were unexpected forms—pieces that defied the potter's wheel. These were crafted instead at worktables, where artisans constructed rectangular-shaped birdcages and flat-sided sleigh-shaped pipe stands with architectural precision. Freely modeled human figures and animals appeared in dynamic poses, some riding, others standing, crouching, or sitting, each capturing a moment in motion.

An unbridled profusion of ceramics, the Dutch Delftware was displayed without any apparent order. In my mind's eye, I began to rearrange the pieces. Moving them backward and forward, switching cases, I grouped them by age, maker, painting style, technique, and function. With each imaginary reorganization, the pieces revealed deeper meaning. This was not just a random display of blue and white; it was, in fact, a ceramic narrative.

Before me, I realized, lay the story of Dutch Delftware. Woven into this array was a narrative thread that recounted the history of the iconic blue-and-white ceramics. The collection illustrated the breadth of Delftware production from a specific period—roughly 1650 to 1800—unveiling how it began and evolved both stylistically and technically. Each piece seemed to introduce the major potteries of Delft while offering a glimpse into life in the seventeenth and eighteenth centuries in the Dutch Republic. It reflected customs, traditions, and even historic turning points.

This was no mere assemblage; it was a collection with a story to tell.

Behind each collection is an individual—a collector. As described by the twentieth-century art critic Aline Saarinen, these collectors are ". . . not objective spectators. By purchase and patronage, they declared their convictions and supported or shaped different levels and kinds of taste." As important as the story that is told, collections are the legacy and reflection of the person or people who actively created them. It mirrored their goals and aspirations, the time in which they lived and how they wanted the world to see them. This Delftware was someone's declaration.

As I walked through the room, I noticed what first appeared to be a blue-and-white pitcher, partially hidden in a case by the window behind two chargers. This ceramic jug featured a gently curved handle that echoed the shape of its ovoid body, distinguished by cobalt flowers framing stylized rocaille panels of river landscapes.

Stepping closer, I took a longer look. The handle was longer than it should have been, connected to the body slightly lower than was customary. The lip was decorated with multiple protruding spouts and its wide cylindrical neck was pierced with trelliswork openings seemingly flaunting its undrinkability. Not a common pitcher; it was something rarer. Intricately constructed in the eighteenth century to confound, fool, and mislead—or as it is called in Dutch a *fopkan*, or in French a *pot trompeur*, a *pot à surprise*—it was in fact a puzzle jug.

Puzzle jugs were popularly used for drinking games in seventeenth- and eighteenth-century Europe. Once filled with wine, they were intended as a game or conversation piece. What the guest may or may not know was that the hollow tubular rim has one functioning nozzle, and two or more "dummy" nozzles connected to the hollow handle. The solution to the puzzle was for the drinker to place a finger over one particular hole in order to create the vacuum that allowed them to drink without splashing wine in every direction at the host's sumptuous table. Some jugs even had a hidden hole to make the challenge still more confounding. The trick to solving the puzzle was in understanding its unique and complex design.

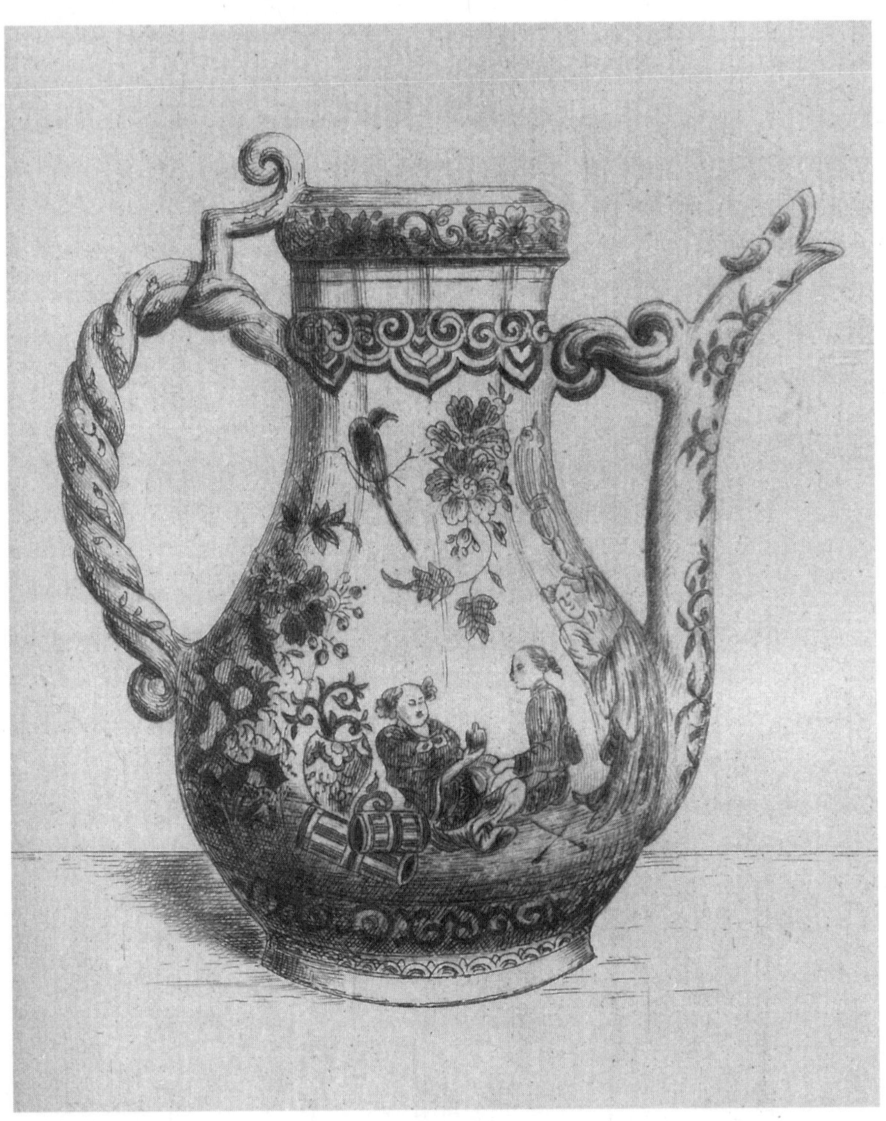

Charles Antoine Goutzwiller's detailed illustration of a Dutch Delft blue and white *pot à surprise*, or puzzle jug, from Henry Havard's *Histoire de la Faïence de Delft* (1878). Author's collection.

Heavier models had been made since the thirteenth century, and used in pubs and taverns. But a Dutch puzzle jug like this one, with its fine details and delicate painting, was probably produced on special order and as a result was particularly unique. A luxurious amusement, this piece would have been brought out with ceremony during a dinner, gently placed on a white linen-covered table among large green glass goblets with knobbed stems at the home of a wealthy eighteenth-century gentleman or lady.

It's probably been more than twenty years since these cases have been opened. Their interior ivory velvet panels and padding have gently bowed and discolored with age. The brass pins that were delicately inserted to hold the backing in place have begun to loosen and turn. I slowly swung open the heavy glass door and gently removed the puzzle jug from the cabinet. Cradling the ceramic work in both hands, I carefully supported its cool, smooth body.

I imagined the potter at their wheel in Delft, shaping several pounds of soft, damp clay to create the jug's body and parts. As the pottery wheel spun quickly, they skillfully brought up the clay, throwing delicate spouts, then pulling it to form a channeled handle and the rounded, belly-shaped vessel. The piece was crafted slightly larger to account for shrinkage during firing. Once the jug had dried and was firm enough to be trimmed and assembled, the spouts and hollow handle were carefully attached, piercings were made on the neck, and the secret hole was meticulously created. After the initial bisque firing, the jug was dipped in a tin glaze, readying it for decoration.

The painter then dipped a thin brush into a cup of dark cobalt slip and applied the intricate design with practiced precision. The creation of this piece was a lengthy and collaborative process, requiring not only adept technical knowledge but also the combined expertise of multiple skilled artisans.

I inverted the jug to inspect the base, where a maker's mark, if present, would typically be found. Not all pieces of Dutch Delftware bear the signature or mark of their creator; some are simply bare and white. But this one was different. Painted boldly in dark cobalt in the center of the base were three initials: **GVS**. These were the initials of the pottery's owner—a woman named Geertruij Verstelle.

In that moment, the blue initials beneath the glaze became more than a mark; they were like a sparkling ceramic fragment, an archaeological *sherd* unearthed in rough soil, focusing my vision and my thoughts. Alone in the room, holding this Delftware, I felt the distant yet powerful presence of another life, a woman's hand intertwined with the creation of art.

Decades of handling countless objects have taught me how rare it is for women to leave their names, signatures, or marks on works of art, be they paintings, sculptures, or ceramics. In the early modern era—spanning from the Renaissance to the Enlightenment—the contributions of women in the decorative arts often went unnamed. The list of women who marked their works is short, but it includes remarkable figures like Suzanne de Court, who crafted luxurious enamel masterpieces in sixteenth-century Limoges, and Hester Bateman, the celebrated eighteenth-century silversmith and entrepreneur in Georgian London. But considering the greater body of decorative arts, few women received recognition in their lifetimes or even in the centuries that followed.

Yet here I was, holding evidence—fused in cobalt—of another woman's life in the arts.

I imagined Geertruij nearly three hundred years ago, surrounded by Delftware in her bustling warehouse or salesroom, or perhaps standing in a workroom as skilled painters meticulously applied decorations to countless plates and bowls. She wasn't merely a pottery owner; she was a master orchestrator, guiding a team of artisans to craft ceramic masterpieces. Over the centuries, her life and achievements were buried under layers of history, forgotten like so many others. Yet her initials—three small letters—endure as a vestige of her presence. Who was she? Were there others like her?

Standing in that room above the streets of New York, surrounded by an ocean of blue-and-white Delftware, I studied the forms and the hues, each piece a testament to craftsmanship. But I wondered, what had Geertruij seen in her own time? What were the circumstances that allowed her to create this work and mark it with her name?

This piece, a source of pride crafted along the canals of Delft, had traveled nearly four thousand miles over the course of three centuries. In the eighteenth century, that voyage would have taken six to ten weeks. How had it come to be here in New York? Who brought it? What motivated them to collect not just this jug, but the entire trove of Delftware surrounding me?

The name "Delft" comes from the Middle Dutch *delven*, meaning "to dig, to excavate, to unearth." What began as an observation had turned into a mystery, inviting further inquiry. The surface had only been scratched.

It was time to dig.

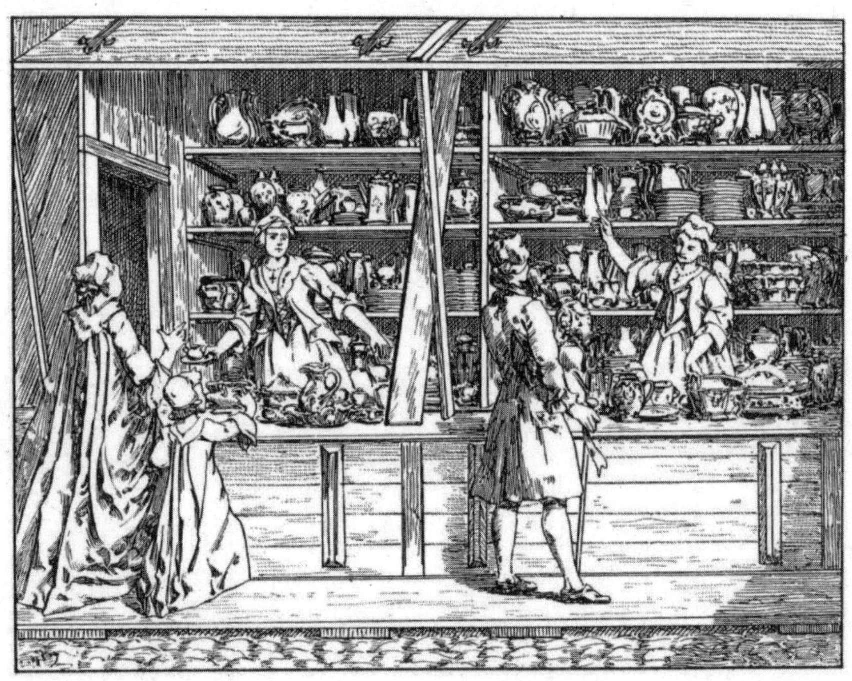

ABOVE: Charles Antoine Goutzwiller's illustration, *La boutique de la Marchande de faïences* (after J. Kilian), from Henry Havard's *La Céramique Hollandaise* (1909), captures the bustling world of female Delftware sellers. Courtesy of the Getty Research Institute. OPPOSITE: Charles Antoine Goutzwiller's 1878 illustration for Henry Havard's *Histoire de la Faïence de Delft* depicts the pottery sign of De Drie Porceleyne Flessies (The Three Porcelain Bottles), based on an eighteenth-century manuscript preserved in the Delft City Archives. Author's collection.

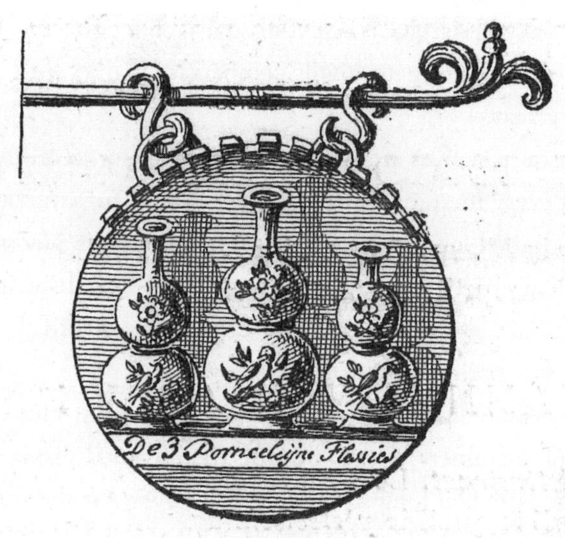

2

Shop Daughter

"The women of Holland are verie faire, wise, paynfull, and so practised in affaires of the world, that they occupie thēselues in most part of mens excercises, especially in marchandize."

–Lodovico Guicciardini, *Descrittione di tutti Paesi Bassi*, 1567

"Winkeldochter (f) A Young woman train'd up in a shop"

–Willem Sewel, *Groot Woordenboek der Nederduytsche de Engelsche*, 1708

The Delftware shop buzzes with activity as customers drift through the wide-open door. Outside, a wooden placard bearing the pottery's symbol swings gently in the breeze, inviting passersby to step inside. It is

1651, and distinctive signage is essential; at least ten potteries operate in Delft during this period, making it a highly competitive market with new workshops opening every year.

Inside, the deep shelves are well-stocked from floor to ceiling with rows of Delftware in every imaginable form—from bowls, jugs, tazzas, and vases to wall plaques, lidded jars, and luxurious blue-and-white *bloempotten* (flower-pots). Plates in a variety of sizes, including small butter dishes and generously wide chargers, are spread across broad tables. The plentiful blue-and-white pieces sit in anticipation, awaiting their buyers.

A young woman stands poised behind the counter. Her eyes follow the movements of customers as they admire the crowded displays of blue-and-white earthenware. Her long woolen petticoat sways as she shifts her weight, while a fine white linen hood drapes over her hair, framing a face of concentration amid the activity of commerce around her.

The scent of damp cool clay and slip wafts from unseen areas, seeping under doors from spaces beyond the salesroom. A series of contiguous buildings and areas, each with a specific purpose, lie nearby—an earth house for storing clay, workshops for throwing pots and painting, drying attics, a woodshed, a hayloft, a warehouse, and the pottery kilns themselves. The industrious rhythm of this world hums just beyond the customers' view.

While potential purchasers browse in the salesroom, the true commerce of the pottery unfolds behind closed doors. In a private room, her parents oversee large-scale transactions that will shape the pottery's success. These deals are not measured in single vases or dishes but in hundreds or even thousands of pieces—bowls, teacups, and saucers—destined for bustling markets, elegant shops, lively fairs, and street vendors across the Dutch Republic and beyond.

Occasionally, an even more luxurious chamber is reserved for the most affluent patrons. In this opulent space, surrounded by paintings, an ebonized *kast* (cabinet), and walls lined with gilt leather panels, burghers or members of the nobility can leisurely consider their purchases. The grandeur of this setting mirrors the interiors where the Delftware will eventually reside.

The young woman standing behind the counter is part of this world. A gentleman gestures for her to bring him a vase, and she carefully holds the piece for his inspection. His gaze lingers on the intricate cobalt-blue flowers painted on its shiny surface before shifting to her hands. He notices the faint stains on her fingers, the light marks of black ink on the young woman's right thumb, index, and middle fingers.

As he deliberates, she glances at other customers. A woman and her child browse nearby, perhaps considering a special commission—a plate with initials or a family coat of arms to commemorate a wedding or the birth of a child. Merchants from Paris or Rotterdam come and go, placing large orders for their shops.

At the counter, she prepares her *schryf pen* (writing pen) to finalize the transaction. Snipping the quill tip with practiced care, she opens the calf-bound ledger and reviews the day's sales. She records prices in Dutch *guilders* and *stuivers* as well as foreign currencies, tracking payments received, pending, and outstanding. For now, it is her responsibility to manage the receipts, but at the end of the day, the ledger and the box of currency will be handed to her parents for review and safekeeping.

The shop is not just a place of artistry and commerce; it is also her home. Above the pottery, her family lives in well-appointed quarters with salons and chambers, some containing paneled box beds. Like many families in Delft, her parents run the business together, and her mother often handles the accounts. The young woman is learning these skills from her mother and already taking on greater responsibilities.

One day, she may run a pottery with her own family—or perhaps even own one herself. She is preparing for that opportunity, honing her skills in both artistry and business.

But today, she remains a shop daughter.

Who was the girl behind the Delftware counter?

She and her family may have come from any number of towns and villages across the Dutch Republic, moving to Delft from places like Haarlem or Rotterdam to join the growing business of Delftware. However, it is most

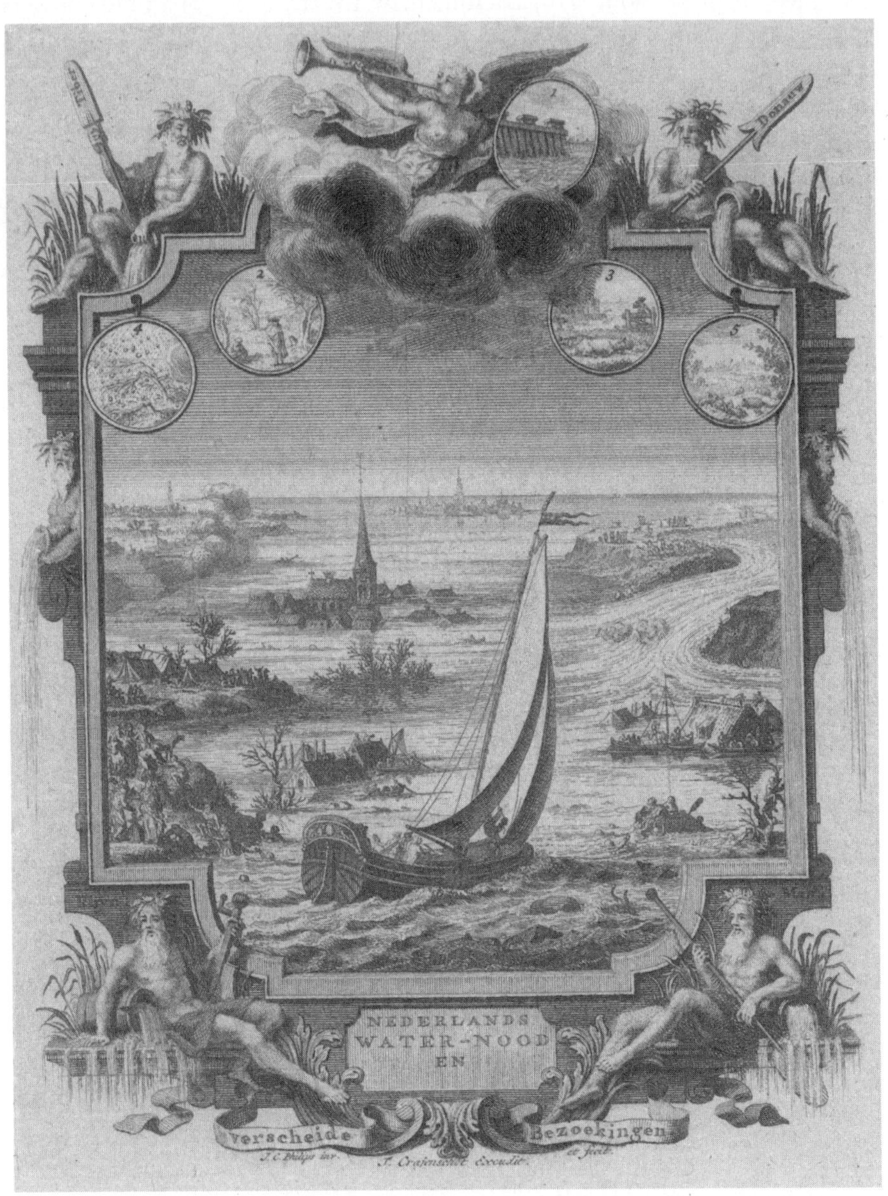

A yacht sails over flooded land and past submerged villages in Jan Caspar Philips's 1741 title-page etching and engraving for *Nederlands water-nood van den jaare MDCCXL en MDCCXLI* (*Dutch Water Emergency in the Year MDCCXL and MDCCXLI*), depicting the aftermath of the December 1740 dike breaches. Rijksmuseum, Amsterdam.

likely she was a daughter of Delft itself, raised in one of the city's many pottery families and taught trade secrets by her mother or father.

Perhaps, on a late spring day in the 1650s, she stood behind the counter of a pottery shop in Delft, part of a blue-and-white legacy that will define this era for centuries to come.

The city of Delft, her home and the center of this vibrant industry, was one of the preeminent cities in the Dutch Republic, which at the time was known formally as the *Republiek der Zeven Verenigde Nederlanden* (The Republic of the Seven United Netherlands). As described by the eighteenth-century Leiden artist and scientist Johannes le Francq van Berkhey, the Dutch Republic, with nearly a third of its land below sea level, was "rightly called a low country; because, compared to all neighboring countries, it is very low and swampy . . ." The Dutch Republic was a kingdom of marshy lands whose people fought to maintain its footprint in the face of the ever-encroaching North Sea.

In the constant battle for self-preservation, clay was part of the Dutch arsenal. Master dike builder Andries Vierling in 1570 described the ongoing fight and the means to win it:

> Our enemy the sea never rests. It sleeps neither by day nor by night, but charges savagely like a roaring lion to devour the entire land. God has given us the weapons to beat it; they are willow twigs, turves, stones and clay.

Yet despite these seemingly inhospitable conditions, the Dutch were able to not only defend their territory but reclaimed and even gained new land starting in the thirteenth century. Implementing a complex system of drainage canals, dikes, dams, sluices, and pumps powered by windmills, they created an extensive network regulating water levels, continually pumping from the lowest points to the highest canals, which transported water to rivers, allowing it to flow back to the sea. Drained marshes and bogs were transformed to establish cities, construct roads, and create *polders*—agricultural fields used for growing crops such as valuable hemp, madder, and flax, as well as for grazing cattle.

Luminous landscapes painted in the seventeenth century by artists such as Aelbert Cuyp depict an idyllic Dutch countryside, where cloud-filled blue skies stretch over vast expanses of flat, fertile green terrain. The scenery is criss-crossed by rivers, dotted with clusters of trees, punctuated by the occasional windmill or recumbent cow. But what's not visible in these bucolic depictions, lying in beds beneath the miles of turf in coastline regions or nestled within river embankments, was a hidden asset—natural clay.

The Netherlands is a country with little or no native stone. There may be glacial boulders, large masses deposited from receding ice sheets—marl (pale crumbly calcite knobs) and bog ore (clumps of dark iron formed in decomposing swamps)—but natural stone suitable for building purposes was rarely found. Stone was reserved for only the most important edifices or used in moderation for decorative elements on facades and main entrances. When required, stone was often imported at great expense, transported by ship from across Europe.

Clay, however, occurs in abundance. Formed over millions of years, this dense material is composed of mainly fine-grained mineral particles of decomposed sedimentary rock, weathered and disintegrated beneath the earth's surface. Its coin- or plate-shaped molecules when joined create a slippery material, often described by terms including fatty, oily, greasy, or even glassy.

Clay eluded scientific definition for centuries. As remarked by van Berkhey in his *Natural History of Holland*, printed in Amsterdam between 1772–1776:

> Various ideas, and not infrequently completely unfounded opinions, have arisen from time to time because of this fat and soft material of Klai. There are those who want it to be a nitrous slime; others, that it consists of the silt of the Sea Salt; and some think this to be a remnant of vitriolic acid; in short, most people consider that substance to be a kind of slimy residue of salts; which, when separated from their earthly parts, leave behind a certain fatty and seep-like substance.

Beginning in the eleventh century, the Dutch began digging canals by hand, unearthing vast quantities of clay in the process. This durable, water-resistant material became essential for building and maintaining the thousands of miles of dikes that protected the waterlogged Dutch landscape. Once extracted, the clay was inexpensively loaded onto barges and transported quickly throughout the country.

Dutch clay, however, was far more than a material for fortifying land; it became the foundation for a vast array of practical and decorative innovations. From bricks and roof tiles used to build cities to wall tiles that adorned homes and earthenware pottery ranging from the everyday to the extraordinary, clay was remarkably versatile. Malleable when moist, cohesive after drying, and rock-hard when fired, it offered endless creative possibilities.

Reviving ancient Roman techniques, Dutch clay was harvested and molded into bricks along riverbanks by the eleventh century. The character of the bricks depended on the clay's composition and the firing process. Iron-rich clay fired to a deep red, while chalk-rich clay produced a soft yellow hue. Placement in the kiln created further variation: bricks nearest the flames emerged darker, while those farther away stayed lighter. This natural variability meant no two bricks were ever identical. These bricks, produced by the millions, became essential for global architecture and a valuable export from the Dutch Republic, traded as far afield as Africa and North America.

By the fifteenth century, Dutch clay was also used in roof tile production. Lightweight, inexpensive, and fire-resistant, overlapping s-shaped roof tiles or *pantiles* were developed by the Dutch. Pantiles helped safeguard towns from the devastating fires that often consumed timber-built homes. After Delft's Great Fire of 1536, sparked by a lightning strike on the *Nieuwe Kerk* tower, much of the city was rebuilt with bricks and clay roof tiles. This transformation not only strengthened Delft against future blazes but also infused its urban landscape with the warm, earthen tones of red ocher and umber.

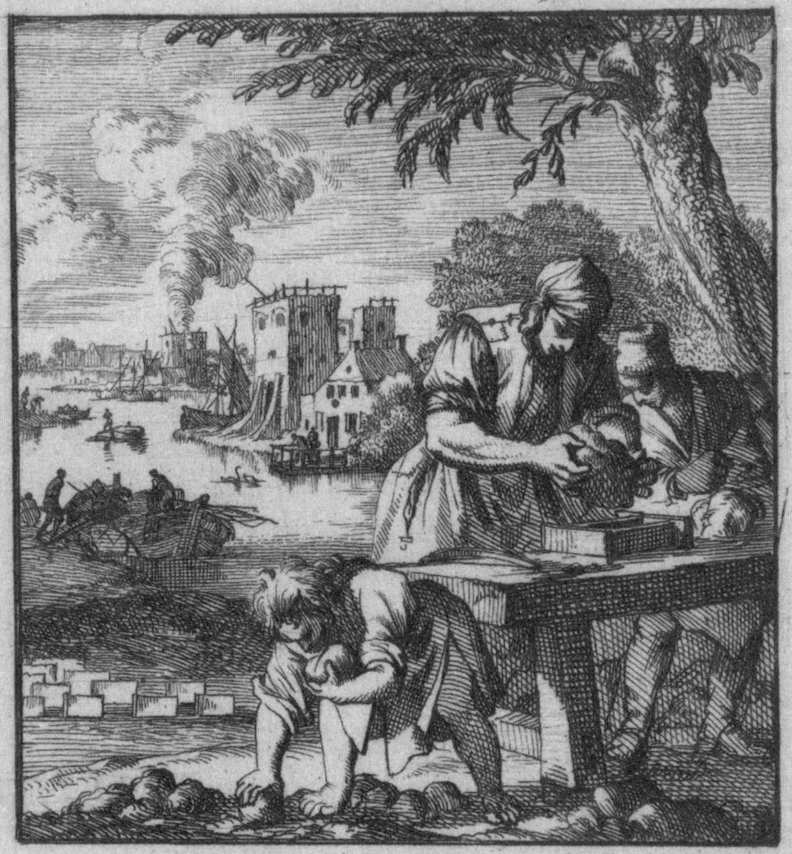

By the river's edge, *De Tichgellaar* (*The Brick Maker*) expertly molds clay into bricks using wooden forms, as depicted in a 1694 etching by Caspar Luyken and Jan Luyken. Rijksmuseum, Amsterdam.

Clay's role extended indoors as well. By the sixteenth century, factories across the Dutch Republic were producing tiles for floors and walls. These tiles, celebrated for their beauty and functionality, became a distinctive feature of Dutch homes, lining walls, covering kitchen and cellar floors, and surrounding fireplaces. Van Berkhey, writing in the 1770s, praised Dutch tiles not only for their aesthetic appeal but also for their practical qualities as they were "exceptionally good at repelling the damp exhalation of the soil, in walls and floors; why it is now used everywhere in Holland with good results to that end."

But ultimately, Dutch clay would assume its most pivotal and widely recognized role in the ceramic arts.

Early examples of Dutch pottery date back to the fifteenth century, when earthenware was painted with watery slip and finished with a clear lead glaze. However, the late sixteenth century marked a transformative period for Dutch ceramics. Following the fall of Antwerp in 1585, artisans fleeing Spanish forces brought the craft of colorful tin-glazed earthenware to the Northern Low Countries, areas later known as the Dutch Republic.

Tin-glazed earthenware, coated with a glaze containing tin oxide, created a brilliant white surface, ideal for intricate designs in blue or polychrome. These designs featured a vibrant palette including deep blues, yellow-greens, and ochreous oranges. The technique, which originated in Mesopotamia over a millennium earlier, spread through Spain and Italy before reaching Northern Europe. Known as *maiolica* in Italy and *faience* in France, pottery of this type flourished worldwide.

Dutch tin-glazed ceramics of the sixteenth and early seventeenth centuries—precursors to Delftware—exhibited distinctive signs of their production and the unique qualities of Dutch clay. Small *spur marks* from triangular spacers, used during firing, left subtle scars on the glossy surfaces of plates and bowls. The reverse sides, coated with a transparent lead glaze, revealed the warm tones of Dutch earth. These early innovations paved the way for the development of Dutch Delftware.

~

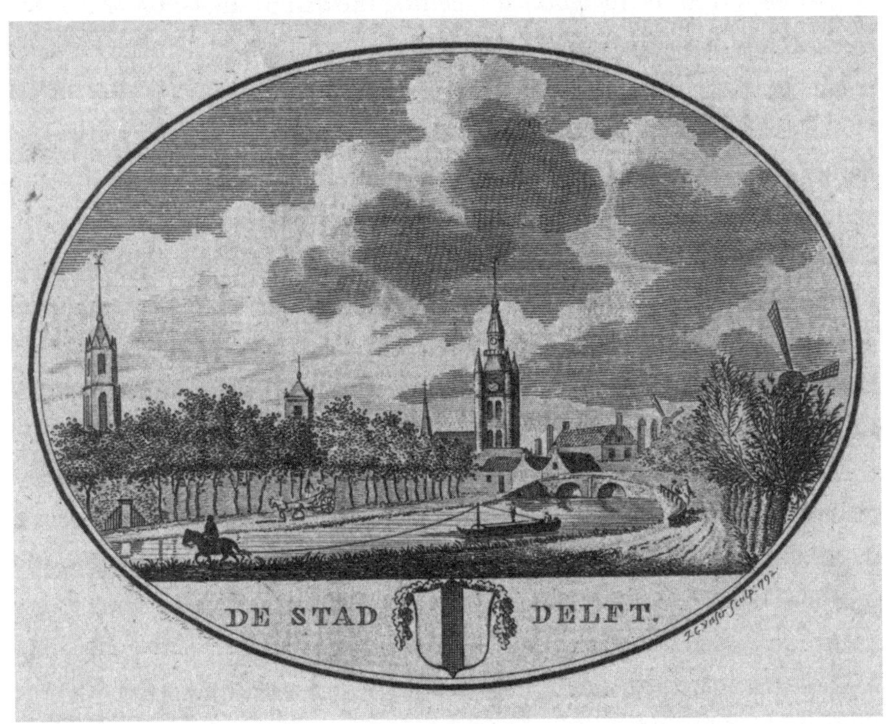

Jan Gerritsz. Visser's 1792 etching presents a picturesque view of Delft, featuring a towing barge gliding along the water, led by a horse on the towpath, with the city's coat of arms displayed below. Rijksmuseum, Amsterdam.

Clay shaped the Dutch as much as the Dutch shaped clay.

It built cities, adorned homes, and provided a canvas for creativity and cultural exchange. From the dikes that held back the sea to the bricks of gabled houses and the tiles lining Dutch kitchens, clay was more than a material—it was intimately intertwined with Dutch existence. Walking the streets of the Dutch Republic was, as it still is now, an experience of clay.

But of all the Dutch towns, none would develop a more unique relationship with clay than the city of Delft.

Delft, as described by the Florentine diplomat and merchant Lodovico Guicciardini in 1567, was "a goodly large town wel built thrughout, with broad and pleasant streetes, and beautified with sumptuous and stately churches." Since receiving its founding charter in 1245, Delft had been a noted destination, attracting visitors from around the globe.

Arriving in the seventeenth century, a traveler entered the walled town of Delft with its ramparts, towers, and encircling moat through one of its fortified gatehouses. Once across a drawbridge, they would find themselves in, as described the English diarist Samuel Pepys in the spring of 1660, "a most sweet town, with bridges, and a river in every street." Like so many Dutch medieval cities, Delft was reclaimed from the soggy marshland and characterized by a system of gently curving brick-lined canals created by hand, dug from the earth. The oldest canal, the *Oude Delf,* was built in the eleventh century. The canals of Delft not only discharged water but allowed commercial goods and travelers to be easily transported to and from Delft, connecting the small town of around 20,000 inhabitants in the 1620s to cities and trade routes not just within the Republic but throughout Europe and via the North Sea to the greater world.

Windmills punctuated the inner wall of Delft at intervals, their broad turning sails gently providing power for a variety of uses from controlling water to milling grain to cutting wood. Some windmills in the Delft area

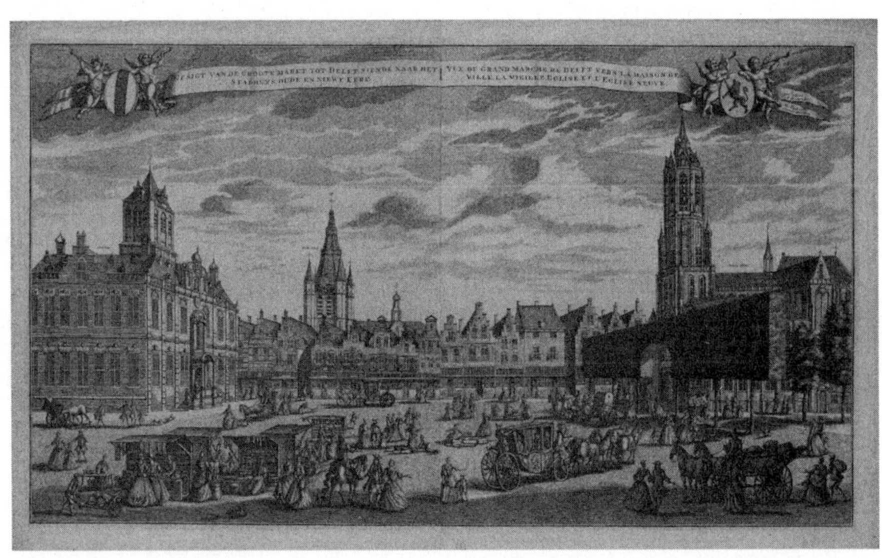

Leonard Schenk's etching (1706–1767) captures Delft's *Groote Markt*, teeming with pedestrians, dogs, vendors, and carriages as men and women sell goods from doorways and stands. Rijksmuseum, Amsterdam.

were also owned or shared by the potteries. By the mid– to late–seventeenth century, the need for vast quantities of finely processed minerals required for glazes was considerable. These paint mills powered by the Dutch wind were in constant movement, grinding hundreds of thousands of pounds of tin oxide, lead, and cobalt needed for making the blue-and-white.

Continuing down the brick-paved streets, past tree-lined canals and over small bridges, visitors encountered rows of gabled red brick facades—homes, warehouses, and businesses—juxtaposed along the way. Among them were numerous Delftware potteries, leading toward the area known as the *Grote Markt*, *Gootemarkt*, or simply the *Markt*.

Only a few minutes' walk from the city gates, the *Markt* with its sprawling stretch of brick paving in bands of herringbone was one of the most expansive and historic market squares in Europe. Towering over this market square was the *Nieuwe Kerk* (New Church), built beginning in 1381. The carillon of its monumental brick and stone tower, rising 326 feet above Delft, provided a constant melodic background to the otherwise quiet city. Lying opposite, facing the *Nieuwe Kerk*, was the *Stadhuis* (City Hall). In the distance over the tiled rooftops was the leaning tower of the *Oude Kerk* (Old Church), founded in 1246.

Delft was often noted for these imposing architectural landmarks, but for many foreign visitors to the Dutch Republic, eliciting descriptive responses ranging from surprise and curiosity to consternation, equally noteworthy was the observation of not a building or work of art but the unique Dutch female presence.

Whether walking the streets of Delft or riding one of the many horse-drawn *trekschuiten* (commuting barges) along its canals, Dutch women moved freely and unaccompanied. Girls and boys played together in the streets, chasing wooden hoops as dogs darted around their feet. Through the open doorways of shops selling everything from silk to silver to books, or at stalls offering cheese, fruits, and vegetables during the *markt* each Thursday, women could be seen managing employees, handling transactions, and orchestrating trade with practiced efficiency.

In his travel journal *The Delights of Holland*, printed in 1696, Sir William Montague comments on his visit to the Dutch Republic:

> Tis very observable here, more Women are found in the Shops and Business in general than Men; they have the Conduct of the Purse and Commerce, and manage it rarely well, they are Careful and Diligent, capable of Affairs, (besides Domestick) having an Education suitable, and a Genius wholly adapted to it.

Beyond just scrubbing stoops, women of the Dutch Republic were actively participating in a life flourishing with the energy of commerce, industry, and creativity. But not all visitors were as complementary. Although delighted by the charms of Delft, Florentine merchant and writer Guicciardini seems also to have been taken aback by the overt public presence of Dutch women. One of the earliest diarists of the Dutch, he expressed disdain when noting widespread female activity in commerce in his description in 1567 that in Holland:

> The Women governe all, both within the doores and without, and make all bargaines, which joyned with the naturall desire that Women have to beare rule, maketh them too too imperious and troublesome.

Like their mothers, precocious Dutch girls did not go unnoticed. Fynes Moryson, the son of a Lincolnshire gentleman, visited the Dutch Republic in 1592 at the age of twenty-five, fulfilling his desire to explore lands beyond England. In his journal of newfound sights and wonders, he remarked on his observations of the "Netherland," expressing surprise: "Nothing is more frequent than for little girls to insult over their brothers much bigger than they, reproving their doings, and calling them great lubbers."

Shocked foreign observers like Guicciardini, Montague, and Moryson may not have understood that the laws and common culture of the Dutch Republic granted daughters rights that were unparalleled elsewhere in Europe. Among

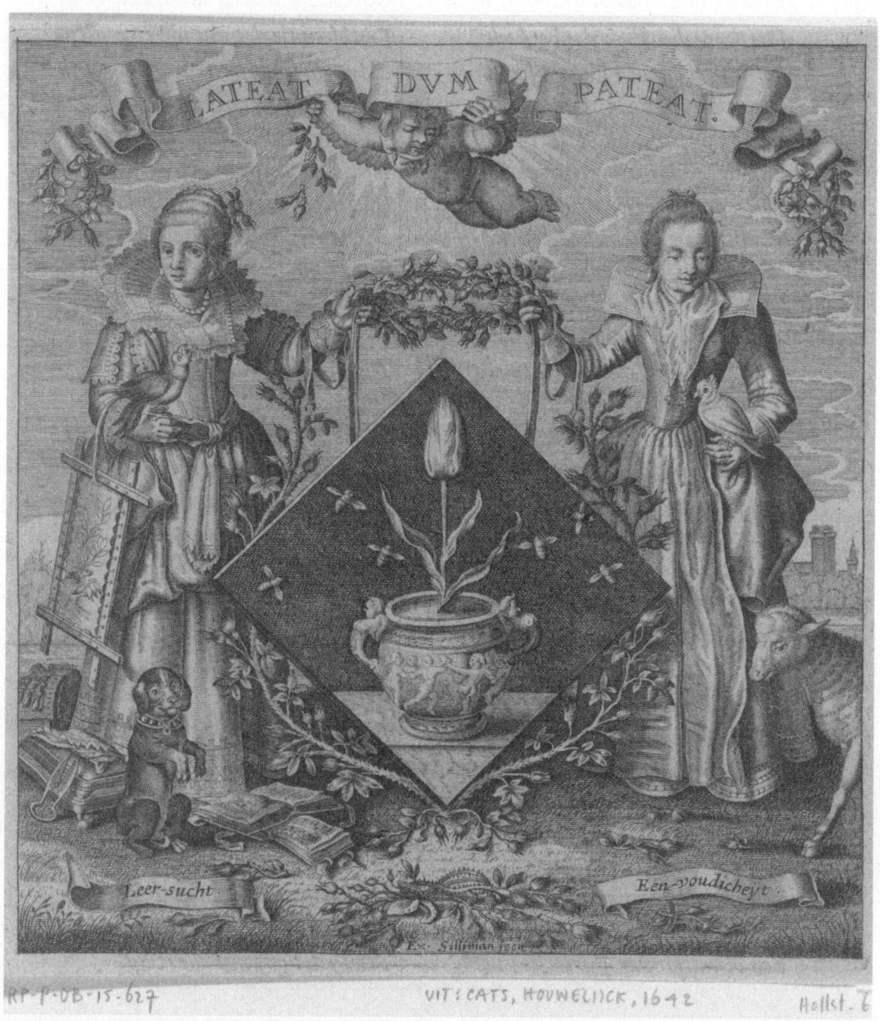

Experiens Sillemans's engraving, *Maeghde-wapen* (*The Maiden's Coat of Arms*), from Jacob Cats's *Houwelyck* (*Marriage*), 1642, reflects a Dutch female ideal, depicting a tulip in a pot flanked by two women symbolizing "Learning Curiosity" and "Simplicity." Rijksmuseum, Amsterdam.

these was the right to inherit equally with their brothers in the event of their parents' deaths. This system allowed Dutch girls the opportunity to establish and maintain their own households without depending on male relatives. Moryson, intrigued by these practices, further noted:

> Upon the Mothers death the children may compel
> their father to devide his goods with them, least
> perhaps he should consume or waste the same.

Such inheritance laws continued to bewilder and astonish Europeans for the next century.

Yet, for a girl or young woman in the Dutch Republic, even with these unique rights and abilities, life was not without conflicting societal expectations.

Dutch presses struggled to keep pace with the soaring demand for mass-published emblem books and advice literature, including works by the celebrated poet and statesman Jacob Cats. His *Houwelick* (*Marriage*), published in 1625, became a widely influential guide for young women, promoting strict adherence to traditional gender roles. Cats emphasized female conformity, urging wives to embody moderation and self-restraint. The ideal woman, he declared should be "Not too sweet, not too sour" and "Not too meek, not too domineering." Firmly situating women within a domestic sphere, Cats articulated his views clearly:

> De man moet op de straet on sijnen handel gaen;
> Het wijf in het huys de keuken gade slaen.
> Men vin teen seldsaem lant, dear slechts alleeen de wijven
> Ook met het buyte volck den gantscgen handel drijven.
>
> (The husband must conduct his business in the street,
> The wife must look after the kitchen in the house.
> One finds a country strange,
> Where only women conduct business with people outside.)

By 1655, *Houwelick* had sold 50,000 copies, and by 1700, books by Jacob Cats had reached a quarter of all Dutch households owning books, making *Houwelick* the most widely circulated book in the Dutch Republic after the Bible. Yet, despite the immense popularity of Cats's prescriptive vision of female domesticity, many women in the Dutch Republic took on active roles in business—driven, in part, by necessity.

In the seventeenth and eighteenth centuries, the Dutch Republic experienced a notable population disparity between men and women, particularly in densely populated urban centers including Delft. With many men engaged in overseas trade through the Dutch East India Company (VOC), it often became necessary for women to step in and out of roles within families and to manage family businesses in their absence. While the VOC was a highly lucrative venture for its investors, it carried significant risks for those who manned its ships. The loss of life during voyages was so common that it earned a grim moniker: the *Indisch lek* (Indian leak).

If employees of VOC ships, whether sailors or soldiers, managed to survive storms, pirate attacks, and onboard accidents during the journey to Asia, many succumbed to diseases such as malaria upon arrival. For those signing on for voyages that typically lasted two years, survival rates were bleak. Between 1700 and 1794, of the 8,340 seamen departing from Delft, only 5,050 returned. The odds were even worse for soldiers onboard: of the 2,035 who embarked during the same period, a mere 614 made it back alive.

In the face of population disparities and a culture that valued self-sufficiency, girls in the Dutch Republic were trained and educated. As described in the 1770s by van Berkhey, "thus enabling them to earn an honest living; in order that, in cases of adversity, singleness or widowhood, they may find a living in their own skills and abilities." Girls of the Dutch Republic were shaped within the multiple spheres of learning surrounding them—beginning at home within their family, extending to church, art, and literature, and also to schools.

The Dutch took great pride in their educational system, which by the 1590s was government-administered and offered elementary education for its youngest citizens. Across the Dutch Republic, primary schools for children

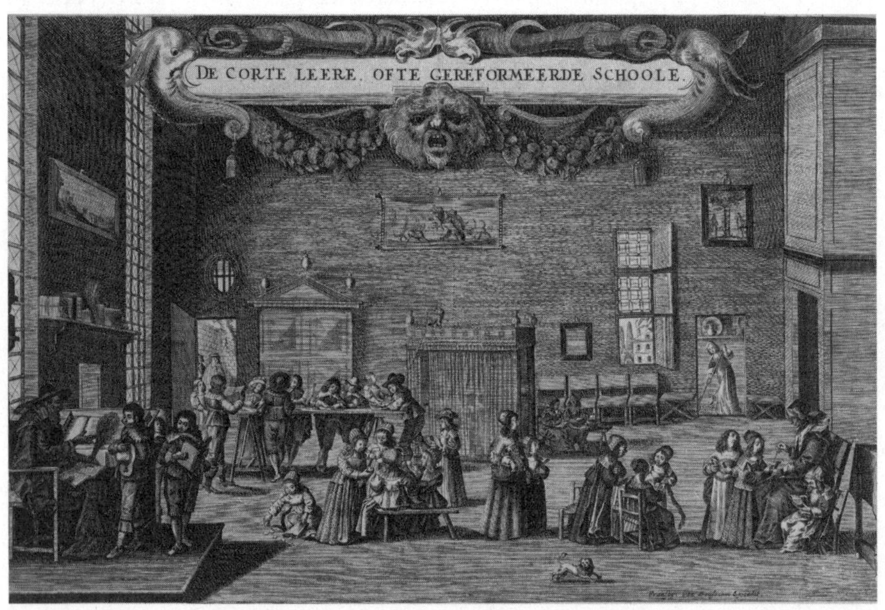

An engraving (1642–1665) of a Dutch schoolroom, ca. 1650, depicts a lively learning environment where a seated schoolmistress teaches three girls, a schoolmaster instructs two boys, boys study at a table, and girls play in the foreground. Rijksmuseum, Amsterdam.

under the age of ten were established, enrolling students from all levels of society. Girls as young as three years old attended school alongside boys, learning together in classrooms. Under the guidance of government-appointed teachers, they were taught sacred history, reading, writing, and arithmetic.

By age ten, boys' and girls' educational paths began to diverge. Boys often attended secondary "Latin schools," where a classical curriculum prepared them for university (both of which admitted only male students), or they began apprenticeships in various trades, ranging from painting to international commerce. Most girls, in contrast, would either return to the home or start work, often contributing to a family business. As further described by van Berkhey in the 1770s, families might:

> . . . place their daughters in a merchant's shop or some feminine profession, as shop or office daughters; in order to make her competent in this way, so that she can then, on that basis, equally take care of herself and her family.

Tales of Dutch girls' education, including financial literacy, reached even eighteenth-century America. In his 1789 memoirs, Benjamin Franklin reflected on the life of Elizabeth Timothy, who was raised in the Dutch Republic before emigrating to America in the 1730s. Elizabeth became America's first female editor and the first woman to own and publish a newspaper. Reflecting on her success, Franklin attributed it in part to her Dutch upbringing, noting that she was "born and bred in Holland, where, as I have been informed, the knowledge of accounts makes a part of female education."

Franklin, sharing the Dutch concern for the challenges faced by unmarried or widowed women, emphasized the importance of female self-sufficiency. He advocated for practical education, stating:

> I mention this affair chiefly for the sake of recommending that branch of education for our young females, as likely to be of more use to them and their children, in case of widowhood, than either

> music or dancing, by preserving them from losses by imposition of crafty men . . .

Trained in financial literacy from an early age, young Dutch women of the seventeenth and eighteenth centuries learned to read and maintain *een koopmans schryf-boek* (a merchant's writing book) or *een reken-boek* (a math book)— a book of accounts. Formal bookkeeping during this period required managing three key records: the memorandum or "waste" book, the journal, and the ledger.

They were taught double-entry bookkeeping, known as the "Italian method," as well as how to balance accounts and track financial transactions with precision. Equipped with these skills, a calf-bound ledger, and pen in hand, they were prepared to manage household finances or run a business—ensuring their family's financial stability and, in turn, contributing to the broader Dutch economy.

The relative wealth of a family significantly shaped a girl's education in the Dutch Republic. Daughters of the wealthiest families often had access to a variety of educational opportunities, including private tutors or enrollment in one of the popular *écoles françaises* (French schools). Beginning in the sixteenth century, these schools provided wealthy young Dutch women with a refined education and were often staffed by male and female migrants, many of whom had fled religious persecution in France.

French, as a second language, was de rigueur for members of the Dutch elite and nobility—not only in the Republic but also at court across Europe, from Germany to England. For merchants' daughters, however—presumed future merchants' wives—French was more than a symbol of affluence and sophistication; it was an indispensable business tool, often serving as the common language in much of Europe's trade.

Sequestered in a curtained cubicle separated from the male students, the first woman to attend a Dutch university and a proponent of women's education was the polymath, artist, and philosopher Anna Maria van Schurman. Proficient in not just French but Latin, Greek, Hebrew, Aramaic, Syrian,

Arabic, and Ethiopian, to name but a few, she was granted the opportunity to attend Utrecht University in Holland in 1636. Anna Maria reflected on the forces that shape women's educational opportunities in her 1657 treatise, published in English under the title *The Learned Maid or, Whether a Maid may be a Scholar*, that:

> some Maids are *ingenious*, others *not* so: some are *rich*, some *poor*: some engaged in Domestick cares, others at liberty. The studies of a Scholar are either universal, when we give our selves to all sorts of Learning: or *particular*, when we learn some one Language or Science, or one distinct Faculty. *Wherefore we make use of these Limitations.*

The moniker "The Dutch Golden Age," popularized in the nineteenth century, once seemed to aptly capture the richness of seventeenth-century Dutch society. However, it failed to recognize the broader picture, the restraints and confines, economic disparities and uncomfortable truths of the era. Not everyone benefited from the Dutch Republic's trade empire and economic prosperity. Populations under VOC control often faced brutal measures to maintain Dutch dominance in territories including present-day Indonesia. Many died or were enslaved and transported to Dutch-controlled regions around the globe, from Southeast Asia to the West Indies. At the same time, in the Dutch Republic itself, the poorest—laborers, farmers, and urban workers, both men and women—struggled to make ends meet despite the Republic's wealth.

In seventeenth-century notarial documents, many Dutch women confidently signed their names in flowing, practiced script, their full names etched in black ink—a clear testament to their literacy and the years spent mastering first chalk and then quill. Others, however, marked documents with a simple "X" or relied on someone else to sign on their behalf.

The ability to sign one's name, a common measure of functional literacy in late medieval and early modern times, reveals the relatively high literacy rates

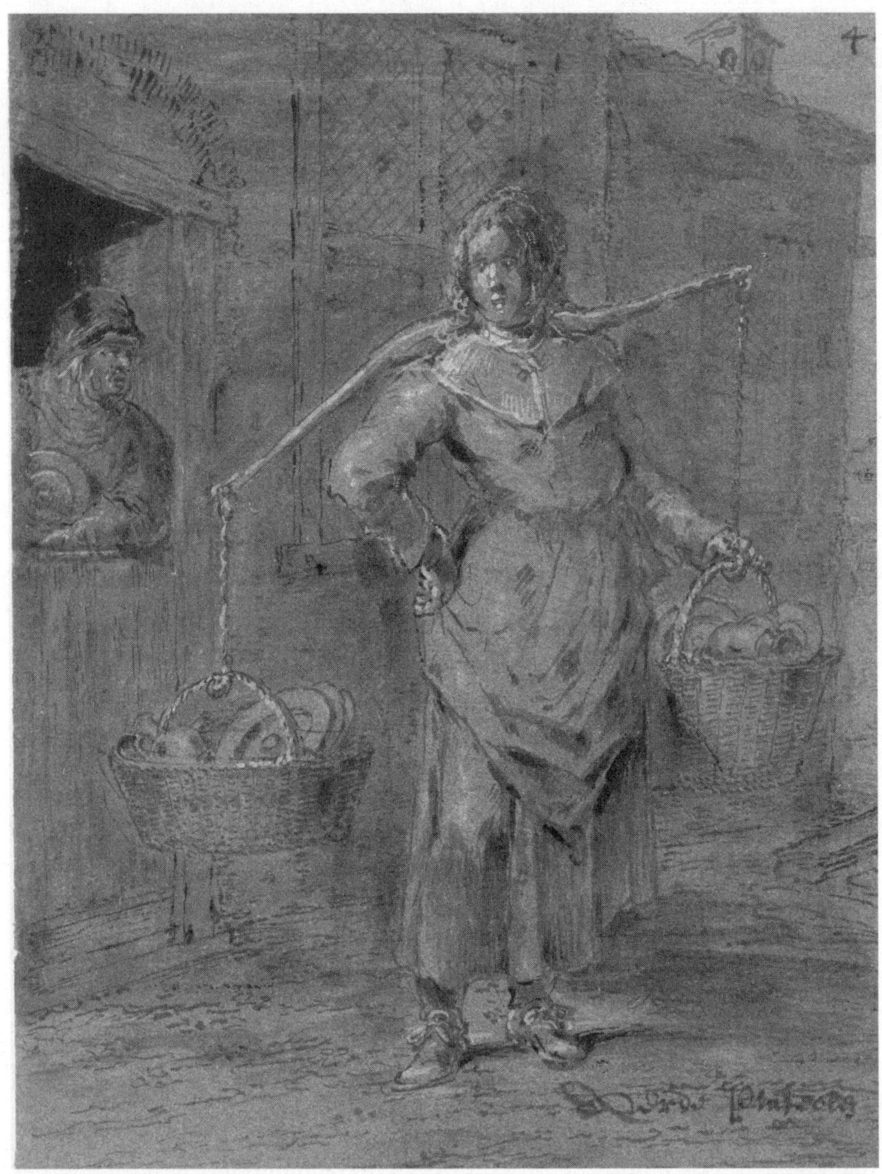

Leonaert Bramer's seventeenth-century pen and ink drawing depicts a female pottery vendor pausing in the street, balancing a wooden shoulder yoke with wicker baskets filled with Delftware dishes and jugs. Universitaire Bibliotheken Leiden.

in the Dutch Republic compared to its European neighbors. By 1650, 70 percent of Amsterdam bridegrooms and 50 percent of brides were able to sign their names in marriage records—remarkable figures when the combined literacy rate for men and women across Europe at the time is estimated at just 35–40 percent. However, outside urban centers like Amsterdam and Delft, a significant portion of Dutch women, particularly in rural areas, likely remained unable to read or write.

Some young women subsisted as Delftware street sellers or peddlers. Balancing wooden yokes on their shoulders, they carried baskets filled with pottery through the streets, selling a plate to a passing customer, or a bowl at a kitchen door on commission from a Delftware merchant. Subsisting on meager earnings, she may have experienced a circumstance more of survival than plenty. On the surface, the seventeenth century in the Dutch Republic was a time of unprecedented wealth—at least for those at the top.

The ascent of the Dutch Republic had been meteoric.

Founded only decades previously, the Dutch Republic in the early seventeenth century was one of Europe's youngest nations. Breaking with the Catholic Spanish Habsburg empire by 1581, the Dutch would create a new geographical and political state. A republic no less. But it was no easy dissolution with Spain. A protracted era of fighting ensued between the two nations. The Dutch fight for independence, the Dutch Revolt, would spread over decades, so lengthy it would also be called the Eighty Years' War. In 1584 the Dutch suffered a major blow when their leader, William of Orange, the *stadholder* known as the "Father of the Fatherland," was assassinated in Delft. Their confederation, The Republic of the Seven United Netherlands (or "of the Seven United Provinces") would not be officially recognized by the Spanish until 1648.

Yet even in the nascent decades after the establishment of their country, despite the political and religious turmoil, continued war, destruction, and hardship, the Dutch economy would not be inhibited. Across the Dutch Republic new businesses large and small were being founded, including an early pottery in Delft recorded in 1598. To effectively fight the Spaniards, the Dutch Republic understood it needed money and a united infrastructure to ultimately undermine Spain's control.

The solution was the establishment of the *Vereenigde Oostindische Compagnie*, commonly known throughout the rest of the world as the Dutch East India Company or simply the VOC. Incorporated in Amsterdam in 1602, the VOC was unlike any business venture ever created in Europe. What has been called the world's first multinational company, the VOC was an amalgamation of small independent trading companies granted a monopoly by the charter from the States General, the highest administrative body in the Dutch Republic. As the author of *Robinson Crusoe*, Daniel Defoe, described in 1728, the Dutch were "the *Carryers of the World*, the middle Persons in Trade, the Factors and Brokers of *Europe*." More than just the right to control a worldwide network of seafaring trade routes, the VOC was given far-reaching authorities including waging war, negotiating treatises, establishing trading posts and colonies and even imprisoning and executing convicts.

The Dutch East India Company rapidly captured markets across Europe and the far reaches of the globe, from Asia to the Americas. With a fleet of over a hundred ships, thousands of employees, and nearly thirty offices in Asia, it was supported by six powerful chambers, or *kamers*, within the Dutch Republic. These chambers—located in Amsterdam, Rotterdam, Enkhuizen, Middelburg, Hoorn, and Delft—served as central hubs of Dutch commerce, each equipped with offices, warehouses, and shipyards.

By the eighteenth century, the VOC's dominance was unparalleled in scale and scope. It managed an extensive network of trading posts and operations across Asia, far surpassing all other European nations combined. Between 1602 and 1796, its ships embarked on nearly five thousand voyages from the Netherlands to Asia—a staggering feat unmatched by its European competitors, who together sent only a fraction of ships and personnel during the seventeenth century.

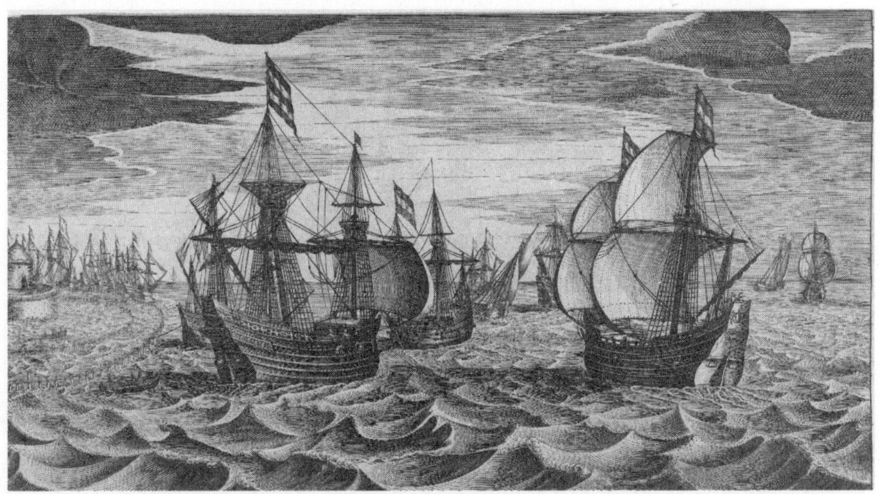

A fleet of nine VOC ships, with sails billowing, embarks from Amsterdam in 1603, bound for the East Indies' riches, in an engraving attributed to Robert de Baudous, possibly marking the second expedition under Steven van der Hagen (1603–1608). Rijksmuseum, Amsterdam.

The vast scale of the VOC's operations was reflected in the sheer volume of paperwork required to sustain its global dominance. This immense administrative legacy endures today in the Nationaal Archief (The National Archives of the Netherlands) in The Hague, where over twenty-five million pages of VOC historical records—ranging from trading post reports and muster rolls to pay ledgers, subscription registers, balance sheets, and committee minutes—stretch across more than 1.2 kilometers of archival shelf space.

What the VOC created would change the world, for better or for worse, and along the way, Dutch Delftware would be born.

In the early morning of February 25, 1603, Dutch ships of the newly founded VOC spotted the *Santa Catarina*, a massive 1,400-ton Portuguese carrack, navigating the warm waters of the South China Sea. The vessel, outbound from Macao and en route to Malacca and Goa, was a formidable sight. With castle-like superstructures towering above the water at the bow and stern, and three or four masts rigged with large sails, the carrack was designed for stability on heavy seas and the capacity to carry substantial cargo on long voyages. This galleon, "so richly laden," was carrying a significant load that would become one of the VOC's earliest and most consequential conquests.

Two Dutch ships, the *Witte Leeuw* and the *Alkmaar*, strategically aimed their cannons at the billowing sails of the *Santa Catarina*, effectively immobilizing the massive vessel while preserving its potentially valuable cargo. Portuguese accounts of the incident describe the chaos aboard the packed ship, as the more than seven hundred Portuguese *soldados* (soldiers) struggled to return fire. Within a day, the fighting subsided, and the Dutch seized the vessel, capturing the soldiers, more than one hundred civilians aboard, including women and children, as well as an immense trove of trading goods stored in innumerable cases below deck.

Hauling the *Santa Catarina*'s valuable cargo back to Amsterdam, the Dutch unloaded countless chests and wooden crates onto the docks, unveiling a vast array of treasures. These included bales of raw Chinese silk, colored damask, *atlas* (polished silk), taffeta, and chests of spun gold, as well as countless sacks of sugar, spices, gum, and musk. Among the haul was thirty *last*—approximately sixty tons—of glistening blue-and-white porcelain, over 100,000 pieces "of every sort and kind." While some had encountered porcelain before, never had they seen such a massive quantity all at once.

Made in the hills of Jingdezhen, a ceramics center in the northern Jiangxi province of China, these deep bowls and wide dishes painted in cobalt featured divided panels with leafy blooms and Buddhist emblems on their wide borders, and central scenes depicting stylized landscapes—often including birds, insects, deer, or mythical creatures. Designed with standard dimensions for easy packing, thousands of pieces could be efficiently loaded into a ship's hold. Often called *kraak* porcelain after the Portuguese carracks that typically transported ceramics of this type, they were the first type of porcelain to be mass-produced for export from China.

The public auction of the carrack *Santa Catarina*'s exotic cargo in Amsterdam in the autumn of 1604 became a landmark event, netting over three million Dutch guilders—a sum according to historians equal to half the paid-in capital, the initial fund raised for the selling of stock, of the VOC. The sale attracted merchants not only from the Dutch Republic but from across Europe. Its overwhelming success underscored the vast potential for trade throughout Asia, while the carrack's treasure, particularly its blue-and-white porcelain, captivated the European imagination.

Once discovered, the European thirst for Chinese porcelain was unquenchable. Holding the delicate blue-and-white porcelain in their hands, Europeans were captivated. Its smooth, glassy sheen, hard and durable yet light and thin, seemed almost otherworldly. It was cool and smooth to the touch, and when struck, it emitted a clear, resonant ring. Unlike earthenware, made from clays in shades of light brown or buff, porcelain clay was pure white and translucent. Seemingly magical, Chinese porcelain embodied the ethereal.

How was it made? Europeans were desperate to uncover the secrets of porcelain production, from the precise clay recipe to achieving the exceptionally high firing temperatures required. Yet these techniques remained closely guarded in China. In the meantime, ships of the Dutch East India Company

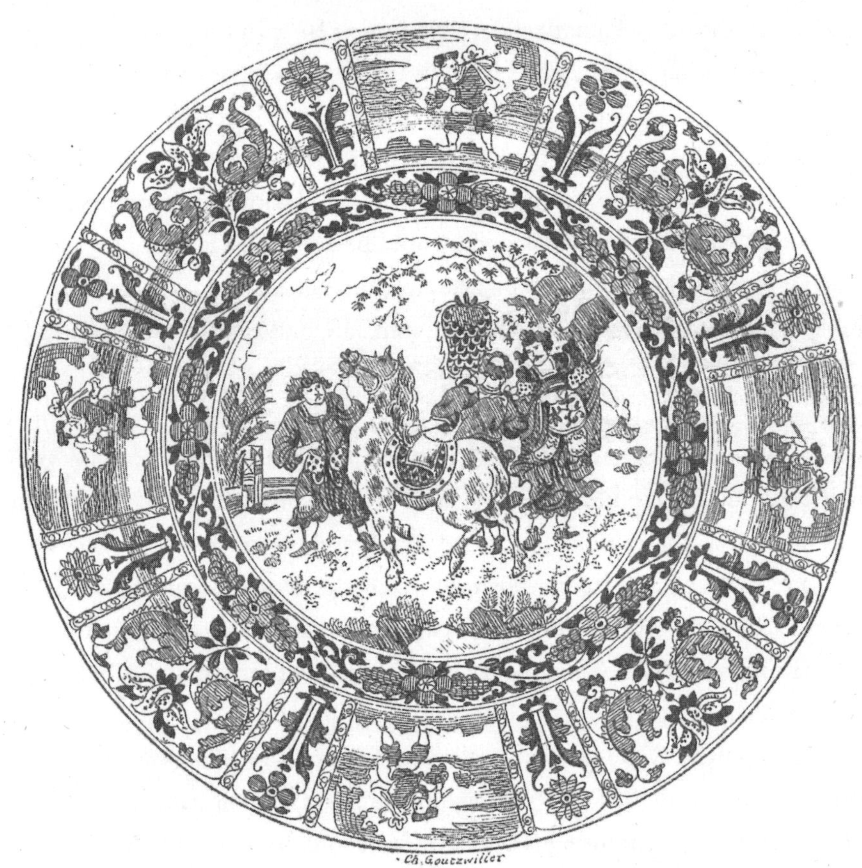

Charles Antoine Goutzwiller's 1878 illustration in Henry Havard's *Histoire de la Faïence de Delft* of a seventeenth-century Delftware dish closely inspired by Chinese ceramics. Author's collection.

set sail in droves, determined to bring back as much of this coveted and mysterious treasure as their holds could carry.

Faced with the soaring popularity of Chinese porcelain, the potters of Delft, who had been producing tin-glazed earthenware, confronted a critical question: how could they compete with the influx of Chinese blue-and-white ceramics? Rather than succumbing to potential ruin, they chose innovation over surrender. They resolved to create their own version of Chinese porcelain.

But how could the potters of Delft transform soft, porous earthenware into something as mystical and precious as porcelain—a material so valuable it was called "white gold?" By the 1620s, working from examples of Chinese porcelain brought through the Delft VOC kamer, they began experimenting. They studied Chinese forms and painting styles with determination, striving to replicate the beauty and allure of Chinese porcelain.

Their efforts led to the development of new clay recipes, incorporating marl for added hardness and imported European clays for enhanced plasticity. To conceal the natural buff color of the clay, each piece was dipped in a white coating and finished with a sparkling lead glaze, achieving a luminous, porcelain-like sheen.

To advance their techniques further, they improved the firing process, using *saggars*—protective earthenware tubes with discreet pins that left firing scars on the back edges of pieces, making them less noticeable. Their ingenuity paid off. By enhancing their materials and methods, the Delft potters succeeded in producing thinner pieces with clean, bright white surfaces. Their skilled painters then replicated the intricate designs characteristic of Chinese ceramics—crafted, however, in earthenware.

The result was a refined and highly collectible product: a more affordable yet equally appealing alternative to imported Chinese porcelain. The success of the Delft potters was undeniable. By 1625, eight potteries in Delft were already producing thousands of pieces of this new, in-demand commodity—Dutch Delftware, or, as it was called in the seventeenth century, *Delft porcelyne*.

By the mid–seventeenth century, civil war had engulfed China. What began as unrest in 1644 with the fall of the Ming Dynasty and the rise of the Qing soon escalated into widespread conflict. In 1645, the kilns of Jingdezhen, the heart of Chinese porcelain production, were destroyed. Dutch traders quickly reported to the VOC kamers about "the great mortality among the porcelain makers." As a result, official Dutch trade with China was suspended in 1647.

With Chinese porcelain production crippled, what had been a quarter million pieces arriving per year on the docks of Amsterdam, Middelburg, and Delft dwindled to just a few crates. Dutch trade with China would not fully resume until after 1680. With the market wide open, Delft potters seized the opportunity to fill the vast ceramic void. Their innovative spirit drove a remarkable evolution in tin-glazed earthenware.

As the seventeenth century progressed, fueled by a vibrant market eager for fresh designs, Dutch Delftware rapidly moved beyond imitation. Drawing inspiration from both Asian influences and European shapes, motifs, and decorative elements, Delft artisans blended these styles into a distinctive synthesis. The success of Dutch Delftware was exponential, and by the 1690s, Delft boasted more than thirty potteries, cementing its reputation as a seventeenth-century global center for ceramic artistry.

The seventeenth century was a time of innovation across the Dutch Republic in fields from ceramics and painting to science and philosophy. Underlying that creativity and contributing to that success was a Dutch tradition of tolerance for diverse ideas and beliefs. The Republic's nearly two million inhabitants included refugees from across Europe—from merchants and scholars to artists and artisans, including those of Jewish and Protestant faiths—whose contributions shaped Dutch culture and strengthened its expanding dominance in global trade. A thriving Dutch economy gave rise to a wealthy merchant class eager to support the vast output of fine and decorative arts emerging from countless studios, workshops, and potteries across the country.

Despite being one of the smallest states in Europe—with a population one-eighth that of France and limited natural resources—the Dutch Republic rose to lead one of the greatest economic and cultural renaissances the world had ever known.

The Dutch Republic was, as described by the diplomat and author Sir William Temple, the "Envy of some, the Fear of others, and the Wonder of all their Neighbours."

Curious competitors throughout Europe were determined to identify the possible conditions whether intellectual, cultural, or economic, that contributed to the Dutch rapid ascendency. From inquisitive economists to members of royalty including Peter the Great, Tsar of Russia, the world came to the Dutch Republic's doorstep to observe, learn, and take note. The inquiring competition needed to know.

In 1669, while scouting for information in the Dutch Republic, Cosimo III de' Medici, the twenty-six-year-old heir to the Grand Duke of Tuscany, visited Delft. He was impressed by the city's churches, the stockpiles of Holland's munitions at the *Armamentarium* (Arsenal) and the vast shipments at the VOC warehouse, but also notably, its Delftware.

As described by his travel companion Lorenzo Magalotti at the conclusion of their tour: "Finally, a shop of Delft earthenware is visited, where Z. H. makes large purchases." Upon returning to their inn on the central *Groote Markt*, Magalotti reflected on the quality of Delftware, even noting the superiority of Dutch ceramics:

> Si vedono con amirazione le majoliche di questa città così ben fatte, dipinte, e si fine, che si scambierebbero per vere porcellane dell'Indie
>
> (One sees with admiration the majolica of this city so well made, painted, and so fine, that they would be mistaken for real Indian porcelain)

Theories regarding the Dutch abounded. Was it Dutch ingenuity, work ethic, cleanliness, "contriving and building of great Ships to sail with small charge," or "parsimonious or thrifty Living?" Myriads of potential explanations were suggested by amazed foreigners to explain the Dutch success.

But a certain hypothesis also arose from the pages of analytical reports of England's East India Company (EIC), the Dutch East India Company's most aggressive competitor, which, in its ceaseless pursuit to overtake its rival, left no stone unturned. That theory included "Daughters."

As Governor of the East India Company and one of the wealthiest men in England, the fittingly named Sir Josiah Child in the 1660s set his sights on the Dutch Republic, addressing the "Dutch threat" by attempting to decipher the secrets of its success. His succinct report, *Brief Observations Concerning Trade and Interest of Money*, from 1668, lists his fifteen possible reasons and his findings—one of which may have been surprising to his company. Amongst the various uniquely Dutch factors from low interest rates to liberal immigration, he describes:

> Seventhly, The education of their Children, as well Daughters as Sons; all which, be they of never so great quality or estate, they always take care to bring up to write perfect good hands, and to have the full knowledge and use of *Arithmetick* and Merchants Accompts; the well understanding and practice whereof, doth strangely infuse into most that are the owners of that quality, of either Sex, not only an ability for Commerce of all kinds, but a strong aptitude, love, and delight in it.

The young woman in the pottery saleroom in Delft pulls out a small rectangular fruitwood case from behind the counter. Unlatching the lid, she opens the box to reveal her coin balance.

A Delftware vase has been selected by the gentleman; it sits on the counter between them. It will be prepared in a basket or box carefully stuffed with hay and delivered to his home. He places several coins on the surface between them. But she is skeptical of their quality, eyeing the uneven metal edges, already measuring and weighing them in her mind's eye.

Her coin balance is her essential tool to ensure fairness and accuracy in transactions. At a time when the Dutch Republic and its merchants conducted business with partners and customers from all over the world, her balance helped determine the value of coins from different regions or countries efficiently. There was always the chance an unscrupulous purchaser could "clip" a little gold or silver from the edge of the soft metal coins.

She gently lifts its delicate steel beam and copper pans, one circular, one triangular suspended by a green silk cord. Holding her scales in her right hand, she deftly calibrates it as they stand in silence. She places the coin on the pan followed by the standardized weights to the opposite pan until the beam was balanced once again.

She maintains the balance. She carefully observes the pans, noting the subtlest differences. Surrounded by the myriads of blue-and-white Delftware on display, the gentleman waits in anticipation for the young woman's pronouncement.

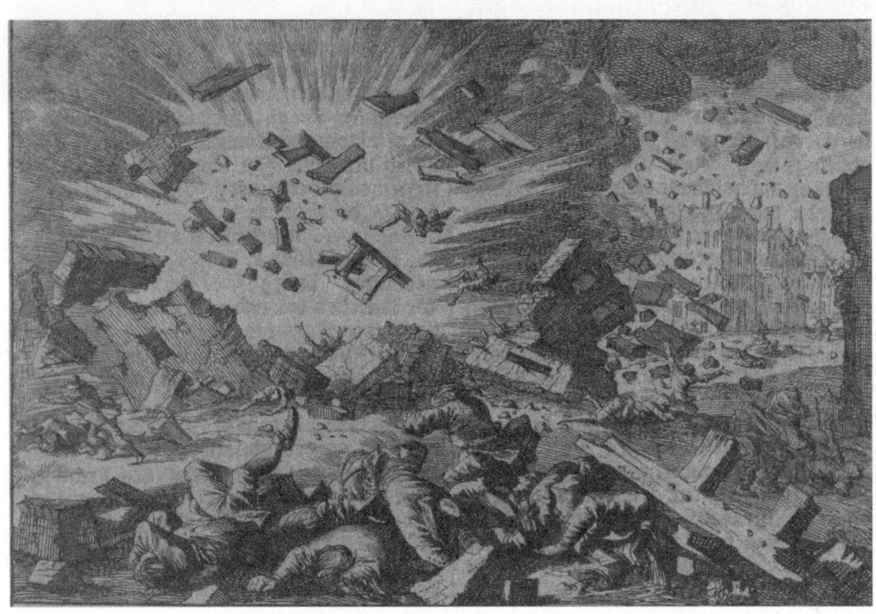

ABOVE: Casper Luyken's 1654 etching, *Explosion of the Gunpowder Tower in Delft*, vividly captures the catastrophic blast that shook the city, featured in Johann Ludwig Gottfried's 1698 *Historical Chronicle*, a compendium of the world's most memorable events. Rijksmuseum, Amsterdam. OPPOSITE: Simon Fokke's 1654 etching depicts the aftermath of the Thunderclap, as survivors survey a gaping crater, Delft residents frantically dig through rubble, motionless figures lie amid the devastation, and a lone figure slips away, burdened with heavy sacks. Rijksmuseum, Amsterdam.

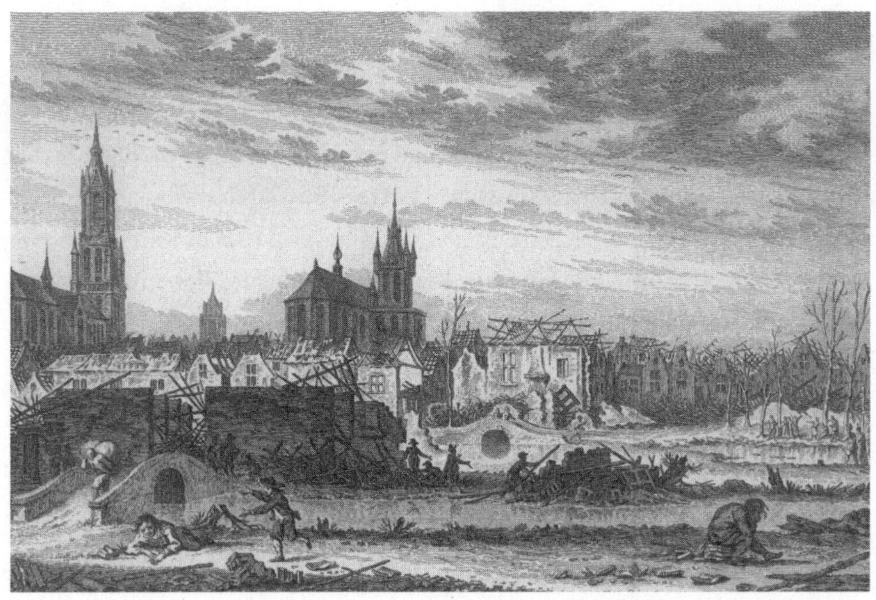

3

The Delft Thunderclap

"One spark, one moment destroys a city . . ."

—Joost van den Vondel, "On the thunderstorm of the nation's gunpowder at Delft," 1654

"She is very clever, too clever for a woman. She lacks the indefinable charm of weakness. It is the feet of clay that make the gold of the image precious. Her feet are very pretty, but they are not feet of clay. White porcelain feet, if you like. They have been through fire, and what fire does not destroy, it hardens."

—Oscar Wilde, *The Picture of Dorian Gray*, 1891

October 12, 1654, began as a typical Monday in the town of Delft. Horse-drawn barges were busily ferrying passengers and goods on the brick-lined canals, artists in their studios were preparing their pigments, grinding minerals with their mortars and pestles, and potters sat at their wheels throwing clay, forming vessels for the next firing. The tree-lined streets were quieter than usual—a number of the residents of Delft had traveled that morning for shopping at the market in Schiedam and a fair in The Hague. Punctuated by the monumental stone church towers of the *Oude* and *Nieuwe Kerk*, the sky was clear above this city of distinctively Dutch step-gabled brick homes.

But at half past ten, a catastrophe occurred that forever shaped Delft and its inhabitants.

In a split second, there was "such a horrible rush and force, that the arc of heaven seemed to crack and to burst, the whole earth to split, and hell to open its jaws," described Delft historian Dirck van Bleyswijck in 1667. A series of five deafening explosions threw bodies into the air, ripped tiled rooftops off buildings, shattered medieval stained glass, and sheared trees to their roots. Acrid waves of heat, debris, and piercing sound emanated from the blast, transforming Delft, a city celebrated by artists of the seventeenth century for its soft fluid light, into a clouded chasm enveloped in darkness.

It would be called *De Delftse Donderslag*, the Delft Thunderclap.

Almost 100,000 pounds of black gunpowder from the Dutch ammunition reserve had been stored in a magazine located in a former convent. The magazine was so concealed—even from Delft residents—that it was nicknamed the *Secreet van Holland* (Secret of Holland). Intended for the protection of their city during an era of ongoing conflict, most notably with the Spanish during the Eighty Years' War or the Dutch Revolt, their defensive cache instead detonated in the largest man-made blast the world had ever seen.

How the explosion occurred remains a mystery to this day. Was it caused by the keeper of the magazine, Cornelis Soetens, who was reported to have gone that morning with his assistant for their customary check of the supply and to collect a sample? Had they created the fatal spark fumbling in the dark in this underground storage space, dropping their metal lantern on the stone flooring between the rows of barrels?

No one will ever know.

All that remained of Soetens, the magazine, and the surrounding section of the city known as the *Doelenkwartier*, only a few hundred meters from central Delft, was scorched earth centered around a fifteen-foot-deep crater filled with water. Doors slammed and windows broke as far as The Hague seven miles away, and a sonic boom was heard in the coastal area of Texel seventy miles to the north.

When the vapor and smoke finally cleared, the residents were faced with a landscape resembling the aftermath on a battlefield. A quarter of the city had been destroyed.

Initial estimates suggested thousands had perished. Eventual counts concluded over one hundred residents were immediately killed in the explosion and thousands were horribly maimed or deafened by the blast. Entire families were wiped out, including that of the noted thirty-two-year-old Dutch painter, Carel Fabritius. Thought of by many as the most promising pupil of one of the Dutch Republic's most revered artists Rembrandt van Rijn, Fabritius was at his easel that morning, located in his family's home, unknowingly not far from the magazine, creating a portrait while a client patiently posed. All that remained of Fabritius's anticipated legacy was a handful of paintings including the jewel-like tromp l'oeil panel now in the collection of the Mauritshuis in The Hague, *The Goldfinch* (1654). Painted just months before the Thunderclap, some believe this diminutive picture depicting a brown and yellow bird restrained to its perch by a gold chain may have in fact been pulled from the wreckage of the Fabritius home and studio, surviving the explosion, unlike its ill-fated maker.

Many left the city after the Thunderclap, away from the constant reminder of tragedy and loss, to make a fresh start. But in the face of surrounding catastrophic devastation was a woman, a recent widow and mother of three young children, who remained in Delft to rebuild her life. She not only recovered from disaster but also seized the opportunity to begin a unique new path—a blue-and-white path. A pioneer, she would step into her role as one of the first known women to found and develop her own successful pottery business in Delft. She would sign business documents in bold traditional Gothic script—she was called by her maiden name—Barbara Cornelisdochter Rotteveel.

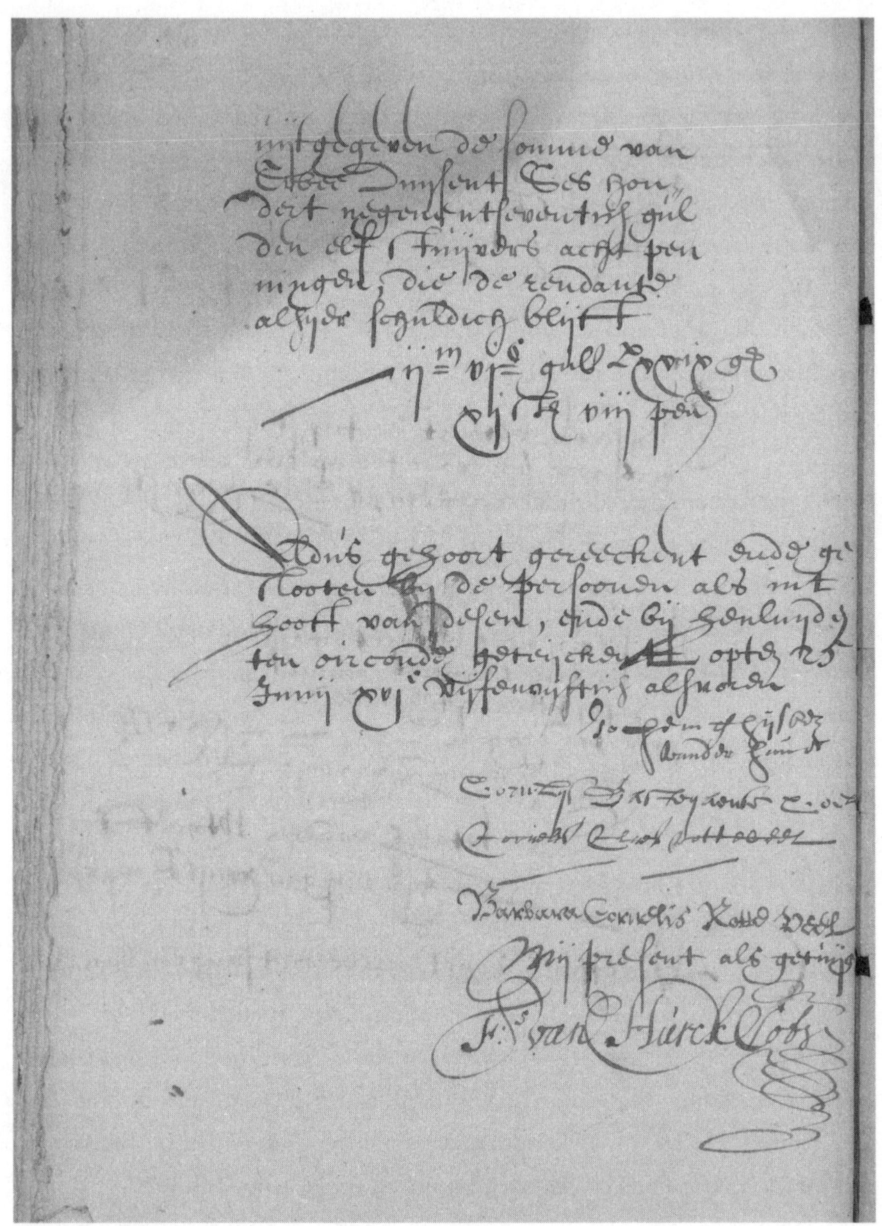

Barbara Cornelisdochter Rotteveel's signature on a notarial deed dated June 25, 1655, reflects her handwriting training, rooted in the Gothic cursive style favored in late sixteenth- and early seventeenth-century Dutch copybooks. Stadsarchief Delft (Delft City Archives).

Baptized in Delft on December 3, 1627, Barbara grew up in a canal house "behind the *Nieuwe Kerk*," or the New Church, in the center of town, characterized by the market square and the Town Hall. It would have been an especially bustling area, a crossroads of sellers and buyers on market days at covered stalls, governing officials heading to their offices, and congregants convening for services. Barbara was five years older than her neighbor, a boy whose parents owned a house and inn a few streets away. He would later create such masterpieces as *Girl with the Pearl Earring* in 1665 and come to be known as one of the most famous artists in history—Johannes Vermeer.

With a tall and narrow red-tiled roof, shaped brick facade, and large windows, Barbara's childhood home may well have been depicted in one of the few remaining paintings by Thunderclap victim Fabritius in his *A View of Delft, with a Musical Instrument Seller's Stall* (1652). Painted two years before the Delft Thunderclap, this mysterious masterpiece has riveted art historians for centuries because of its unique optic perspective, which affords a glimpse behind the *Nieuwe Kerk*—Barbara's neighborhood as she would have known it.

It was in the *Nieuwe Kerk* that Barbara was baptized, as were her contemporaries Johannes Vermeer and another Delft native, Antonie van Leeuwenhoek, the celebrated self-taught "Father of Microbiology." An early developer of the microscope, van Leeuwenhoek was among the first to observe such organic matters as blood cells. The *Nieuwe Kerk*'s austere nave and chapels would bear witness to virtually every pivotal and celebratory moment of Barbara's life, from family baptisms to weddings and funerals.

Growing up in the shadow of the *Nieuwe Kerk*, a short distance from the Markt where she could run and play on its brick-paved expanse, Barbara was the eldest of five children. Although not from a family of regents or wealthy merchants, she was certainly of relatively comfortable means. Barbara's mother also grew up in a home on a canal, on one of the wealthier streets in Delft at the time called *Turfmarkt*. From notarial documents, we know her father participated in real estate and commercial transactions, which would suggest they had ample income.

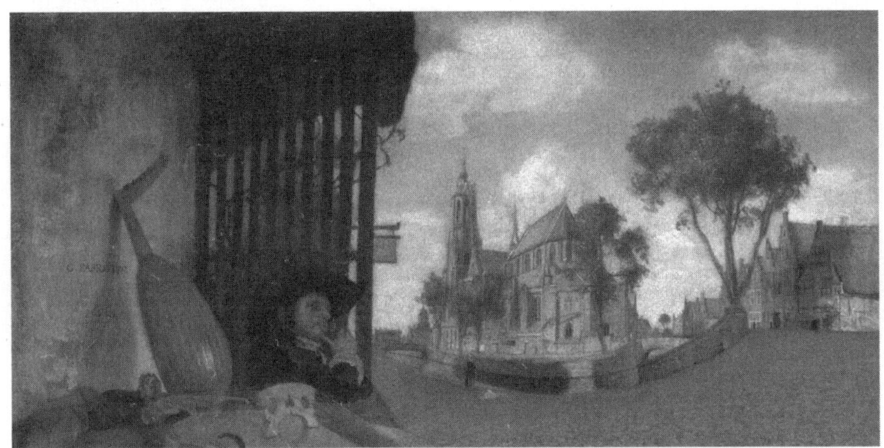

In Carel Fabritius's 1652 painting, *A View of Delft, with a Musical Instrument Seller's Stall*, the instrument seller gazes toward the brick facades of homes behind the *Nieuwe Kerk*, an area that included the Rotteveel family residence. The National Gallery, London.

Barbara was an archetypal "Golden Age" girl, living through the ascendency of the Dutch Republic. To inhabit this dynamic place and time would have been an experience characterized by Dutch military might and trading prowess but also more social mobility and tolerance of different religions and ideas than its neighboring contemporary states. This afforded its residents freedom of thought and opportunity, which in turn reaped economic, scientific, and artistic riches.

Just as the United States would later be known, the Dutch Republic had quickly become a "land of opportunity," drawing talented immigrants from throughout Europe. Perhaps Barbara's parents had heard of the group of English seeking religious freedom that had been living just fifteen miles away from Delft in Leiden. Later known as the Pilgrims, they set off for the first leg of their journey to America from the port of Delft called Delfthaven in July 1620.

The *Geoctrooieerde Westindische Compagnie* (Dutch West India Company), granted a monopoly on trade in the Americas and Africa in 1621, also looked across the Atlantic Ocean for new opportunities, which led to the settlement of New Amsterdam and the so-called "purchase" of Manhattan in 1626—just one year before Barbara's birth.

The first half of the seventeenth century in the Dutch Republic was also a time marked by risky speculation. As Barbara grew, so too did the markets for commodities, including exotic imports like tulips. Dubbed "Tulipmania" by nineteenth-century historians, the frenzied tulip bulb trade of the 1630s saw single bulbs sold for staggering sums—the equivalent of six ships—before the market dramatically collapsed in 1637. The crash left some investors and bulb dealers, known as "florists," reeling, as fortunes were lost as quickly as they had been made.

Equally alluring to Dutch consumers was the insatiable market for Chinese porcelain brought to the Dutch Republic thanks to the endeavors of the Dutch East India Company. Barbara's parents were possibly among the lucky few who were able to purchase the elusive Chinese porcelain due to their close proximity to the firm's Delft kamer, one of the five VOC locations in the Dutch Republic. Decorating their home, the treasured exotic import would have been prominently displayed on cabinets, tables, chimneys, or wall brackets. If not the coveted porcelain, Barbara's family would have had an ample supply of the local copies—the equally brightly hued but more accessible blue-and-white Delftware.

Growing up in this era of speculation and entrepreneurship, Barbara, like most young women of her time and class, prepared for this commerce-focused Dutch society with an education either at home or boarding school and a curriculum that included math. It is also possible, as was the custom, that she would have had the opportunity to learn day-to-day transactions in a shop or office, assisting her family's businesses as a young woman.

As the abundance of notarial records penned in ink on pages of paper held today in the Delft City Archives show, from contracts with employees to loans she made to Delft residents, it would seem likely she excelled at her studies and its applied uses such as accounting. These tools together with a healthy dose of Dutch entrepreneurial spirit would accompany her for the rest of her life in her passion for business until the day she died.

On September 28, 1650, at the age of twenty-five, Barbara was married at the *Nieuwe Kerk* to Simon "the Notary" Mesch. In the Dutch Republic, where magistrate's courts considered only the most serious offenses, such as murder, it was the notary who oversaw legal acts, from wills and prenuptial agreements to property transactions and divorce. Appointed by public authorities at the national, not local, level, the *notaris* was often a role held by the sons of powerful regents.

But Barbara's life with Simon the Notary was cut short. Just weeks after the birth of their third child, as Barbara recovered, Simon lay dying in bed. A notary, one of Simon's peers, was called on January 8, 1654, and a last will was signed. Eight days later, Simon died.

That October, when the Thunderclap roared, shook the earth, and sent roof tiles hurtling through the air, was Barbara alone at home with her children, including her recently born son? In the aftermath of the explosion, from 1654 through 1656, the Secretariat of the City Council compiled lists of compensation for those whose homes had been damaged. Delft residents recorded their expenses for reimbursement, and among these records is a claim for 800 guilders, attributed to Barbara's "large house."

At a time when 300 guilders represented the annual wages of an unskilled laborer, the amount suggests the damage was extensive. As windows shattered, objects flew from their shelves, and chaos engulfed her home, had Barbara shielded her children, struggling to protect them? The records remain silent, leaving these questions unanswered.

As Barbara raised her children following the Thunderclap and through the 1660s, she would have been aware of the proliferation of blue-and-white pottery in Delft as it soared in popularity. Before the Delft Thunderclap in the 1640s, Delft was home to eleven potteries with an average of fifteen painters and servants each. By 1670, as reported by the historian van Bleyswijck, the number of these "makers of Delft Porcelain" had more than doubled in number to twenty-eight, many with approximately sixty employees. This rise was in response to the great demand worldwide, "because Dutch Porcelain is nowhere wrought more subtly or delicately than in this town, in which they seem to copy the Chinese to perfection."

It is at this moment of flowering in the production of Delftware in the late 1660s that Barbara—now in her mid-forties—and her children, now young adults, seized the opportunity to capture a part of this lucrative trade and step into a role that was, on the surface, dominated by men. She would establish a pottery of her very own.

Perhaps during her walks through the southwestern section of Delft, the heart of Delftware production, she noticed the vacant potential of premises by the canal. This two-story house and workshop, with large windows overlooking the canal and bridge where the Korte Geer and Korte Breedsteeg intersected, seemed ideal. A map from the period reveals the strategic nature of her choice. Prominently located on a busy corner with canal access for transporting goods, her workshop was also in close proximity to the prestigious Delft offices of the Dutch East India Company. Diagonally across the canal stood one of her fiercest competitors in Delftware, the renowned *De Griekshe A* (The Greek A) pottery, which would be later favored by royals. Her ambitions were high, and her choice of location reflected her determination.

Like The Greek A, Barbara's pottery was the site of a former brewery. At the time there would have been ample opportunities to buy such buildings in

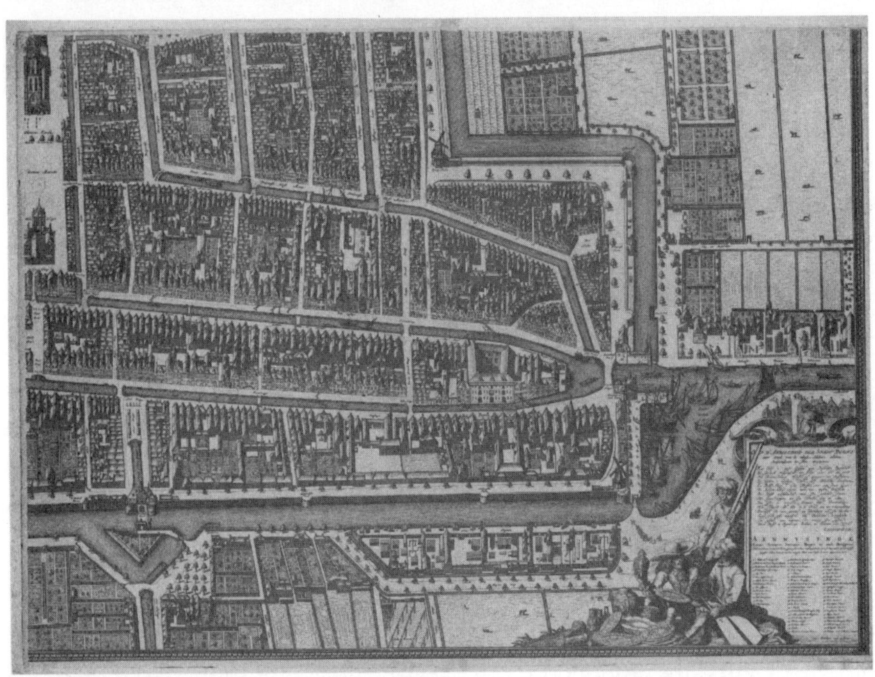

Bottom right section of *Figurative Map of Delft* (1703–1752) by Johannes de Ram, from the second state of the *Kaart Figuratief* (Figurative Map), commissioned by Delft in 1678 and produced under Dirck Everts van Bleyswijck. Its three-dimensional relief creates a striking miniature of the city, including The Three Bells pottery. Rijksmuseum, Amsterdam.

Delft, left empty after the precipitous decline in the Delft brewing industry. Once a central product of the city, with more than a hundred beer-makers in Delft in 1600, by 1650 the city had fewer than thirty. What had provoked this precipitous demise of brewing in Delft?

Is it possible the quality of the Delft water had been affected by another lucrative local trade—textiles? Had the makers in the production of fabrics polluted the water sources? The cause remains in question, but we do know the space the brewers abandoned provided the ideal location for potteries that would also require ample works areas and storage, easy access to the canal to transport materials and products, and the ample availability of water necessary for the preparation of clay. Immortalizing their previous tenants, most Delftware potteries simply retained the titles of the beer businesses that preceded them, with their works of art forever identified by names easily mistaken for those of inns or taverns such as The White Star, The Peacock, or The Double Jug.

Acquiring the location on the Korte Geer was no simple task, and Barbara approached it strategically—and anonymously. The sale was set to take place at public auction, and perhaps to ensure her plans remained discreet, she enlisted the help of her brother-in-law, Joris Mesch, to bid on her behalf. By December, Joris revealed the true buyer to the residents of Delft—Barbara Rotteveel. The property included a house, yard, warehouse, coach house, and stables, all of which Barbara intended to transform into her own pottery. By December 29, 1670, the property, known as *De Drie Klokken* (The Three Bells), officially became hers.

But Barbara's greatest challenge was yet to come. The optimal property, ample capital, artistic talent, and initiative were not the only requirements for Barbara to make Delftware in the town. No blue-and-white could be made or sold in Delft without the express consent of the rigorous and exclusive Guild of St. Luke, the professional trade organization of Delft for artists and artisans. Without their approval, any Delftware created by Barbara would be seized and destroyed.

In order for Barbara to gain entrance into the field of blue-and-white, she would need to be elected as a full dues-paying member, a Master of Delft's Guild of St. Luke.

We do not know when the Delft Guild of St. Luke was founded, but according to the historian Michael Montias it was probably in existence by the fifteenth century. The Guild Hall, located around the corner from the *Nieuwe Kerk*, the *Stadhuis*, and her childhood home, would have been a building Barbara knew well. Passing by this brick building with its four prominent stained-glass windows, she would have noted the carved sandstone festoons mounted on the facade depicting the main trades of the Masters, which at the time included painting, pottery, bookbinding, and glassmaking.

Named after the patron saint of artists, the Guild of St. Luke's main function was to enforce the monopoly of production and trade against other cities and non-guild competitors, and to control the training of the workforce, the quality, and the prices of the products. Masters who wanted to produce and trade in Delft were required to become citizens of Delft and were registered after paying an entrance fee. Apprentices and *kneck* (journeymen) were not full members. Each major city in the Dutch Republic had its own self-governing guild that protected, promoted, and defended the interests of its members. Once a member, Barbara would be expected to pay not only an entrance fee but annual dues, and even attend funerals of fellow members—and be fined if she didn't.

At the top of the Guild's organizational pyramid was a small elite group of leaders, six *hoofdmannen* (headmen) representing the most important areas of artists and artisans. Convincing the headmen that she had the ability to uphold the standards of the Guild as well as fulfill financial requirements of entrance fees and regular dues was Barbara's goal. She needed their approval; without it there would be no Delftware business.

It was 1671 and the headmen of the Guild were comprised of two Delftware makers, two glassmakers, and two artists—one of which was none other than the respected Johannes Vermeer.

Although the Dutch Republic was a nation-state where women enjoyed more agency than any of its neighboring countries, it would still have been quite unique for a woman to come forward to join a Guild in her own right. How was it that Barbara could successfully appeal to the headmen? The answer lies in the preserved ledgers of newly enrolled members, the Master Book of

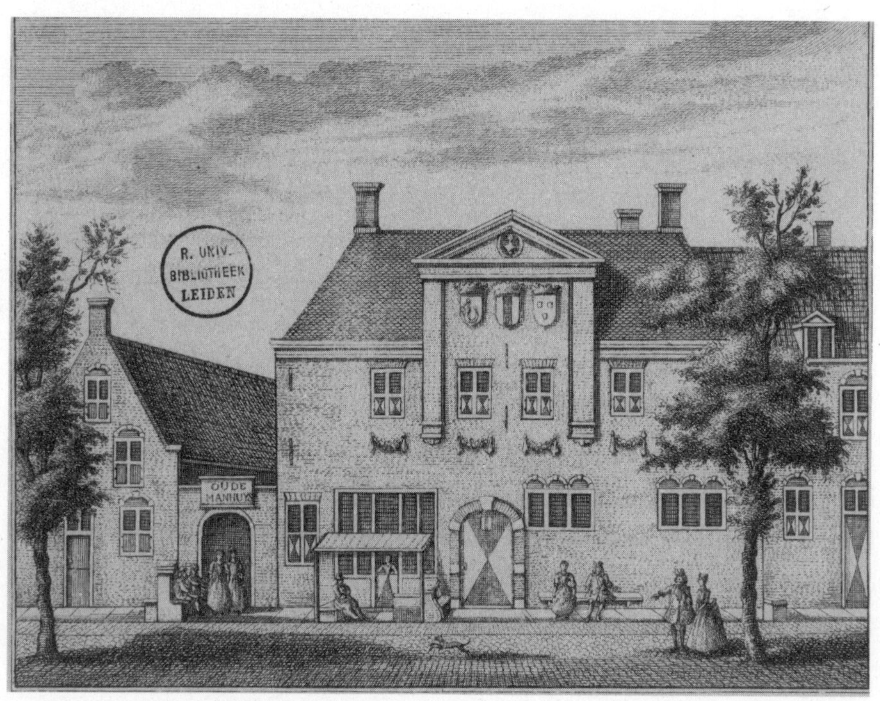

Leonardus Schenk's 1736 engraving, *View of Delft's St. Luke Guild House*, highlights the decorative brick facade featuring an arched doorway, pediment, sandstone festoons, and stained glass windows. Universiteitsbibliotheek Leiden.

the Guild of St. Luke of Delft, discovered in the Koninklijke Bibliotheek (Royal Library), today known as the KB National Library of the Netherlands.

Founded in 1798 and located in The Hague, seven miles from Delft, the KB National Library of the Netherlands collects and conserves Dutch national heritage in written, printed, and, today, also digital form. Its shelves contain all that remains of the records of Delft's Guild of St. Luke. After more than two hundred years as the center of artistic and artisanal life in Delft, by the early nineteenth century the once venerable group was disbanded. The Guild Hall fell into disrepair and was eventually torn down in 1879.

Miraculously, two small vellum-bound booklets containing a list of members, or Masters, from 1611 to 1715 survived and were identified by researchers in the early nineteenth century. Within the pages of these Master Books, Vermeer's name appears intermittently, as he served as Headman during four one-year terms: 1662, 1663, 1670, and 1671. During these years, he enrolled other members—including Barbara.

Penned in a variety of cursive hands, the Master Book contains only the most basic information regarding the Guild's recent inductees—the date of induction, name, title or métier, dues, and whether or not those dues had been received. The brevity of the descriptions suggests the succinct efficiency of the members and an organization with little time for or interest in lengthy formalities—there was art to be created and, moreover, money to be made.

Although sparsely written, these entries disclose a wealth of revealing familial connections that illuminate the context of Barbara's life. We are introduced to Barbara's extended family including her brothers-in-law: Joris Mesch, whose name would appear in 1661, the founder of *'t Fortuyn* (The Fortune) factory and Johannes Mesch, entering the Guild in 1667 as a Master potter or *plateelbacker*, who would become owner of *De Vier Romeynse Helden* (The Four Roman Heroes).

The Mesch brothers, Joris and Johannes, together with her nephew Simon Simonsz. Mesch (owner of *t' Hart* or The Stag pottery) would all achieve the status of headmen of the Delft Guild of St. Luke, representing the interests of potters from the 1680s through 1705. Had the Mesch brothers appealed to the Guild on behalf of their sister-in-law? Had Barbara wanted or been required to take the rigorous five-day examination to produce a sample piece of Delftware, as required for Master potters?

The details of what exactly transpired have been lost but we do know that on March 31, 1671, Johannes Vermeer and his fellow Headmen entered Barbara's name in the Master Book of the Guild of St. Luke as "Winckelhouster haer Plateelbackerije de 3 Klocken" (owner of her pottery The Three Bells). She was one of only eleven Masters entered in 1671. Paying her entrance fee of six guilders, the standard for Delft-born Masters whose parents were not in the trade previously, she was officially enrolled.

It was on this early spring day that Barbara stepped out of the Guild Hall onto the brick-paved street, finding herself now a full member of the Guild of St. Luke of Delft. She had successfully purchased a property, established a pottery, and gained entrance to the Guild—feats certainly worthy of celebration. Perhaps Barbara gathered the extended Mesch family, including the brothers, wives, and children as well as friends for a festive evening of wine, dinner, songs, and speeches to commemorate the auspicious occasion, as was often the custom. This festive pause to reflect on her accomplishments was most likely brief. Given the effort and expense entailed, Barbara was probably eager to fire up the kilns and start production as quickly as possible.

What would it have taken for Barbara to own and oversee a successful Delftware pottery? On a day-to-day basis, thanks to a description of the production of Delftware captured at the end of the eighteenth century by Gerrit Paape in his *De Plateelbakker of Delftsch Aardewerkmaaker*, 1794, we can visualize the complex process that the production of Dutch Delftware necessitated and therefore Barbara's many concerns and interests.

At the outset, she would require significant space, time, staffing, artistic skill, and organization. The process for any ceramic could take as long as two weeks, from preparing the clay to cooling the finished product and preparing it for sale. A Delft pottery would usually need to be a large complex with one or more kilns for firing the pots. Other facilities were also needed on-site: drying lofts, woodsheds, painting rooms, warehouses, and a salesroom. Everyone at her pottery had their own specialization and was responsible for a particular part of the production process. Proprietors like Barbara would often have their home within the complex, too.

The clay used for Delftware was a carefully crafted combination of materials. It included a local clay from the Delft area, a fattier, more malleable clay from Germany, rich in minerals that gave it a greasy texture and enhanced plasticity, and dry *marl*—a light-colored, rock-like material containing calcium carbonate, which added strength and hardness. This unique recipe distinguished Delftware from other types of earthenware. In the quest to make more refined objects that closely imitated porcelain, it allowed for the refinement of forms, from thinner dishes to finer handles and spouts, allowing Delft potters to blur the lines between earthenware and the elusive porcelain.

The clays were mixed and purified in a clay washery. The pottery would store square blocks of clay in pits. When it was time to make the Delftware, the clay had to be made soft and pliable again. This was the job of the *aardetrapper*, a "soil stomper" or "earth treader," who would knead the large amounts of clay with their bare feet to bring the material to a pliable consistency.

The softened clay would go to the throwers and shapers, who would turn it into objects. Throwers used the potter's wheel to produce dishes, bowls and other circular items. Other items that consisted of several parts, such animals and figures, would be made by the shapers. They used plaster molds to repeat a shape. Components like knobs and handles would be shaped by hand and stuck on using clay slurry.

At this point the pieces coming from the throwers and shapers still contained a lot of water, so they had to be dried in the drying loft to avoid fracturing in the kiln. Lifting the pieces with long wooden boards, the pottery assistants would carefully store the items on tall racks.

After successfully drying—a process that could take anywhere from several days to over a week, depending on the size and thickness of the piece—the pottery underwent its initial firing in preparation for glazing and painting. Stokers heated the kiln to approximately 800–1000°C, consuming large quantities of wood. During this firing, the wares hardened and developed a buff-colored appearance.

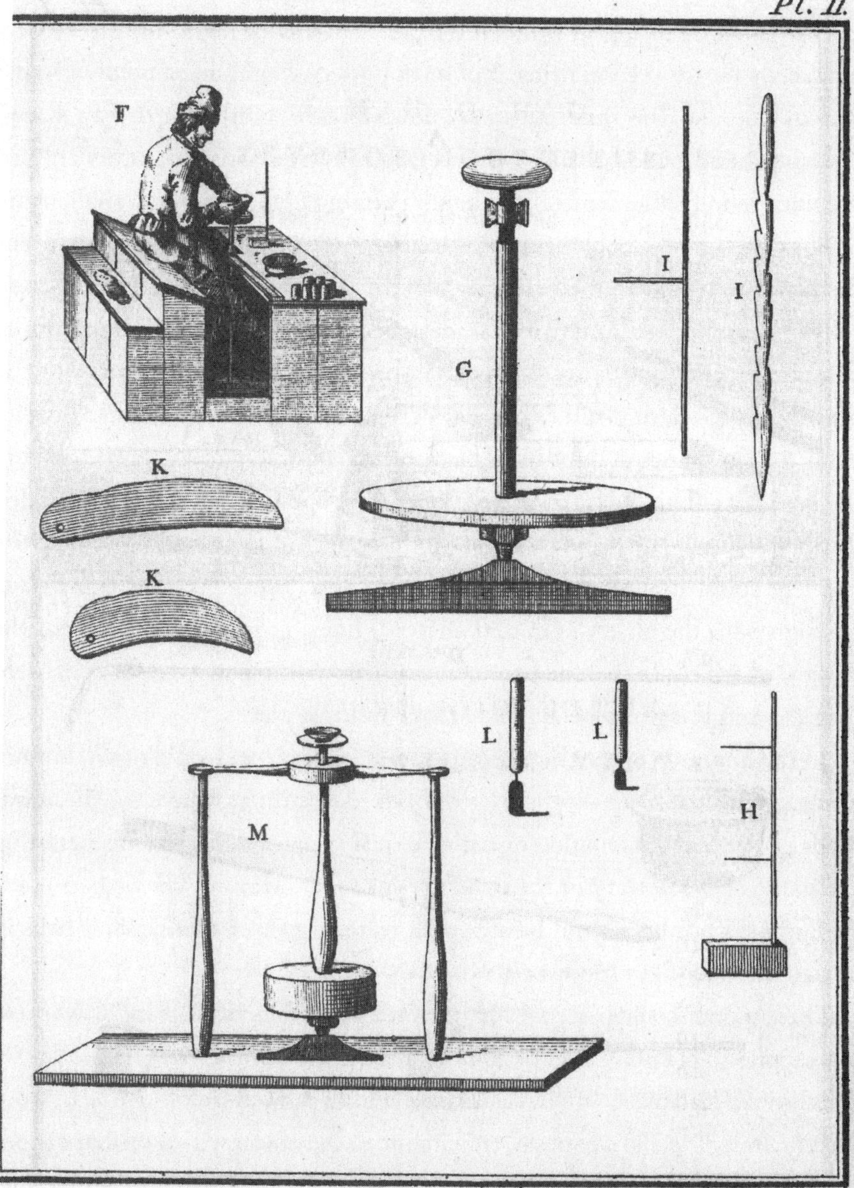

In Gerrit Paape's *1794 De Plateelbakker of Delftsch Aardewerkmaaker*, the "thrower" expertly shapes clay on his potter's wheel, setting it in motion with his foot while using measuring instruments and a cutter to refine and remove the finished vessel. Universiteitsbibliotheek Utrecht.

Fired pieces were scrubbed clean then entirely dipped in the *wit*, a bath of tin glaze to make them appear white. If the pieces were to be plain white, they were now ready for the second firing. But most pottery would be painted with that famous blue, and The Three Bells was known for its beautiful deep cobalt shades.

Using handmade brushes, often crafted by the artist, painters applied decorations to Delftware freely by hand. Painting Delftware was a challenging task, as the painter could not let the brush rest on the surface; the porous earthenware would immediately absorb the paint. These brushes were typically long and of medium firmness, designed to hold just the right amount of paint for precise application. Many Delft pottery painters began their work by drawing *trek*—dark outlines of their designs—directly onto the fired object using a deep shades of dark blue, black or manganese-purple pigment before the layers of cobalt blues of varying tones were applied. These outlines added distinctive depth and dimensionality to the surface of Delftware. Alternatively, painters could use a pounce—a perforated piece of paper that transferred a design onto the object as dotted charcoal lines—to create a shadow of the design, which could then be painted over. This method allowed for consistent patterns and images to be applied across multiple pieces.

In the final step of the decorating process, the painter would often, but not always, mark the piece on the base or back to document where the piece was made. Pottery marks could consist of letters or figurative symbols denoting the name of the pottery or the owner or manager. Many of the objects made by Barbara's pottery would bear a mark featuring three small cobalt bells in a triangular configuration.

Once painted, the piece was handed off to the *vloerwerker* (floor worker), who applied a colorless layer of gloss over the glaze using a short-haired brush. This layer of lead glaze, known as *kwaart* (a term derived from the Italian word *coperta*, meaning blanket or cover), enhanced the object with a brilliant sheen reminiscent of porcelain while also providing an added layer of protection. With this final coating, the piece was ready for its second firing in the kiln.

Placed in *saggars*—cylindrical earthenware containers—these vessels ensured that flames and gases did not damage the pottery or its glaze. Inside the protective saggars, the pieces were separated by pins to prevent them from

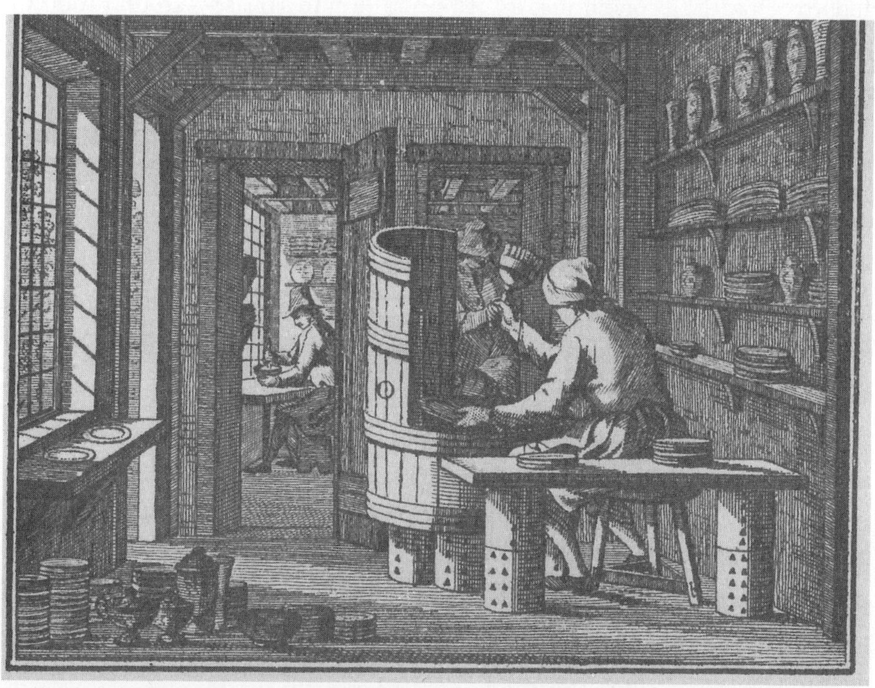

In Gerrit Paape's 1794 *De Plateelbakker of Delftsch Aardewerkmaaker*, artisans enhance Delftware's post-firing sheen by sprinkling and spreading a thin, clear lead glaze over the surface—a technique known *as kwaarten*. Universiteitsbibliotheek Utrecht.

fusing together during firing. Once the saggars were filled, they were placed in the kiln, which was then sealed, leaving a few small holes for observation.

The carefully monitored second glaze firing would take several days to complete, with the pots being gradually fired and cooled. A variety of things could go wrong during this process. If the kiln was too hot, the earthenware could become misshapen; if it cooled too quickly, cracks could form. While many colors could be applied before the second firing, the temperature of this phase—around 1000°C, hot enough to be called the *grand feu* (large fire) technique—was so high that colors like gold, red, and black would burn away.

If decoration incorporating gold, red, or black was needed, the pieces would be returned to the painter for these additional colors before being placed in the kiln for a third and final firing at around 600°C—a cooler temperature known as the *petit feu* (small fire) technique. Archaeologists excavating the former site of Barbara's pottery have uncovered sherds confirming that colors such as yellow, green, purple, and black were also used at The Three Bells in the complex and highly skilled dance of ceramic production.

Successfully completed Delftware would then be sold at the pottery itself, in shops and markets, or handled through brokers for international trade. At the height of the industry, around 1700, it is probable that The Three Bells, like many of the Delftware potteries, could produce in the region of tens or even hundreds of thousands of pieces annually, which were packed in straw-filled willow baskets or wooden crates and loaded on barges on the canal to be taken to the awaiting ships to be sold all over the world.

The nineteenth-century French art historian Henry Havard described the products of Barbara's pottery as being "highly esteemed. They consist the most often in vases, cones, plates, dishes and bottles, decorated in blue shades. The paste is fine, sonorous; the slip is white, the shape graceful, the décor simple, yet elegant . . ."

But the production of refined blue-and-white vessels for discerning clients was not the only vital aspect of the business of Dutch Delftware. A successful and competitive enterprise such as The Three Bells required Barbara's management of some thirty to fifty workers. It also called for the coordination of a constant flow both regionally and internationally of materials, including the essential

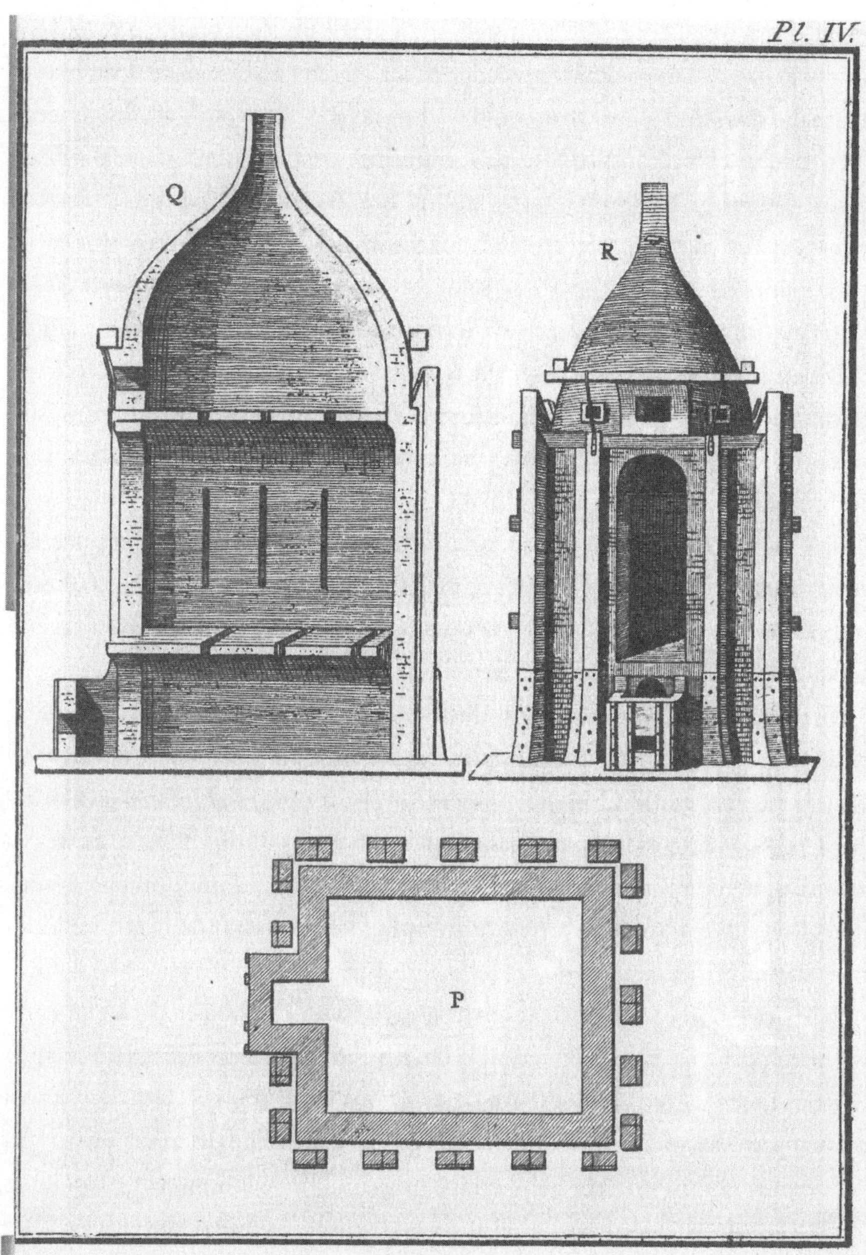

An illustration from Gerrit Paape's *De Plateelbakker of Delftsch Aardewerkmaaker* (1794) includes a cross-section of a Delft kiln, revealing its design that allowed for the precise stacking of ceramics to fire thousands of pieces at once. Universiteitsbibliotheek Utrecht.

cobalt, from suppliers as well as distribution of the finished products to buyers. As owner she had to possess knowledge of the closely held scientific formulas to create the clays and glazes that could withstand the rigors of the firing process. Then Barbara would utilize astute accounting, enabling the financial wheels to run smoothly. Building a team around her, Barbara would hire a series of managers and master potters to assist in the execution of her vision.

Barbara would own The Three Bells for thirty-three years, overseeing *haer* pottery until the age of seventy-six in one of the longest stewardships of any Delftware pottery. Turning over the ownership of her business in 1706 to her grandson Pieter Mesch, who had joined the Guild of St. Luke as a master potter in 1700, she completed her final task. Just a year following the transfer, Barbara passed away in Delft in 1707.

On October 10, 1707, nearly a half century after the Delft Thunderclap struck their city, a notary with several assistants gathered at Barbara's home and pottery to create, in a process that could require hours or often several days, an inventory of her final assets and possessions.

The notary was prepared to produce descriptions of each object, searching every room, closet, and drawer, even exploring under each bed, to create a document that would ultimately include over fifty pages of financial instructions and a listing of her personal property in flourishing calligraphy. It is a record that today, more than three hundred years old and yellowed with age, allows us a glimpse of the private sphere of a woman behind the blue-and-white Delftware.

Barbara's home and pottery on the canal were demolished in the early twentieth century to make way for Delft's red brick neo-Renaissance-style District Court. From the effusive descriptions from the 1670s of Dirck van Bleyswijck, Delft's city biographer, we can imagine that her home located on the premises of the pottery had high ceilings and tall windows of broad panes of glass, proudly asserting that visitors and writers admired the city because "the houses of Delft are as beautiful, as elegant, as large and as high as can be found anywhere else in the Netherlands."

Carrying their writing utensils, ink, paper, and measuring equipment, the notary and his assistants began their work by climbing the steep stairs of

Barbara's home to the uppermost reaches, passing the large salons of the lower floors as they ascended.

It is in a curtained chamber, a storage or work room described as a "Small Upstairs Room," that the notary chose the first object to begin the inventory—a simple black trunk. Its understated form may have piqued his curiosity. Opening the lid, it afforded the most appropriate first introduction to Barbara: they found a hoard of "old paper receipts," hundreds of business papers most likely documenting the many transactions of materials and purchases generated by her Delftware pottery.

But not to be discouraged, next entering "a Small Back Room," the notary continued the search and shortly thereafter came upon an *Eyken kist*, an oak box. Perhaps expecting even more paperwork, perhaps he was surprised to discover the lustrous cache of silver—from large silver bowls, salt cellars, and mustard pots to the monogrammed utensils of family members including a baby's pap spoon. Probably conserved in cloth, he carefully unwrapped and inspected each piece, noting any marks or monograms. Just as he thought he had finished unpacking the box, upon reaching the bottom he found ingots of gold and foreign currency. Pulling out a portable scale, he paused the search to weigh each piece and note their value.

Continuing throughout the house, we follow the notary on a winding path passing through plain workrooms, storage rooms, cellars, and several kitchens to refined upper and lower salons. A rich sanctuary of objects reflecting a lifetime in the business of Delftware, its spaces are filled with countless stacks, garnitures, and wall-mounted quantities of Dutch Delftware. But it is equally a reflection of the unique riches and habits of the Golden Age as afforded by the international scope of the Dutch East India Company. Large amounts of Chinese *fyne porceleyne* were artfully arranged on chimneypieces and furniture made of rare tropical woods including ebony filled the rooms. There are delicate bowls for drinking chocolate, the popular and luscious treat grown by the Dutch in the West Indies.

Like many Dutch, Barbara was also a painting collector. Covering the walls throughout the house, from the functional kitchens to the richly furnished salons, were a multitude of oils-on-canvases depicting a variety of genres—landscapes, seascapes, and portraits—including one of herself, a "*syned portrait Barbara Rotteveel.*" The notary, apparently familiar with contemporary art, was careful to note her collection included such popular artists as the Dutch artist "van de Venne" (Delft-born Adriaen van de Venne, 1589–1662), the renowned Flemish painter "Jordaens" (Jacobs Jordaens, 1593–1678), and "Vosmaar" (possibly Daniel Vosmaer, 1630–1666, a Delft native who started out with landscapes but soon switched to Delft townscapes, perhaps due to their popularity following the Delft Thunderclap).

Foreign visitors to the Dutch Republic were constantly amazed at the quantity and quality of pictures in Holland. The English traveler, Peter Mundy, visiting Amsterdam in 1640, commented on the Dutch love of paintings. He observed, "As For the art off Painting and the affection off the people to Pictures, I thincke none other goe beyond them. . . . All in generall striving to adorne their houses, especially the outer or street roome, with costly peeces. . . ."

But in the last room, "The Upper Front Room," we have been afforded an intimate reflection, a peek of Barbara's life behind closed doors. It was a room filled with memories of family; the notary described a chamber with walls lined with portraits. Seated in this room, Barbara would have been surrounded by relatives past and present, including a "*sygned*" portrait of Barbara's eldest daughter, Elizabeth. Two years old at the time of the Thunderclap, she not only survived childhood but married a goldsmith and continued to live in Delft.

This room overlooking the canal was also an homage to another element close to her, a subject Barbara would have known intimately—the color blue. In every shade, from sapphire to aqua, in a luxurious array of materials, this chamber would have delighted the eye with its plentiful supply of "blue flowered seat cushions," "blue glass" that probably included ultramarine Venetian-style beakers, flutes, goblets, and serving bottles, and a trove of cobalt fine Chinese porcelain artistically arranged across the chimneypiece, as well as eleven pieces of fine Chinese porcelain atop a *kast*, a massive Dutch cabinet.

Traditionally descending with a family's daughter when she marries, the *kast* with its adjustable shelves and drawers would have held a bride's valuable linens and silver. The typically neoclassical design of this traditional cupboard

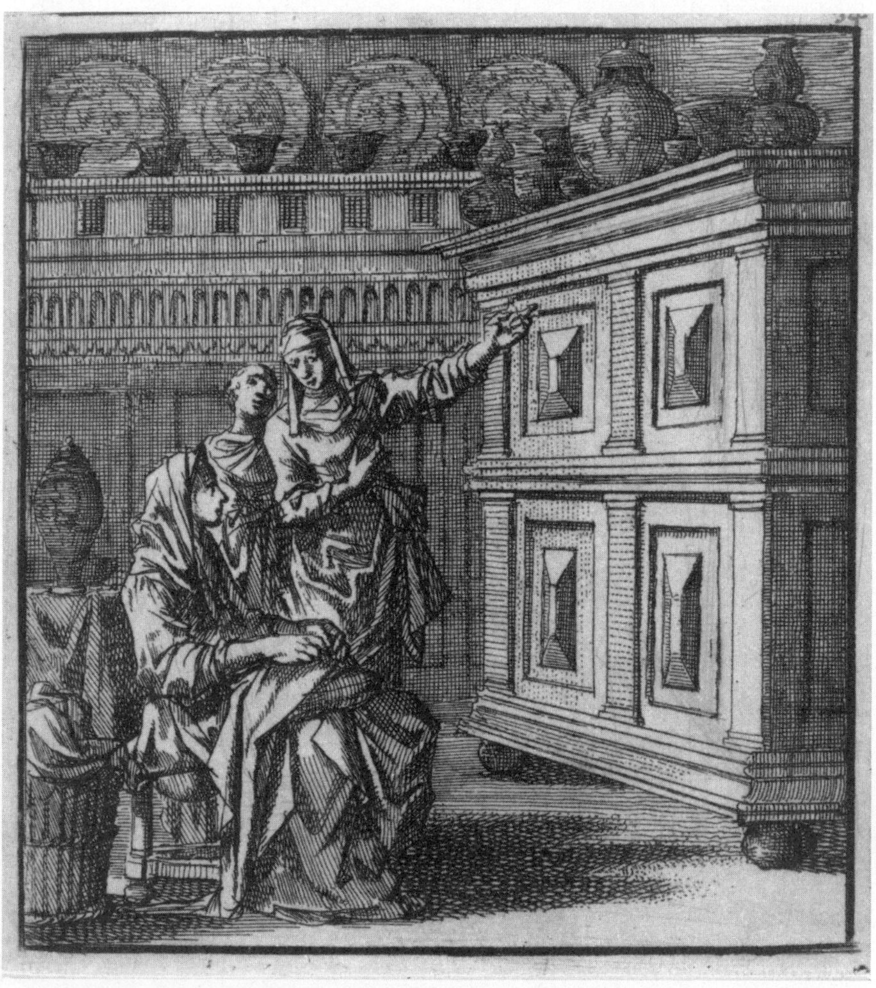

Jan Luyken's 1711 engraving *Het Porselyn: 't Is maar een Vertooning (Porcelain: It's Just a Display)* depicts the *kast* as an elegant, elevated showcase for treasured porcelain and Delftware, emphasizing their beauty and prestige. Rijksmuseum, Amsterdam.

dated from the Renaissance and was often characterized by bold moldings and massive feet. Made usually of fine-grained European oak, it would have been veneered or accented with ebony from the Dutch East Indies. The door would have had a working lock. A prized piece of heirloom furniture, this grand armoire, some over seven feet wide at the crown, also often contained a secret compartment to hold valuables.

But what was in this *kast*? The notary must have relished the moment of unlocking the cabinet, swinging open its doors. Locating the hidden compartment, probably with the help of a family member, the notary had finally located some of Barbara's most valuable personal possessions—her long gold chain necklace for "twice around the neck," her monogrammed gold hairpin "marked BR" worn to secure her hair tightly under her linen and lace cap, and gold rings, including one with seven round diamonds and another with seven square diamonds. Conveying devotion, prestige, or authority, these gold objects were worn by Barbara to commemorate moments of her life—her marriage? The birth of her children? Her Delftware business?

Joining her fellow Masters of the Guild of St. Luke Johannes Vermeer and Carel Fabritius as well as other prominent citizens of the Dutch Republic, Barbara's body was laid to rest in Delft's oldest church, the *Oude Kerk*, located just west of her factory on the same canal that had provided water for pottery production and a convenient route of transportation for her finished blue-and-white Delftware.

The Three Bells, like its founder, would prove resilient. In the years following Barbara's death, though the Dutch Republic found itself gradually losing its place as a dominant world power, the pottery continued to successfully produce Delftware for more than another century. Despite the surrounding ever-increasing political and economic instability, the subsequent owners—both male and female—were able to hold onto the property, even as the once unrivaled Dutch Republic finally unraveled by the end of the eighteenth century. At war with England, invaded by French revolutionaries in 1795, and ultimately becoming a Napoleonic vassal state in 1805, the Dutch Republic would regain its freedom in 1815. By this time both its as well as The Three Bells's best years were now behind it. The Kingdom of the

Netherlands would be the final owners of The Three Bells, purchasing what had been Barbara's property and closing its doors in 1841.

Barbara's legacy outlasted the venerable Guild of St. Luke of Delft, dissolved in the 1830s following the breakup of the guild systems across Europe. Turning the pages of the Guild of St. Luke's Master Book, reading the lists of its distinguished membership of Delft's artists and artisans, we see that Barbara was one of just a handful of women noted in its extant ledgers. On the surface the apparent lack of female names might suggest that women were an anomaly of the Delft trade.

But while openly acknowledging Barbara's unique position as a woman founding her own successful Delftware factory, the Master Book at the same time obscured the full extent of other women's roles in the world of blue-and-white. Awaiting on archival shelves were the identities of the many female pottery owners whose names had not been inscribed.

In 1703, during the last years of her life, gazing out the windows of her The Three Bells pottery across the canal and up the street, noting the smoke rising from the brick chimneys of the neighboring potteries, Barbara would have been aware that not one, but all three of her nearest neighboring Delftware factories—The Greek A, The Peacock, and The Porcelain Claw—were at that moment under the ownership of women.

In truth, nearly a quarter of all Dutch Delftware pottery owners from the mid–seventeenth through the mid–nineteenth century had been consistently female. Running production, directing employees, shipping works, managing accounts, as well as maintaining their families and homes—these were women just like Barbara—but they shared one unique difference, a defining status that held them apart and yet allowed them the freedom to make blue-and-white.

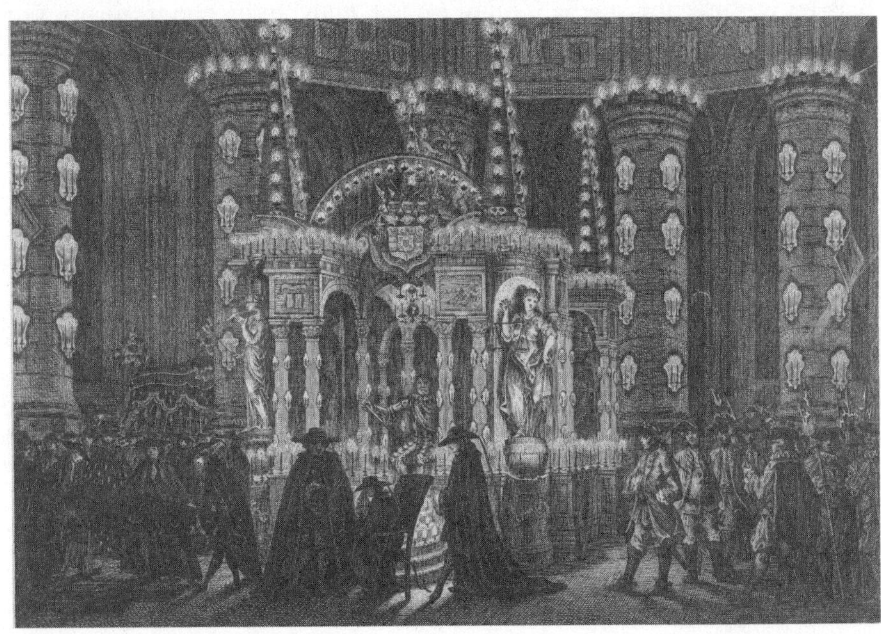

ABOVE: Simon Fokke's 1760 etching captures the 1759 night funeral of Anna of Hannover, Princess of Orange-Nassau, in the *Nieuwe Kerk*, Delft, where countless candles in mounted sconces and obelisk-shaped towers cast a flickering glow over the tomb. Rijksmuseum, Amsterdam. OPPOSITE: Charles Antoine Goutzwiller's 1878 illustration in Henry Havard's *Histoire de la Faïence de Delft* showcases rare examples of black Delft (*fond noir*) from a garniture of five pieces. Author's collection.

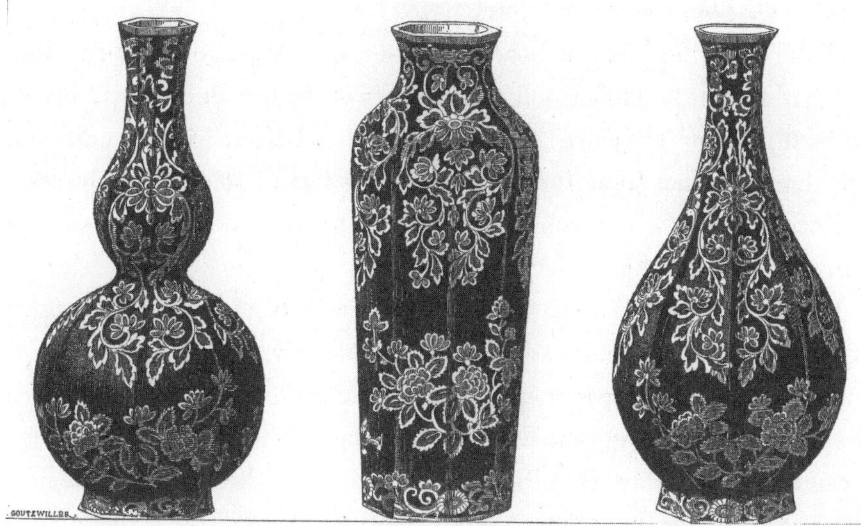

4

Weduwes

"Their was not Widdow, Wife, or Maid,
But to a hair she had her Trade"

—Anonymous, *Hogan-Moganides: or, the Dutch Hudibras*, printed for William Cademan, 1674

On the winter evening of January 24, 1701, a light wind swept across frozen canals, under low footbridges, and through the dark, narrow streets of Delft. The chill settled on the windows of *De Griekscke A* (The Greek A) pottery located on the Geer, frosting its thick glass panes. Inside, however, candles flickered in wall-mounted sconces and large fires crackled, warming the assembled guests.

That night, in place of the usual sounds of stoking kilns, the rhythmic hum of pottery wheels, and the quiet concentration of painters, the air was alive with celebration. Violins and flutes played lively tunes, laughter and singing filled the rooms, and the floorboards creaked under the weight of dancing feet.

Johanna van der Heul stood at the center of the festivities, joined by her husband, Pieter Adriaensz. Kocx, along with relatives, friends, staff, and neighbors. Production at The Greek A, one of Delft's preeminent potteries, had been halted for two consecutive days of feasting to commemorate the transition of leadership at the pottery.

Johanna was the wife of the heir apparent, Pieter, when he took on the mantle of his father Adrianus Kocx as the head of the family business. The Greek A, with its history of royal patronage and celebrated craftsmanship, had long been the pottery of choice for both wealthy Dutch burghers and European royalty, including Queen Mary II of England. Now, the time had come for the next generation—Pieter and Johanna—to continue its legacy. The gathering was both a personal and professional triumph.

Johanna surveyed the room, surrounded by the many faces that, in their own ways, played specialized and vital roles in the success of the business. From the *aardetrappers* (earth treaders), *draaiers* (potters), and *schilders* (painters) to the *vloerwerkers* (floor workers), *kokermakers* (container makers), and *houtklovers* (wood choppers)—every member of The Greek A was present, husbands and wives, families and friends in what may have been over one hundred guests.

The Dutch were famous for their feasting traditions, regardless of the event's scale, and on this occasion, the Kocx family would have spared no expense. Long tables draped in fine Dutch linen were covered with pewter platters of winter delicacies: golden-skinned goose, suckling pig, and savory pies with thick, flaky, fluted crusts ordered from Delft's finest baker. Sweet confections included fruit-filled *taerten* glistening with jewel-toned preserves, Delftware bowls brimming with cherries and quinces preserved in syrup, and rose-scented marzipan shaped into delicate fruits and flowers.

Heavy glasses of French wine and tankards of Dutch ale were raised as toasts filled the air, including one from the potter Pieter van Hurk, who composed a poem for the occasion. His twenty-three-stanza "*Vreugde-Gezang*" ("*Joyful Song*") was an ode of gratitude to their generous host, Adrianus Kocx, an acknowledgment of the vital contributions of The Greek A staff, and a celebration of Johanna and Pieter, the *Jonge Lui* (young people) who would lead the pottery into its next chapter. Van Hurk urged the guests to lift their voices in song, letting their joy echo across the pottery and "reverberate to the warehouse."

Johanna moved gracefully among the guests, exchanging toasts and sharing in the laughter and music that filled the rooms. Delftware bowls with mounds of scented tobacco were handed around. As the clay pipes were lit, sweet smoke wafted. Caterers came and went to replenish the copious courses as the food and drink was enjoyed and a group of musicians accompanied the gathering late into the night.

For Johanna, this was a moment of pride and happiness, both as a partner in the business and as a wife. She had been married to Pieter just three years earlier, on March 28, 1698, at Delft's *Nieuwe Kerk* (New Church), at the age of twenty-nine. Tonight, she was not only celebrating the future of The Greek A, but also the promise of a life to build with Pieter—in business and, perhaps in time, as a family. As prominent makers of Delftware, with a history of royal patronage behind them, they would have been the envy of the city's potters.

Yet, just two years after this celebration, on a spring day—May 7, 1703—Johanna stood silently in the *Nieuwe Kerk*, overseeing Pieter's funeral.

Gathered in the church's choir, family, friends, and colleagues of The Greek A were once again brought together—but now enrobed in black mourning cloaks. The coffin, placed on a carriage, had solemnly processed through the streets of Delft. Pieter was to be interred beneath the church's choir, not far from the burial site of the Dutch royal family. This privileged location underscored not only his wealth but also his status and significance within the Delft community.

Inside the church, gray stone pavers had been lifted from the dark floor and propped against the nave's columns, revealing the raw red clay earth beneath. A long trench lay open, prepared to receive Pieter's body. While tradition called for four to six attendants, his sixteen pallbearers reflected

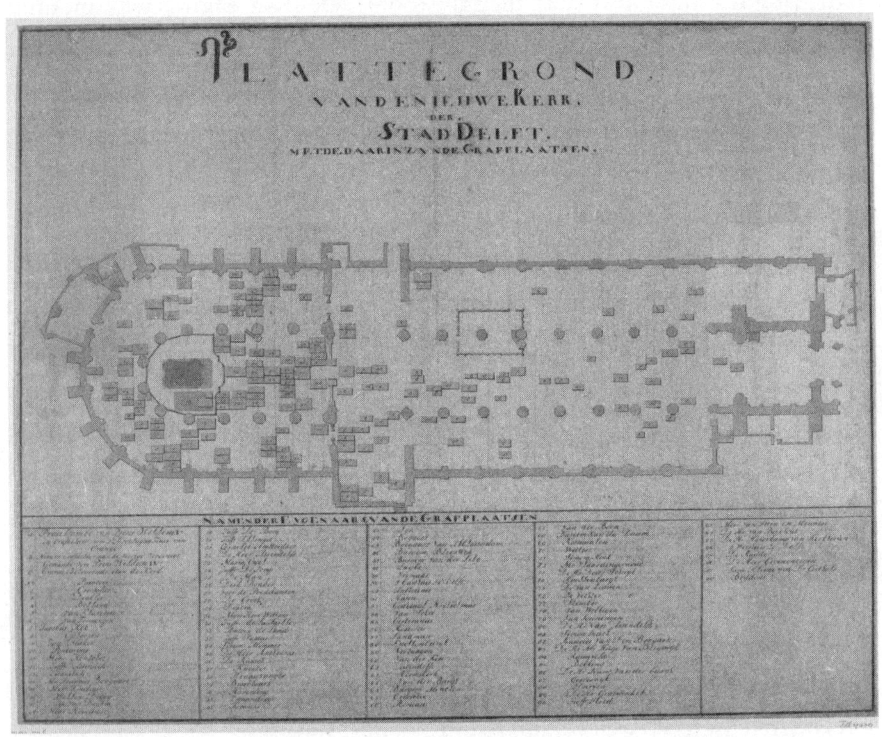

A grave map of Delft's *Nieuwe Kerk*, 1751, rendered in pen, ink, and pencil, reveals the precise locations of burials within the church's interior. Rijksmuseum, Amsterdam.

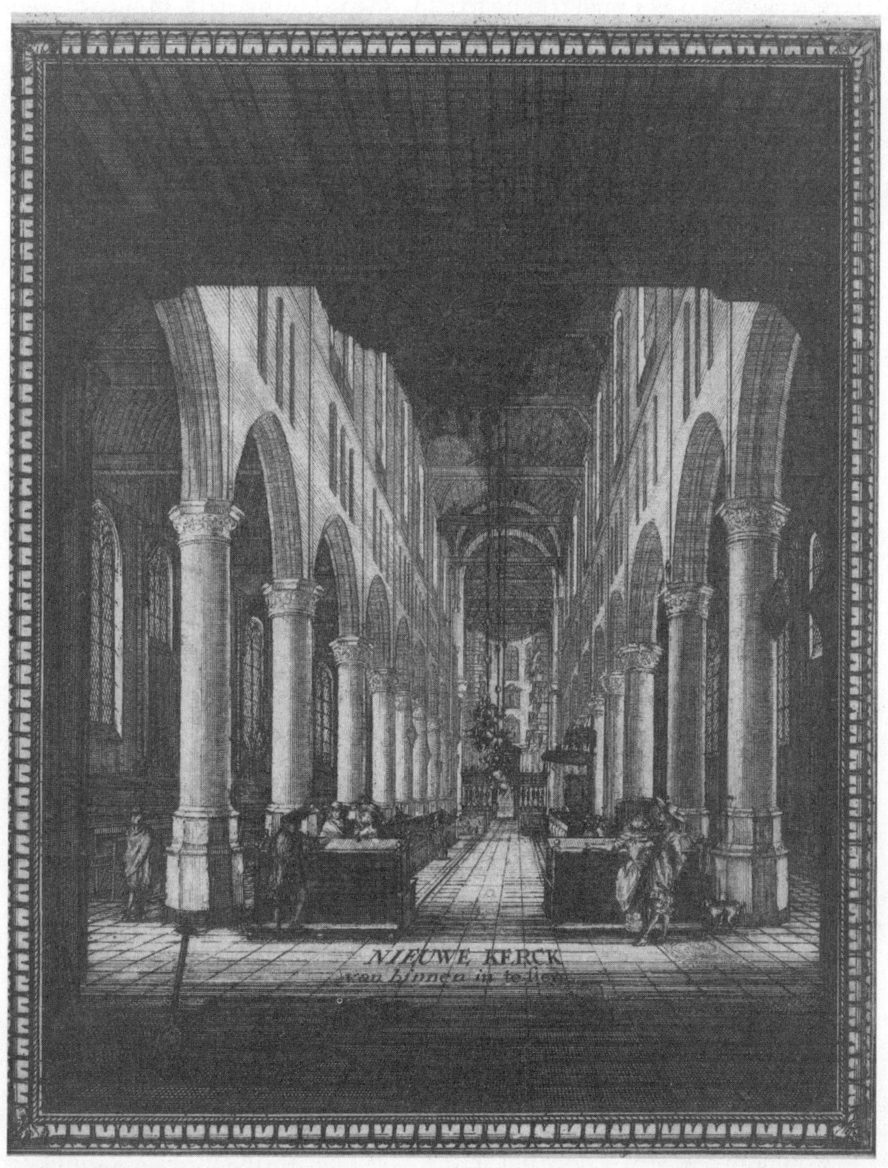

Attributed to Coenraet Decker, a 1680 etching of the *Nieuwe Kerk* in Delft offers a striking view of the nave from the entrance, with a recently removed grave slab and scattered tools. Rijksmuseum, Amsterdam.

his exceptional stature—not just within the community, but in the legacy of The Greek A. It was a final tribute to a life shaped by mastery, influence, and enduring renown. Standing beside Johanna in their broad-brimmed black hats were his "Guild brothers," members of the Guild of St. Luke—not only the potters but artists and artisans from painters to bookmakers. Guild protocol required they attend; if they didn't, fines would be procured.

Johanna stood in solemn silence as her young husband's body was gently lowered between the rectangular stones, coming to rest beside his father. Pieter's death, at just thirty-eight, leaves unsettling questions. Was it illness? An accident? The records left behind in Delft offer no answers. Left to grapple with the suddenness of her loss, Johanna gazed down the nave of the church, her mind likely swirled with uncertainty about what lay ahead.

Her days had only recently been punctuated with the excitement of new beginnings—a new century, a new union in marriage with Pieter, and a new partnership as owners of one of Delft's most prestigious businesses. But Johanna's path had taken an abrupt, unexpected turn. She was now alone, referred to by the Dutch term for a woman whose husband had died—a *weduwe.*

The Dutch term *weduwe* and its English equivalent "widow" share the base ancient Indo-European stem *widh* or *weidh* meaning "to be separated," but also "to be empty." Like an overturned vase or ewer having spilled water or wine in a sudden rush, these women were compared to vessels with their contents poured out, losing all that they contained in an instant.

For a Dutch woman who had been known since birth—even when married—by her maiden or family name, widowhood added a distinctive, permanent coda to her identity. Redefined, signing her name on each notarized document for the rest of her life as:

Johanna van der heul weduwe pieter kocx

But for Johanna, like many other Dutch women, this flowing away of one life would give way to a slow but bittersweet replenishment—the gaining of new independence, an establishment of autonomy, and for some, as a *weduwe*, there was opportunity.

Stepping out of the *Nieuwe Kerk* at the conclusion of the service onto the expanse of alternating bands of staggered and herringboned brick pavement

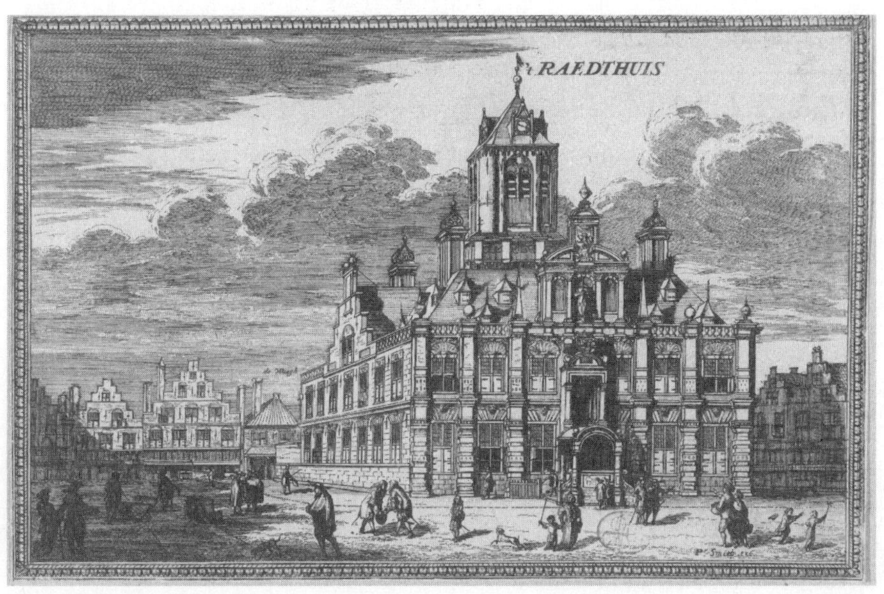

An etching (1678–1703) attributed to Coenraet Decker captures Delft's Renaissance-style *Raedthuis* (*Stadhuis* or town hall) in the *Markt*, the heart of the city's civic life. Rijksmuseum, Amsterdam.

of the *Markt*, the central square of Delft, Johanna faced the *Stadhuis*, the City Hall. The imposing classically conceived building with red shutters, constructed around a central limestone tower dating from the fourteenth century, was the seat of city government that administered both civil and criminal law. Behind its massive stone walls and large wooden doors, in rooms decorated with sumptuous tapestries woven in Delft and paintings, were the meeting rooms of the members of the *Heeren van de Wet* (Gentlemen of the Law). Twice a week in Johanna's time, on Wednesdays and Saturdays, its front rooms became the *Vierschaar*, a public court of justice where official business was made public, from city laws to civil and criminal penalties.

The *Stadhuis* was a building Johanna would have rarely visited in a legal context. Her last visit may had been to register her and Pieter's betrothal—a public act required before their church ceremony. Women in the Dutch Republic were prohibited from holding public office and, as a married woman, Johanna was legally subject to her husband.

While marriage was viewed as the union of two entities of equal value, the management of their combined property was considered the husband's domain. Wives in Delft could not pursue legal matters, such as selling property or goods (even their own), buying property (unless for household use or as public vendors), or representing themselves without their husband's consent. Husbands even had the right to sell property originally belonging to their wives without their permission.

Despite these restrictions, married women were not entirely without legal protections. Many Dutch couples arranged mutual wills and premarital contracts, offering safeguards for both husbands and wives.

Widowhood in the Dutch Republic often represented a reversal, an unwinding of the legal and social bonds of marriage. Notably, and to the surprise of many Europeans at the time, if a Dutch couple had no will or marriage contract, the widow was entitled to half of the marital estate. This division was considered just in seventeenth- and eighteenth-century Holland, as both the bride and groom were generally perceived to have contributed marriage portions of approximately equal value.

In widowhood, women experienced a unique shift in agency. They not only regained control over their own property but also acquired the right to buy and sell goods. Widows were often entitled to manage the estate and any communal property accumulated during marriage. Women like Johanna, as widows, gained significant authority as decision-makers, holding influential positions both privately and publicly—whether managing their assets or owning lucrative enterprises such as a Delftware pottery.

As the funeral attendees departed the *Nieuwe Kerk*, the potters and painters of The Greek A considered the newly widowed Johanna with compassion but probably also with guarded trepidation. They knew she had a variety of options. Would she sell the pottery? Johanna had no children, no dependents, no son or daughter to train in the craft and to hand the business to in time. Perhaps she would remarry. Or she could return to her family, which had its own wealth. Before her marriage, she was a van der Heul.

The van der Heuls were a family that, for many generations beginning in the sixteenth century, was responsible for a vital substance for the Dutch Republic, bringing them great wealth but leaving the city of Delft with haunting associations—gunpowder.

A family of *cruytmackers*, the van der Heuls produced gunpowder, supplying not only the Dutch Council of State but also the VOC Chamber of Delft. This essential substance, made from ground saltpeter (potassium nitrate), sulfur, and charcoal, was critical for a Republic engaged in ongoing warfare and for the VOC's ships, whose reliance on artillery and firearms made gunpowder the lifeblood of the Company's defenses. Each VOC ship departing from the Dutch Republic carried up to even ten thousand pounds of gunpowder, carefully stored belowdecks.

In 1572, the States General, the central leadership of the young Dutch Republic, designated Delft as the primary storage site for its weaponry and gunpowder. Beginning with Johanna's great-grandfather, Moijses Jansz van Nederveen, in the late sixteenth century, the van der Heul family played a key role in meeting the Republic's and the VOC's demands. This arrangement ensured generations of substantial profits for the van der Heul family.

Although lucrative, gunpowder was a dangerous business. The family's horse-drawn *kruitmolen* (gunpowder mill), located outside the city walls, exploded twice in the early 1600s. By the mid–seventeenth century, the van der Heuls had become one of four leading gunpowder producers in Delft. It is likely that gunpowder produced by their mill was among the stockpiles stored in the city on the day of the Thunderclap. The proximity of their operations and their ongoing ties to the Republic strongly suggest that Johanna's family contributed, at least in part, to the Dutch Republic's ill-fated store. But despite the catastrophe, as a quarter of Delft lay ruined, the van der Heul business in the mid–seventeenth century not only survived but continued to grow exponentially.

Johanna was one of four children born to the van der Heul family in Delft and baptized on April 25, 1668, at the *Oude Kerk*. Given her family's affluence, it is likely Johanna not only attended primary school but also received private tutoring from a young age or attended a French school. Her education included reading, writing, performing mathematical calculations, and possibly becoming proficient in French—a skill that would later prove invaluable when The Greek A established exclusive dealings with Parisian merchants.

As the daughter of a gunpowder maker, did Johanna also gain any knowledge of chemistry? As part of the fourth generation in a family whose livelihood depended on precise measurements and an understanding of chemical properties, it's possible she had some familiarity with the science. Perhaps she accompanied her father to the gunpowder mill located just beyond Delft's walls. Operating since 1672 and safely positioned away from most of the city's inhabitants, the mill may have been where she observed the production process under her father's watchful eye.

Their home, situated near the family's gunpowder mill on the Buitenwatersloot, showcased their wealth and cultural refinement. Its rooms displayed porcelain, silver, and paintings. According to Arnold Houbraken, as noted in his three-volume biographical study of Netherlandish painters, *De groote schouburgh der Nederlantsche Konstschilders en Schilderessen* (1718), Johanna's father owned a work by the Delft artist Adriaen Cornelisz. van Linschoten

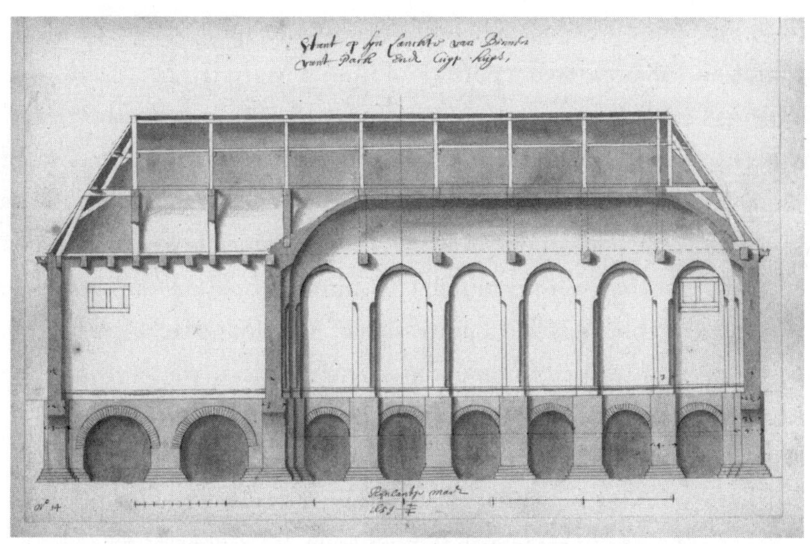

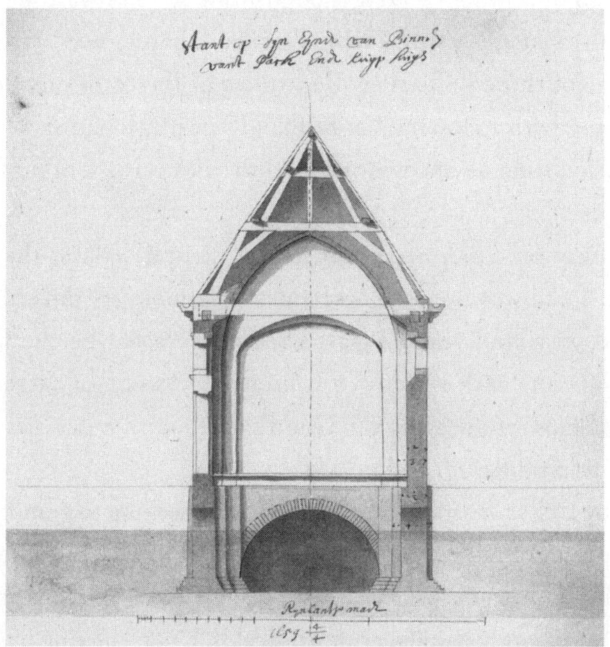

TOP: Architect and artist Pieter Jansz. Post's 1659 pen drawing, a horizontal cross-section of the Gunpowder House, or State Warehouse, on Schieweg, Delft—a fortified brick structure standing just beyond the city limits. Stadsarchief Delft (Delft City Archives). BOTTOM: Architect and artist Pieter Jansz. Post's 1659 pen drawing of the Gunpowder House from the perspective of "standing at the end of the inside . . ." Stadsarchief Delft (Delft City Archives).

and commissioned portraits of his children by Jan Verkolje I—the same artist who, around 1688, painted a portrait of Queen Mary II.

Johanna's mother, Rusge 's Gravesande, passed away in 1692, shortly before Johanna's wedding. Her funeral, surpassing even that of Johanna's wealthy father-in-law, Adrianus Kocx, was held at night at the *Nieuwe Kerk*—the most expensive time to conduct a burial. Evening funerals were considered so extravagant that they were eventually discouraged by the Dutch authorities. With sixteen torchbearers and a procession of luxurious coaches, her mother's body was solemnly carried through the streets of Delft to the awaiting church, which glowed with the light of countless candles.

Her father Salomon lived well into old age, even ordering a new coach shortly before his death in 1722. Until his final days, he resided in the mansion near the gunpowder factory, though from 1698 onward he also owned two impressive houses within Delft. Perhaps Johanna was contemplating a return to one of those properties. Regardless of the emotions she may have been grappling with following her husband's death, Johanna would need to make a decision soon, as she was required to inform the Guild of St. Luke of her intentions.

Tucked away on a side street off Delft's central square, the hall of the Guild of St. Luke was nonetheless hard to overlook. Its broad brick facade was adorned with four stained-glass windows, crafted by the Guild's own glassmakers. Below each window, a contrasting festoon of carved sandstone depicted emblems representing the Guild's four main trades: painting, glassmaking, book production, and pottery.

Inspired by Delft's artistic heritage and perhaps seeking to grandly associate it with classical antiquity, the structure's pediment featured a niche centered with a bust of Apelles, the legendary Greek painter and portraitist of Alexander the Great, surrounded by vibrantly painted armorial shields. Upon entering the Guild Hall, as described by Dirck van Bleyswijck in *Beschryving der Stadt Delft* (*Description of the City of Delft*, 1667), members would ascend the stairs to a "very large and airy room" complete with fireplace. Here, seated in chairs donated by Delftware potters as a gift to the Guild, members debated rules, resolved disputes, discussed their works, and elected officers.

Banquets celebrating new members were also held in this richly decorated space. The surroundings were as inspiring as the gatherings themselves: the intricately coffered ceiling was adorned with illusionistic paintings by Guild member and Johannes Vermeer's colleague Leonaert Bramer, and a canvas mural by Cornelis de Man wrapped the walls, depicting a classical scene featuring a triumphal arch.

The Guild of St. Luke represented a diverse array of crafts, occupations, and activities in Delft. As articulated in its complete set of regulations, the Guild Letter of 1661, its membership included:

> all those earning their living here with the art of painting, be it with fine brushes or otherwise, in oil or watercolors; glass-makers; glass-sellers; dishbakers; tapestry-makers; embroiderers; engravers; sculptors working in wood, stone, or other substances; scabbard-makers; art printers; booksellers; [and] sellers of prints and paintings.

As both advocate and governing body, the Guild was responsible for protecting its members' livelihoods. To achieve this, it sought to limit foreign competition and uphold the value of locally produced goods. The Guild established a host of exacting regulations, covering membership criteria, mastery qualifications, the hiring of apprentices, entrance fees, and dues. Ensuring adherence to its rigorous standards, infractions were met with swift "fines and punishments."

The hired staff member, the Guild "servant" or "dean," was poised to collect the *stuivers* or *guilden* from guilty or tardy members. Those who did not obey the rules could face seizure of artwork or pottery or even expulsion from the Guild. Guild membership was required either as a Master craftsman or as a proprietor, a *winkelhouder*, in order to make or sell earthenware to the public or to hire apprentices or employees. To join the Guild one had to be a tax-paying citizen of Delft, or *poorter*. Children of *poorters* automatically received this status but nonresidents or foreigners were required to purchase the right.

The rank of Master in the Guild of St. Luke of Delft, particularly for Delftware makers, was held to exceptionally high standards. Achieving this status required apprentices to complete six years of training under three Guild Masters and pass a rigorous Master's test before a jury of Master potters to demonstrate their skill.

According to the Guild records of 1654, a Delftware "thrower" was required to craft three specific items from a single piece of clay to illustrate their expertise: a salt cellar with a hollow stem, a syrup-pot (a pear-shaped vessel with a handle and spout, often used by apothecaries for medicinal tinctures), and a salad bowl.

The salad bowl may seem an unlikely form required to master in the seventeenth century, given the abundance of Dutch still-life paintings depicting rich compositions of roasted meats, breads, butters, and cheeses, and platters of glistening oysters. But raw vegetable salad or *salat* was in fact very popular, so much so it was even the first listed recipe in *De Verstandige Kock of Sorghvuldige Huyshoudster* (*The Sensible Cook or Careful Housekeeper*, 1669), the bestselling and most favored Dutch cookbook of the seventeenth century.

Pottery painters, on the other hand, were required to demonstrate their skills by decorating an entire fruit bowl with intricate designs ranging from floral motifs to human figures across its curved surface. They also had to show consistency in their craftsmanship by reproducing patterns across six large dishes. After successfully completing these tasks and gaining admission to the Guild of St. Luke, the newly accepted member was required to pay mastery dues before officially beginning their work.

The Guild of St. Luke in Delft was renowned for its strict rules and rigorous mastery tests, designed to ensure only the most skilled artisans earned its approval. Yet, amid this rigid structure, there was one fascinating exception—certain women were allowed to bypass some of the Guild's most exacting protocols.

Unaware of the tragic loss of life that would soon follow—including the deaths of members of the Guild of St. Luke—an amendment was added to the ordinance books of the Weth, Delft's legal code, in the spring of 1654, just five months before the devastation of the Thunderclap. This timely "amplification" stated:

> With the exception and on the understanding, however, that the widows of masters after the death of their husbands may continue to exercise the trade without making a proof. (They may do so) their life long, but if they should remarry and, being remarried, die, then their husbands wishing to continue in the trade shall be obliged to make their proof within six weeks after his wifes death, in the manner specified above.
>
> Thus done and confirmed by the lords of the Weth on the 20th April 1654 and announced with the great clock on the 21st following

With the ringing of the *Stadhuis*'s midnight bell over Delft, a rare exception to the Guild's many rules was put into effect. Free to proceed with the abilities of a guild member for her lifetime without taking the requisite test of the Guild of St. Luke, a widow now officially had the right to carry on her and her husband's work, allowing the continuation of business production without interference or interruption.

It was the summer of 1703, three months after Pieter's funeral, yet the Guild books still bore no notations of Johanna's intentions. She would have been acutely aware of the unique opportunity the Guild afforded her as a widow, and they awaited her response.

When her decision was finally made, did Johanna walk from The Greek A to personally notify the Guild that she would take on the pottery as her own? Perhaps waiting outside the Guild she paused at its front door, gazing up at the stone sculptural swag that celebrated the pottery makers—its sandstone renditions of plates, bowls, and ewers centered by a covered jar, before heading in to convey her message. Or did she instead send a letter, entrusted to one of her young assistants, to be hand-delivered to the Guild servant, the employee responsible for distributing information and paperwork, announcing her choice?

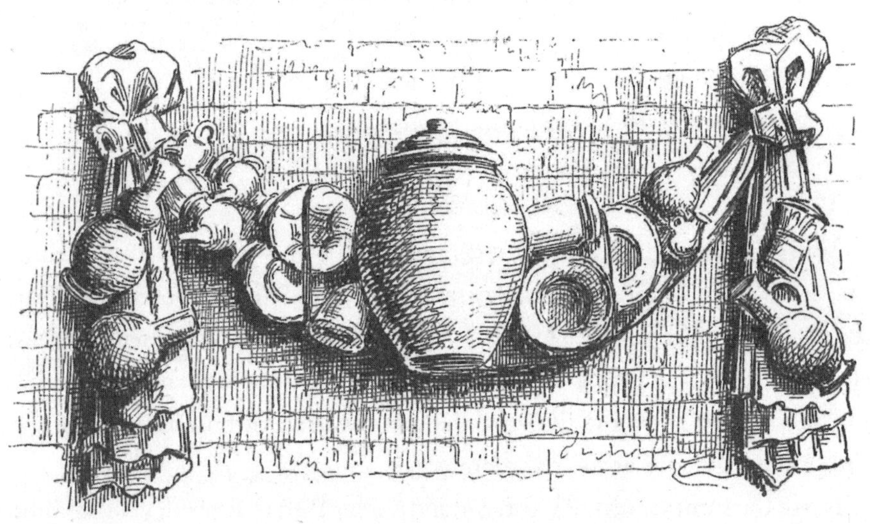

Charles Antoine Goutzwiller's illustration in Henry Havard's *Histoire de la Faïence de Delft* (1878) captures the sandstone sculpture of a swag adorned with a covered jar, dishes, and bowls, from the facade of the guildhall of Delft's Guild of St. Luke. Author's collection.

We don't know the chain of events surrounding Johanna's joining the Guild of St. Luke of Delft. Working with one of the few remaining references, a ledger, we do know that on August 14, 1703, "*Johanna van deer Heul, Wideue*" was formally listed. Having reflected for more than three months, through the spring and into the summer, in the end Johanna chose the life of Delftware. Informing the Guild of St. Luke that summer, she made it official: The Greek A would be hers alone.

It wasn't long after assuming her role as *winkelhouder* or proprietor of The Greek A that Johanna made a strategic decision: she hired a master craftsman as nominal head to help run the business. In 1705, she appointed Pieter van Hurk to the pivotal role of *meesterknecht*. An experienced potter of many talents, van Hurk was someone Johanna had known for years and who had even penned the celebratory poem *Vreugde-Gezang* for The Greek A banquet in 1701.

But was Johanna herself a potter? The answer is unclear. In a culture that produced exceptional female Dutch artists—including Judith Leyster, renowned for her genre works and portraits in the seventeenth century, and Rachel Ruysch, the still-life painter of flowers who joined The Hague's painters' guild in 1701—it seems likely that women also participated as potters and painters of Delftware. Yet Delftware, an artform rarely marked by artists' signatures and lacking, thus far, documentary evidence of women in these roles, leaves us without a definitive understanding of their contributions at the pottery wheels and painter's benches in seventeenth- and eighteenth-century Delft.

Johanna propelled The Greek A into the eighteenth century, continuing to produce blue-and-white Delftware inspired by the classic underglaze Chinese aesthetic while also embracing new styles, techniques, and palettes. Among these innovations were Delft interpretations of the colorful and highly coveted Japanese porcelain, often referred to by Europeans as *Imari* and *Kakiemon* styles.

Japanese porcelain was a relatively new commodity in the early eighteenth century. While Chinese porcelain had been perfected by the Tang dynasty in the seventh century, Japanese production only emerged in the seventeenth century. The civil uprisings in China during the 1640s disrupted Dutch access to Chinese porcelain, boosting the European market for Delftware and prompting Dutch traders to turn to Japan as an alternative source. Granted exclusive trading rights in 1609, the Dutch became the only Europeans permitted to trade with Japan for much of the Edo period (1615–1868).

Initially imitating Chinese blue-and-white designs, Japanese artisans soon developed their own distinctive styles. The Imari style, known for its bold use of gilding and vibrant overglaze enamels—particularly red and blue—quickly gained favor in Europe. Meanwhile, Kakiemon porcelain, named after the Japanese potter Sakaida Kakiemon (1596–1666), featured a softer palette of red, yellow, blue, and turquoise-green. These richly ornamented wares captivated European consumers, and The Greek A, one of the few Delft potteries capable of replicating such colors and intricate designs, excelled in adapting them to earthenware.

Under Johanna's leadership, The Greek A produced some of the most striking Imari-style Delftware. Dishes adorned with exotic landscapes, elegantly robed female figures, dragons, and butterflies were rendered in iron-red, salmon, and gold over underglaze blue. Unlike traditional Delftware, these elaborate pieces required multiple firings, increasing both complexity and risk. Achieving a stable red pigment demanded precise kiln temperatures and advanced scientific expertise, while gilding required highly skilled artisans. Recognizing the value of this specialized craft, Johanna secured an exclusive contract in 1713 with three gilders, ensuring their expertise remained dedicated to The Greek A as long as she remained in charge.

Equally challenging to produce and mesmerizing in design, "cashmere" Delftware emerged during Johanna's tenure, reflecting a striking fusion of global influences. Nineteenth-century ceramic collectors later coined the name, inspired by the luxurious, vibrantly colored scarves imported from India and prized by Europe's most fashionable women. This exquisite Delftware style encompassed dishes, garniture sets, and tea wares, drawing heavily from the *famille verte* palette of Chinese porcelain—deep cobalt-blue, rich red, vivid green, and occasional accents of yellow or black—that had captivated European collectors since the late seventeenth century.

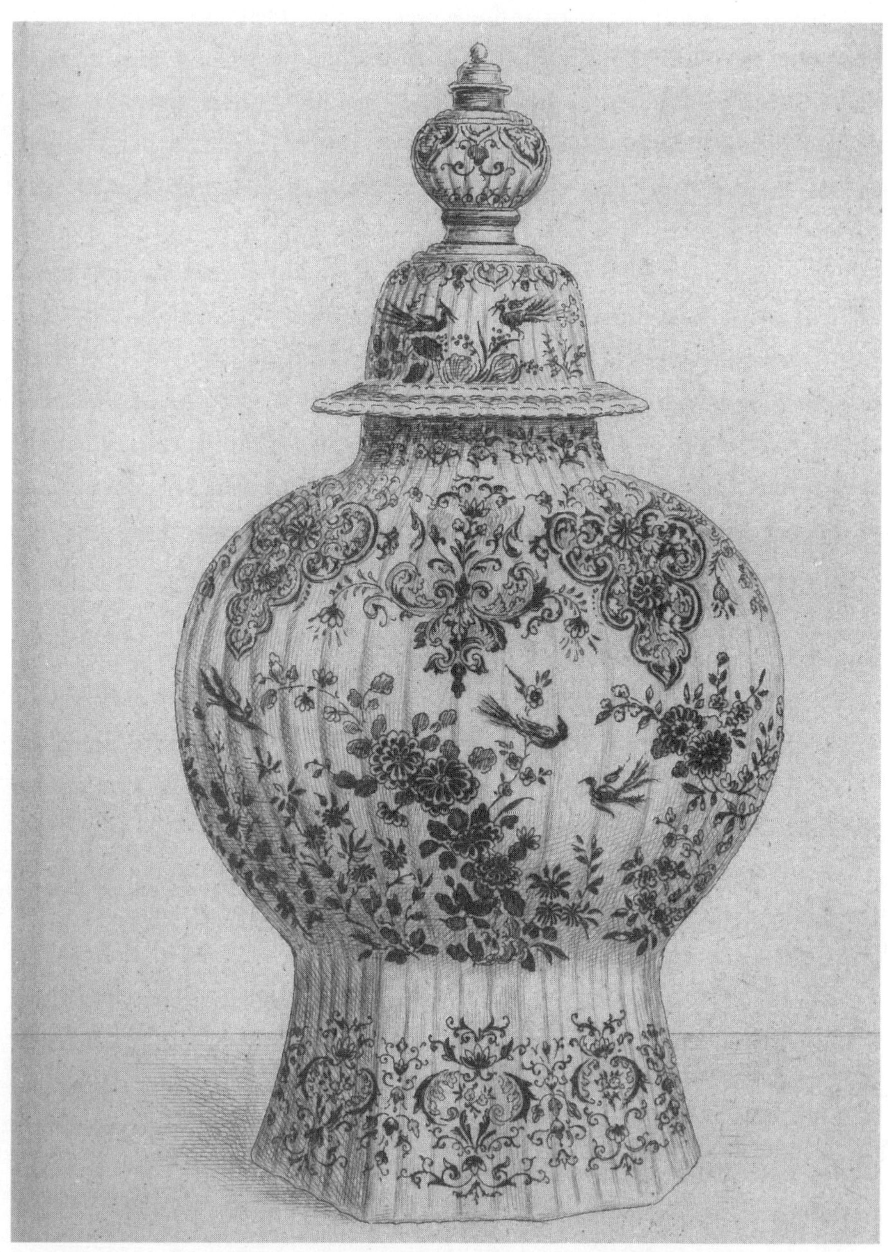

Charles Antoine Goutzwiller's illustration of Delftware in the vibrant cashmere style, featured in Henry Havard's *Histoire de la Faïence de Delft* (1878). Author's collection.

Seamlessly merging artistic influences, cashmere Delftware combined the vivid hues of Asian ceramics with the ornate scrolls, pendants, and arabesques of the French Baroque, the lush floral patterns of Chinese design, and the elegant forms of European silver. Some of the most opulent pieces featured ribbed or reeded surfaces, their delicate ridges catching and reflecting light to heighten their brilliance.

Yet, among Johanna's many innovations at The Greek A, one stood apart—a rare and daring feat of craftsmanship. Defying tradition, her workshop transformed the familiar white tin glaze into something entirely unexpected: a deep, light-absorbing ceramic of striking elegance. Achieved through a highly specialized process, this elusive creation demanded the skill of only the finest artisans. A rarity even in its own time, it remains one of the most coveted and enigmatic achievements in Dutch ceramics—*black Delftware.*

Emerging in the late seventeenth and early eighteenth centuries, black Delftware was inspired by a wave of luxurious, ebony-toned imports from China and Japan. Ships returning from Asia carried *famille noire* and *mirror-black* porcelain, as well as exquisite black lacquerware objects and furniture. The deep, glossy allure of black lacquer—mysterious, almost otherworldly—captivated the European imagination. Its seemingly magical properties fueled an obsession with imported black materials, weaving its way into Dutch culture in unexpected ways.

So much so, in fact, that black lacquer found a place in *Het natuurlyk tover-boek, of 't Nieuw speel-toneel der konsten*, a popular seventeenth-century conjuring book first published in 1679. The book contained 1,600 tricks (*tover-konsten*), from card games to small chemical experiments performed "for fun." Among its many recipes was the *Chineejche manier van verlakkin* (*The Chinese Method of Lacquering*), a testament to Europe's enduring desire to unlock the secrets of black lacquer's mesmerizing finish.

Much like a magician's most guarded trick, the technique for achieving a flawless black Delftware glaze was one of a pottery's most closely kept secrets. Few Delft workshops possessed the technical mastery to produce black glazes, as they were notoriously temperamental during firing. When combined with other colors, the glaze often risked running, melting, or destabilizing due to delicate chemical reactions.

Through a ceramicist's sleight of hand, the potters at The Greek A perfected the extraordinary illusion. The process began with a base layer of white tin glaze, followed by carefully applied polychrome enamel designs. Next, artisans meticulously filled the remaining blank areas with a rich black glaze before firing—a highly unpredictable, labor-intensive technique so challenging that few factories dared to attempt it, and even fewer achieved success.

Adding to its mystique, most black Delftware pieces were left unmarked, making attribution elusive. Of the few marked examples, the majority were produced at The Greek A, likely during Johanna's tenure as sole proprietor or in the years of her brief co-ownership with Pieter. Today, only about seventy known pieces of black Delftware survive. These rare, often diminutive works—teapots, brush backs, dishes, and small bowls—were more than functional objects; they were exquisite statements of beauty and exclusivity, designed to captivate and astonish.

Johanna van der Heul was an exceptional businesswoman who not only successfully transitioned the company after her husband's death but led it to further commercial success as sanctioned by the Guild of St. Luke. Through her vision and strategic leadership, she not only safeguarded the company's legacy but also positioned Delftware at the forefront of European ceramic innovation. But like black Delftware, was Johanna a rare example, an exotic anomaly in the history of Dutch Delftware? Or were there other women like her?

The need for the 1654 amendment to the laws of the Guild of St. Luke, sanctioning widows to continue their work after their husbands' deaths, would suggest that by the mid-1600s a number of widows had been already actively pursuing this right. And yet, their names remain conspicuously absent from the Guild's ledgers. Who were these widows of Delftware?

Locating sources to determine their identities requires traveling outside the historic center of Delft, to an area that in the seventeenth and eighteenth centuries would have been growing fields or *polders*, where now resides the *Stadsarchief Delft*, the Delft City Archives.

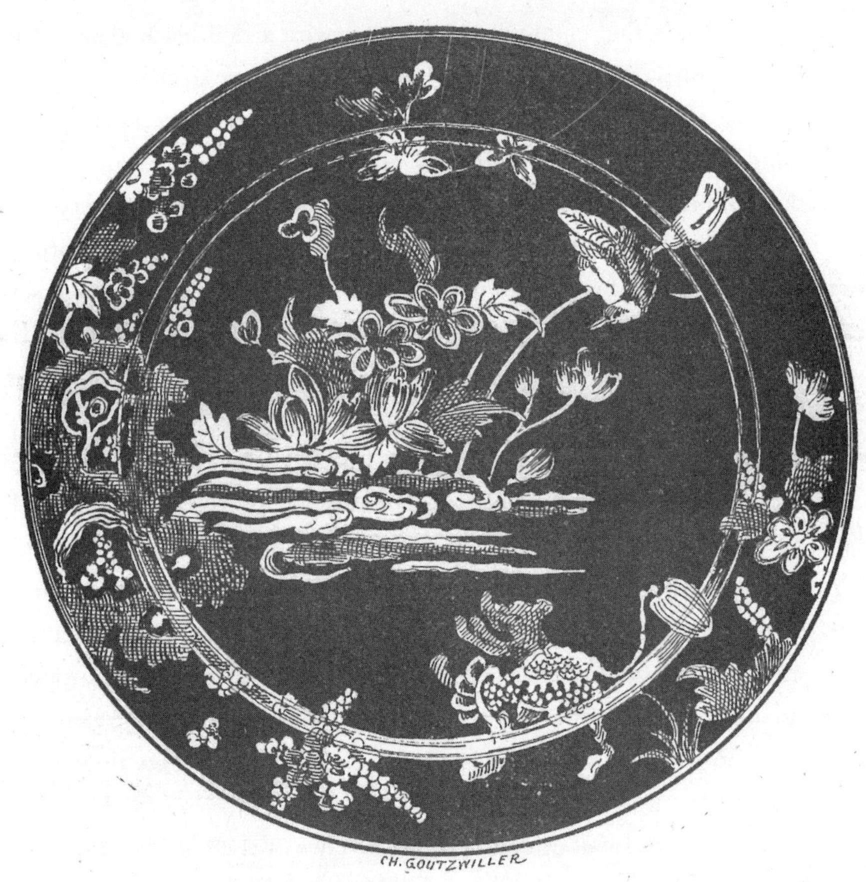

Charles Antoine Goutzwiller's illustration of a rare black Delftware plate, featured in Henry Havard's *Histoire de la Faïence de Delft* (1878). Author's collection.

Completed in 2017, the modern home of the Delft City Archives features a striking facade of staggered red brickwork, resembling an abstract bookcase standing alone on a quiet suburban Dutch street. Geometric arrangements of slender prefabricated concrete slabs form the shelves, while brick pilasters, evocative of book spines, protrude at varying lengths.

To protect the collections from water damage during a severe storm surge or torrential rain, the archive storage is located on the upper floors, securely housed behind solid red brick walls. This design creates an impenetrable safe haven for Delft's invaluable historic collections—part research library, part vault.

In the sixteenth century, documents now housed in the Delft City Archives were stored in the *Stadhuis* (City Hall). During the Dutch Republic, an era when official records were essential for the efficient functioning of a complex mercantile society, the Dutch became meticulous record-keepers. They compiled a vast array of documents detailing nearly every aspect of life and business—baptismal books, marriage contracts, betrothal and burial records, carefully curated estate inventories, legal depositions, notarial attestations, tax records, deeds, and *Kamer van Charitate* (Chamber of Charity) donations.

By the nineteenth century, archivists undertook the monumental task of preserving these countless records while contending with threats like mold, moths, and even theft. In 1865, Delft's first archivist managed to reclaim what was believed to be the trunk containing the papers of the Guild of St. Luke, only to find it empty. While most of the Guild's records did not survive, a wealth of alternative sources remains, offering insights into Delft's past, particularly the lives of its widows. Hidden deep within the City Archive's extensive storage, amid hand-calligraphed minutes penned by the twenty or so Delft notaries of the seventeenth and eighteenth centuries and their clerks, lies evidence of not just a handful of widows engaged in the Delftware business, but many.

Exploring the documentation of everyday life in Delft reveals a broader picture of the city's potteries and the women who played an integral role in their operations. Across Delft, from The Fortune, The Hart, and The Young Moor's Head to The Porcelain Bottle, The Porcelain Dish, and The Metal

Pot, female ownership and involvement were consistently present throughout their histories.

For some widows, ownership was short-lived. Financial records, including property sales, indicate that some widows managed potteries for only a year or two after their partner's deaths before selling them. However, many widows ran their businesses for years, even decades. The archives document the busy lives of these women—hiring employees, purchasing properties, suing vendors, paying taxes, and lending money. These widows not only assumed full responsibility for their potteries but also expanded and innovated, adapting to new ideas and opportunities. As a result, certain widows achieved remarkable success and prosperity.

Inventories taken after the death of Margaretha van der Gucht, owner of *De Klaauw* (The Claw) pottery in the early eighteenth century, reveal the valuable contents and lavish decoration of both her factory and home. Twice widowed, Margaretha likely hosted her most important Delftware clients in a *grote zaal* (grand salon), adorned with *goudleer* (gilt leather) wall coverings. These painted, gilded, and often embossed leather hangings were manufactured in panels and assembled to cover walls, serving as an opulent alternative to tapestry. In the Dutch Republic, the craft of gold leather-making thrived in seventeenth-century Amsterdam, where at least eleven gilt leather-makers were active. Margaretha's home also boasted a large garden, where she walked along gravel paths past more than twenty Delftware flowerpots to a gilt-bronze fountain.

Similarly opulent accounts from the period include the home of Elizabeth Elling, owner of *'t Fortuyn* (The Fortune) in the 1760s, who kept exotic pets, including a caged parrot in her front parlor to greet visitors. Another example is Cornelia van Willigen, who owned The Greek A for more than twenty years starting in 1745, succeeding Johanna van der Heul. Cornelia entertained lavishly at her residence on Delft's Lange Geer. Her estate inventory revealed an astonishing 203 chairs—an extraordinary number at a time when even twenty chairs would have seemed extravagant for an average household.

Although some Delftware widows are remembered for the luxurious amenities their success afforded, most were known primarily for their business acumen and tireless determination. Among them were Jannitge Claesdr. van Straten and her mother, Adriaantje Jansdr. van der Sande.

Jannitge grew up immersed in the operations of potteries. Her parents became the owners of *De Lampetkan* (The Porcelain Ewer) pottery in 1649. When her father died just four years later, her mother managed the family business for nine years. Jannitge continued in the pottery trade, marrying Jacob Wemmersz. Hoppesteijn, the owner of *Het Moriaanshooft* (The Moor's Head). However, Jannitge too became a widow. In 1671, she assumed control of The Moor's Head, which she managed for the remaining fifteen years of her life.

Examining Delftware produced by The Moor's Head during Jannitge's tenure as proprietor reveals an interesting detail: although her husband had passed away, the pieces were marked not with her initials, but with his—IW, for Jacob Wemmersz. Hoppesteijn. Why was this done?

The study of Dutch Delftware *marken* (marks) is an enigmatic subject. In Delft, there were no rules for potters marking Dutch Delftware. Some pieces were marked, others not. Marks on Delftware can include painted symbols or letters or a combination of both and can represent the company, the owner (past or present), the maker, or the manager. Marks could be over the glaze or under the glaze. They could be any number of colors, including red, but most were blue or black. A comprehensive listing of the pottery marks of Delft wasn't inaugurated until the eighteenth century when the Delft municipal government required that all potteries submit a list of their marks for reference in response to systemic copying between the potteries. Today, marks on Delftware are just one factor in the consideration of authenticity or attribution.

While pottery marks are often analyzed for identification purposes, could they also reflect the individual women behind Dutch Delftware? Upon assuming ownership of a pottery, a widow had the discretion to decide how her pieces would be marked. The choices she made in marking her pottery varied significantly, offering a glimpse into her personal and professional identity.

Some widows marked their pottery by adding a "W" for *weduwe* (widow) to their late husband's initials. For example, Elisabeth Elling, the widow of Pieter van den Briel, registered a mark in 1764 composed of the letters WVDB. This mark appeared on the works of the pottery The Fortune for over twenty years.

WVDB.

Henry Havard's *Histoire de la Faïence de Delft* (1878) features the WVDB mark, referring to *Weduwe* (Widow) van Den Briel, owner of *'t Fortuyn* (The Fortune) factory from 1759 to 1771. Author's collection.

Other widows, however, chose to use their own initials. Geertruij Verstelle, the notable and successful widow and proprietor of *Het Oude Moriaanshooft* (The Old Moor's Head) factory in the 1760s, boldly marked her pieces GVS, a proud reflection of her identity as a pottery owner.

When Johanna assumed ownership of The Greek A in the summer of 1703 and production resumed, a crucial question arose: how would the pottery's pieces be marked? As painters completed their decorations, did they pause and seek her guidance? As the leader of one of Delft's most esteemed pottery firms, the decision rested solely with her.

Examining pieces produced by The Greek A after her husband's death, we find objects marked with the letters PAK or APK, representing Pieter Adriaensz. Kocx. Like Jannitge Claesdr. van Straten of The Moor's Head, Johanna continued using her husband's initials rather than her own. This choice may have been a tribute to his legacy or a practical decision to maintain the workshop's established reputation. Whatever the reason—tradition, strategy, or sentiment—her decision ensured that, like many other widows who led Delftware workshops, her contributions remained invisible on the pottery itself.

Johanna led The Greek A for nearly twenty years, overseeing the production of hundreds of thousands of pieces. As owner, she took on the unyielding demands of the trade—managing the flow of raw materials and finished wares, reviewing accounts to ensure workers were paid, and bearing the weight of looming deadlines and the ever-present risk of financial loss from shipments damaged in transit after months of painstaking labor. Rather than relying on others for support, she became the foundation of the workshop, responsible for more than thirty employees and their families who depended on her leadership.

Yet, in choosing this demanding life, she also found moments of creative triumph. She had the rare privilege of shaping new forms, pioneering innovative styles, and witnessing the magic of transformation as the kiln door was removed, revealing the fired pottery. What had once been dull, gray-painted clay emerged in a dazzling alchemy of deep, glossy cobalt, layered with vibrant hues and finished with luminous touches of gold. These exquisite works—and her unwavering pursuit of technical mastery—became her legacy, elevating Delftware to new heights and securing its place among the most celebrated ceramic traditions in the world.

In 1722, almost twenty years after Pieter's death, Johanna finally sold The Greek A. Living the rest of her life on the *Oude Delft* in comfort, one of the wealthiest areas of Delft, she died at the age of seventy years old and was buried nearby on June 15, 1736, in the *Oude Kerk* by the canal.

Widows of the Dutch Republic and their entrepreneurial acumen did not go unnoticed in their day. As the world looked upon the Dutch Republic with envy and curiosity, many surmised that women too had a contributing effect on the success of its economy—during both marriage and widowhood. Reflecting on the effects of commercially active Dutch widows, Joseph Child in 1668 postulated that their abundance "doth incourage their Husbands to hold on in their Trades to their dying days, knowing the capacity of their Wives to get in their Estates, and carry on their Trades after their Deaths."

Rather than accidental players, widows were a continuation of women's already prevalent roles in the ongoing development of Dutch Delftware. Leadership wasn't necessarily thrust upon them following the death of their spouse. Married women took on their roles as entrepreneurs, central contributors in businesses including potteries that had been made invisible. Their transformation into widows brought degrees of visibility, giving us a view of the actual level of involvement of women in the decorative arts.

As *weduwes*, the hidden businesswomen of Dutch Delftware were revealed.

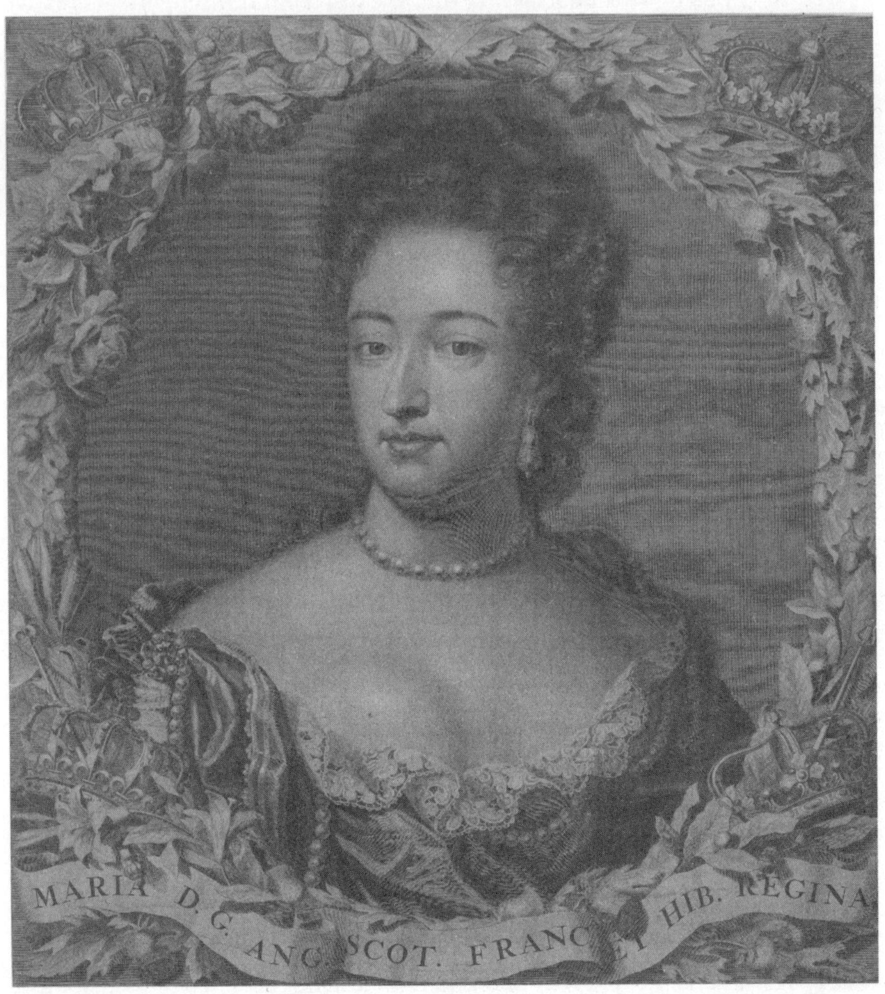

ABOVE: Pieter van Gunst's 1694 etching presents a regal portrait of Queen Mary II, adorned with pearls and encircled by an oval including roses, lilies, oak leaves, and thistles, while crowns in each corner underscore her sovereignty. Rijksmuseum, Amsterdam. OPPOSITE: A photomechanical print *Hampton Court Palace West Front* (John Swain & Son Ltd., London, ca. 1910). Author's collection.

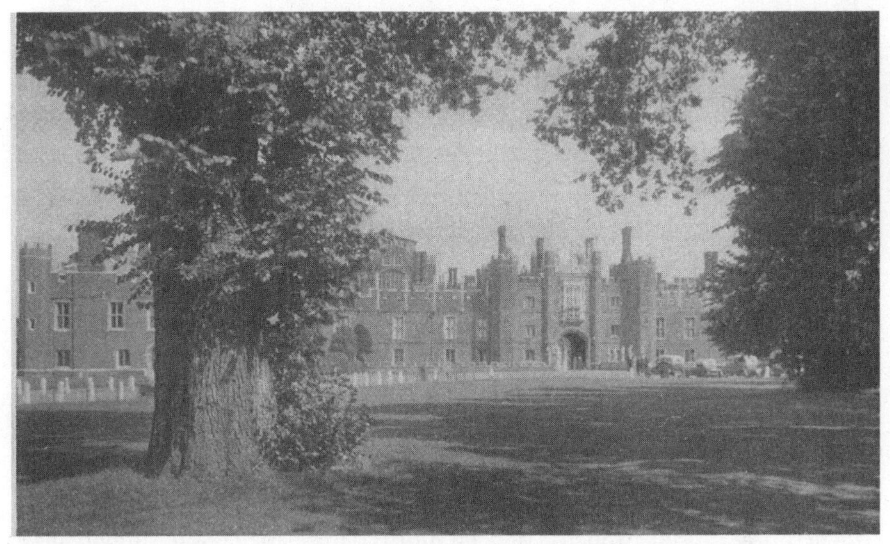

5

Queen of Blue-and-White

"She strikes the Rock, the Rudest Rocks Obey,
New Life invades, and animates our Clay"

—"A Poem on the Arrival of Queen
Mary, February the 12th, 1689,"
Thomas Rymer, 1689

"The Queen brought in the custom or humour . . . of furnishing houses with china-ware, which increased to a strange degree afterwards, piling their China upon the tops of cabinets, scrutores, and every chymneypiece, to the tops of the ceilings . . . ."

—Daniel Defoe, 1724

Shortly after the death of Queen Mary II in 1694, a young woman mounts her horse, setting off on a journey following the dirt roads from London to Hampton Court, the royal palace ten miles west of the city on the River Thames. Wearing a wide-brimmed hat, gauntlets, fitted jacket, and matching full skirt, her long train gently drapes over the horse's back, covering her ankles. She is an unmarried daughter of an English politician. Her name is Celia Fiennes.

Once beyond the city limits, the landscape quickly transformed from crowded shops and rows of houses to stretches of trees and open fields. Celia is wary of riding too close to lush hedgerows, as she knows the densely planted shrubs are often the hiding places of highwaymen. The journey from London would take two hours and, luckily, so far, has been without incident. In an age when road maps are vague at best, English roads are rarely marked, potentially treacherous with ruts, trenches of deep mud, or mirey patches of slippery clay, not to mention populated with robbers. Her trip is not an endeavor to be taken lightly, especially for a woman journeying alone on a sidesaddle.

Traveling for pleasure in the seventeenth century is still very unusual—but Celia, diarist and pioneering female traveler, is intrigued. It is her obsession to see England in its entirety. Before setting off on an endeavor that would take her throughout England and Scotland on horseback between 1694–1705, one of her first destinations is a home of another woman of uncommon strength, courage, and curiosity.

She was not only a young princess who had become England's co-reigning monarch, she was Dutch Delftware's most influential patron and a veritable blue-and-white muse—Queen Mary II.

Up ahead above the tree line, Celia catches sight of her destination—the undulating red brick rooflines and chimneys of Hampton Court Palace. As Celia notes in her journals, later published in the nineteenth century, the palace "looks Like a little town ye buildings runn so great a Length on ye ground, Ye old buildings and ye New part wch King William and Queen Mary built. Ye Queen took Great delight in it." Her journey is almost complete.

Arriving at Hampton Court Palace, Celia dismounts and—remarkably unimpeded—walks freely along its gravel paths, through private gardens and secluded courtyards, and even into the royal inner sanctums.

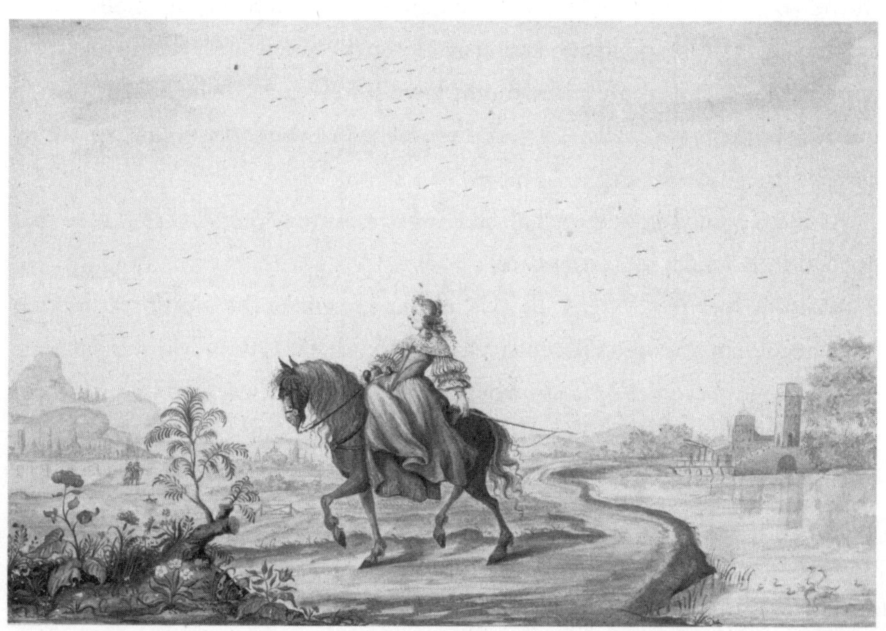

Gesina ter Borch's 1660 pen and ink drawing offers a rare glimpse of a woman riding side-saddle alone through the Dutch countryside—an unusual subject captured by a female artist of the time. Rijksmuseum, Amsterdam.

But it is not just the great halls or royal apartments that capture her attention.

Standing at the Palace, she looks out across the Privy Garden toward something unexpected—a curious architectural confection nestled at the very edge of the Thames. Unlike the palace's restrained Tudor facades, this small, detached brick building is adorned with ornate balconies and circular towers, its onion-shaped cupolas painted a striking shade of ultramarine blue.

The walk to this enigmatic structure is a long one, tracing the path through the newly designed parterres, where clipped yews, round-headed hollies, and exotic flowers form intricate patterns along the finely packed gravel walkways. As Celia approaches, she might have simply turned the handle to step inside—perhaps hesitating for just a moment in the entryway, awestruck by the opulence before her.

As she recorded in her journal, she had discovered "the Water Gallery that opened into a balcony to ye water."

Stepping into the Water Gallery, Celia enters one of the most breathtaking interiors of late seventeenth-century England. This is Queen Mary II's private sanctuary—a *maison de plaisir*, where her passion for Dutch Delftware is not just displayed but brought to life in spectacular fashion.

The space is a theatrical masterpiece of blue and white, a color scheme dominated by the dazzling gleam of Delftware, heightened with opulent touches of silver and gold. Across two floors, the rooms unfold like a staged fantasy, each one surprising and delighting with Dutch Delftware that defies scale, expectation, and convention.

The Water Gallery holds ceramic marvels of unprecedented size—from towering nearly five-foot-tall Delftware flower vases, their countless spouts for fragrant blooms, to tiled walls, each tile a gargantuan two feet wide, creating a spectacle of Baroque refinement.

Beyond these monumental showpieces, the entire interior is adorned with hundreds—possibly thousands—of additional porcelain and Delftware pieces, carefully arranged throughout the long central gallery, four private cabinets, and the lower level, where a grotto, bathroom, and a luxurious pleasure dairy continue the ceramic spectacle.

Even the furnishings were designed to complement the Delftware aesthetic. Tables, chairs, and picture frames were painted in Delft-inspired hues, their ornate surfaces mimicking porcelain. Upholstered in sky-blue satin and damask, edged in blue silk fringe, the textiles further extend the ceramic palette, ensuring that every corner of the Water Gallery reflects Mary's singular artistic vision.

Its visitors, like Celia, were enamored. In 1695, Constantijn Huygens Jr., King William III's secretary and diarist, describes this retreat as "a very nice thing, in the parterres." In 1720, Daniel Defoe recalls it as "the pleasantest little Thing within Doors that could possibly be made."

And yet, despite its grandeur, the Water Gallery's reign is fleeting.

By 1700, barely a decade after its creation, it is dismantled and destroyed. No renderings survive, no architectural plans remain. The blue-and-white wonderland that once captivated all who entered vanishes, erased by time and circumstance. Only by piecing together scattered historical accounts—including the rare journal of an unlikely visitor, Celia—and by examining the few surviving pieces of Mary's Delftware, can we begin to reimagine this extraordinary royal retreat.

The Water Gallery was more than just a royal indulgence. It was an assertion of taste and authority, a monument to Mary's artistic vision, and a defining moment in the elevation of Dutch Delftware to an unparalleled level of prestige.

The story of this lost masterpiece—and of the queen who brought it to life—is as remarkable as the Delftware itself.

Mary was born "Her Highness the Lady Mary" at St. James's Palace in London on April 30, 1662, as the English monarchy reestablished itself to its former sumptuousness following more than a decade of Cromwellian austerity. Mary's grandfather, King Charles I, had been executed in 1649 by Oliver Cromwell and her uncle King Charles II had just reassumed his title. Third in the line of accession to the crown at birth, Mary was one of two surviving children of James, Duke of York, later King James II, and his first wife, the commoner Anne Hyde.

It was a time of rampant disease in England, with outbreaks of measles, smallpox, and even the bubonic plague. The Great Plague of London struck in 1665, just three years after Mary's birth, claiming over 100,000 lives—nearly one-third of the city's population. To safeguard their health, Mary and her younger sister, Anne, were raised outside the city in the relative but secluded safety of Richmond Palace, located along the River Thames.

Mary grew up as a child of the state, shielded from the dangers and unhealthy conditions of the city yet deeply immersed in the world of fine and decorative arts. Her family was celebrated for their extraordinary collections, which spanned everything from exquisite paintings to delicate porcelain. At the heart of this legacy was her grandfather, King Charles I, a voracious collector who amassed the most remarkable and expansive art collection of any English monarch, filling his palaces with masterpieces, including works by Leonardo da Vinci, Raphael, Titian, Anthony Van Dyck, and Artemisia Gentileschi. His was also the first royal collection in England to include a work by Rembrandt van Rijn.

At the time of Mary's birth, her father, James, Duke of York, was Lord High Admiral, the head of the English Royal Navy. Although he differed from his Protestant family in matters of religion—having converted to Catholicism—he shared their passion for the arts, much like his brother, King Charles II. James had a particular appreciation for paintings, fine furniture, silver, and an extensive collection of porcelain. By the late seventeenth century, porcelain, once a rare treasure confined to cabinets of curiosities or *kunstkamers* in the sixteenth century, had become a fashionable element of interior design. No longer hidden away, it was prominently displayed in symmetrical arrangements atop cabinets or elegantly showcased on tiered steps above mantels, transforming it into a centerpiece of refined taste.

When Mary was two years old, English ships, acting on the orders of her father, captured a small Dutch outpost in North America. On September 8, 1664, Dutch director-general Peter Stuyvesant surrendered New Amsterdam, the capital of New Netherland, to an English naval squadron. In honor of Mary's father, New Amsterdam was renamed New York.

Just four days later, on Monday, September 12, 1664, Samuel Pepys, diarist and "clerk of the acts" of the Navy Board, observed two-year-old Mary at St. James's Palace. Amid what would have been the activity of the fleet's staff, advisers, and high admiral in conference, she entered her father's chambers. Despite the business of state, the Duke of York paused to enjoy a moment with his young daughter, "with great pleasure play[ing] with his little girle like an ordinary private father of a child."

Mary's childhood, with fleeting moments resembling the life of a typical girl, was brief. As she grew into a strikingly tall yet graceful young woman, standing at five-foot-eleven, her future became a matter of vital national interest. In a Europe dominated by wars and shifting alliances, her marriage was seen as a crucial diplomatic tool to advance England's position. Among those considered as potential partners were some of the most illustrious figures of the era, such as Louis XIV's son, the Dauphin of France, a match that could have allied England with the most powerful monarchy in Europe.

Ultimately, Mary was engaged to her first cousin, William, Prince of Orange, a man twelve years her senior. As *stadtholder* of the Dutch Republic, William was a stark contrast to the opulent court of Louis XIV. A soldier and strategist, his life was consumed by a single goal: resisting French domination. Though often plagued by poor health, William devoted himself to countering the ambitions of Louis XIV, the Sun King, who relentlessly sought to expand his empire, with the Dutch Republic his frequent target.

For England, the alliance with William reinforced its ties to the Dutch Republic, creating a crucial stronghold against French aggression. For Mary, however, it meant leaving the vibrant cosmopolitan world of London for what she likely viewed as the windswept marshes of the Dutch Republic, where life seemed austere by comparison. According to Mary's tutor Edward Lake, Archdeacon and Prebendary of Exeter, the fifteen-year-old princess was far from enthusiastic about her impending marriage and deeply unsettled by the prospect of leaving England for the Dutch Republic:

> "October 21, 1677—The Duke of York din'd at Whitehall; after dinner returned to Saint James', took Lady Mary into her closet, and told her of the marriage designed between her and the Prince of Orange; whereupon her highness wept all that afternoon and the following day."

Mary never expected to see England again.

William and Mary were married in an expedient ceremony in her bedchamber at St. James's Palace on November 4, 1677, and at William's insistence they departed for the Dutch Republic as quickly as possible. Arriving in The Hague, Mary was introduced to the center of Dutch court life—a world vastly different from the structured splendor of London's palaces. While her affection for William took time to grow, she found herself falling in love with something else almost immediately—her new home.

The Dutch Republic was unlike anything Mary had ever known. Vast green polders stretched to the horizon, dotted with windmills, while meticulously tended pleasure gardens bloomed beneath skies that shifted dramatically from golden light to stormy gray.

In Amsterdam, boats glided through mirror-like canals, reflecting rows of stately gabled houses. The streets bustled with markets overflowing with the exotic—brilliantly plumed tropical birds, fragrant spices, and lush plants never before seen in England.

Down at the harbor, a different spectacle awaited. The masts of Dutch East India Company ships, packed so tightly they resembled a dense forest, loomed over the bustling quays. Dockworkers moved swiftly between endless rows of crates freshly unloaded from Batavia—each containing treasures from across the world. Lacquered boxes, shimmering textiles, and gleaming porcelain flowed from ship to shore, a testament to the Dutch Republic's vast global reach.

For Mary, raised in the formal confines of the English court, this dynamic, kaleidoscopic world was mesmerizing—and among its many novelties, one in particular would capture her imagination: Delftware.

For someone accustomed to the translucent elegance of Chinese porcelain, Delftware must have felt strikingly different—heavier in her hands, lacking the glass-like delicacy she had known since childhood. Yet, Delftware's possibilities were endless. With skilled ceramic artists in nearby Delft, Mary could commission pieces that reflected her own taste and vision, transforming earthenware into something uniquely hers. She was intrigued.

The origins of Mary's Delftware patronage remain a mystery. Did she wander Delft's brick-lined streets, watching potters at their wheels and painters at their benches? Or did she rely on trusted agents, acquiring pieces from afar? The details of her commissions—who arranged them, how designs were selected, and how involved she was—are lost to history. No records survive, but blue-and-white ceramic fragments unearthed in her former Dutch residences hint at the scope and artistry of her growing collection.

By the 1680s, Mary was actively seeking out the finest Dutch artisans, particularly those at The Greek A factory, one of Delft's most renowned workshops. From 1678 to 1685, it was led by master potter Samuel van Eenhoorn, a period that coincided with Mary's early years in the Dutch Republic. After van Eenhoorn's death in 1685, his widow, Cecelia Houwaert, briefly took over, before selling the business in 1687 to her brother-in-law, Adrianus Kocx. Under Kocx's leadership, The Greek A entered a new era of craftsmanship—one that would play a defining role in shaping Mary's collection.

Meanwhile, William and Mary embarked on a sweeping transformation of their surroundings. Between 1677 and 1684, they rebuilt and refurbished eight residences, from grand city palaces to secluded hunting lodges. These spaces were lavishly decorated with fine furniture, art, and, for Mary, an ever-expanding collection of porcelain—both Chinese and Japanese imports as well as Delftware. Her plates, dishes, bowls, and vases were not merely functional objects; they were centerpieces of decorative display, arranged in ways that would be later defined as porcelain rooms.

In the seventeenth-century Dutch Republic and increasingly throughout Europe, porcelain rooms became the ultimate expression of aristocratic luxury, where ceramics were seamlessly integrated into architecture. These immersive interiors showcased newly imported porcelain from East Asia, brought by the Dutch East India Company, and displayed in breathtaking profusion—adorning cornices, moldings, overdoors, wall brackets, and grand mantelpieces. Often enhanced with mirrors, gilding, and lacquer, these spaces became theatrical spectacles, reflecting boundless wealth and global influence.

One of the earliest champions of this trend was William's grandmother, Amalia van Solms-Braunfels, Princess of Orange, wife of Frederik Hendrik, Prince of Orange and *stadtholder* of the Dutch Republic. Born in 1602, Amalia became one of the most renowned female ceramic collectors of the seventeenth century. She assembled an extraordinary collection of over 1,200 Chinese and

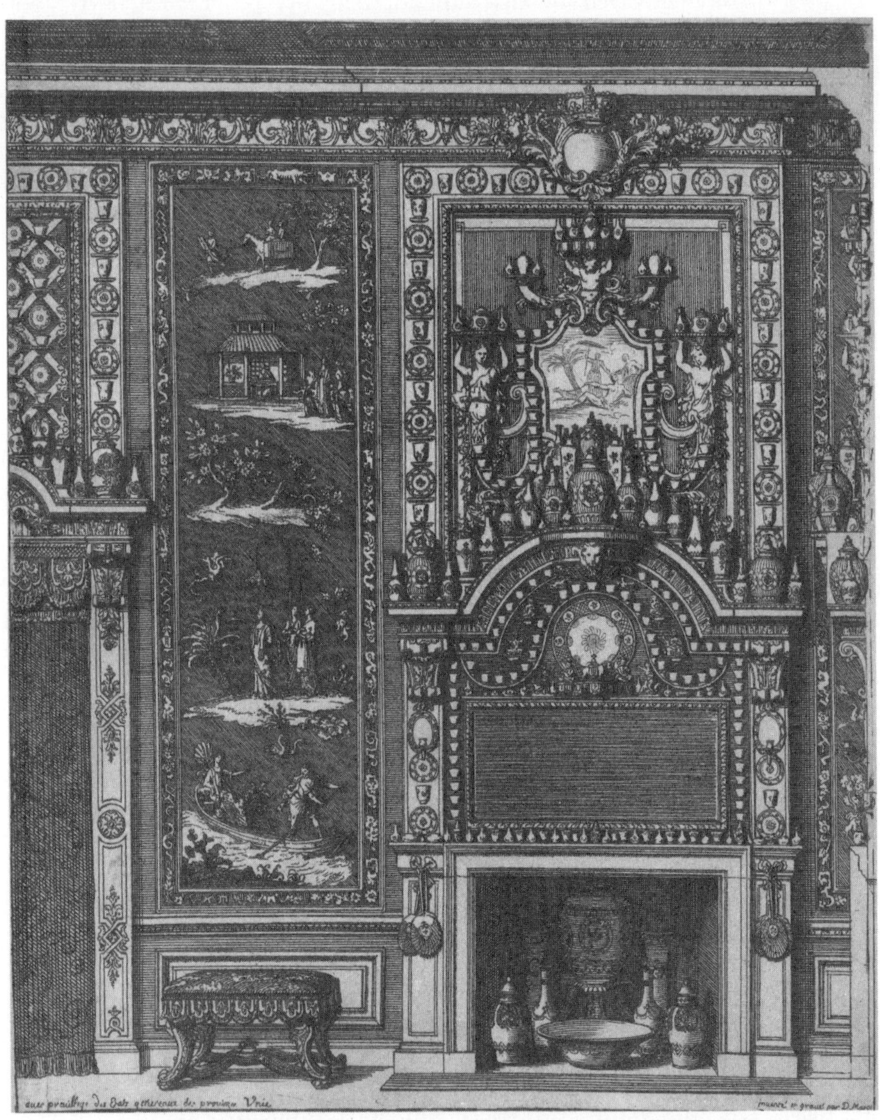

Daniel Marot's *Design for a Chimney Wall with Lacquered Panels and Porcelain* (etching and engraving, 1673–before 1703) showcases a lavish display, where a profusion of porcelain enhances the opulence of the intricately decorated interior. Rijksmuseum, Amsterdam.

Japanese ceramics, which she displayed in grand, immersive settings, including her *groote porceleyn cabinet* (large porcelain closet). Her passion for porcelain extended throughout her residences, from Noordeinde Palace in The Hague (then known as the *Oude Delft*, or Old Court) to *Huis ten Bosch* (House in the Woods). Amalia's decorative innovations set a trend that swept across seventeenth-century Europe, flourished in the eighteenth century, and continued to shape interior design well into the nineteenth century and beyond.

Although Amalia died in 1675, just before Mary's arrival in the Dutch Republic, her vision for porcelain display left a lasting mark. She set a precedent—one that Mary would embrace, weaving it into her own decorative style across the many residences she and William would build or transform.

Among these, one residence stood above the rest—their most personal and ambitious undertaking: Het Loo Palace.

Located thirty miles east of Amsterdam, in the heathland of the Veluwe near Apeldoorn, Het Loo was once a hunting lodge before William and Mary transformed it into a magnificent royal summer retreat. Commissioned in 1684 and completed by 1686, the palace served as both an elegant venue for entertaining the Dutch court and a peaceful escape from the demands of political life, allowing the couple to immerse themselves in the tranquility of the countryside. Overseeing the palace's interior design was a new arrival in the Dutch Republic—a young French architect and designer who would play a crucial role in shaping Mary's decorative world: Daniel Marot.

Daniel Marot was born in Paris in 1661, the same year Louis XIV began his grand transformation of Versailles. Growing up in the shadow of the former hunting lodge as it evolved into an opulent palace and the seat of royal power, Marot honed his skills within its artistic and architectural community. This milieu, rich with carpenters, gardeners, weavers, silversmiths, and cabinetmakers, shaped his creative vision. Marot's engravings capture the grandeur of the Louis XIV style, showcasing the scale, elegance, and modernity of Versailles. His work spanned furniture, silver, clocks, ceramics, garden architecture, and interior design, all characterized by extravagant yet symmetrical compositions. These designs often featured bold decorative motifs, including flower-filled strapwork, scrolling arabesques, *mascarons*

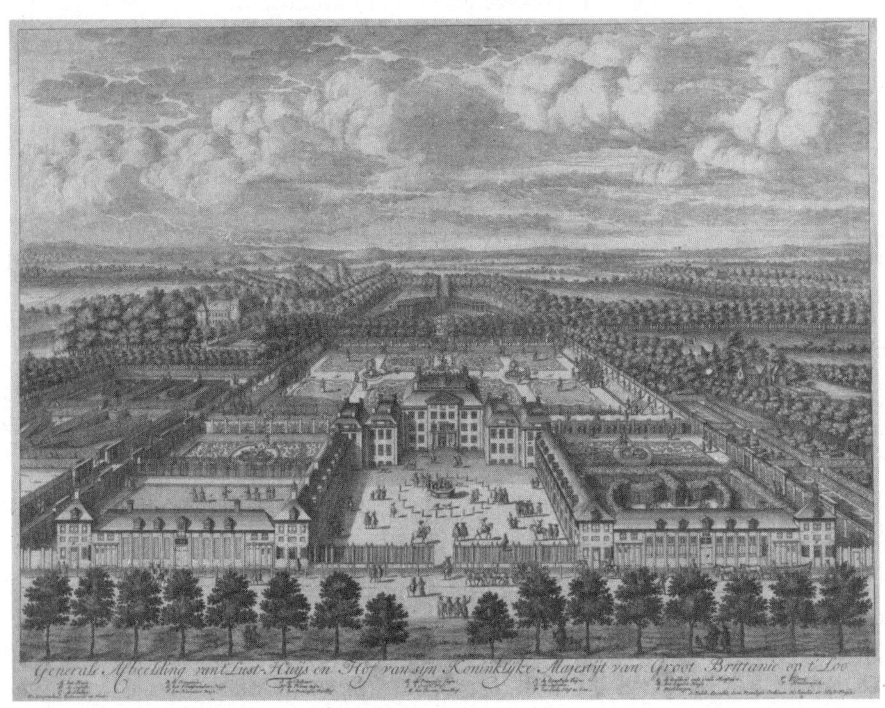

Bastiaen Stopendael's 1689–1693 etching and engraving, *Gezicht op Paleis Het Loo* (*View of Het Loo Palace*), offers a bird's-eye perspective of the estate, showcasing its grand architecture and meticulously designed gardens. Rijksmuseum, Amsterdam.

(masks), and ribbon-suspended foliate canopies, blending opulence with meticulous precision.

But Marot was also a Protestant, part of France's embattled religious minority. For years, his right to worship had been protected by the Edict of Nantes, but in 1685, just three years after the grand inauguration of Versailles, Louis XIV revoked the edict, unleashing a wave of persecution. Protestants were forced to flee, facing imprisonment or even death if they remained. By 1686, Louis XIV boasted that his policies had reduced France's Protestant population from nearly a million to fewer than a thousand. Despite his royal connections, Marot was left with no choice but to abandon his work and seek refuge in the Dutch Republic, where he would start a new life and continue his artistic legacy.

Although the Dutch Republic was at war with France, its nobility remained eager to adapt French grandeur to the unique Dutch aesthetic. Daniel Marot quickly found favor with William and Mary, who enlisted him to bring the latest French style to their court. Just a year older than Mary, Marot became one of her most trusted creative collaborators, shaping the visual splendor of her reign.

At Het Loo, Marot transported the opulence of Versailles to the Dutch countryside. The palace's exterior embodied the elegance of classicizing Dutch baroque style of architecture, its red brick facades accented with German sandstone and crowned with gray slate-hipped roofs. Yet beyond its dignified facade, Het Loo was designed to inspire awe—both inside and out.

As Mary strolled the gravel paths of her vast symmetrical gardens of Het Loo, she passed through ornamental parterres of grass, gravel, and intricately arranged plantings. Along the pathways, striking blue-and-white Delftware *jardinières* adorned with Marot-inspired motifs overflowed with exotic flora, creating a vivid contrast against the lush greenery. At the heart of the garden, a towering fountain soared over forty feet into the air—the highest in Europe—commanding attention and reinforcing the palace's sense of grandeur.

Inside, Marot curated an atmosphere of stately magnificence. The Grand Staircase, with its painted wood balustrade, led to the first floor, where private chambers featured elaborate cornices, brackets, and moldings, each designed

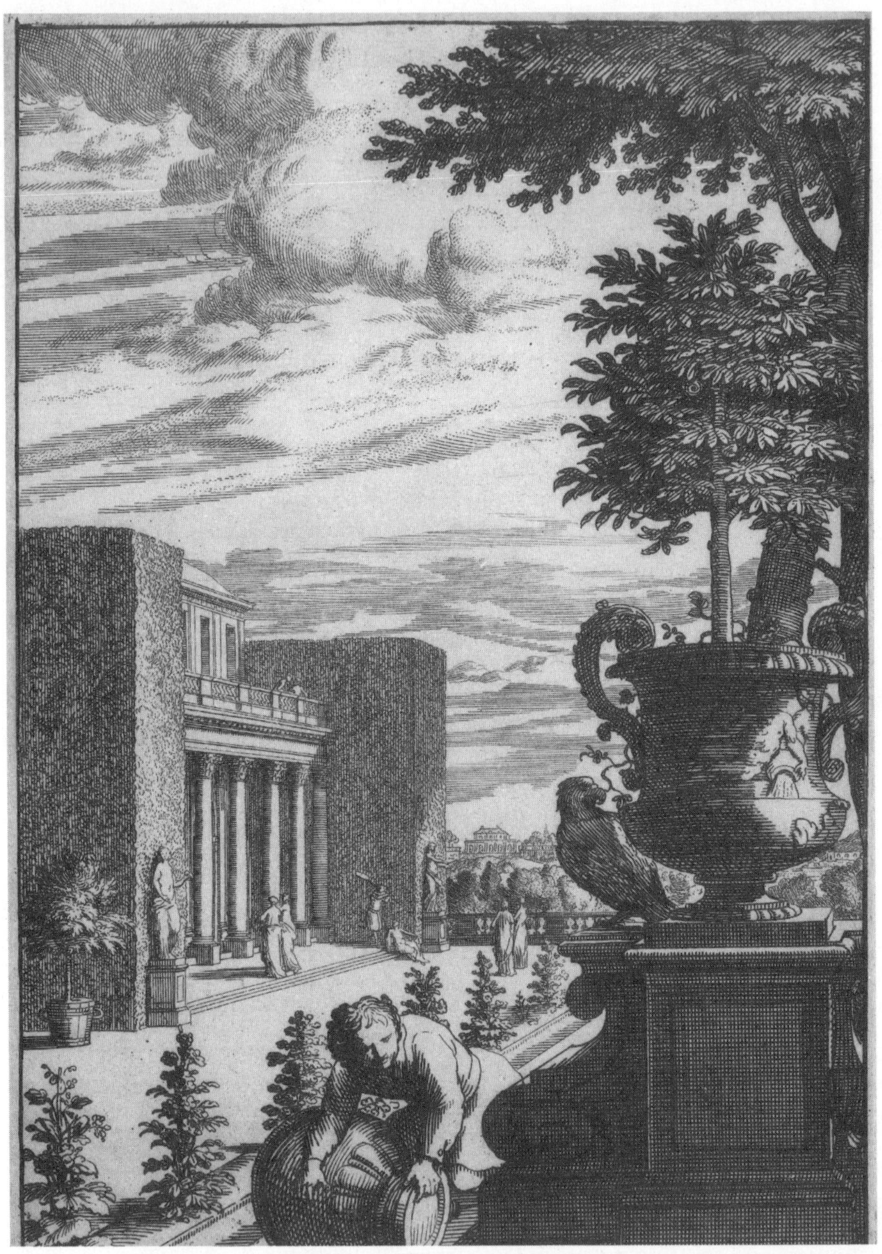

An etching, *Paviljoen tussen twee hoge heggen* (*Garden Pavilion Between Two Hedges*), possibly by Daniel Marot, 1703–1712, illustrates the use of pots in Dutch garden design, some of which were made of blue and white Delftware. Rijksmuseum, Amsterdam.

to showcase Mary's prized porcelain collection. Towering state beds, draped in imported Chinese silk and crowned with high-mounted canopies, were finished with finials of ostrich feathers, adding a touch of regal extravagance.

Het Loo stood as a testament to the Dutch Baroque, its imposing formality designed to inspire awe. Yet, beneath its stately halls lay an architectural secret—a hidden intimate sanctuary entirely Mary's own—where her Delftware took center stage.

Descending from her first-floor apartments through a series of stairs, she entered a colorful basement suite designed for her personal enjoyment—a private retreat filled with some of the objects she cherished most. This secluded space featured a tearoom, a grotto, and, in keeping with Dutch tradition, a tiled kitchen cellar. Identified in 1705 as the *Coninginen Confituir Camer* (*Queen's Confection Room*), it was here that Mary indulged in one of her favorite pastimes: the art of jam-making.

As described by the English traveler John Farrington in 1710, the *Queen's Confection Room* was "a small cool room very pleasant in summer where there is an abundance of china; it is floored with Dutch tile and the sides of the room are tiled with the same." The walls were adorned from floor to vaulted ceiling with vibrant tiles produced in Rotterdam, featuring shades of cobalt-blue and manganese-purple. These tiles were intricately painted with images of flower-filled vases, landscapes, ribbon-like strapwork, and geometric patterns, creating a rich tapestry of color and design.

In this lively and fragrant space, long wooden tables would have been piled high with baskets of fruit, freshly harvested from Het Loo's gardens and greenhouses. Cherries, apricots, pears, and apples sat alongside prized exotic offerings—lemons and oranges. Preserving fruits and preparing sweetmeats and jams was a favored pastime among the Dutch elite, who embraced these culinary arts in their grand country homes, surrounded by expansive gardens and greenhouses. Inspiration for such endeavors often came from popular recipe books of the time, including *De Verstandige Confituur-maker* (*The Sensible Confectioner*) in *De Verstandige Kock* (*The Sensible Cook*), part of Jan van der Groen's 1669 compilation, *Het Vermakelijck Landt-leven* (*The Pleasurable Country Life*).

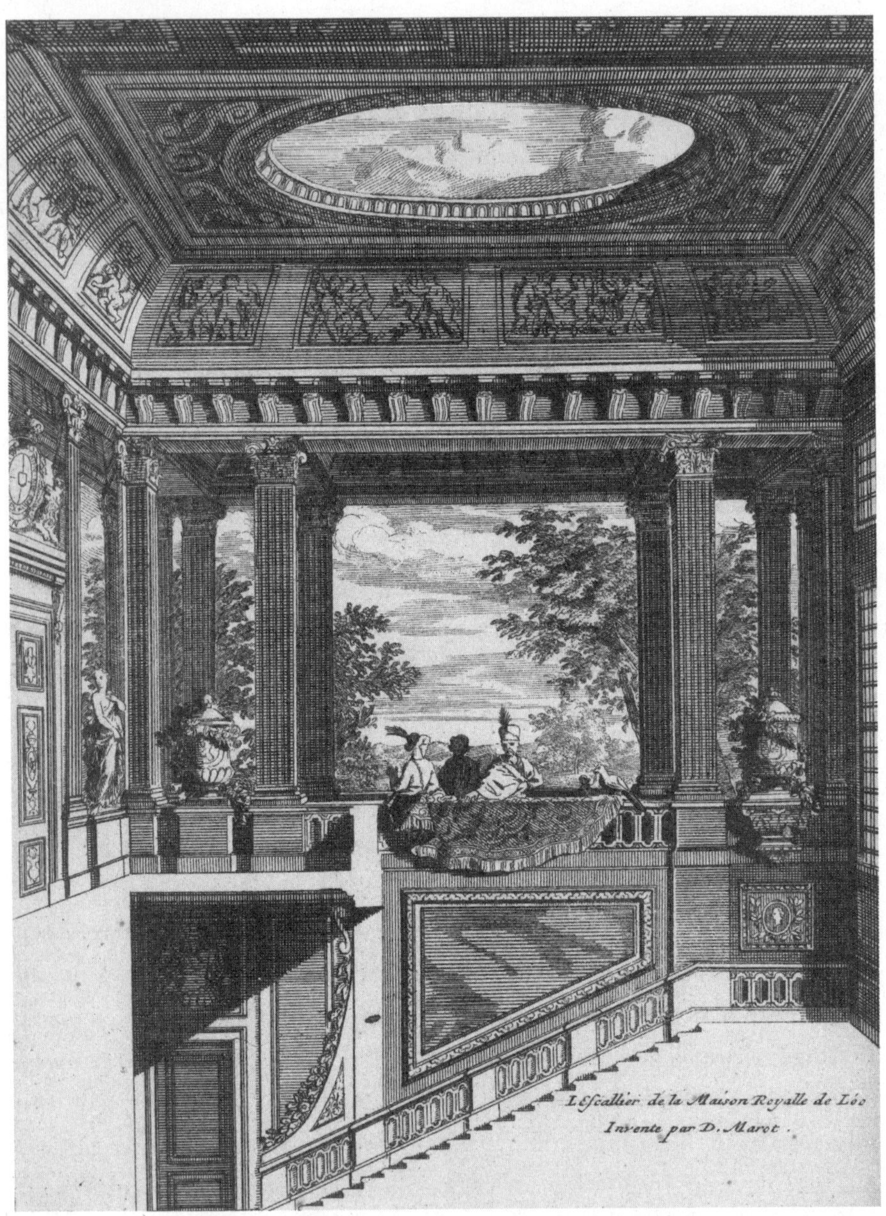

Etching after Daniel Marot (1703–1800), *L'Escalier de la Maison Royalle de Loo* (*Staircase of Palais Het Loo*), illustrates the grandeur of Marot's architectural vision. Rijksmuseum, Amsterdam.

Standing at the copper stoves, Mary and her jam-making assistant, or *confiturier,* worked amid the rich, heady aromas of melting sugar, citrus zest, ripe berries, and spiced fruits. The warm air carried the scent of slowly simmering preserves, while Delftware pots and tiles, ideal for preparing and cooling, provided the perfect tools for the craft. A recipe from *De Verstandige Confituur-maker* (*The Sensible Confectioner*) offers a glimpse into this meticulous process, detailing a popular technique of the time:

> To preserve the fruit-marrow of Cherries, Plums, Apricots, etc. for a whole year.
>
> Take Cherries that are somewhat sour, take off the stems, boil them in an earthenware pot without liquid on a low fire. When they start to cook in their own juice, stir them so they do not burn. They are done when the outer skin comes off and the meat has become a thick porridge; let them cool and rub them through a turned-over Sieve. take the resulting porridge and spread it on glazed tiles, let it dry this way in the sun or in an oven when the bread has been removed. Take it from the dish and save it . . . .

With a doorway leading directly to her private garden, the *Queen's Confection Room* also provided convenient access to the abundance of blooms from Mary's nearby plantings and greenhouses. Roses, tulips, hyacinths, carnations, poppies, and irises were among the many varieties brought inside and placed on long tables ready for arrangement. Situated on the lower level of the palace, this subterranean tiled room maintained a consistently cool temperature, making it an ideal space for the cutting, storing, and arrangement of fresh flowers.

Designed to elevate the art of floral display, Mary's blue-and-white Delftware vases and flower holders, crafted by The Greek A with Chinese-inspired floral motifs, came in a striking array of forms. Her collection featured two distinct types: vases with spouts and flower holders with perforated openings, each designed to create carefully arranged, artful compositions.

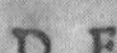

DE

VERSTANDIGE KOCK,

Of Sorghvuldige Huyshoudster:

BESCHRYVENDE

Hoe men op de beste en bequaemste manier alderhande Spijsen sal koocken/ stoven/ braden/ backen/ en bereyden; met de Sauffen daer toe dienende: Seer dienstigh/ en profijtelijck in alle Huyshoudingen.

Oock om veelderley slagh van TAERTEN en PASTEYEN toe te stellen.

Vermeerdert met de

HOLLANDTSE SLACHT-TYDT.

Hier is noch achter bygevoeght / de

VERSTANDIGE CONFITUURMAKER,

Onderwijsende/ hoe men van veelderhande Vruchten/ Wortelen/ Bloemen en Bladen/ etc. goede/ en nutte Confituren sal konnen toemaken/ en bewaren.

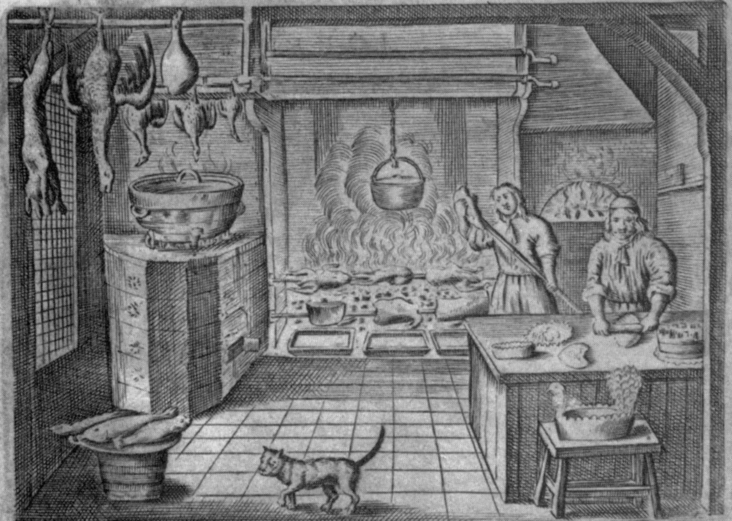

t'Amsterdam, By GYSBERT de GROOT, Boeckverkooper tusschen de twee Haerlemmer-sluysen in de groote Bybel, Met Privilegie.

The title page of *De verstandige kock, of sorghvuldige huyshoudter* (*The Sensible Cook or Careful Housekeeper*, 1683) depicts chefs at work in a bustling seventeenth-century Dutch kitchen, with Dutch tiles lining the counters and walls. General Research Division, The New York Public Library.

The vases with spouts, influenced in part by Nevers ceramics from France as early as 1650, featured multiple openings to cradle individual blooms. Among them were elegant fan-shaped quintel vases with five spouts and more elaborate ovoid or baluster forms, their circular bases supporting cascades of flowers. The Het Loo inventory even records small flower pyramids and obelisk-shaped flower holders, showcasing the diversity of Mary's collection. In contrast, her flower holders with perforated openings allowed for intricate arrangements, ensuring each stem had its own designated space. Among these were shallow Delftware "flower baskets," inspired by seventeenth-century wickerwork, which incorporated delicately perforated plates to secure individual blooms.

Each piece was a unique synthesis of European and Asian influences, transformed into a distinctly Dutch creation. Using these flower holders, fresh, artful arrangements adorned Mary's rooms daily—a tradition reminiscent of the French court, yet expressed in a style entirely her own.

In her Confection Room, whether cutting and arranging flowers or preparing slow-simmering preserves, Mary found a momentary escape from the demands of court life, immersing herself in pastoral pursuits.

Yet, even as she embraced the pleasures of her "Pleasurable Country Life" in the Dutch Republic, she remained keenly aware of the rapidly deteriorating political situation in England.

Shortly after Mary's departure for the Dutch Republic, fears among the English public began to escalate, culminating in the Popish Plot of 1678. This alleged conspiracy, in which Roman Catholics supposedly planned to assassinate King Charles II and replace him with Mary's Catholic father, James, Duke of York, sparked nationwide panic. The event even inspired the production of commemorative English tin-glazed earthenware, allowing citizens to recount the political drama through ceramics. Blue-and-white tiles, plates, bowls, and jugs were decorated with scenes depicting various moments of the plot, turning political tension into tangible art.

Tin-glazed earthenware had been produced in England since the sixteenth century, initially known as "galleyware" or "white ware." By the seventeenth century, it became known as "delf" or "delft," reflecting its stylistic similarities to Dutch Delftware, a connection reinforced by the

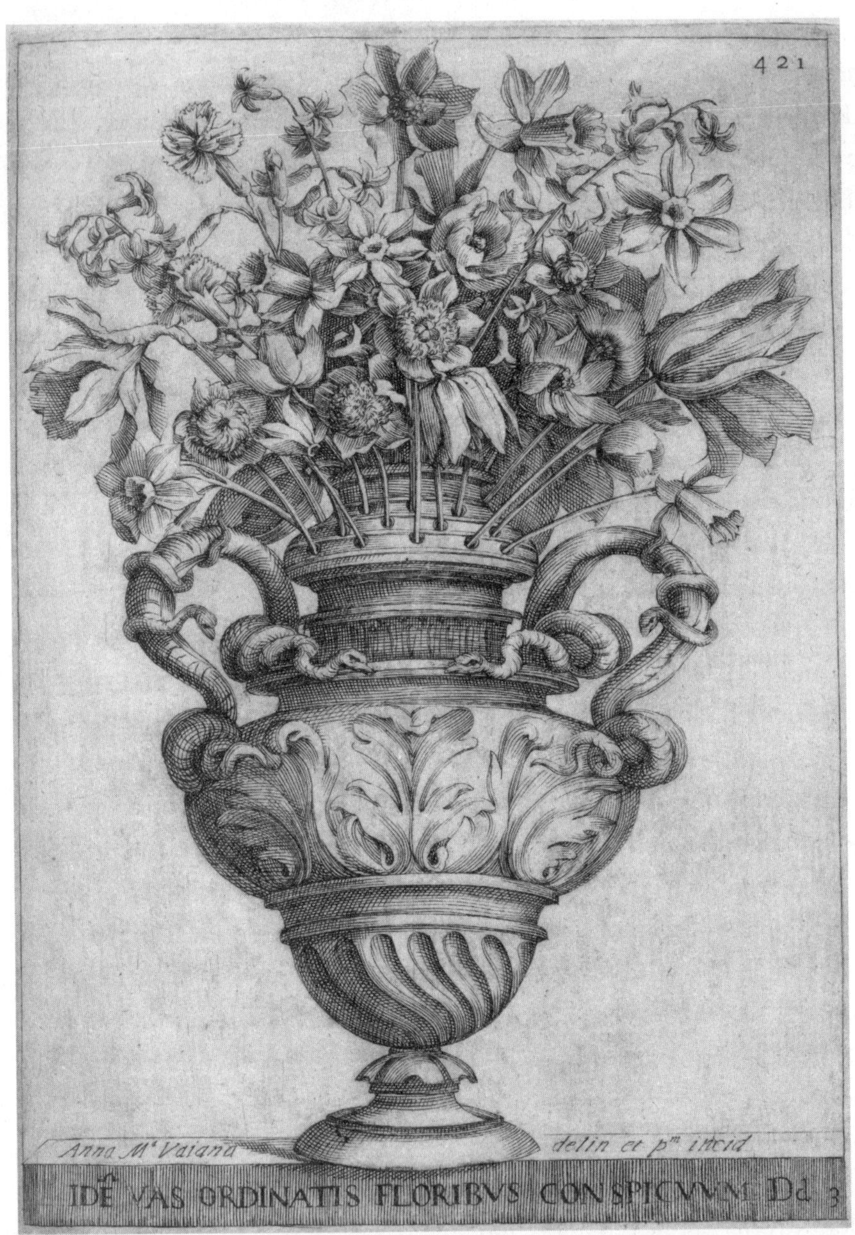

Anna Maria Vaiani's 1633 engraving from Giovanni Battista Ferrari's *De florum cultura* showcases the artistry of seventeenth-century floral arrangements, which included the use of specialized flower holders with individual holes to elegantly display each stem. Dumbarton Oaks Research Library and Collection, Trustees for Harvard University, Washington, D.C.

establishment of potteries in England by migrating Dutch artisans. Over time, the term "Delftware" was often broadly applied not only to ceramics produced in Delft but also to similar pieces made elsewhere in the Dutch Republic and in England. Today, these blue-and-white ceramics from sixteenth- to eighteenth-century England are referred to as "English delftware."

When Charles II died suddenly in 1685 without a legitimate heir, he was succeeded by his brother, Mary's father, James. As King James II, however, James's Catholic faith and his attempts to rule with unchecked royal authority created widespread unrest. When his wife gave birth to a Catholic son, signaling the possibility of an indefinite Catholic dynasty, public and parliamentary outrage reached a breaking point. In response, King James's leading opponents invited William and Mary to intervene, offering them the Crown as joint sovereigns. For William, this was an opportunity to bolster his campaign against France. For Mary, it was an act of devotion to her Protestant faith and her country, but one that came at a personal cost—she would have to turn her back on her father. It also meant an unexpected journey back to England. Having spent nearly half her life in the Dutch Republic, she arrived at the age of twenty-nine to be crowned. The events surrounding her arrival and the transfer of power remain one of the most debated transitions in royal history, known as the Glorious Revolution.

William was the first to arrive, landing in southwestern England in November 1688 with the Dutch navy, comprising more than 250 ships and over 7,000 Dutch soldiers. Mary followed on February 12, 1689. Shortly afterward, James, having lost the support of Parliament, the army, the aristocracy, and even his own daughter Mary, fled to France. He would never return to England or see his daughters Mary or Anne again.

On April 11, 1689, William and Mary were crowned at Westminster Abbey in a historic and unprecedented ceremony as the only co-reigning monarchs in England's history. The event featured two coronation chairs and sets of regalia, with duplicates made for Mary. Although she was the heir apparent, Mary declined to rule alone, agreeing instead to co-reign with William, who held the primary authority. By her own admission, Mary felt unprepared for the role she would assume as queen. Despite her reservations, Mary became a symbol of national loyalty and security, a trusted leader who anchored the co-reign. Together, William and Mary steered England through a revolutionary era toward greater stability, including the enactment of the English Bill of Rights in 1689. Members of the English nobility who supported their succession were generously rewarded.

In England, loyal supporters of William and Mary received not only titles and land but also coveted Delftware crafted by the finest Dutch potters. Blue-and-white Delftware flower vases, adorned with the monarchs' arms and cyphers, were gifted to their closest allies. Some nobles, eager to demonstrate their continued loyalty, went further, commissioning Delftware directly from Delft's potters, including The Greek A, to display prominently at their estates.

English country houses, from Chatsworth in Derbyshire to Dyrham Park in Gloucestershire, showcased these exquisite Delftware flower vases integrated within their art collections. Often placed near mantels or, during summer months, within empty fireplaces, the bright blue-and-white surfaces and dramatic silhouettes of the vases stood out against the dark recesses, adding vibrancy and visual interest to rooms.

Meanwhile, in the Dutch Republic, supporters of William and Mary celebrated their coronation by purchasing widely available, colorful Dutch tin-glazed earthenware featuring the new king and queen of England. Produced quickly and affordably, these commemorative dishes often depicted painted double portraits of the royal couple, inspired by popular woodblock prints of the time. Made for display, they were mounted on walls or placed in plate racks or cabinets, serving as symbols of allegiance and pride.

Shortly after their coronation at Westminster Abbey in London, William and Mary turned their attention again to architectural pursuits, focusing on a royal residence outside the city: Hampton Court Palace. This historic Tudor palace, once the seat of monarchs including Henry VIII, was located upstream of London on the River Thames. Planned as their principal residence, Hampton Court Palace offered refuge from the dense coal smoke that filled London's air—an environment believed to be detrimental to William's health.

With the same energy and decisiveness demonstrated in their building projects in the Dutch Republic, William and Mary quickly initiated plans

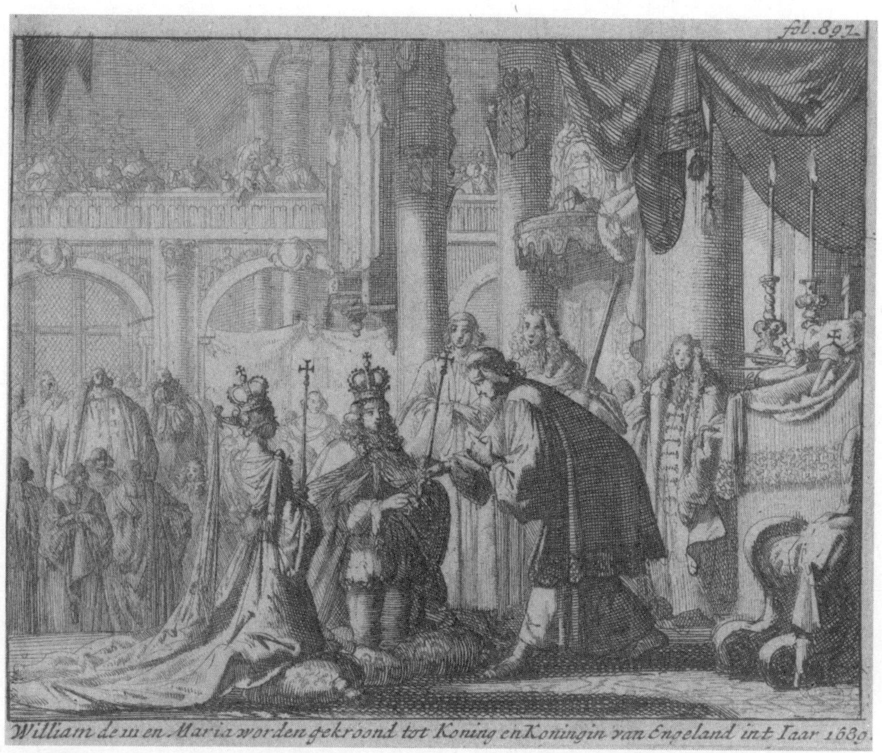

Jan Luyken's 1689 etching captures the grand coronation of William III and Mary II in Westminster Abbey on April 21, 1689, an event that sparked Dutch demand for images celebrating the Dutch-born prince's ascension to the English throne. Rijksmuseum, Amsterdam.

to renovate Hampton Court Palace under the direction of Sir Christopher Wren, the architect and Surveyor General of the King's Works. However, their decision to relocate to Hampton Court faced criticism from members of the government, who feared the royal couple's distance from London would reduce their accessibility and hinder official business. To address these concerns, William and Mary acquired a mansion west of the City of London, in what is now Hyde Park. After renovations and expansion, this residence became known as Kensington Palace.

Meanwhile, Mary envisioned transforming Hampton Court Palace, a sprawling and dimly lit structure, into a Versailles of her very own. While awaiting the completion of the palace renovations—amid the constant noise and dust—her attention turned to a small rectangular red brick building nearby. This former boathouse or "watergate," located just a few hundred yards across the garden, caught her eye.

Originally built in the 1560s by Henry VIII to receive the royal barge and its distinguished guests arriving from London's palaces, the Water Gallery took its name from its stunning perch on the edge of the River Thames. When Mary claimed it for her private use, she transformed it into a jewel-like retreat, a dazzling expression of her taste and vision. Unlike her beautiful yet secluded basement suite at Het Loo, the Water Gallery stood proudly in the open—vibrant, unmistakable, and a bold declaration of artistry, authority, and power.

Following the precedent of an earlier opulent *maison de plaisir*, the Water Gallery was not a blue-and-white first of its kind. Featuring blue-and-white tin-glazed earthenware made by both Dutch and French potters, the *Trianon de Porcelaine* at Versailles had been built by King Louis XIV in 1670 for his mistress Madame de Montespan. Known for its sensorial excesses, its interior and exterior of blue-and-white featured a series of rooms, from a *Cabinet des Parfums*, for the purpose of collecting essences from the profusion of surrounding Trianon flowers, to a luxurious *Chambre d'Amour*.

As the nephew of Pierre Gole, *ébéniste du roi* (official cabinetmaker to the king), who supplied furniture for Louis XIV's Trianon de Porcelaine, Daniel Marot likely collaborated with architect Christopher Wren in designing the Water Gallery. Combining their talents, they brought Mary's love of

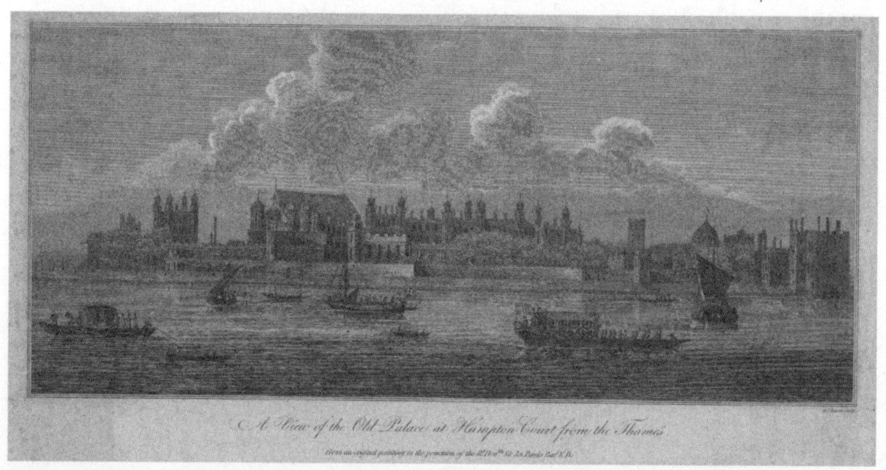

James Basire's undated engraving, *A View of the Old Palace at Hampton Court from the Thames*, captures the royal residence, including the Water Gallery, before Queen Mary II's transformative renovation. Yale Center for British Art, Paul Mellon Collection.

blue-and-white splendor to life, rapidly transforming it into an exquisite masterpiece worthy of both French and English royalty.

Records from carpenters, plasterers, and furniture makers reveal that the Water Gallery featured all the details and luxuries a seventeenth-century monarch or noblewoman could desire. The design included terraces, bedrooms, grand galleries, and intimate salons, all equipped with the newest fittings and architectural advancements, including movable sash windows—an innovative feature of the period.

On the lower level of the Water Gallery, as noted by Celia Fiennes, "There was the queen's Bath and a place to take boat in the house"—a bathing room outfitted with hot and cold running water, alongside a grotto adorned with rusticated faux rock formations. Adjacent to these spaces of relaxation was a room of particular delight for Mary: a blue-and-white Dutch Delftware pleasure dairy.

Although pleasure dairies are often associated with Marie Antoinette's *laiterie d'agrément* at Versailles in the 1780s, the concept had captivated noblewomen for centuries. Catherine de' Medici had established a dairy at Fontainebleau in the sixteenth century, and such refined spaces allowed queens and aristocratic ladies to entertain guests while sampling fresh dairy products in settings designed as elegant retreats.

In Mary's pleasure dairy, visitors entered a serene space where Dutch-tiled walls and marble or tiled ledges displayed rows of decorative Delftware milk pans. Traditionally used for cooling milk and separating cream, these wide, shallow bowls—typically plain earthenware—became canvases for Delft painters. Scenes of pastoral life emerged in vivid cobalt: figures tending cattle and goats, animals resting near thatched farmhouses, and rustic buildings dotting rolling fields. Framed by decorative bands and festoons of husks, these milk-pans elevated the simple act of dairy-making into an artistic experience, blending function with beauty.

With her "dairy women" at hand, Mary's guests were served an array of milk, cream, yogurt, and cheese in Delftware cups, bowls, and on finely painted dishes. These dairy delicacies were prized not only for their fresh, wholesome qualities but also for their association with purity and well-being.

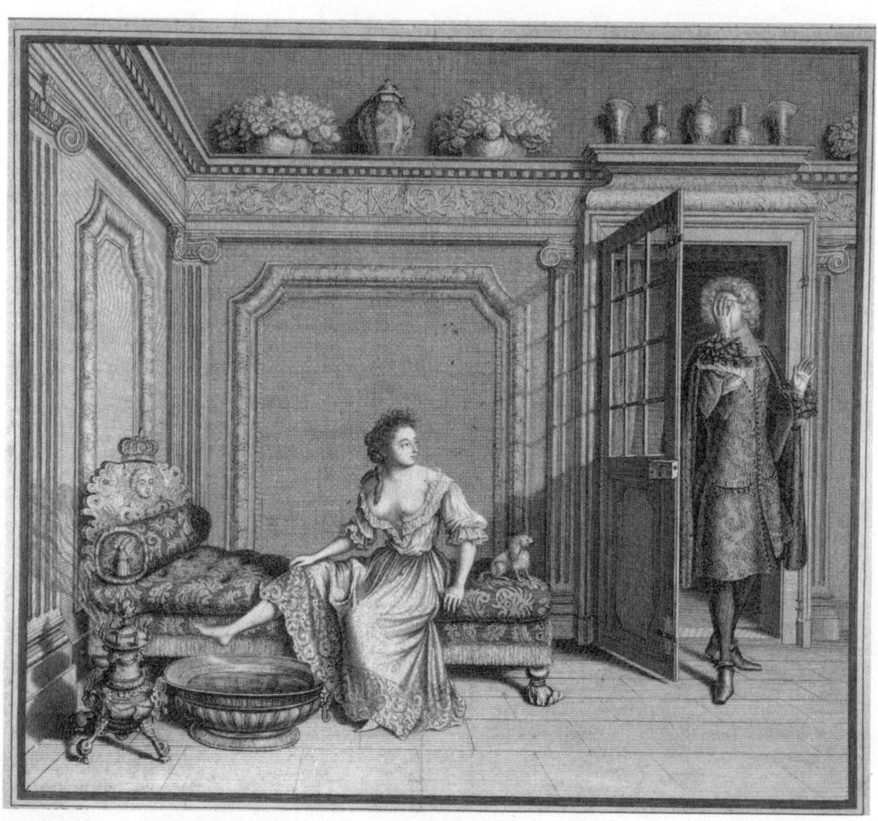

Nicolas Bazin's 1683 etching, *Femme de qualité déshabillée pour le bain* (*A Woman of Quality Undressed for Bathing*), illustrates an elegant seventeenth-century bathing room, adorned with a daybed and ornate cornices lined with ceramics. Musée Carnavalet - Histoire de Paris.

Dutch tin-glazed earthenware was the perfect material for dairy use—its smooth, cool surface preserved freshness, while its easy-to-clean glaze made it both practical and refined.

Mary's love of her dairy did not go unnoticed. An anonymous writer in the 1705 publication *The Royal Diary* remarked on her temperate nature, recalling that she "was so far from being fond of great Dainties, that I heard her once say, That she *could live in a Dairy.*"

Ascending the stairs from the Dairy to the upper level of the Water Gallery, guests entered its largest and most dazzling space: the central gallery. Tall windows flooded the long rectangular room with light, reflecting off the gleaming ceramics and painted surfaces. As Celia Fiennes described, "fine pictures of ye Court Ladyes drawn by Nellor" adorned the walls between the windows. These eight full-length portraits, painted by Sir Godfrey Kneller and commissioned by Mary in 1689, became known as the *Hampton Court Beauties.* Depicting her closest female allies and court supporters, the paintings were set in elegant blue and white painted frames, harmonizing with the gallery's overarching ceramic aesthetic.

The central gallery was a breathtaking fusion of art and display. Cornices, mantels, and brackets overflowed with meticulously arranged vases, cups, and dishes, their symmetrical configurations transforming the gallery into a theatrical showcase of porcelain and Delftware. As Daniel Defoe marveled, the space was "fill'd with this china and every other place, where it could be plac'd, with advantage." At the heart of this carefully curated spectacle stood some of Mary's most extraordinary Delftware commissions—pairs of towering, pyramid-shaped flower vases, their intricate tiers designed to hold cascading floral displays.

Almost as tall as the *Hampton Court Beauties* themselves, these *bloemenpiramides* or "pyramid flower vases" represented the pinnacle of blue-and-white Dutch Delftware artistry. Standing nearly five feet high, these obelisks of tin-glazed earthenware were created by The Greek A under the leadership of Adrianus Kocx. Each vase was composed of nine hexagonal tiers, gradually decreasing in size, with multiple spouts designed to hold cascading floral arrangements. Like pieces of a puzzle, each tier fit seamlessly into the one below, forming a towering structure supported by a footed base. Every part of the vases was covered with intricate blue-and-white motifs inspired by the style of Daniel Marot. These designs ranged from floral garlands, animals, and grotesque masks to *putti* (winged cherubs) and even portraits of William, making each piece as much a work of art as a functional object.

The obelisk or pyramid form, associated with sovereignty since ancient Egypt, was reimagined by Delft potters as a grand yet functional sculpture. This striking combination of monumental strength and nature's fleeting beauty would have delighted Mary. Each tier could be filled with water to nourish individual flower stems, resulting in cascading displays of textures, colors, and scents—becoming a living masterpiece of ceramic and botanical artistry.

By the nineteenth century, as historic interest in Tulipmania resurged, these flower holders became popularly known as *tulipières* or tulip vases. However, in the seventeenth and early eighteenth centuries, their use extended far beyond tulips, accommodating a wide variety of floral arrangements. Much like Dutch floral still-life paintings, where cascades of blooms spill from carefully arranged compositions, these vases overflowed with seasonal splendor—from hyacinths, narcissi and jonquils to guelder roses, lilies, and fritillaries—creating a spectacle for the senses.

Mary's passion for flowers and horticulture had flourished during her years in the Dutch Republic, shaping both her gardens and her artistic pursuits. At Hampton Court, she cultivated over two thousand plant varieties, earning acclaim for her vast and meticulously curated collection, which included rare *Exotiks* and *Aurunculae*. Her gardens flourished with over a thousand orange and lemon trees, alongside rare specimens sourced from the Mediterranean, the Caribbean, Mauritius, and even the American colony of Virginia. These Delft vases were not simply ornamental—they embodied her passion for art, nature, and innovation, transforming interiors into living gardens of rare and exquisite beauty.

At the corners of the central gallery, as Celia Fiennes described, "were little roomes like Closets or drawing rooms." Each of these intimate chambers showcased a distinct artistic technique or material, creating a series of immersive, visually striking spaces. Among them were rooms embellished

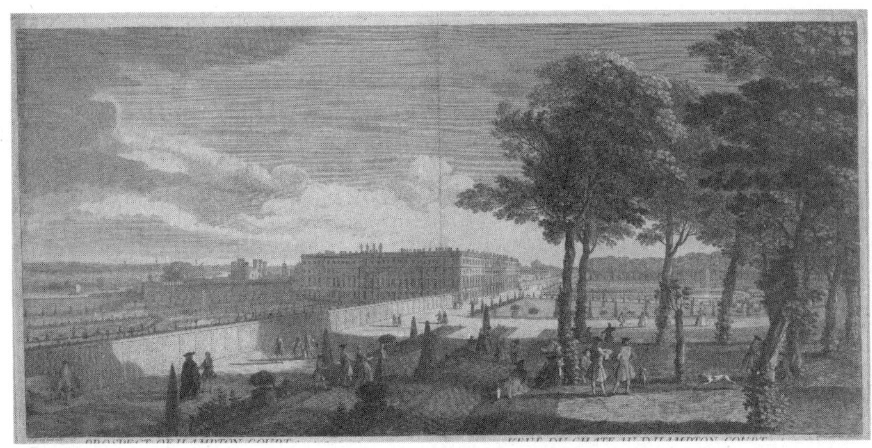

Jacques Rigaud's 1736 engraving, *Prospect of Hampton Court from the Garden Side,* offers a view of the Privy Garden and the grand facade transformed by William and Mary's renovations. Yale Center for British Art, Paul Mellon Collection.

with Chinese lacquerwork, paintings on glass, mirrors, and, most notably, Mary's "Delft-Ware Closett."

While the exact contents of Mary's "Delft-Ware Closett" remain unknown, it may have housed one of her most extraordinary commissions—a series of Dutch tiles crafted by The Greek A. Though they may have been mounted in her pleasure dairy, it is also possible that these tiles, distinguished by their exceptional size, quality, and artistry, once lined the walls of this enigmatic space, transforming it into an immersive Delftware display.

Mary's monumental tiles, nearly two feet wide, provided an expansive canvas for Delftware painters, allowing them to showcase their artistry on an unprecedented scale. Rendered in cobalt-blue with bold Baroque motifs inspired by Daniel Marot's engravings, the tiles depicted military drummers and trumpeters, flags bearing William and Mary's royal cypher, exotic birds, birdcages, and elaborate baskets of flowers. When arranged, they created the illusion of soaring architectural columns, seamlessly merging artistic splendor with structural grandeur. By transforming the modest domestic wall tile into a regal statement of power, these Dutch tiles were designed to astonish and inspire. They stood as both a celebration of Mary and a striking declaration of her royal authority.

In the evening, the Water Gallery glowed softly with candlelight from Delftware sconces, suspended from blue-and-white silk cords with matching tassels. Mary and her guests sat on blue silk-covered stools and sapphire lacquer-painted cane chairs, surrounded, as Defoe described, by "her Majesty's fine Collection of Delft Ware, which indeed was very large and fine; and here was also a vast stock of fine China ware, the like whereof was not then to be seen in England." The air was filled with the delicate scent of blooms held in surrounding Delftware vases. In this serene retreat by the river's edge, Mary sat immersed in a world of blue and white—a vision entirely of her own making, finally realized.

But the tranquility would not last.

On the morning of December 21, 1694, Mary awoke to find a rash spreading across her arms and chest. Within five days, at just thirty-two years old, the queen succumbed to smallpox in her bedchamber at Kensington Palace amid the porcelain collection she had assembled. News of Mary's sudden death spread quickly, and soon, Kensington Palace was overwhelmed by a mourning public unprepared for the loss of their Queen.

Although Mary had requested a modest funeral, the country's immense grief ensured it became one of the most elaborate in English royal history. After two months of preparation, her funeral took place in March 1695 at an unprecedented cost of more than £50,000. London was transformed into a city of mourning, its streets draped in black fabric, creating a solemn passage for the funeral procession as it made its way to Westminster Abbey. Crowds gathered in silence, watching as more than a thousand mourners, including both Houses of Parliament, followed in tribute. Yet, despite the wide attendance, two absences were striking—her sister Anne and William. Celia Fiennes, witnessing the ceremony, noted the omission observing that the King "ommitted noe Ceremony of Respect to her memory and remains." Even as the months passed, London remained shrouded in mourning, black bunting still hanging long into the spring.

In the summer of 1695, Anne van Goldstein, one of Mary's "favoured Ladies, First Woman of the Bedchamber, and Keeper of the Privy Purse," sat at her desk in Kensington Palace. Although the queen had died six months earlier, Anne remained occupied, meticulously finalizing an eighty-five-page document that itemized Mary's most recent purchases. Among these were bills for Delftware, including one from The Greek A. In one of her final official missives, Anne wrote one of the few surviving references to Mary's Delftware commissions:

> I do certify there is due unto Adrianus Koex of Delft for Dutch China or ware sent to her late Mary the sum of Thirteen hundred & fifty Guilders 3 Styvers; of English Money £122 14s. 9d.

The silk curtains were drawn, Mary's Delftware sat untouched, and the Water Gallery—once a luxurious retreat and an opulent venue for entertainment, where guests gathered amid the shades of blue and white—was now shuttered, silent, and forgotten. Though William never remarried and solemnly marked the anniversary of Mary's passing each year, he moved swiftly to erase the last traces of her presence.

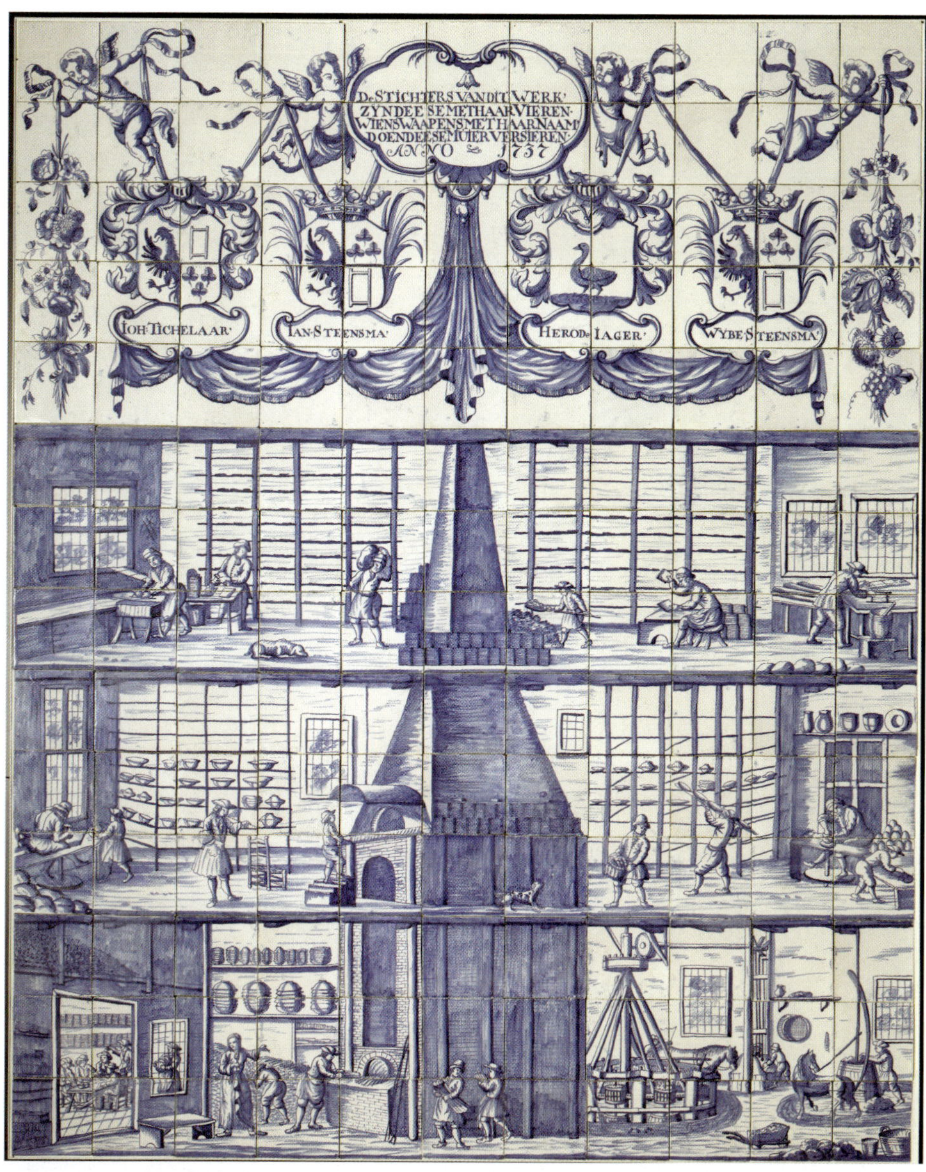

Figure 1. A Dutch Tile Panel Depicting a Tile and Pottery Factory in Bolsward. Painted decoration attributed to Dirk Danser (1698–1763), Bolsward, ca. 1745–1765. Rijksmuseum, Amsterdam. This Dutch tile panel commemorates the 1737 founding of the Bolsward tile and pottery factory with a detailed workshop scene. Stokers fuel the kiln, painters decorate ceramics, and potters shape wares above, while the colossal kiln towers through all three levels.

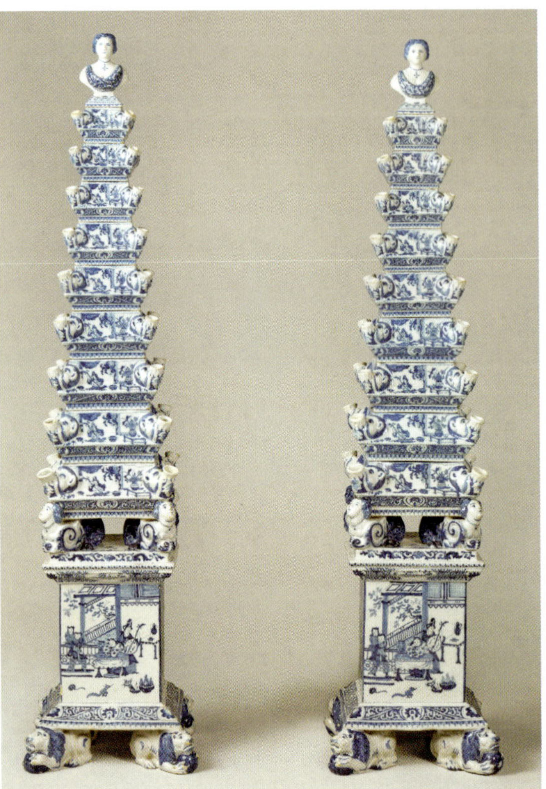

Figure 2 (left). A Pair of Dutch Delft Blue and White *Bloem-piramides* (Flower Pyramids). Attributed to De Metaale Pot (The Metal Pot) Factory (Lambertus van Eenhoorn), ca. 1692–1700, three segments and top executed by Tichelaar, Makkum, 2004, glazed earthenware. Rijksmuseum, Amsterdam.

Figure 3 (below). Disassembled View of a *Bloempiramide* (Flower Pyramid). Each spout of this tiered "flower pyramid," composed of stacked segments, once held delicate cut flowers. The towering vase design, sometimes called a tulip vase or *tulipière*, originated at the court of William and Mary, whose passion for flower arranging, porcelain, and pottery shaped its creation. Rijksmuseum, Amsterdam.

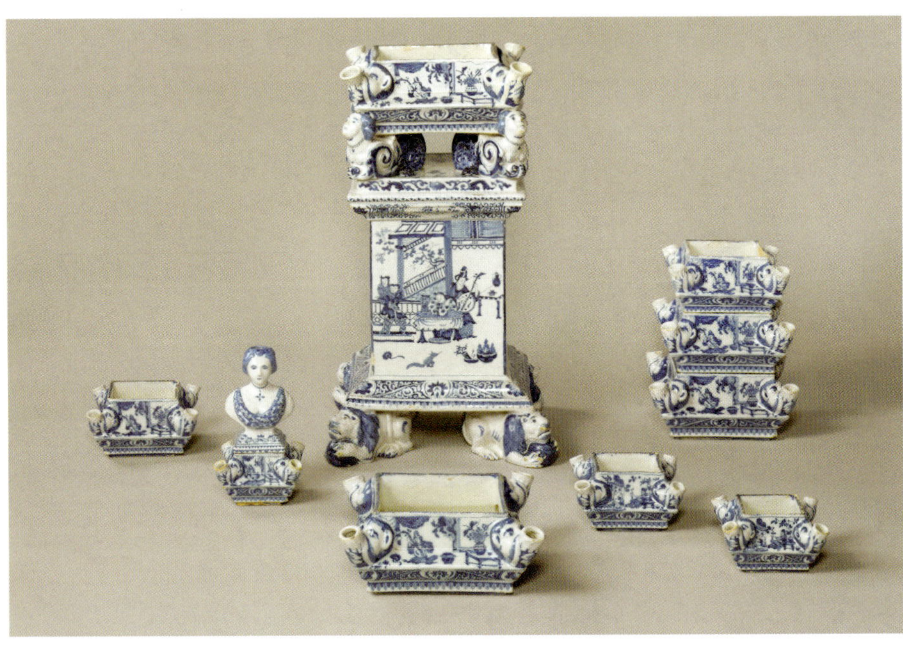

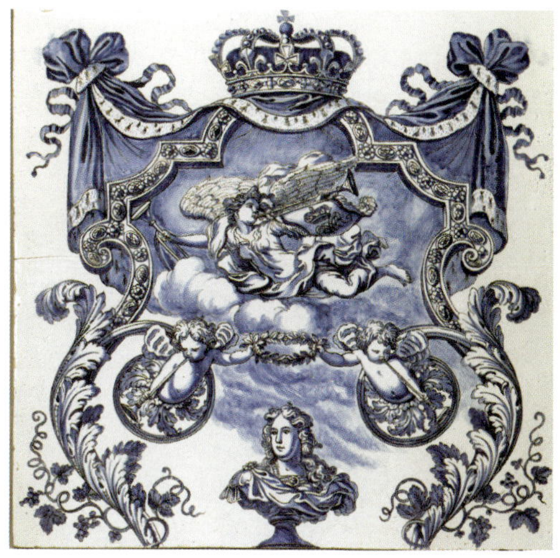

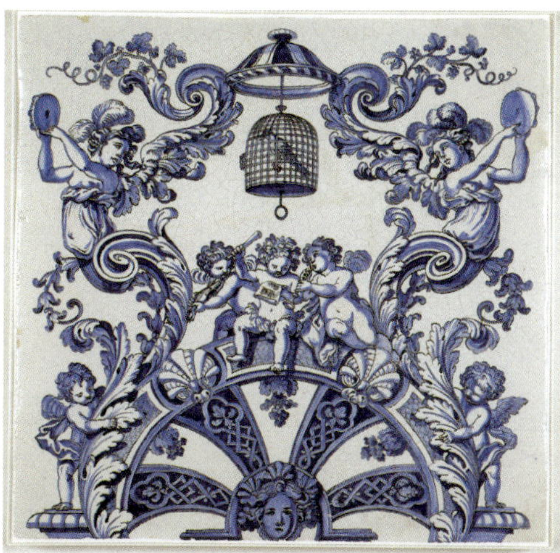

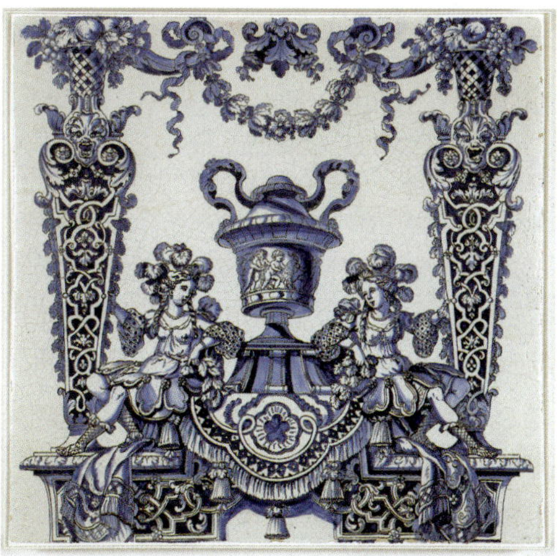

In the sumptuous Water Gallery at Hampton Court, ca. 1690, Queen Mary II indulged her passion for Delftware, displaying monumental blue-and-white tiles inspired by Daniel Marot's designs. These tiles combine classical motifs with Baroque exuberance, with symmetrical strapwork providing structure, while decorative elements—from curling acanthus leaves to figures of female warriors—add dynamic ornamentation.

Figure 4 (top). A Dutch Delft Blue and White Large Tile with a Bust of William III. De Grieksche A (The Greek A) Factory, period of Adrianus Kocx, ca. 1694. The Metropolitan Museum of Art, New York.

Figure 5 (center). A Dutch Delft Blue and White Large Tile with a Birdcage and Putti. De Grieksche A (The Greek A) Factory, period of Adrianus Kocx, ca. 1690. Rijksmuseum, Amsterdam, loan from the Royal Antiquarian Society.

Figure 6 (bottom). A Dutch Delft blue and white large tile with a covered urn flanked by two female warriors. De Grieksche A (The Greek A) Factory, period of Adrianus Kocx, ca. 1690. Rijksmuseum, Amsterdam, loan from the Royal Antiquarian Society.

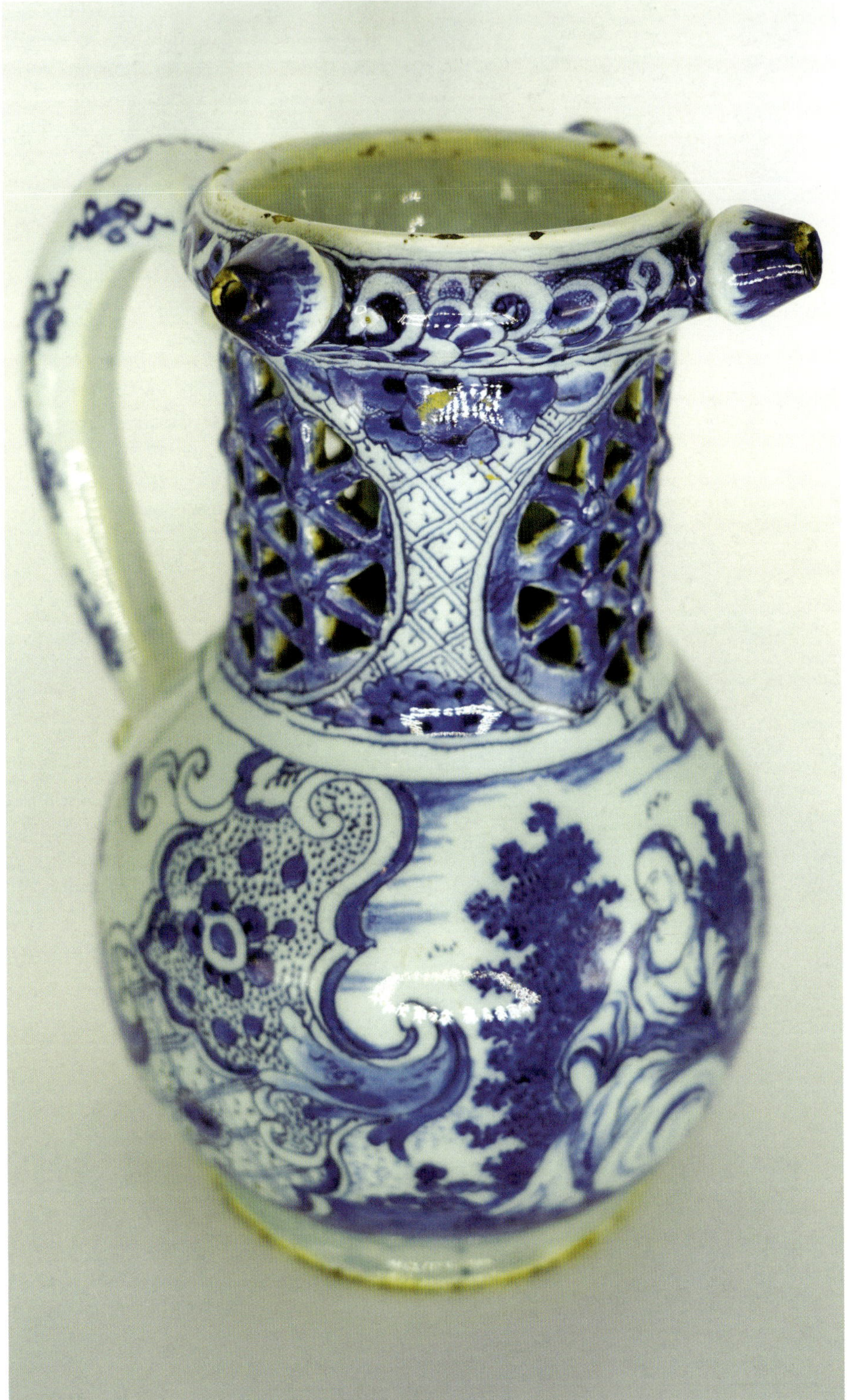

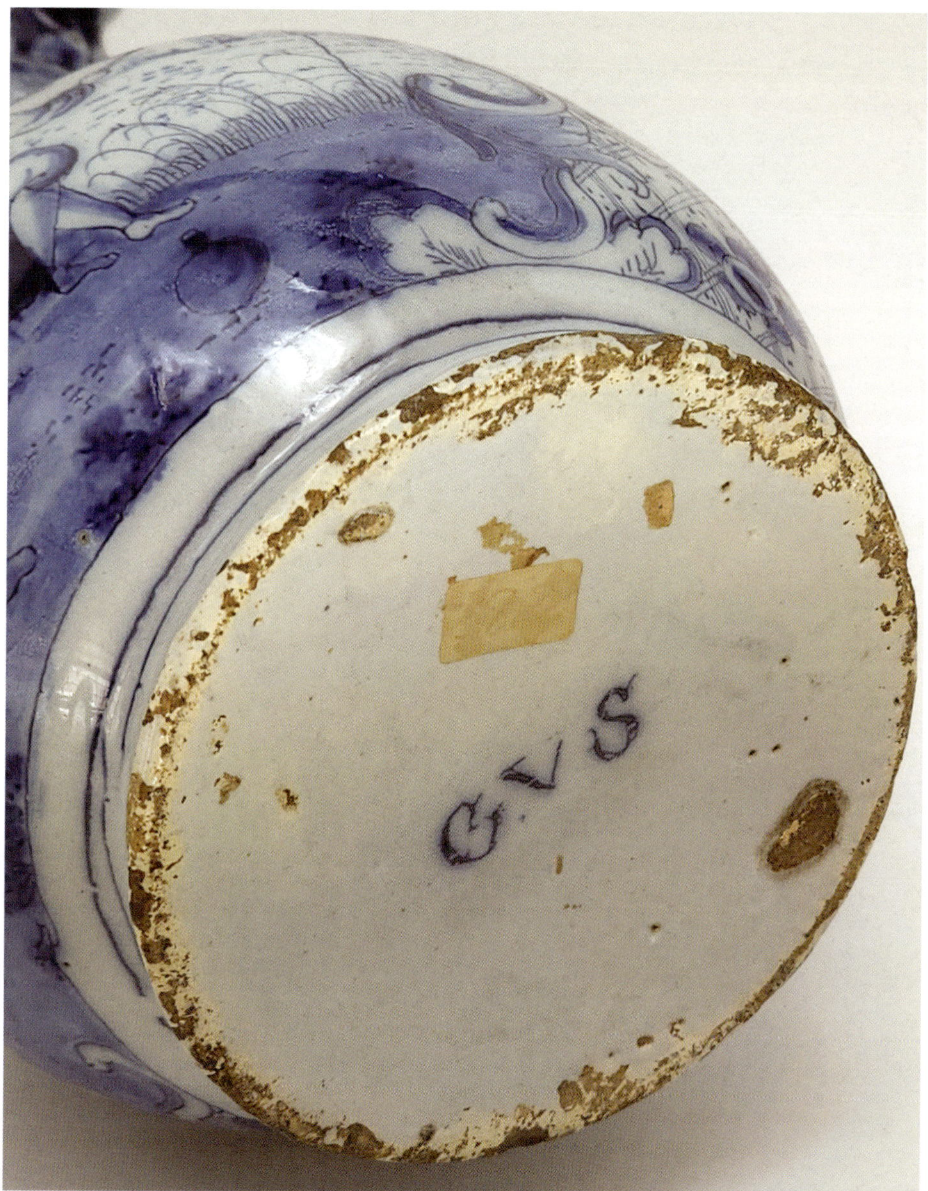

Figure 7A (opposite). A Dutch Delft Blue and White Puzzle Jug. Het Oude Moriaanshooft (The Old Moor's Head) Factory, marks G.VS for Geertruij Verstelle, ca. 1769. The spherical body painted with a couple fishing between stippled, trellis-patterned and cailloute panels edged in rococo scrollwork with the date 1769 and issuing floral sprigs, the cylindrical neck with a trellis diaper ground pierced with three trelliswork roundels, the roundel on the front above the initials I:K and beneath a tubular rim issuing three nozzles and a hollow tubular loop handle painted with beribboned artemisia leaves. Provenance: The William Randolph Hearst Collection. The National Society of Colonial Dames in the State of New York.

Figure 7B (above). (Base view of the puzzle jug)

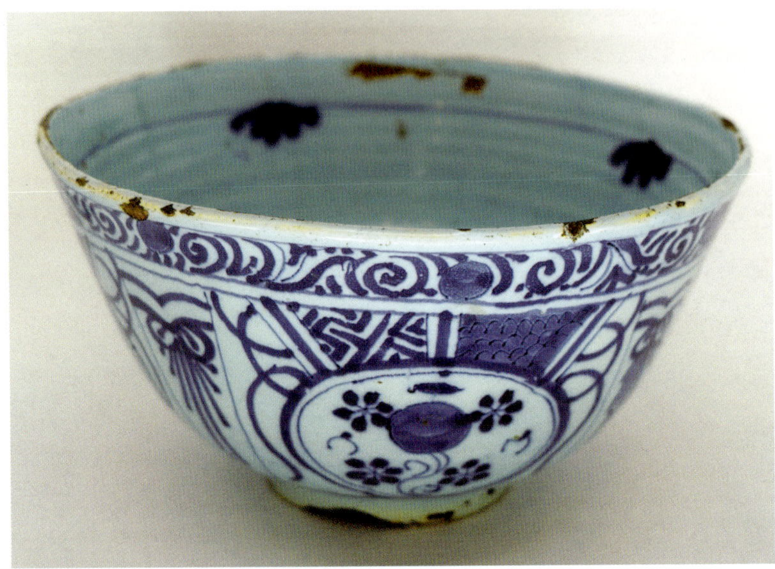

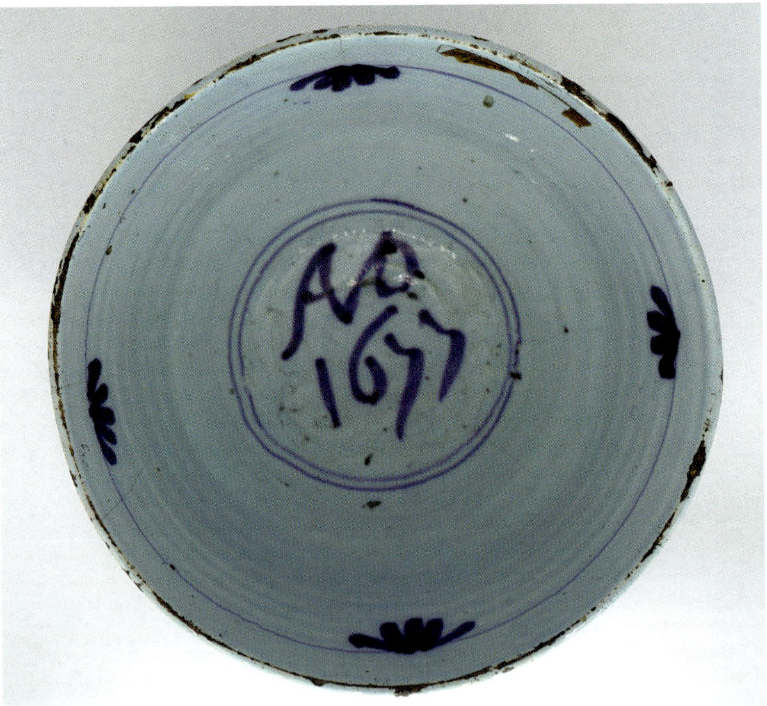

Figure 8A (top). A Dutch Delft Blue and White "Wanli" Style Deep Bowl, 1677. Painted around the exterior with four large panels of Chinese motifs within quatrefoils, the interior inscribed with the monogram AVO above the date 1677 within a double roundel beneath four foliate sprigs pendent from a single line near the rim. Provenance: Smith-Jordan Collection, gift of Mrs. George Pratt. The National Society of Colonial Dames in the State of New York.

Figure 8B (bottom). (View of the bowl interior)

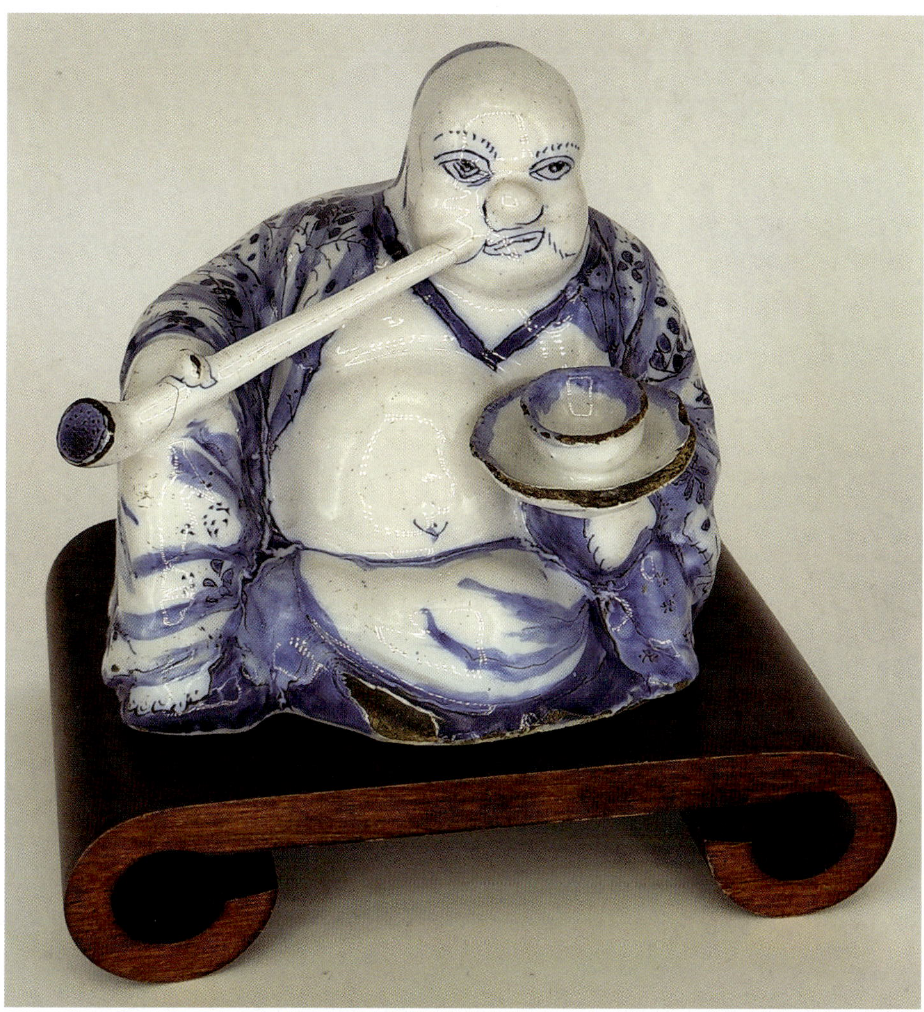

Figure 9. A Dutch Delft Blue and White Seated Figure of Budai Heshang, ca. 1720. Modeled seated wearing an open robe, smoking a long pipe held in his right hand supported on his raised right knee, and holding in his left hand a teabowl and saucer. Provenance: James A. Lewis & Son, Inc. The National Society of Colonial Dames in the State of New York.

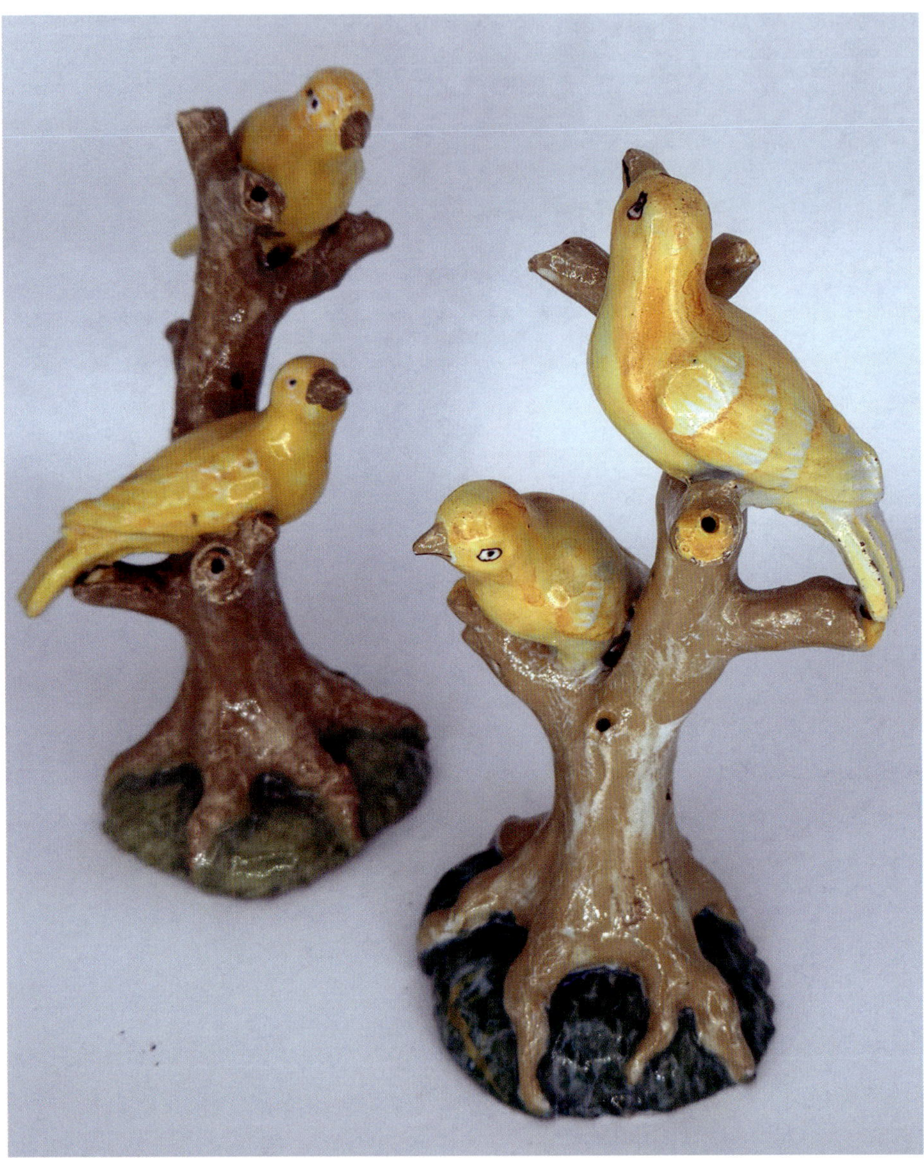

Figure 10. Two Dutch Delft Polychrome Groups of Birds Perched in Trees, ca. 1760. The first modeled as two yellow canaries with tan beaks and manganese eyes, the upper bird looking upwards, perched on the truncated branches of a tan tree, its roots extending over a green mound base. The second almost identical to the preceding but the upper bird looking outwards and the mound base of a pea-green color. Provenance: Ginsberg & Levy, Inc., Robinson Bequest. The National Society of Colonial Dames in the State of New York.

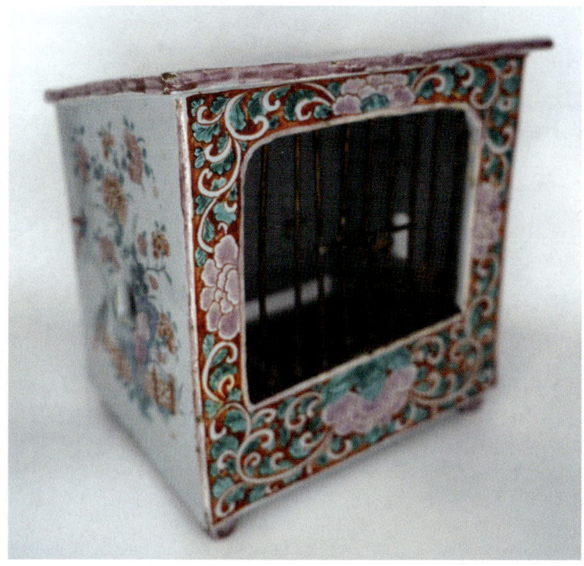

Figure 11A (above). A Pair of Dutch Delft Doré Birdcages, ca. 1730. Each rectangular with a rose-edged slanting roof, an open front mounted with metal bars and door, and painted in pink and green with scrolling peonies on an iron-red ground, the pierced sides painted in iron-red, green, pink, blue, black, and gold with a bird in flight above another perched on a fence beneath peonies growing by a rock, the interior with a feeding trough and the reverse with an opening for a food drawer and a pierced aperture for suspension. Provenance: The William Randolph Hearst Collection. The National Society of Colonial Dames in the State of New York.

Figure 11B (below). (Bird cage b)

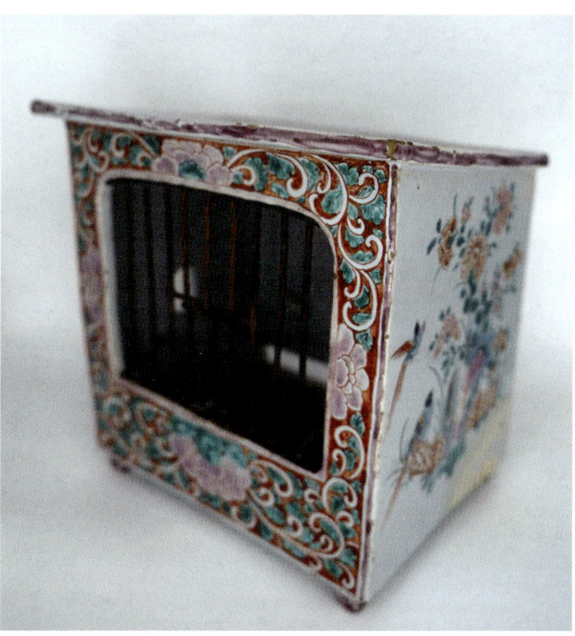

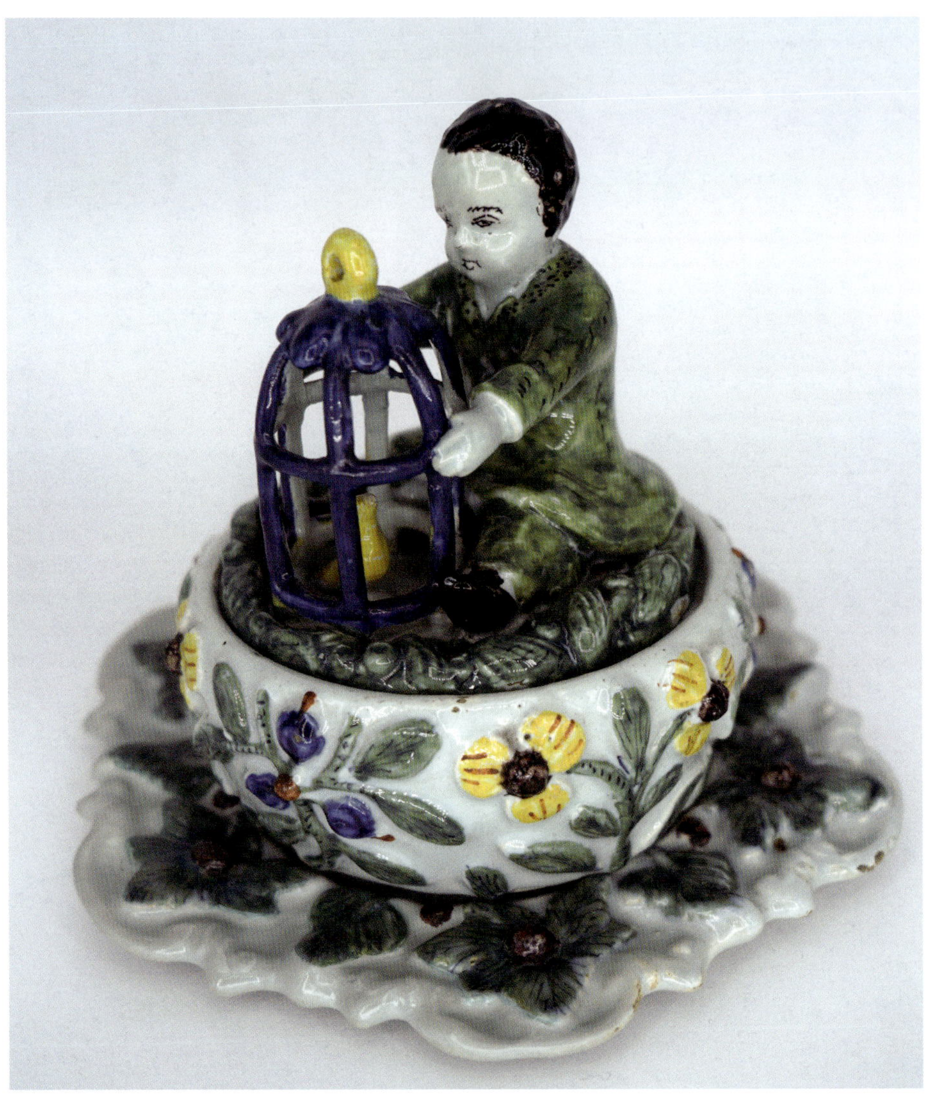

Figure 12. A Dutch Delft Polychrome Circular Butter Tub, Cover, and Stand Depicting a Child with Birdcage. De Witte Ster (The White Star) Factory, ca. 1764. The cover modeled as a manganese-haired child wearing a green tunic and trousers, and seated with a blue and yellow birdcage between his manganese shoes, a singing canary within, the rim molded with curling leaves. Provenance: Ginsburg & Levy, Inc. The National Society of Colonial Dames in the State of New York.

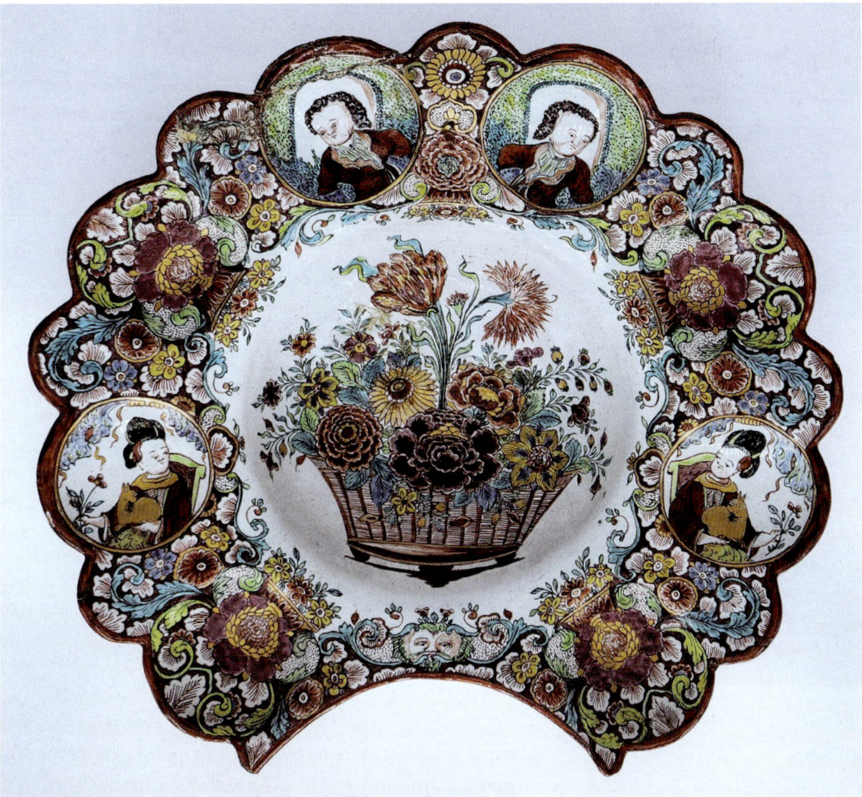

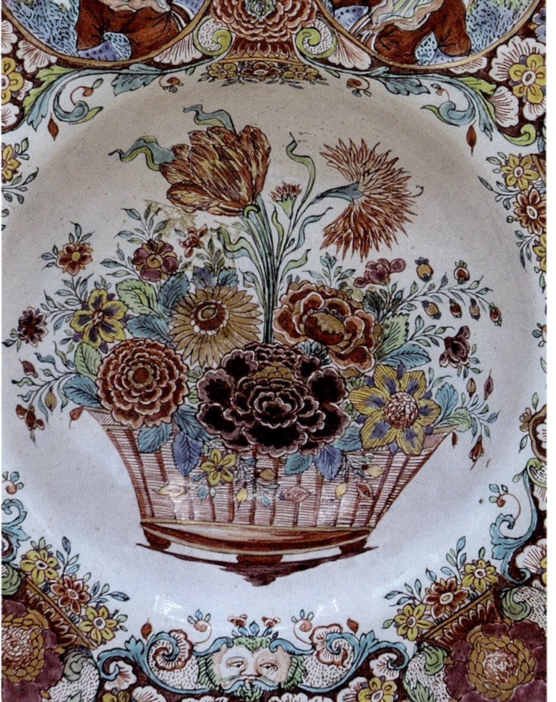

Figure 13A (above). A Dutch Delft Doré Circular Scalloped Barber's Bowl, ca. 1720–30. Painted in shades of rose, iron-red, turquoise, green, yellow, blue, russet, black, and gold in the deep well with a basket of lush flowers, and around the manganese-ground rim with a profusion of blossoms and leaves in and around four circular depressions at the sides, two with a seated Chinese lady holding a rabbit, and two at the top with a half-length Dutch gentleman, all within an iron-red edge. The National Society of Colonial Dames in the State of New York.

Figure 13B (left). (Barber's bowl detail)

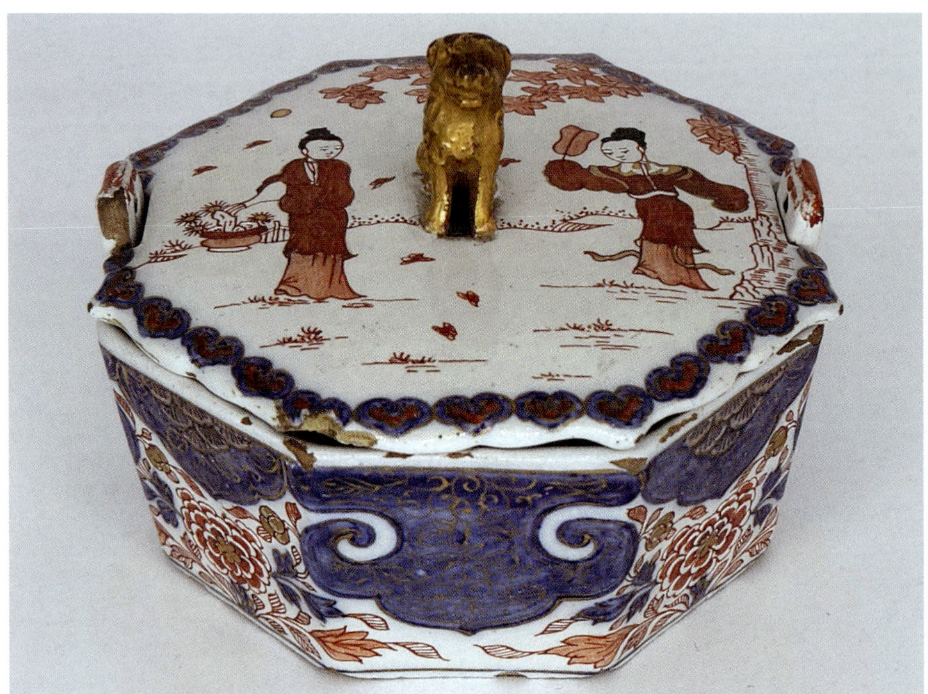

Figure 14A (above). A Dutch Delft Doré Butter Tub and Cover, ca. 1740. Painted in an Imari palette around the tub with four flowering peony plants beneath a gilt peony-patterned blue lappet border, the sides with pierced upright tab handles, and the flat cover painted with two Chinese ladies in a garden flanking the gilt seated lion knop, the scalloped and barbed rim with a ruyi-head border. Provenance: Ginsburg & Levy, Inc. The National Society of Colonial Dames in the State of New York.

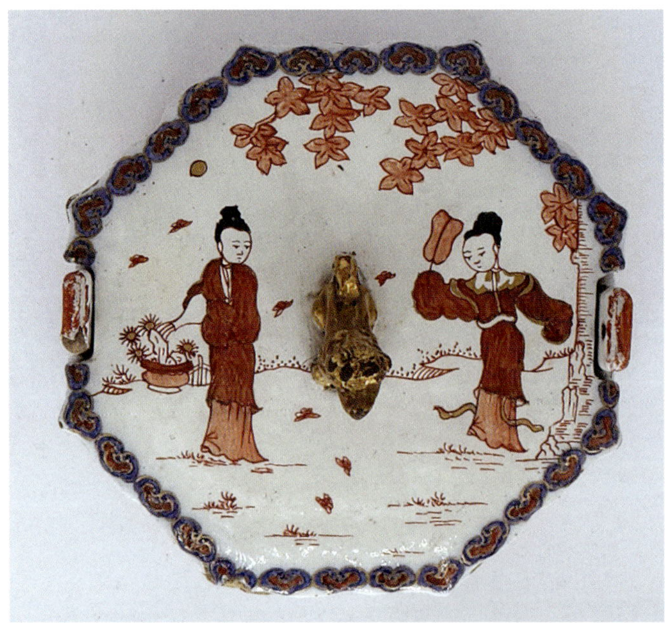

Figure 14B (left). (Detail cover)

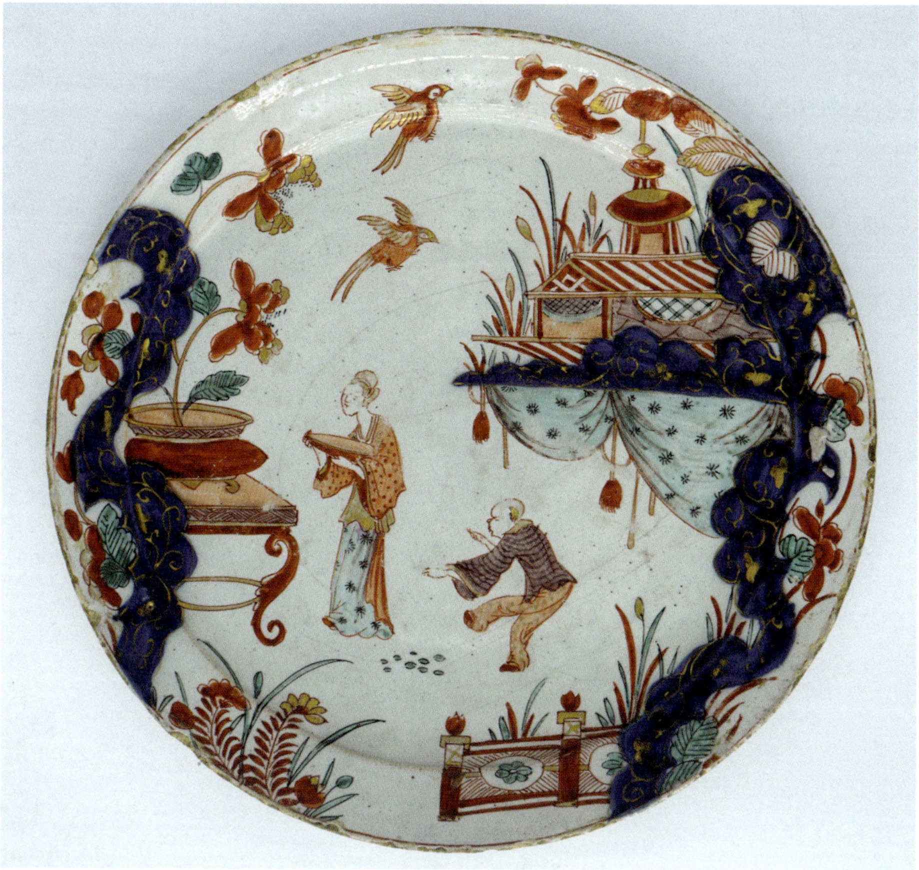

Figure 15A (above). A Dutch Delft Doré Plate. De Grieksche A (The Greek A) Factory, ca. 1710, marked PAK in iron-red for Pieter Adriaensz. Kocx, the owner of The Greek A from 1701 to 1703, or his widow Johanna van der Heul, the owner of the factory from 1703 to 1722. Painted in blue, iron-red, salmon, turquoise-green, black, and gold with two birds flitting above a female figure and a boy walking toward a jardinière on a table, a pavilion beyond above a tasseled drapery at the right and floral panels at the sides. Provenance: Harry S. Koopman. The National Society of Colonial Dames in the State of New York.

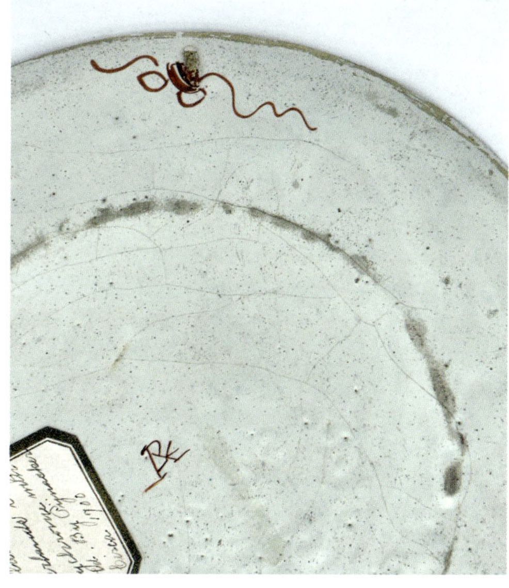

Figure 15B (right). (Detail of the reverse)

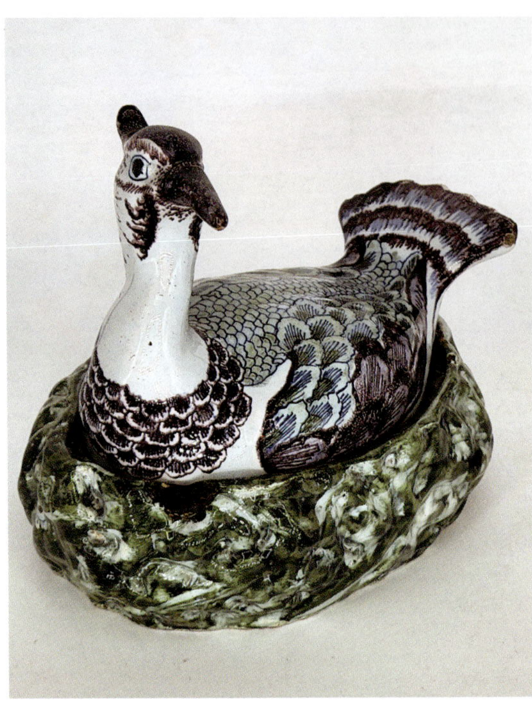

Figure 16. A Dutch Delft Polychrome Oval Butter Tub and Cover. De Grieksche A (The Greek A) Factory, ca. 1758–64. The cover formed as a plover with a manganese beak, crest, neck, and eyes, and manganese, green, and blue plumage, the underside of the tail feathered in iron-red, and modeled perched on a nest-form tub mottled in green. Provenance: Ginsburg & Levy, Inc. The National Society of Colonial Dames in the State of New York. For centuries, the Netherlands—especially South Holland near Leiden and Delft—was celebrated for its rich, high-quality butter, a prized export across Europe and a particular favorite of the English.

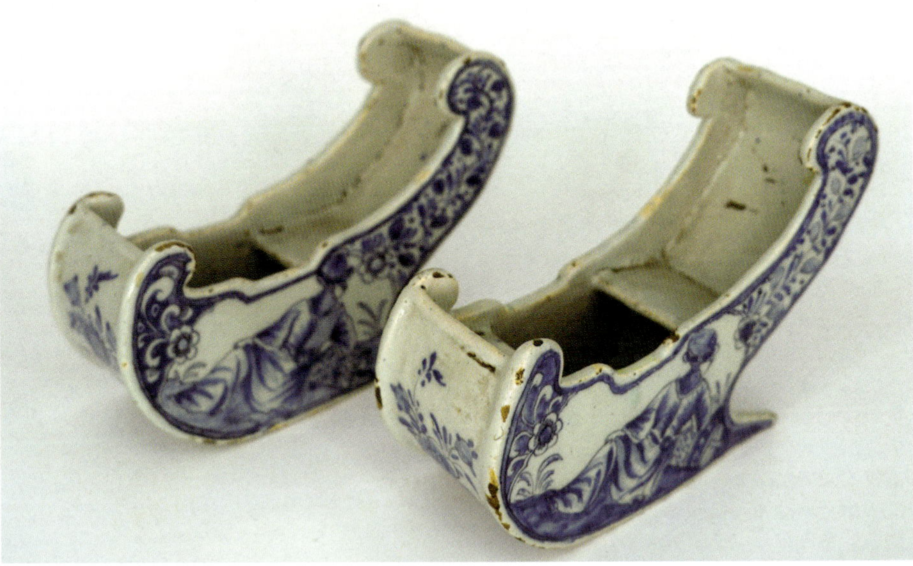

Figure 17. A Pair of Dutch Delft Blue and White Models of Sleighs, ca. 1740. Each painted on either side with a lady reclining against a barrel between a floral sprig and a budding vine extending up the tall sides, the curved front and the scrolling back with a floral spray, and the interior with two "seats." Provenance: Ginsberg & Levy, Inc. The National Society of Colonial Dames in the State of New York. Delft sleighs, often described as pipe stands, were likely decorative rather than functional. Delft potters crafted these pieces after popular ice sleighs, in which seated ladies would glide gracefully across the ice, propelled by skating gentlemen.

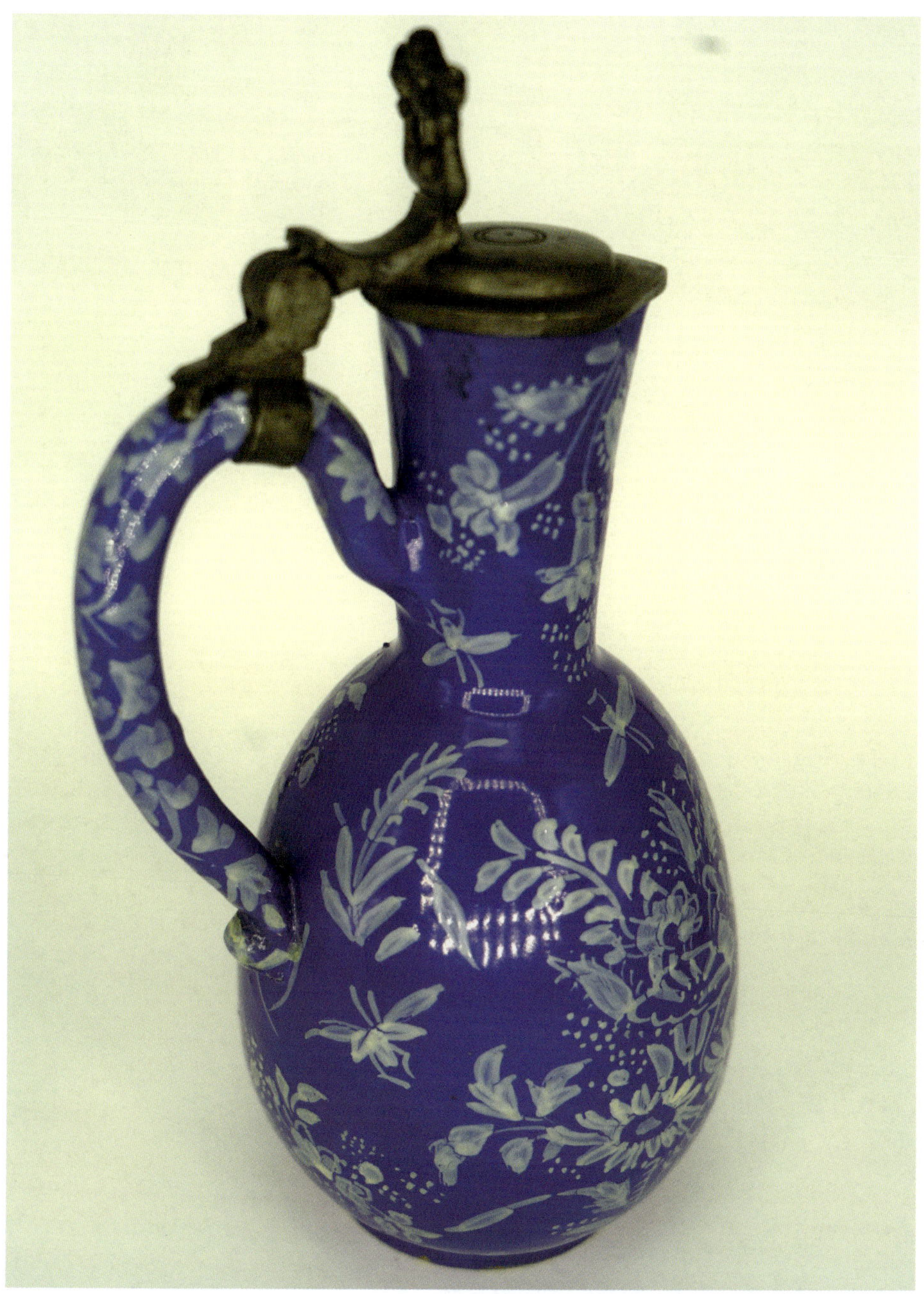

Figure 18. A Dutch Delft "Persian Blue" Pewter-Mounted Ewer. De Paauw (The Peacock) Factory, ca. 1690–1710. The ovoid periwinkle-blue body painted in white on the front with a bird looking upward and surrounded by large flowering plants on the sides and beneath the flowering vine–decorated loop handle, and the tall neck with floral sprigs, mounted with a pewter cover hinged and affixed with a double-tailed mermaid thumbpiece, marked. Provenance: The William Randolph Hearst Collection. The National Society of Colonial Dames in the State of New York.

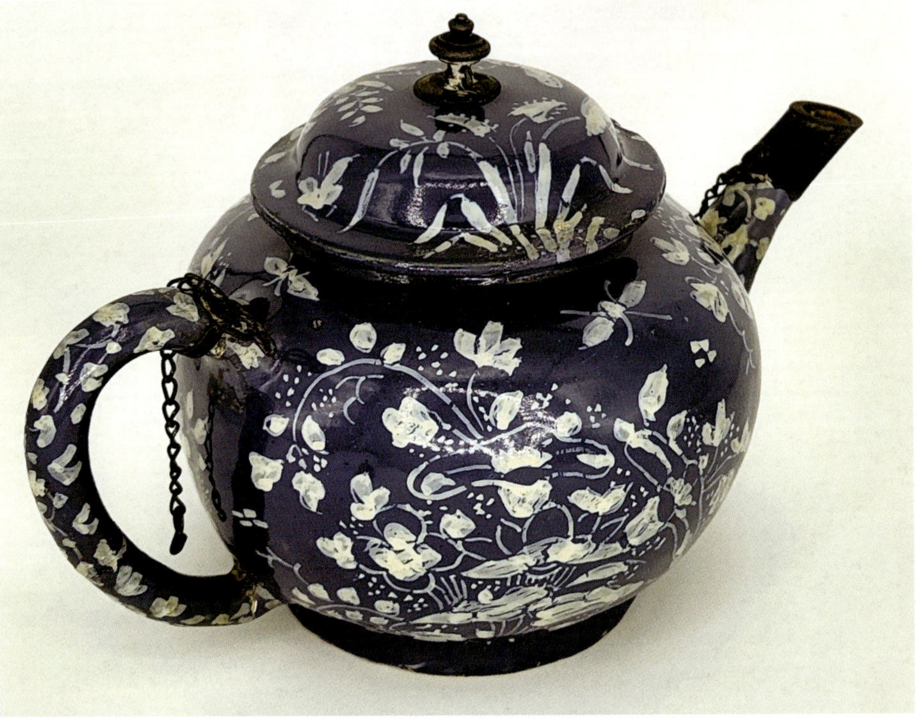

Figure 19A (above). A Dutch Delft "Persian Blue" Teapot and Cover. De Paauw (The Peacock) Factory, ca. 1690–1710. The slightly compressed spherical blue body and cover painted in white with insects, flowering plants, and floral sprays. Provenance: M. Keezer & Fils, Amsterdam; Collection of Mrs. Russel S. Carter. The National Society of Colonial Dames in the State of New York.

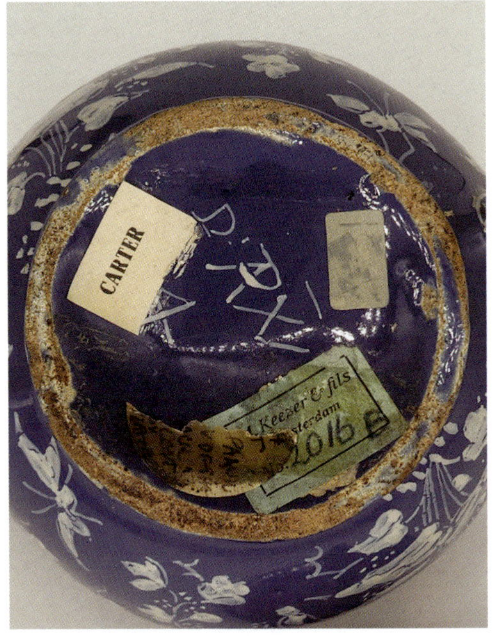

Figure 19B (left). (Base view of the "Persian Blue" teapot)

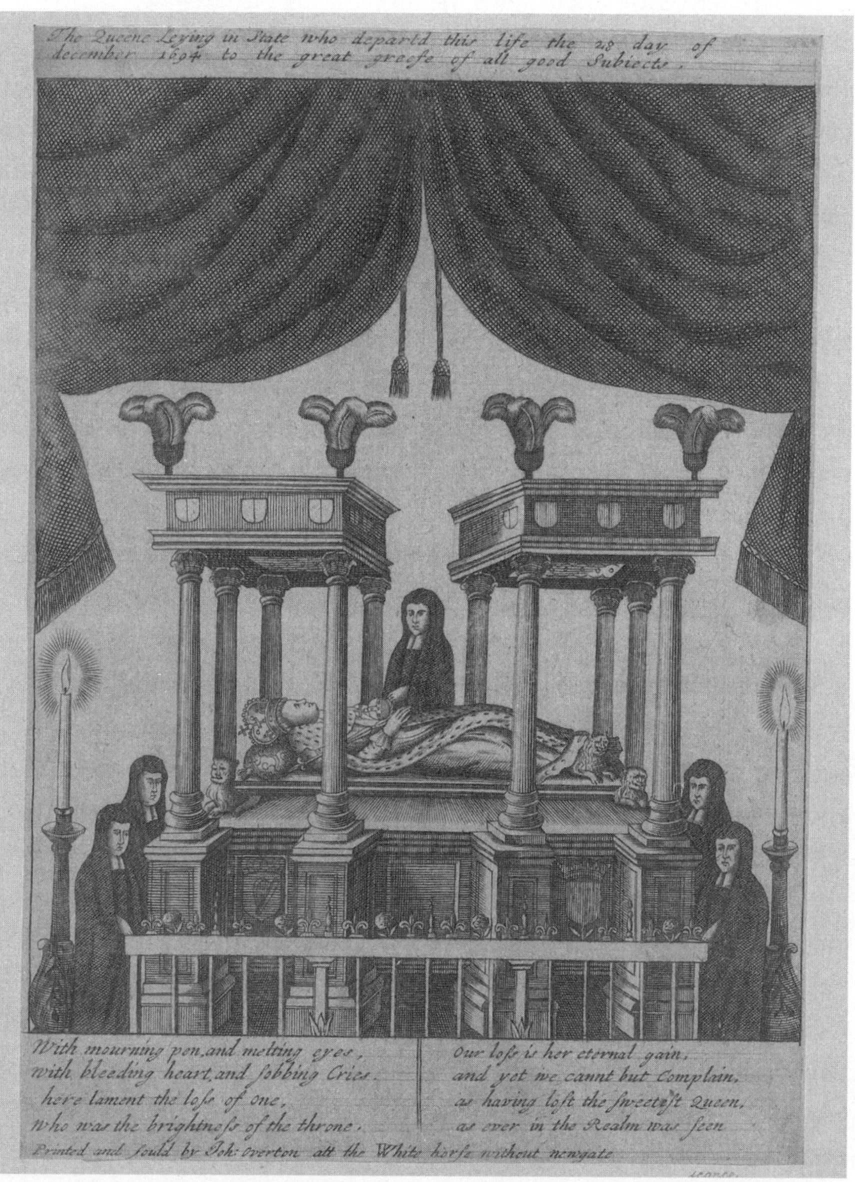

Publisher John Overton's 1695 engraving of Queen Mary II lying in state reflects the widespread mourning following her sudden death from smallpox in December 1694, which was swiftly commemorated in sermons, poems, and printed images. Wellcome Collection, London.

By 1700, at William's request, the dismantling of the Water Gallery had begun. Cornices, mantels, and brackets were cleared; cabinet doors swung open, and shelves were emptied. Once meticulously arranged displays were undone, their careful order disrupted. Tiles were pried from walls, shattering their intricate patterns, while vases that had once overflowed with carefully chosen blooms were packed up, stored, or given as gifts. One by one, Mary's Delftware and porcelain vanished, her work of art quietly unraveled.

That July, William ordered the Water Gallery's demolition to extend his Privy Garden to the Thames. Brick by brick, timber by timber, the structure was dismantled. By November, at his request, gardeners had begun lowering the ground to improve his view of the river from the palace. When the foundations were finally excavated, even the last shadow of the Water Gallery had disappeared.

Yet, while her Water Gallery and much of her Delftware were lost, Mary's blue-and-white legacy endures.

By the time of her death in 1694, Dutch Delftware had evolved into something bold, innovative, and distinctly its own. Under her patronage, Delft potters pushed the boundaries of scale, form, and decoration. What began with small tabletop vases—delicate enough for Mary to hold as she arranged flowers at Het Loo—grew into towering ceramic sculptures. Dutch tilework expanded to the scale of paintings, while ornamental motifs became ever more intricate. Mary transformed everyday objects into statements of grandeur, elevating Delftware to a regal art form. Without Mary, Delftware might never have reached such expressive, dynamic heights.

The monumentality of Mary's commissions not only captured the imagination of the English and Dutch but also fueled Delftware's rise across Europe and, eventually, the American colonies. Her influence ensured that Delftware became an enduring symbol of artistic ambition and royal taste.

What little remains of the Water Gallery's Delftware is now scattered across the world, from the shelves of the Victoria and Albert Museum in London to the walls of the Metropolitan Museum of Art in New York. Many of her ceramics may have been broken, discarded, or unknowingly absorbed into other collections. Yet the essence of her vision persists—in every piece of

Delftware that continues to enchant, inspire, and tell the story of a queen who saw art in Delftware and transformed it into something extraordinary.

While Mary contributed greatly to the art of Delftware, what did she receive in return?

The Water Gallery was the creation of a queen who, at fifteen, wept bitterly for two days at the prospect of leaving England for a foreign land. Yet when she returned fifteen years later, her first and most personal artistic act on English soil was the creation of this radiant jewel box—a sanctuary bathed in blue and white, encapsulating the essence of the Dutch world she had come to cherish.

In Delftware, Mary found more than decoration; she discovered a medium through which to shape her artistic sensibility, assert her authority, and visually proclaim the global significance of her English and Dutch monarchy. The tiles that lined her walls, the pyramidal vases that towered in her galleries—each piece was a statement, a reflection of her cultivated eye and the deep bond she had forged with the artisans of Delft.

Yet, beyond its political and artistic symbolism, perhaps the Water Gallery offered something more intimate. Surrounded by blue-and-white Delftware, from milk pans to towering flower vases, Mary may have felt something simpler, more personal—a connection to a place that had, against all expectations, become home. Contemporary accounts speak of the "great delight" the Water Gallery brought her and the "great joy" she found at Hampton Court.

Mary could have chosen to express herself through the gleaming metals of London's silversmiths or the grandeur of oil paintings from master studios. But instead, she embraced the soft, malleable clay of the Dutch Republic—formed from its earth, shaped by its artisans, and tied to the land where, in her own words, she had led "a life so suitable to my humour . . . where in a word I had all earthly content, and sufficient means to bring me to Heaven."

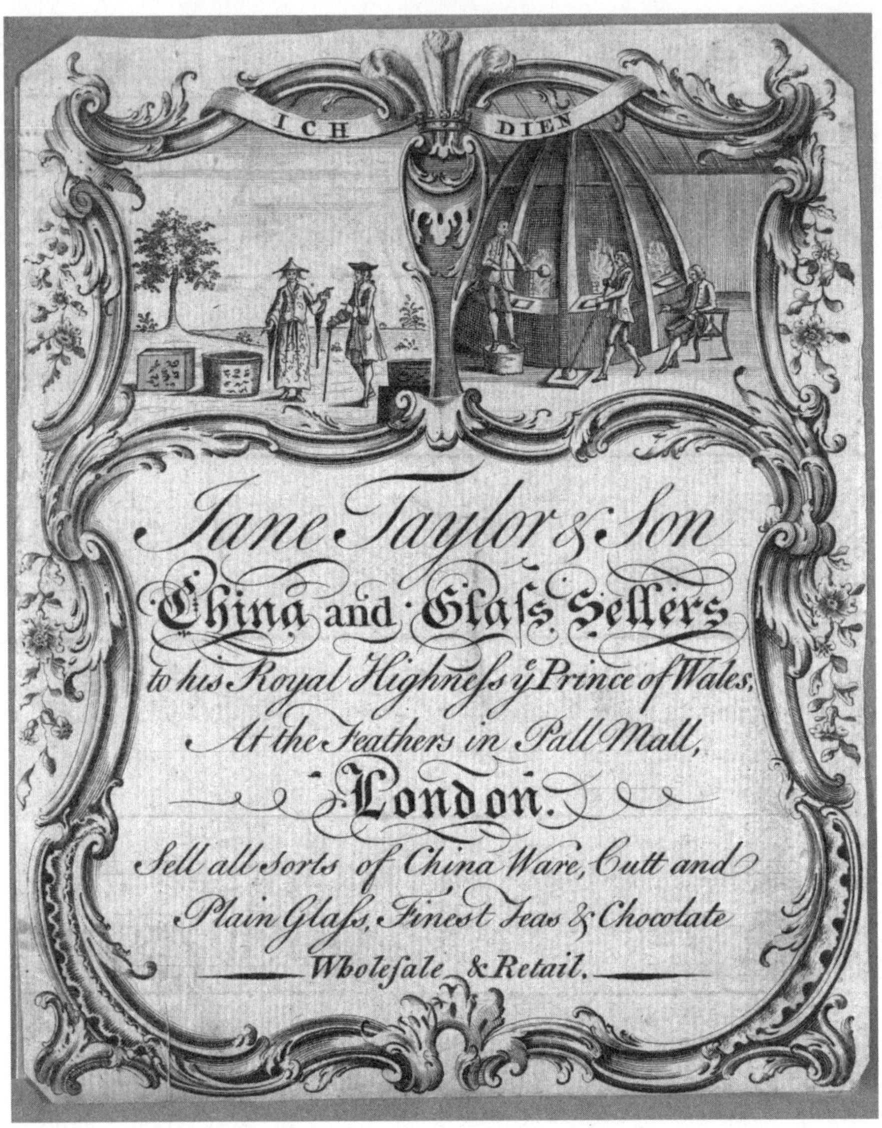

ABOVE: Jane Taylor's trade card, an etching and engraving ca. 1750–1770, features the Prince of Wales's feathers and the motto Ich Dien ("I serve"), symbolizing her status as a London china-woman with royal patronage.

OPPOSITE: A satirical 1750 etching portrays a wealthy woman in her gilded carriage blocking the pavement outside Mrs. Chenevix's "toyshop" at Charing Cross, where elegant vases and figures fill the shop window—a scene reportedly based on a true incident.

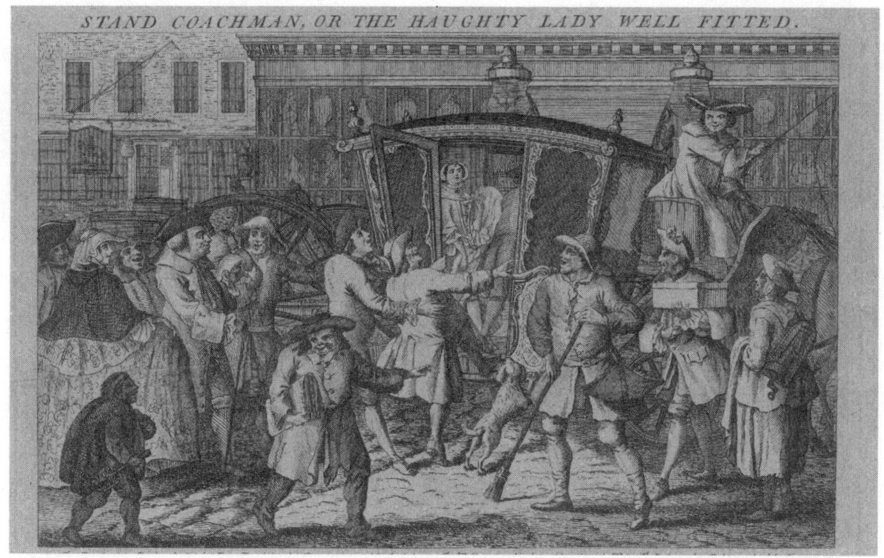

6

China-Women to China Hunters

"*China's the passion of her soul;*
A cup, a plate, a dish, a bowl,
Can kindle wishes in her breast,
Inflame with joy, or break her rest."

—John Gay, *To a Lady on Her Passion for Old China*, 1725

"A true china hunter will drive for days through the country asking for 'old crockery' at every house with a gambrel roof, has a great square chimney or an old sweep, without even hearing of one old tea-cup; and yet will start up again the next week cheerful, hopeful, undaunted, and courageous."

—Alice Morse Earle, *China Collecting in America*, 1892

To step into London's streets in the mid–eighteenth century was to enter a chaotic maze of bustling street vendors, jostling carriages, sedan chairs, and swirling dust—not to mention the occasional pack of roaming dogs, a frequent topic in the weekly newspapers. Even a routine outing carried unexpected hazards, including the very real risk of a run-in with stray cattle. The phrase "a bull in a china shop" is a relic of this era, when livestock yards still operated within city limits, and such incidents were far from rare. One particularly dramatic account from 1733 describes the plight of a china-woman:

> "This morning an over-drove bullock rushed into the China shop of Miss Powell, opposite Sant Andrews Church in Holbern, where he frightened the lady into a hysterical fit and broke a quantity of glass and china."

The love of "china" had reached a fever pitch since the death of Queen Mary II. What had once been the exclusive domain of nobles with their cabinets of curiosities and porcelain rooms had become accessible to ceramic enthusiasts across the social spectrum. By 1724, Daniel Defoe observed that the nation was in the grip of a craze:

> the custom or humour, as I may call it, of furnishing houses with china-ware, which increased to a strange degree afterwards, piling their china upon the tops of cabinets, scrutores, and every chymney-piece, to the tops of the ceilings, and even setting up shelves for their china-ware, where they wanted such places, till it became a grievance in the expence of it, and even injurious to their families and estates.

Fueling this "contagion of china-fancy" were the staggering numbers of porcelain imports—more than ten million pieces brought in by the Dutch and English during the eighteenth century alone. London, home to the busiest port in the world, had become the epicenter of international trade. By this time, the English East India Company (EIC) had finally overtaken its Dutch rival, securing England's dominance in global commerce.

As trade and banking flourished, so too did London itself. The city's population surged from about 630,000 in 1715 to over 740,000 by 1760, at a time when the second-largest English city held only 30,000 residents. The immense wealth generated through commerce was reflected in the extravagant townhouses, pleasure gardens, and grand squares that reshaped the urban landscape—and in the flourishing shops that catered to both the wealthy and those who aspired to luxury, selling everything from books and wine to fans and "china."

In 1755, Samuel Johnson had recently completed *A Dictionary of the English Language*, creating one of the most influential dictionaries in English history. What had once been an elusive mystery was now a common definition, marking a turning point in Europe's understanding—and production—of porcelain. At last, the recipe for porcelain was widely understood and formally defined:

> Chi'na. *n.s.* [from *China*, the country where it is made.)
>
> China ware; porcelain; a species of vessels made in China, dimly transparent, partaking of the qualities of earth and glass. They are made by mingling two kinds of earth, of which one easily vitrifies; the other resists a very strong heat: when the vitrifiable earth is melted into glass, they are completely burnt.
>
> Spleen, vapours, or small-pox, above them all,
> And mistress of herself, tho' *china* fall. *Pope's Epist.* ii.
>
> After supper, carry your plate and *china* together in the same basket.
>
> *Swift's Directions to the Butler.*

Discovered around 1708 in Meissen, in what is now Germany, a team of sequestered alchemists finally unlocked the long-sought formula for Europe's first porcelain—a white, translucent, high-fired ceramic akin to the prized wares of China. Contrary to earlier theories, including the belief that it was made from crushed eggshells, Chinese porcelain was actually crafted from a precise blend of two natural materials: kaolin, a fine white clay that provided plasticity and structure, and petuntse, a feldspathic rock that contributed hardness and translucency.

Once this long-held secret was uncovered, it ignited a wave of porcelain production and ceramic experimentation across Europe. Meissen mastered hard-paste porcelain in Saxony, Sèvres refined soft-paste porcelain in France, and Wedgwood revolutionized English ceramics with his elegant creamware. The obsession spread rapidly through royal courts and workshops, fueling an era of relentless innovation and insatiable demand. In Germany, it was called *porzellankrankheit*; in France, *la maladie de porcelaine*—a phenomenon aptly named "china fever."

The potters of Delft, meanwhile, attempted to keep pace with their now numerous rivals. With the voice of a seasoned "china-fancier," Johnson warned his readers,

> Delf.
> Delfe. *n.s.* [from delwan, Sax. to dig.]
> 2. Earthen ware; counterfeit China ware, made at *Delph*.
> Thus barter honour for a piece of *delf*:
> No, not for China's wide domain itself. *Smart.*

Johnson's description of Delftware reflects a public increasingly attuned to ceramic materials and discerning in their tastes. His wording also underscores a pivotal decision made by Delft's potters in the eighteenth century: unlike their competitors, they chose not to adopt the newly discovered porcelain formula. Instead, they remained committed to their traditional tin-glazed earthenware techniques, innovating not through composition but through the introduction of new forms, styles, colors, and glazes—adapting to a changing market while staying true to their craft.

In eighteenth-century London, the booming ceramics trade was dominated by the "china-man" and, as recorded in the *1763 Directory of London*, the "china-woman." Between 1699 and 1778, at least 124 female ceramic dealers were listed as china-women, actively participating in the market alongside their male counterparts. Mirroring the work of china-men, as described in the 1747 manual *A General Description of All Trades Digested in Alphabetical Order*:

> Their business is altogether shopkeeping, and some of them carry on a very considerable trade, joining white flint glass, fine earthenware and stoneware, as well as teas, with their china ware. They usually take with an apprentice from 20 to 50£, give a journeyman 20 to 30£ a year and his board, and employ a stock of 500£ and often more.

Beyond selling ceramics, china-women also offered repair services for their clients' fragile purchases. Jane Taylor, a china-woman in Pall Mall, was known for arranging "riveting" repairs for the avid collector Mrs. Mary Bowes in 1743–44. The Bowes family, among the wealthiest in northern England, had amassed their fortune through the coal industry, a driving force of the Industrial Revolution. Yet even collectors of their stature often chose to conserve broken ceramics rather than discard them.

When a vase or other delicate item shattered, it was carefully restored. Drilled and reassembled, the fragments were secured with wire or with silver or copper staples that clamped the pieces back into place. This method of ceramic conservation—dating back centuries—was typically entrusted to a "china mender." With minimal tools, requiring little more than a delicate drill, it was a trade practiced by many women, either as itinerant workers or in established shops, ensuring that prized porcelain remained part of daily life rather than being lost to breakage.

One of the earliest references to a china-woman appears in the theater. In 1609, English playwright and poet Ben Jonson—a contemporary of William Shakespeare—mentions a "rich China-woman, that the courtiers visited so often" in his play *Epicœne, or The Silent Woman*. However, a seventeenth-century audience would have recognized the double meaning, as "china-houses" or "India-houses" were often euphemisms for brothels, adding a suggestive undertone to Jonson's words.

Like the early china-houses, china shops were sensorial destinations. China-women were the curators of this experience, crafting a world with theatrical flair to showcase their wares to maximum advantage. Trade cards and journals often noted that, alongside cups, saucers, and pots, china-women would "generally deal in Tea, Coffee and Chocolate." Stepping into a china shop was more than a transaction—it was a carefully orchestrated sequence of intimate interactions, often beginning with the ceremonial act of taking tea.

The nutty aroma of oolong or vegetal scent of green tea filled the air, poured into cups that could also be purchased. Transitioning to the viewing of pieces, dishes, vases, or anything that might catch a customer's eye were brought down from shelves for handling, inspection of marks, or consideration of condition. A china-woman's stock of the most up-to-date ceramic trends was vital and according to *The London Tradesman*, 1747, ceramic sources included ". . . several Houses in England, from Holland, and at the Sales of the East-India Company."

The interlude concluded with the discussion of price. Bargaining was central to this commercial dance—the wealthier the customer, the greater their leverage. Discussions would continue until a final price was mutually agreed upon. Women, whether as consumers or vendors, were far from passive participants; the sale of china required a keen understanding of value and the art of persuasive negotiation from both sides.

One of the most effective and influential china-women, "Famous for her high prices and fine language," was Elizabeth Deards Chenevix. In 1725, she opened her exclusive "toy shop" in Pall Mall, specializing in the amusements of the very wealthy—from gold-mounted fans to the finest porcelain. As described by the author, aesthete, and collector Horace Walpole, she was "a toy woman à la mode." Trained since childhood in the art of purveying by her china-man father, Madame Chenevix was queen of the Pall Mall shops.

Women in eighteenth-century London were not only skilled sellers of ceramics but also avid buyers and collectors. Purchasing porcelain and earthenware from china shops was considered a socially acceptable activity, one that demonstrated intelligence and sophistication. It also became a new form of informal sociability, allowing women to assert their independence, explore personal interests, and foster social connections.

This growing trend did not go unnoticed by shopkeepers. Reflecting their increasing frustration, the popular daily periodical *The Spectator* featured a fictitious "Grievance" in 1712 from a china-woman, lamenting the rise of "Female Rakes" who frequented china shops. These women, she claimed, were indulging in a new, widespread custom that would today be called browsing:

> *I am, dear Sir, one of the top China-Women about Town; and though I say it, keep as good Things, and receive as fine Company as any o' this End of the Town, let the other be who she will: In short, I am in a fair Way to be easy, were it not for a Club of Female Rakes, who under pretence of taking their innocent Rambles, forsooth, and diverting the Spleen, seldom fail to plague me twice or thrice a-day to cheapen Tea, or buy a Skreen; What else should they mean? as they often repeat it. These Rakes are your idle Ladies of Fashion, who having nothing to do, employ themselves in tumbling over my Ware . . . I am, Sir,*
> *Your constant Reader, and very humble Servant,*
> *Rebecca the Distress'd*
> *March the 22nd.*

For some women, browsing china proved too tempting.

With its high value and portability, china often attracted criminal interest. In eighteenth-century England, stealing china was frequently classified as grand larceny, a serious charge punishable by fines, whipping, or even "transportation." Introduced as a preventative measure, transportation became increasingly common between 1718 and 1780. Convicts were removed from England and sent to the American colonies to serve out their sentences, effectively exiling them as part of their punishment.

Despite the potential severity of the punishment, case records from London's Old Bailey reveal that on March 23, 1743, a young woman named Alice Burk of St. Brides shoplifted from not one but two china shops. She was ultimately caught by a vigilant china-woman, who later testified during the court proceedings that . . .

> the Prisoner at the Bar came into my Shop, and asked for some enamelled China Plates. I turned my Back to her, and took some off the Shelf; I showed them her, and told her the Price; she said they were a great deal too dear; I told her I could not take much less. She said she must have them cheaper, for she had broke three of a Gentlewoman's Plates, and that the Gentlewoman said they cost her 4 s. said I, you had better give the four Shillings to the Person; she stood humming and hawing and would not stir; said I, Good Woman, you had better go away; says she, look a little farther; said I, Prithee go about your Business, and I espied under her Arm something of China; thinks I, she may have been somewhere else and bought some. When she was got two or three Steps from the Counter, said I, Mistress, What have you got there? So I took hold of her, and saw my own Dish.

In a similar incident in 1750, a young woman named Eleanor Hine was apprehended for shoplifting several items, including a group of "Delft plates." When brought before the court, both Eleanor Hine and Alice Burk were found guilty and sentenced to transportation.

Female British convicts receiving the punishment of transportation were typically packed onto ships and sent to colonies like Maryland and Virginia, where they were sold as indentured servants to serve seven-year sentences. Any attempt to return to England was considered a capital crime, punishable by death. Alice and Eleanor were among an estimated five thousand female convicts transported to America in the eighteenth century. For some women, the wealth of Georgian England was so unattainable that stealing a piece of Delftware seemed their only option, despite the grave risks involved.

Aside from the occasional bout of bovine mischief or theft, a china-woman's greatest challenge was intense commercial competition—not only from her peers but also from the growing number of auction houses. Sotheby's was founded in London in March 1744, and auctioneer James Christie established his permanent saleroom in Pall Mall in December 1766.

Christie's would handle historic transactions, including the sale of Sir Robert Walpole's painting collection to Empress Catherine the Great in 1779—works that went on to adorn the Hermitage, in St. Petersburg. Notably, the first lot of Christie's inaugural auction that winter day in Pall Mall consisted of "six breakfast bowls and plates."

Auctions and their public viewings brought together a broad spectrum of dealers, collectors, and fashionable society, and women attended widely. These events were not only places for women to see and be seen but also competitive arenas where prominent women often vied for prized lots, especially ceramics. Among these participants was Margaret Cavendish Bentinck, Duchess of Portland.

The well-publicized auction of the Duchess of Portland's property after her death in 1785 introduced many to a woman now considered to be one of the great collectors of the eighteenth century. Spanning thirty-eight days and comprising over four thousand lots, the sale featured items ranging from "Shells, Corals and Petrifications" to "Fine Old China" and "Exceeding Curious Articles." The auction was accompanied by a catalogue, a coveted yet cumbersome accessory for the fortunate few able to acquire the numbered publication.

The Duchess of Portland was also a member of the Bluestocking Circle, a group of celebrated women writers, artists, and thinkers in eighteenth-century London dedicated to fostering intellectual exchange in the arts and sciences. The group, which included both female and male luminaries such as Samuel Johnson and Horace Walpole, provided a space for collaboration and shared curiosity. However, like female ceramic collectors, the Bluestocking Circle was often viewed dismissively by some in English society. The term "Bluestocking" eventually evolved into a term of derision, reflecting the broader societal belief that women's intellectual capacities were inherently limited.

Horace Walpole was among the many curious attendees at the 1786 auction of the Duchess of Portland's estate, eager to witness—or perhaps acquire—a portion of one of the most celebrated collections of the age.

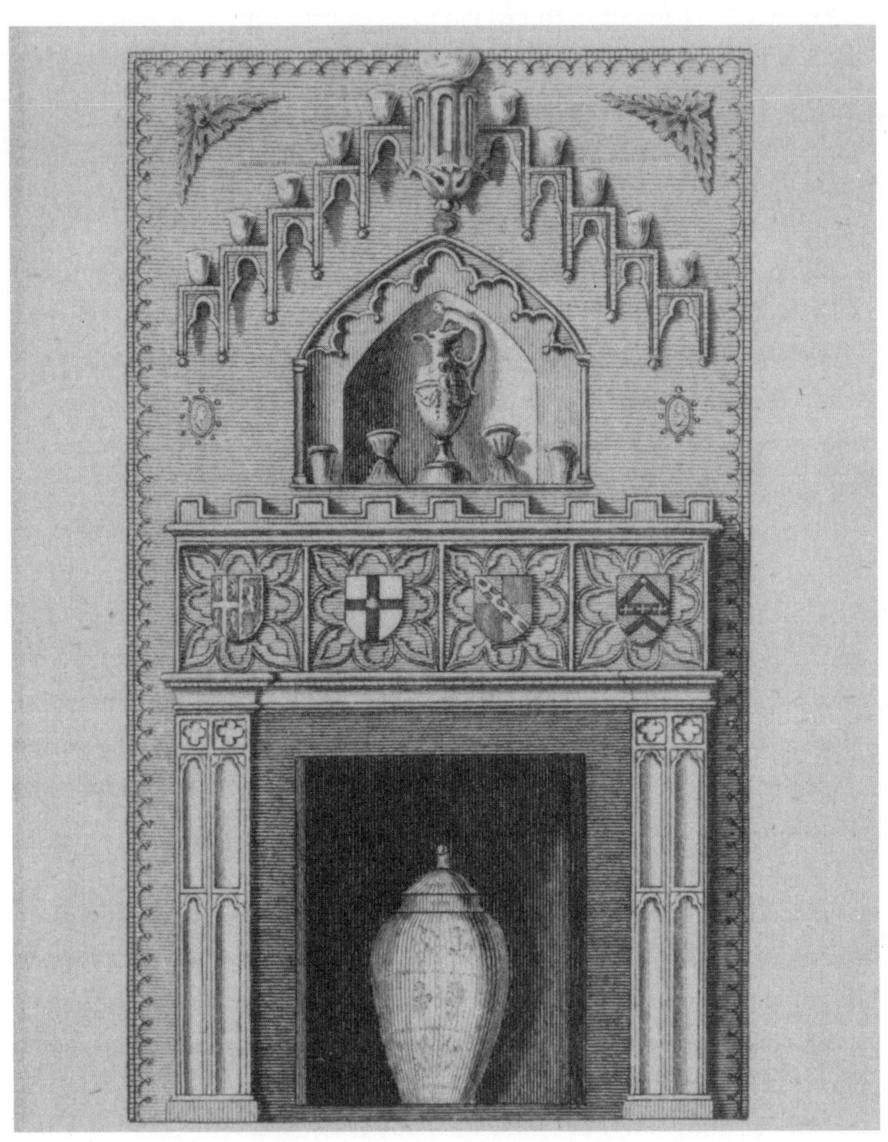

An engraving from *A Description of the Villa of Mr. Horace Walpole . . . at Strawberry-Hill . . .* (Thomas Kirgate, 1784) illustrates the symmetrically arranged ceramics adorning the Gothic-style chimney in the China Room. Yale University, Lewis Walpole Library.

As the owner of Strawberry Hill, his Gothic-revival summer residence outside London, Walpole was no stranger to eclectic treasures. His home, a masterpiece of antiquarian taste, was more than just a residence—it was a theatrical stage for his extensive collection of fine and decorative arts.

Strawberry Hill had an unusual provenance of its own. The estate had been purchased from the heirs of Madame Chenevix, the renowned china-woman. Under Walpole's ownership, the house evolved into a destination so sought-after that he eventually opened it to the public for tours, allowing visitors to marvel at its architectural spectacle and extraordinary collection. One of its most distinctive spaces was the China Room, a dedicated showcase for Walpole's prized collection of Asian and European ceramics. Walpole's display was far from uniform, as he filled the space with a thoughtfully curated assortment of objects, described as "Porcelain, earthenware, glass, and enamel on copper of various ages and countries."

The walls, lined with gleaming "white Dutch tyles with borders of blue and white," provided a striking backdrop for the ceramics arranged upon the tiered shelves. Among the "Sèvres china," "Saxon tankards," and delicate "Nankin china"—sat two Delftware "butterpots and saucers of blue and white," gifts from Lady Ailesbury, a fellow connoisseur.

While Dutch tiles played only a minor role in Walpole's China Room, by the early eighteenth century, they had become dazzling symbols of opulence and grandeur worldwide. From France and Germany to Poland, Russia, Egypt, and even South America, these shimmering tiles adorned aristocratic palaces, pleasure retreats, hunting lodges, and churches. Among the most striking examples was the Pagodenburg (1716–1719), a blue-and-white tiled pavilion in the Nymphenburg Palace complex near Munich, designed by Joseph Effner as a summer retreat where Elector Max Emanuel paused between rounds of *mailspiel*, a game similar to golf.

No longer confined to fireplace surrounds or baseboards, blue-and-white Dutch tiles became integral to sweeping decorative schemes, covering entire walls—and even ceilings—in vibrant, breathtaking displays. Often arranged into intricate pictorial panels, they transformed interiors into immersive works of art, adding saturated color, pattern, and a striking visual narrative to the grandest of spaces.

Keeping pace with soaring global demand, Dutch makers produced tiles in staggering quantities—millions upon millions. Though often called "Delft tiles," their production extended well beyond Delft itself. More than 200 tile factories operated across the Netherlands, with cities such as Rotterdam, Utrecht, Amsterdam, Harlingen, Makkum, and Bolsward, each bringing its own artistic style. More than a decorative surface, Dutch tiles became a popular element of eighteenth-century design, spreading across continents and leaving a lasting imprint on architectural spaces.

But among the world's most opulent blue-and-white tiled interiors, few are as steeped in myth, secrecy, and splendor as those of the Topkapi Palace, Constantinople.

For centuries, Topkapi stood at the heart of the Ottoman Empire, a sprawling architectural marvel first constructed in the fifteenth century. Within its labyrinthine halls, gardens, and private chambers, the sultan, his family, and his harem lived in a world closed to outsiders. With over three hundred rooms, the palace was not merely a residence—it was a self-contained realm, where intrigue, power, and beauty coexisted behind heavily guarded walls.

The palace's interiors were legendary, their grandeur reflecting the empire's wealth. But nowhere was its artistic mastery more apparent than in its extraordinary tilework. Iznik tiles—renowned for their deep sapphire blues, intricate floral motifs, and elegant calligraphy—covered the walls, ceilings, and domes, transforming the palace into a jewel of Ottoman craftsmanship.

Yet, in the late eighteenth century, as the once-thriving Iznik tile industry declined, the Ottomans looked elsewhere to fill the artistic void. They turned to an unexpected source—the Dutch.

While largely unknown to the outside world, blue-and-white Dutch tiles quietly made their way into Topkapi's interiors, beginning under Sultan Mahmud I and continuing through the reign of Selim III. This artistic fusion was perhaps most striking in the Imperial Hall (Hünkar Sofası), the Sultan's Throne Room, where Dutch and Ottoman ceramics met in an unexpected harmony— Rotterdam-produced tiles, featuring delicate roses enclosed within octagonal borders, were set into red-painted wooden frameworks, blending seamlessly with the palace's rococo-era décor.

But the Dutch tiles were only part of the blue-and-white story.

Behind the palace's gilded doors, Ottoman princesses cultivated their own private ceramic collections, amassing vast treasures of porcelain and earthenware. Hadice Sultan the Elder (1658–1743) was renowned for her obsession with Chinese porcelain, acquiring countless blue-and-white Ming and Qing dynasty pieces. Her grand-niece, Hadice Sultan the Younger (1768–1822), however, looked westward, assembling an extraordinary collection of European ceramics—including Delft, Meissen, and Sèvres coffee services. By the nineteenth century, the ceramic holdings of Topkapi Palace had swelled to over ten thousand pieces of Chinese and Japanese porcelain, alongside more than five thousand European wares, creating a collection that rivaled those of Europe's grandest courts.

Yet, this private "china fever" among Ottoman princesses was not without controversy.

Confined to her royal quarters and barred from visiting the collections of her European counterparts, Hadice Sultan the Younger relied on intermediaries to acquire her prized pieces, curating her collection from within the palace walls. Her fascination with European decorative arts raised eyebrows among the Ottoman elite. Many saw her growing assemblage as a symbol of foreign influence, a troubling shift away from Ottoman traditions.

As the eighteenth-century "China fancy" captivated the globe, the late eighteenth and early nineteenth centuries became defined by political upheaval and revolution. From the American Revolution to the French Revolution, transformative events reshaped societies across continents. Amid these global changes, the Dutch Republic underwent its own period of upheaval known as the *Patriottentijd*, the "Time of the Patriots." By the late eighteenth century, the Dutch Republic stood on the brink of civil war, and the rising tensions of this internal revolt found reflection even in its Delftware.

As John Adams negotiated crucial loans from the Dutch Republic in Amsterdam during the 1780s to sustain the fledgling American nation, Dutch citizens, in part inspired by American ideals, were producing pamphlets demanding reforms to their own system of government, where representation was lacking. The Dutch Republic was deeply divided. Supporters of

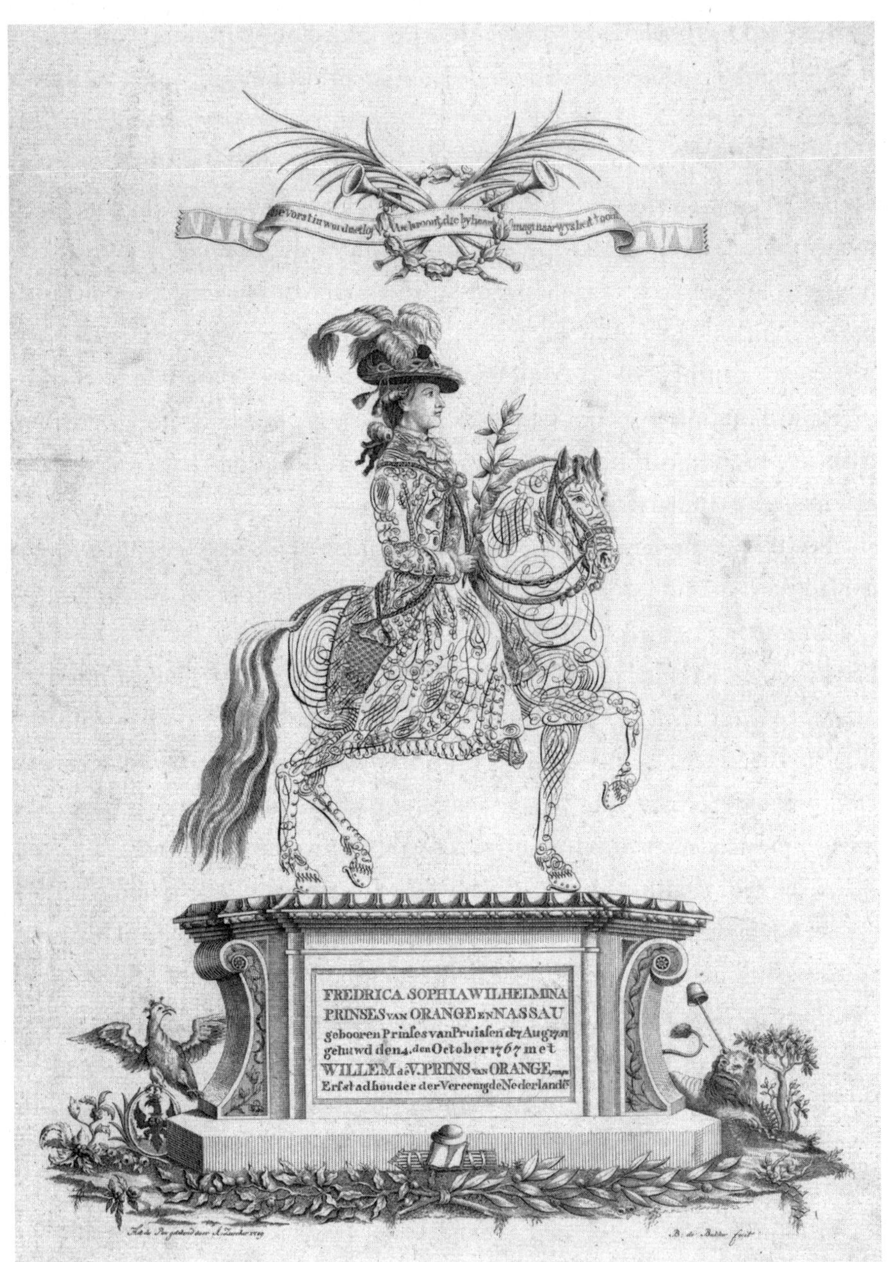

Barent de Bakker's etching (1789–1804) portrays Princess Frederica Sophia Wilhelmina on horseback, reflecting her role as more than a consort—she was the de facto leader of the House of Orange and the counter-revolution during the Dutch Republic's final years. Rijksmuseum, Amsterdam.

the *stadtholder* prominently displayed "Orangist Delftware," adorned with portraits of Frederica Sophia Wilhelmina of Prussia, Princess of Orange, and her husband, the *stadtholder*, William V, Prince of Orange, along with their monograms or orange trees, symbolizing the House of Orange.

The tradition of expressing loyalty to the *stadtholder* through Delftware originated in the seventeenth century but gained significant momentum during the civil unrest of the 1780s. Potteries in Delft produced plates, plaques, bowls, and covered vases depicting the royal couple, which were prominently displayed on cabinets and over doorways in Dutch homes.

Wilhelmina of Prussia, the Princess of Orange, was a strong and ambitious figure who played a pivotal role in preserving the power of the House of Orange. Often regarded as the de facto leader during the final years of the Dutch Republic, she wielded greater influence than her husband, the *stadtholder*. Despite the violent fates of her contemporaries—her cousin King Gustav III of Sweden was assassinated in 1792, and Queen Marie Antoinette and King Louis XVI were guillotined in 1793—Wilhelmina successfully navigated these turbulent times and emerged unscathed.

In 1793, just ten days after the execution of Louis XVI, the French Revolutionary government declared war on both England and the Dutch Republic. By the following winter, French forces invaded the Dutch Republic, forcing Wilhelmina and her family into nearly two decades of exile. Wilhelmina, however, endured the upheaval and lived to witness the fall of French rule. In 1815, she saw her son crowned King William I and the establishment of the Kingdom of the Netherlands. When she passed away in 1820, Wilhelmina was laid to rest in the *Nieuwe Kerk* in Delft.

In the decades following Wilhelmina's death, the once-vibrant town of Delft quietly faded into obscurity.

The Dutch East India Company, weighed down by internal corruption and rising administrative costs, had formally dissolved by 1799, with its Delft VOC kamer and canal warehouses shuttered and sold. The Guild of St. Luke, which had persisted in name until 1833, was finally disbanded. Even the iconic brick and stone city gates featured in Vermeer's *View of Delft* (c. 1659–1661) were dismantled and sold for materials.

By 1835, of the more than thirty potteries that had once flourished in Delft, only a few remained. Several potteries had consolidated, most had shuttered, and only five survived—including Barbara Rotteveel's The Three Bells. A declining Dutch economy and fierce global competition in ceramics proved insurmountable.

European porcelain manufactories were thriving, producing ceramics across the continent from Italy to Germany and France. Most prolific, however, were the towering coal-fired kilns of Staffordshire, England, which flooded the market with mass-produced, inexpensive ceramics including creamware.

What had once set Delft apart—the intricate, hand-painted masterpieces of tin-glazed earthenware crafted by skilled artisans—had become unsustainable in the face of industrialization. The small wood-fired kilns and labor-intensive techniques that defined Delft's golden era could not compete in an age dominated by mass production.

By the 1860s, *De Porceleyne Fles* (The Porcelain Bottle) was the last remaining Delftware pottery in the city. Deep in debt and nearing collapse, it had been taken over in 1849 by Geertruida Piccardt, the daughter of its owner, Henricus Piccardt. In a desperate bid to keep the business afloat, Geertruida repurposed the kilns to produce refractory fire bricks, focusing on building materials instead of Delftware.

The production of Delftware, which once reached hundreds of thousands of pieces annually and included some of the world's finest ceramics crafted for Mary's Water Gallery, had dwindled to a mere trickle in just over two hundred years.

But as Delft potteries struggled and failed under the shadow of industrialized English ceramics, by the 1860s the English themselves began experiencing a lifestyle revolution against the very mass consumerism that had propelled them to worldwide economic domination. This reaction, spurred by disillusionment with the design standardization, repetitive patterns, and cheaply made products showcased at London's Great Exhibition of 1851, gave rise to the Aesthetic Movement and the "rediscovery" of blue-and-white ceramics. Almost three centuries after the first massive shipments of Chinese porcelain arrived on Dutch docks in Amsterdam in 1602—plundered from the Portuguese carrack *Santa Catarina* and igniting waves of ceramic fascination—a new blue-and-white obsession began sweeping the world once again.

Dubbed "Chinamania" by the press in the 1870s, this fervor spread rapidly throughout Europe and across America. Cultural commentators of the late nineteenth century both embraced and poked fun at ceramic buyers as they enthusiastically lined their shelves and cabinets with Japanese bowls, placed countless Chinese vases on mantels, and applied Dutch tiles to fireplaces. Fashionable men and women bought blue-and-white to affirm their cultivated taste and just because they desired them—not because they needed them. For British shoppers, blue-and-white ceramics signified status and cultivated taste.

Shaping the Aesthetic Movement was a new generation of influential artists, artisans, writers, and collectors, including Dante Gabriel Rossetti, William Morris, and the American expatriate painter James McNeill Whistler. They championed a philosophy centered on pure beauty and "art for art's sake," emphasizing the exploration of color, form, and composition to create beauty not only in the "high" arts but also in fashion and interior design.

Advocating for beauty as an integral part of everyday life, they believed the home should serve as an inspirational environment for its inhabitants. The decoration of these idealized spaces was characterized by a rich, eclectic vocabulary drawn from a wide array of visual sources, cultures, and historical periods, ranging from Renaissance painting and Greek sculpture to East Asian art. Collectors often layered these exotic influences, creating interiors adorned with blue-and-white ceramics, including landscapes and mixtures of Chinese and Japanese pieces alongside Iznik pottery and "old Delft."

Oscar Wilde, the era's most famous aesthetic arbiter, was infamous for "finding it harder and harder every day to live up to my blue and white china." For Whistler too, blue-and-white Chinese porcelain was a source of aesthetic inspiration, with vases and plates populating many of his paintings. Influential designers including William Morris revitalized interest in not only Asian ceramics but other forms of blue-and-white including Dutch tiles, Delftware, and Iznik pottery to decorate areas in his home.

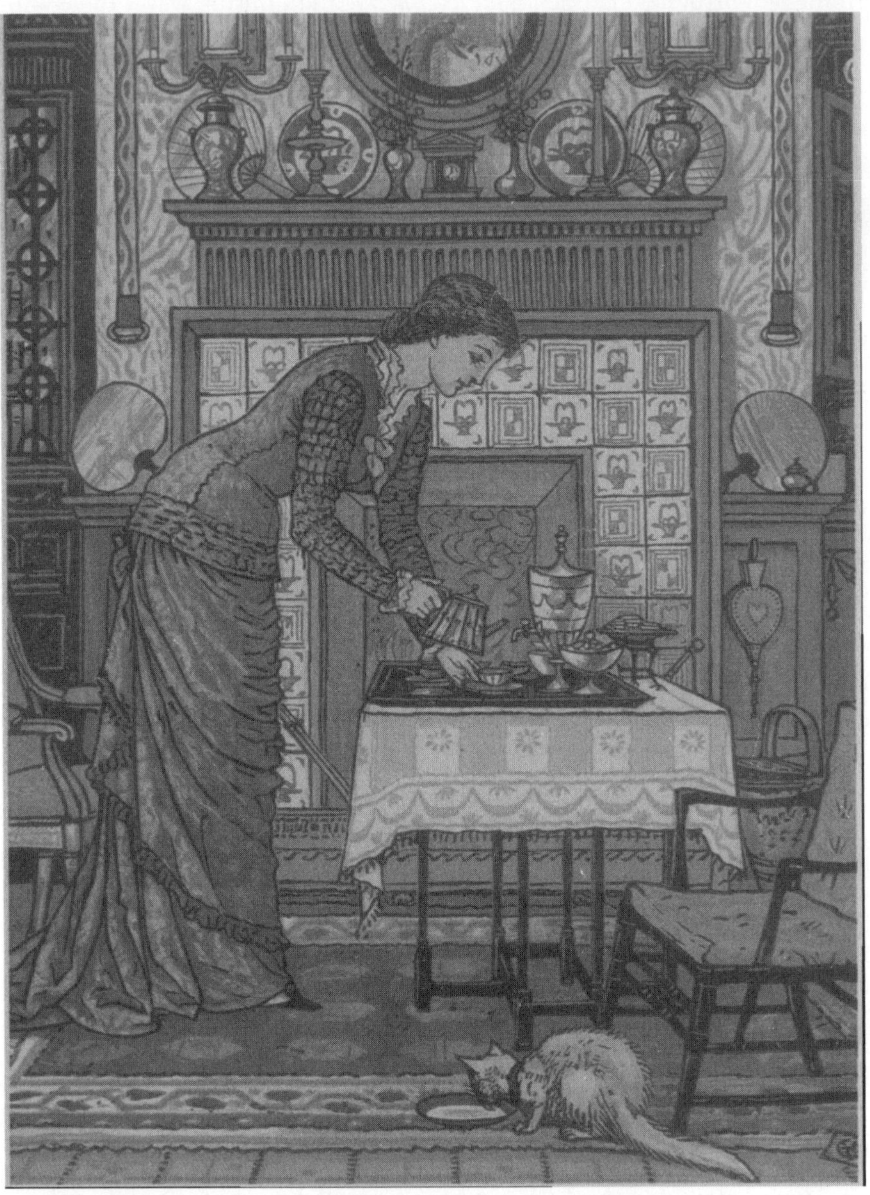

Walter Crane's 1878 color wood engraving, *My Lady's Chamber*, the frontispiece of Clarence Cook's *The House Beautiful*, reflects the popular use of ceramics, including Chinese porcelain and Dutch tiles, in nineteenth-century interiors. Author's collection.

Welcomed at the table of the Aesthetic Movement was American Elizabeth Robins Pennell, a noted journalist, biographer, and food writer. Developing a friendship with the artist James McNeill Whistler, Elizabeth and her husband would often host and attend evenings with influential artists of the era. In 1896, a compilation of her articles was published under the title *The Feasts of Autolycus: The Diary of a Greedy Woman.*

Defying Victorian dining conventions, Pennell redefined food as a creative art form, celebrating cooking, eating, and the dining table itself as avenues for female expression. Her recipes and decorating suggestions, written as descriptive personal essays, offered imaginative advice, such as:

> From your own garden gather a bunch of late tulips, scarlet and glowing, but cool in their shelter of long tapering leaves. Fill a bowl with them: it may be a rare bronze from Japan, or a fine piece of old Delft, or anything else, provided it be somewhat sumptuous as becomes the blossoms it holds.

For Pennell, the dining table was a canvas, and blue-and-white ceramics, such as Delftware, were the paints of her artistic palette.

Purveyors emerged in cities like London and New York to meet the vast demand for blue-and-white ceramics as newly inspired "Chinamaniacs" eagerly filled their interiors. Replacing the china-women and china-men of the eighteenth century were sellers operating out of "antique shops" and "curiosity shops." Catering to the needs of these enthusiastic buyers, nineteenth-century antique dealers were quick to capitalize on the growing demand and rising prices of ceramics, turning the craze into a lucrative enterprise.

Few dealers capitalized on the blue-and-white craze more successfully than the Duveen Brothers. In 1866, Joseph Joel Duveen left the Netherlands for England, determined to build a thriving trade in fine ceramics. He later partnered with his younger brother, Henry J. Duveen, and together they co-founded Duveen Brothers. Initially, their stock consisted primarily of Dutch Delftware and Chinese porcelain, but they soon expanded into both decorative and fine arts, including tapestries, fine furniture, and Old Master paintings.

The business eventually passed to Joseph Joel Duveen's son, later known as Baron Joseph Duveen, who became one of the most influential art dealers of the twentieth century. His prestigious clientele—including Henry Clay Frick, J. Paul Getty, and William Randolph Hearst—created some of the world's most celebrated collections.

Fakes and forgeries thrived in a market where demand for seventeenth- and eighteenth-century ceramics, including "old Delft," far exceeded the limited supply of authentic pieces. Unscrupulous sellers passed off newly made counterfeits as antiques, while ceramics with misleading or fabricated marks were also widespread. By adding fraudulent marks from well-known potteries to the bases of originally unmarked Dutch Delftware, dishonest dealers could instantly and significantly inflate the value of their stock—at the expense of unsuspecting buyers.

Adding further complexity to the ceramics market, reproductions of historic pieces were becoming widely available as affordable copies of objects found in private collections and museums. One of the most prolific producers of these high-quality reproductions was the French ceramic manufactory Samson & Cie, established in Paris in 1845. Samson produced a diverse range of wares in both porcelain and tin-glazed earthenware, drawing inspiration from renowned makers across the world, including those in China, Japan, Sèvres, Meissen, and Delft.

From its founding, the Samson factory took care to clearly distinguish its reproductions, modifying original factory marks and adding a distinctive "S" to set them apart. However, when these identifying marks were removed, the distinction between imitation and authentic masterpiece became dangerously blurred. Unsuspecting buyers could easily mistake Samson's expertly crafted copies for originals, further complicating an already intricate market for historic ceramics.

Helping eager collectors navigate the vast and often challenging world of historic ceramics, a wealth of ceramic "compendiums," histories, and guides emerged in the nineteenth century. Filled with images, descriptions, lists of marks, and pottery histories, these publications became invaluable resources for identifying and authenticating pieces. Notably, several of these guides

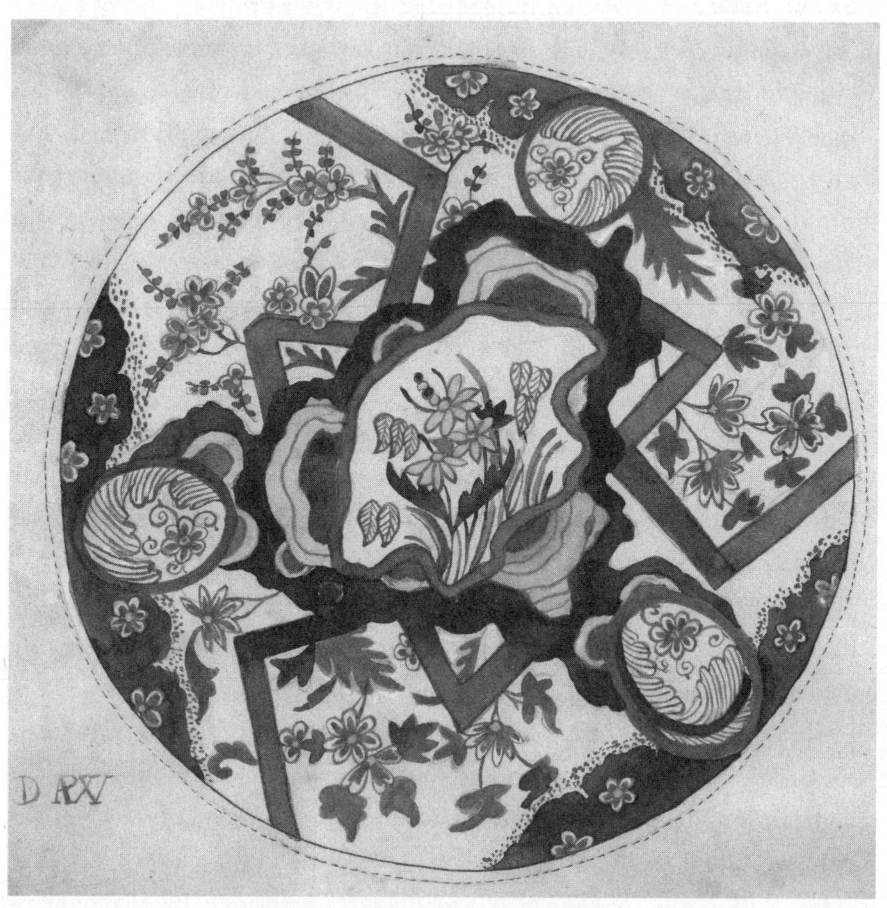

Samson & Cie's pen, ink, and watercolor design, created in Paris ca. 1845 or later, served as a visual prototype for factory painters to replicate a Delft *bliksem* (lightning) dish in the Imari style with masterful precision. Author's collection.

were authored by women, including *The Ceramic Art: A Compendium of the History and Manufacture of Pottery and Porcelain*, published in 1878 by Jennie J. Young, a ceramicist, author, lecturer, and young New Yorker.

With almost 500 pages "with 464 illustrations," *The Ceramic Art* was Jennie's first book and it was an immediate success, securing a third of a page of coverage in *The New York Times* when it was initially published in 1878. Written for the experienced collector as well as the student of ceramics, this "elegant volume" and "concise, comprehensive, and well-arranged treatise" was both systematically informational and entertaining. It taught her readers about the history of ceramics but also encouraged them to engage with contemporary makers, including recently founded American potteries.

Jennie was a popular speaker with regular engagements at Exeter Hall in central London, a venue that could accommodate up to four thousand attendees. In the spring of 1884 Jennie spoke on "The Potter's Art" accompanied by Sir Henry Doulton, the founder, inventor, and head of the English ceramic manufactory later known as Royal Doulton. Addressing the crowd from the stage, "the gifted young lady" described the history of ceramics and for added effect "having at her elbow a potter at his wheel, practically to illustrate her lecture."

In 1874, collector and author Fanny Bury Palliser (Mrs. Richard Bury Palliser) created a "pocket guide" for ceramic collectors. Having previously edited her brother Joseph Marryat's *Collections Towards a History of Pottery and Porcelain, in the 15th, 16th, 17th, and 18th Centuries* (1850), one of the first popular books in English on ceramics, a weighty almost five-hundred-page compendium—Fanny recognized a need for a smaller, more practical version for the popular market.

Her solution was *The China Collector's Pocket Companion*. Pocket companions or "pocket-books" had been produced since at least the seventeenth century on a broad variety of topics, from law to travel. Fanny's *Pocket Companion* was similarly convenient. Small, light, portable, and with a succinct listing of marks, including those of Dutch Delftware, Fanny's *Pocket Companion* allowed the collector to easily access information and conferred mobility. Inquisitive and informed nineteenth-century female ceramic collectors were taking to the road.

Boarding steamships, riding trains, and hiring coaches, Lady Charlotte Schreiber traversed Europe, exploring cities large and small in her relentless pursuit of ceramics. Born in 1812, Lady Charlotte was an industrialist, linguist, philanthropist, and one of the most prominent nineteenth-century English ceramic collectors. Rarely without her shipping baskets and her red velvet bag for particularly delicate finds, she was always prepared for a potential discovery. By 1884, at the age of seventy-two, she had amassed and donated nearly twelve thousand pieces of English, Continental, and Chinese porcelain to the Victoria and Albert Museum, London.

Her collecting diaries vividly capture the ceramic hunt, revealing a woman whose insatiable curiosity and boundless energy propelled her to seek treasures wherever she traveled. For Lady Charlotte, the pursuit of ceramics was not just a scholarly endeavor but a competitive and exhilarating sport. Describing her days scouring dealers' shops, she wrote, "We had some sport in our chasse among the shops." Her travels in the Netherlands epitomized the excitement of the hunt: ". . . went to Gouda, where we had a charming chasse. We had scarcely left the station when we fell upon a curiosity shop, a very small one, but containing several good marked pieces."

Every city, every dealer's shop, and every unexpected discovery fueled Lady Charlotte's passion for the chase. For her, the joy was not just in the acquisition but in the pursuit of ceramics itself—a game of skill, intuition, and determination.

American women, meanwhile, were embarking on their own ceramic chases.

Beginning shortly after the Civil War, the collecting of blue-and-white ceramics became a voraciously pursued passion in the United States. William Cowper Prime, author of the comprehensive guide *Pottery and Porcelain of All Times and All Nations* (1878), described the meteoric rise of American interest in ceramic collecting: "Ten years ago there were probably not ten collectors of pottery and porcelain in the United States. Today there are perhaps ten thousand."

Among these fervent collectors was Prime's wife, Mary Trumbull Prime, an inveterate ceramic enthusiast. Traveling across Europe, Africa, Egypt, Asia, and the Middle East, Mary amassed an encyclopedic collection of ceramics, ranging from Greek kylixes and Iznik pottery from Turkey to European porcelain and

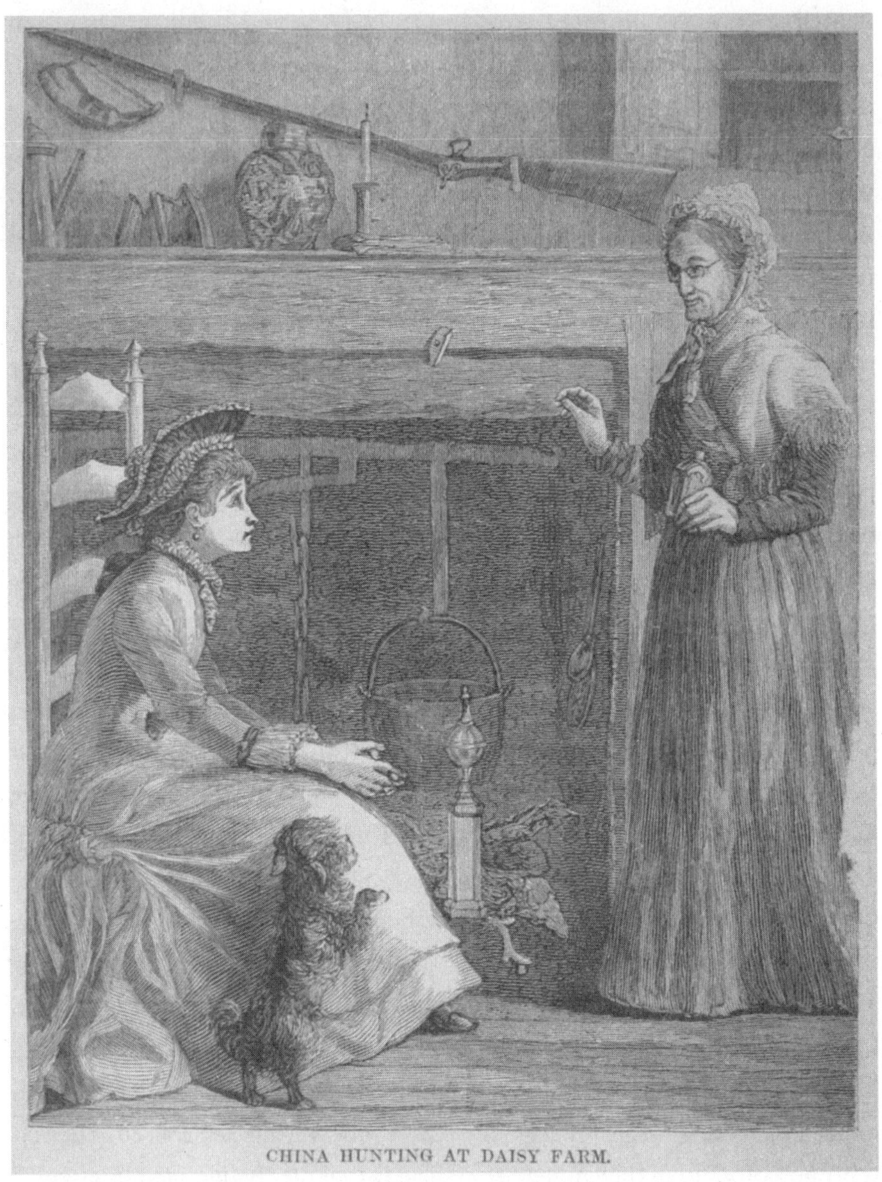

Frontispiece from *The China Hunter's Club* (1878), depicting a fictional young china hunter conversing with her summer host, Arethusa, at picturesque Daisy Farm in New England. Author's collection.

Dutch Delftware. Her collection, comprising hundreds of objects, was loaned to the Metropolitan Museum of Art in 1875. Living in New York, Mary could have conveniently purchased pieces from any number of the city's many antique dealers and auction houses, but there was another available option. Working outside conventional ceramic purchasing channels, in a mode that required time, planning, patience, and stamina, was "china hunting."

China hunting was practiced in the United States beginning in the 1860s following the Civil War, primarily centered in New England, and entailed collectors dealing directly with owners in the purchase of ceramics. Although china hunting could be a lengthy and expensive process, it appealed to collectors as it circumvented dealers and enabled a level of perceived control in a ceramic market plagued by steep prices and potential fakes and forgeries. Reflecting the prevailing sentiment among china hunters, a 1909 article titled *"Old Blue China"* in *Boston Cooking-School Magazine* advised, "It is cheaper to buy from country homes than from town shops, and one feels more certain that her old blue is genuine." Yet, for many American women, china hunting was more than just a pursuit of authenticity—it was an opportunity for adventure.

Often arriving by train at their starting points, "china hunters" climbed into hired carriages and set off on winding journeys through seaside villages and the rural countryside in search of blue-and-white ceramics. They rumbled down unknown dusty lanes, ventured through dense forests, and passed rolling fields and weathered farmhouses. Knocking on doors, they approached local residents to inquire about the availability of ceramics and, if successful, negotiated potential sales. While most finds consisted of bright blue English Staffordshire ceramics, abundantly produced in the nineteenth century, occasional older treasures—such as Chinese porcelain or Dutch Delftware—also surfaced. These dishes, cups, tobacco jars, and "syrop pots" were often among the last surviving ceramics handed down through generations in former English and Dutch territories.

China hunting quickly became a national pastime, with collectors scouring homes from New York and New Jersey to the farthest reaches of Vermont and Maine in search of blue-and-white treasures. The feverish pursuit of ceramics was so widespread that by October 17, 1876, *The Hartford Daily Times* reported:

> Here in Hartford . . . the China Craze . . . has spread very rapidly during the past year . . . Collectors of these articles scour the country round in search of new discoveries and there is scarcely a substantial old farm-house left, in this part of Connecticut, that has not been raided and cleaned out of its hereditary and traditional heirlooms . . .

Joining Mary Prime on her ceramic adventures was her sister and fellow collector, Annie Trumbull Slosson. A celebrated short-story writer and literary critic, Annie authored more than fifteen collections of short stories between 1878 and 1912, with her works appearing in *The Atlantic* and *Harper's Magazine*. Her first book, *The China Hunter's Club* (1878), was part narrative, part ceramic history, and part hunting guide, chronicling a group of Americans who band together to collect rare ceramics. The novel captures the thrill of the chase, immersing readers in the exhilarating world of nineteenth-century collecting. In one particularly evocative passage, Annie transports her audience into the very moment of discovery:

> The day was a hot one in August, but our road was full of shade and beauty, and the air sweet and spicy. For a time I forgot everything but the loveliness about me, and drank it in silently as I leaned back in the easy carriage. But as we passed an ancient farm-house, I spied in a window a broken cup, and, like turkey-cock at sight of scarlet rag, I woke to action.

A decade later, Alice Morse Earle, historian and author of *China Collecting in America* (1892), reflected on the mishaps and misadventures of her own blue-and-white pursuits in her essay "A China Hunter in New England" (*Scribner's Magazine,* September 1891). Her account, laced with self-deprecating humor, proves that the hunt was not always as refined as one might expect:

> It may appear to scoffing outsiders that all this asking and looking become monotonous, but I find no lack of variety. Had you gone to

> an isolated farm house to purchase some Delft jars which you had heard the owner wished to sell, had you found the house locked and empty of its inmates, had you decided not to leave without trying at least to see the jars, and then climbed upon a peaked roof hen-house under a window which commanded a view of the mantelpiece holding the coveted Delft, had you felt the roof of the hen-house suddenly give way and precipitate you down among piercing splinters and broken eggs on which you stood for one hour with only the distracted hens and the scarcely less distracted thoughts for company, until at last the owner of the Delft and eggs came home and kindly and even cheerfully chopped up his own hen-house in order to extricate you from your well-deserved prison—had you experienced all this, I feel sure you would not complain of the lack of incident in china-hunting.

The world of blue-and-white collecting was never just about acquiring objects; it was a pursuit of cultural exchange, adventure, and discovery. From china-women trading porcelain in the elegant salons of eighteenth-century Pall Mall to china hunters scouring the Connecticut countryside for "old-Delft" in the nineteenth century, women played an integral role in shaping this vibrant world. As scholars, merchants, collectors, and storytellers, they navigated both the physical and social landscapes of their time, driven by passion and curiosity.

Yet, alongside the thrill of the chase came the possibility of risk—even misfortune. In the eighteenth-century Ottoman Empire, a princess collecting European ceramics behind closed doors risked scandal and political repercussions, subtly defying traditional norms. In England, the theft of Delftware was a crime severe enough to warrant transportation. And, as Alice Morse Earle vividly recounted, in nineteenth-century New England, an ill-fated treasure hunt might simply end with a tumble through the roof of a henhouse.

All for the love of a single piece of blue-and-white.

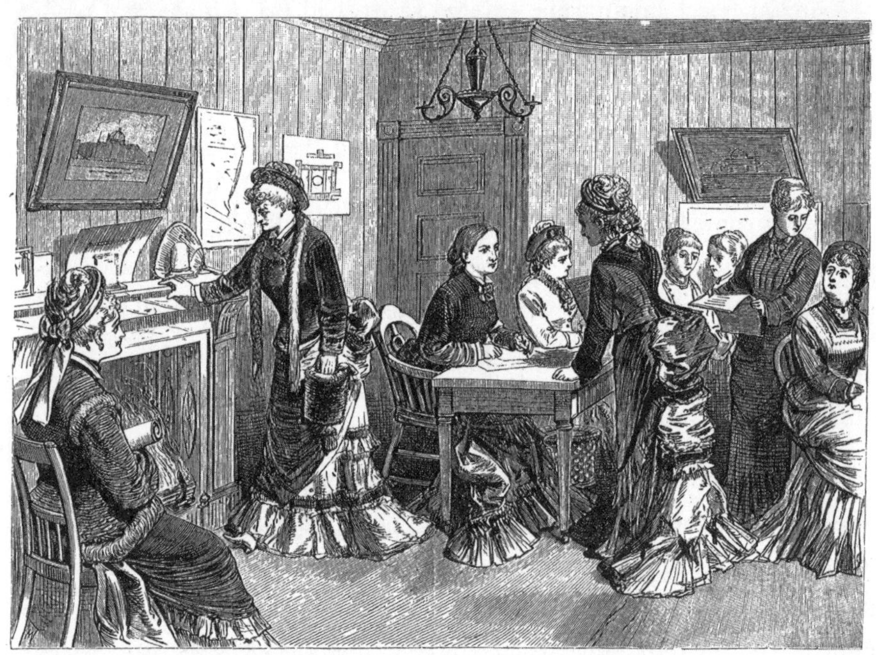

ABOVE: A 1877 illustration from Frank Leslie's *Historical Register of the United States Centennial Exposition* (1876) depicts the Women's Centennial Executive Committee at work in their Philadelphia headquarters, as Elizabeth Gillespie receives reports from the subcommittees. Courtesy of the Free Library of Philadelphia, Print and Picture Collection. OPPOSITE: An illustration from *Frank Leslie's Historical Register of the United States Centennial Exposition* (1876) of the Women's Pavilion in Philadelphia, a 30,000-square-foot wooden structure with a light blue-gray painted exterior. Author's collection.

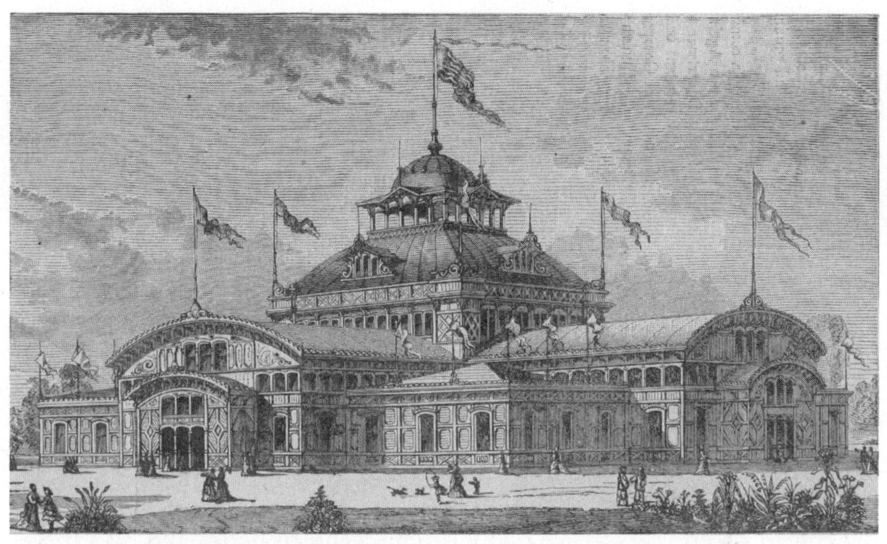

7

Dames

"The common-sense of Americans has long ago perceived the necessity for some women to be self-supporting. Feminine dignity and delicacy, as sung by poets and vaunted by after-dinner orators, when the last toast is drunk and the last best gift to man is gushingly, if somewhat incoherently cheered, is as pretty as painted china.

Until the State is prepared to furnish elegant shelving for such porcelain, in other words, shelter and maintenance, befitting its extreme fragility and preciousness, the financial crash, with its complicated problem of wreck, constantly repeats itself; and the question arises, what is to be done with china, for which there is no place in the world?"

—"Painted China," *The New Century for Woman*, Woman's Centennial Committee, Centennial International Exhibition, Philadelphia, Saturday May 20, 1876

In the early morning hours of January 23, 1909, the American historian and author Alice Morse Earle lay awake in her berth on the RMS *Republic.* Known as the "Millionaires' Ship," the transatlantic liner was fitted with unusual elegance including a dining salon of light hardwoods surmounted by a domed skylight, a library with mahogany book cabinets, and staterooms with molded cornices and Oriental carpets. It was the largest and fastest transatlantic passenger liner in the White Star fleet. Speeding through the darkness on its journey from New York to the Mediterranean on an especially foggy night, it cut through the warm moist air flowing over ice-cold waters. Alice was a known night owl. In her initial years as an author, she would begin her work after her children had gone to bed, subsisting on apples and oranges as she wrote until dawn.

Over fourteen years, Alice had written seventeen books and over forty-seven articles for magazines, a star of Charles Scribner's Sons, Houghton Mifflin, Herbert S. Stone, and Macmillan, with multiple printings of all her books. After her initial successes, including *China Collecting in America* in 1892, emblazoned with a colorful reproduction of a Dutch Delftware charger on its cover, her career had rapidly unfolded with a series of books including *Colonial Dames and Good Wives* (1895), *Home Life in Colonial Days* (1898), and *Two Centuries of Costume in America 1620–1820s* (1903). Americans were voraciously consuming books on cultural history and her bestsellers with repeating profits enhanced her notoriety and influence. Alice's best-selling books brought history to life, gave objects new meaning, and influenced both collecting practices and the way Americans understood the past.

Using both tangible objects—from portrait miniatures to Dutch Delftware—and information gleaned from primary sources, including wills, letters, sermons, and journals—she recreated a vivid picture of not just heroic moments of well-known characters but everyday life in early America, and women's lives in particular. Seeing a need to make historical writing both more engaging and accessible, she sought to move beyond the dry textbooks of her childhood, which she once described as little more than a collection of "ill-balanced facts in its dull pages."

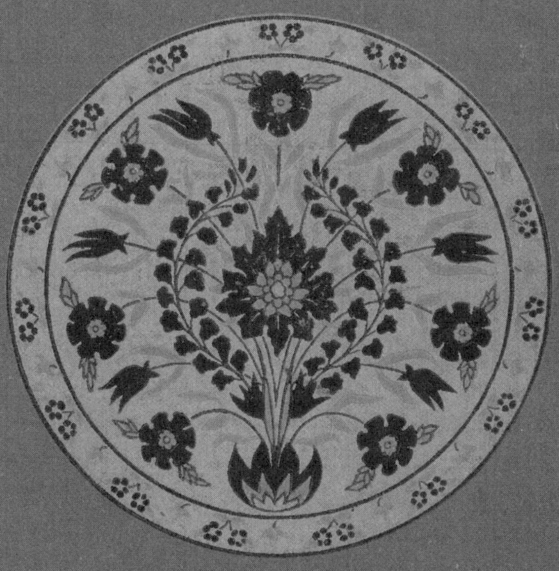

The blue cover of Alice Morse Earle's *China Collecting in America* (New York: Charles Scribner's Sons, 1892) features a Delftware-style dish at its center. Author's collection.

Now, after nearly two decades of constant activity, Alice was finally slowing down and enjoying the rewards of her success. No longer bouncing along the back roads of New England in an open carriage, she now traveled in the comfort of a first-class cabin on the Atlantic. Yet, despite the change in surroundings, her journeys were still driven by a spirit of adventure. This china hunter, New Yorker, influential writer, and now grandmother was bound for Egypt via the Mediterranean, accompanied by her sister Frances—her "Companion of My China Hunts." Setting her glasses aside, she finally rested for the night.

What Alice and her fellow passengers did not realize as they settled in for the first evening of their journey was that their ship was on a direct collision course in the dense fog with an oncoming vessel in one of the most perilous and heavily trafficked waters of the North Atlantic—just fifty miles off the coast of Nantucket, Massachusetts. The SS *Florida* had departed Naples, Italy, two weeks earlier and was now on the final leg of its voyage to New York City. Unlike the luxury liner, it was a transport vessel—an emigrant carrier packed with over nine hundred Italian passengers, each bound for a new life in the United States.

Sleeping passengers were thrown from their berths as the bow of the two-thousand-ton SS *Florida* pierced the side of the RMS *Republic* around 5:00 A.M. The pointed prow sliced through the *Republic*'s metal-clad exterior, damaging the engine room, disabling engines, and shutting down all power, heat, and emergency whistles. The passengers cried for assistance in the darkness as the *Republic* quickly filled with water. The ship began to slowly list forward.

The *Republic*'s Marconi operator, equipped with state-of-the-art wireless telegraphy, frantically transmitted distress signals—marking the first time in maritime history that the technology was used to summon aid. Yet, despite the urgent call, the thick fog obscured visibility, preventing nearby rescue ships from locating the stricken vessel. As the *Republic* took on water, the only option was to transfer passengers—most without coats and many in nightgowns—to the very ship that had rammed them, which, miraculously, remained intact.

While they waited for rescue, the *Republic* continued to sink, slipping beneath the waves within hours.

No one knows exactly how, in the chaos of the morning, as the sun slowly rose and lifeboats were hurriedly lowered, Alice fell into the freezing ocean. According to a local Massachusetts newspaper, she was twice pulled under the waves in 270 feet of icy, turbulent water. The identity of the Italian sailor who rescued her—despite her inability to swim— and how she managed to secure his grasp as she gasped for breath remain a mystery. Taken aboard the smaller SS *Florida*, its prow buckled from the collision and now dangerously overloaded with more than two thousand men, women, and children—they drifted in the open ocean, awaiting rescue.

Hours later, the White Star Line's RMS *Baltic* arrived to transport the stranded passengers back to New York.

As the overcrowded ship approached the city, its decks filled with men and women—some lying down, others sitting, and many standing along the rail—the *Baltic* passed the lightship marking the entrance to the Ambrose Channel. It sailed past the Statue of Liberty toward the awaiting skyline, now dominated by early skyscrapers, before finally returning to New York Harbor.

More than five thousand New Yorkers gathered to welcome the returning ship and its survivors, carrying armfuls of coats, shawls, and jackets to warm the passengers as the vessel finally pulled into the West Side pier off West 10th Street. Miraculously, only a few passengers and crew members lost their lives. Just three years later, however, the White Star Line's next great maritime disaster—the *Titanic*—would not have such a fortunate outcome.

Alice and her sister descended the gangway alongside their fellow passengers, many still dressed in nightclothes, empty-handed, having lost all their belongings. Women stepped ashore with their hair loose or in long braids and, as journalists on hand to cover the headline-making event noted, "without hats." Meanwhile, the Italian passengers, including self-described farm laborers, stone masons, housekeepers, and cooks, were soon transferred to Ellis Island to begin the process of starting their new lives in America. Many would join the nearly 1.5 million people who had arrived from across Europe between 1900 and 1910, shaping New York City into one of the busiest, cosmopolitan, and influential cities in the world.

Alice Morse Earle too had been drawn by the promise and allure of New York as a young woman.

Alice had first arrived in 1874 as a twenty-three-year-old bride from Worcester, Massachusetts. She sought the American city that imbued the spirit of the future with its explosive financial growth, development of the latest technology, and constant rebuilding. Her husband began work as a commodities broker at a time in banking when J. Pierpont Morgan, one of the most storied and powerful financiers of all time, reigned on Wall Street. But when her husband's nascent business failed, Alice turned to writing to contribute to her family's income. They settled in a brick townhouse in Brooklyn Heights.

From across the East River, they watched over the next twenty-five years as New York underwent a dramatic transformation. The Brooklyn Bridge took shape, its steel cables stretched taut and its granite towers rising to form one of the nation's first suspension bridges. The soft glow of gaslight gave way to the brilliance of electricity as Thomas Edison's Pearl Street Station, opened in 1882, gradually illuminated homes and businesses across the city by the late 1880s. Meanwhile, the New York skyline evolved from a low expanse punctuated by church steeples in the 1870s to a soaring landscape of the city's first skyscrapers.

This was the height of the Gilded Age, an era that on the surface encapsulated everything bright, opulent, and new. Alice embodied that spirit by establishing her career as an enterprising female writer. America was blazing a path with its eye on the future, poised to become the world's leader, and had entered a period of great expansion, geographically and economically, together with quickly changing demographics.

Yet the popularity of Alice's works, books, and articles grounded in historic subjects, from food, ceramics, clothing, and furniture to customs, social practices, and daily life reflected an America that in the face of innovation and modernization craved insight into its earliest years. It was an era where Americans, seeking a national identity, cast a gaze on its past. They turned to the stories and objects related to its earliest foundations to create and redefine the American story.

As quickly as the United States was founded in the eighteenth century, even amid uncertainty about its survival as a viable political entity, the country began establishing its first museums and historical societies. These institutions sprang up across the nation, rapidly accumulating collections of art, artifacts, and "relics." While the term "relic" often carries religious connotations of venerated objects associated with saints or martyrs, in the eighteenth and nineteenth centuries it was also commonly used to describe items valued for their age or historical significance.

In 1804, when New York City was home to only 75,000 people and its name was still hyphenated, the city founded its own repository of art and artifacts: the New-York Historical Society. Its founders declared, "Without the aid of original records and authentic documents, history will be nothing more than a well-combined series of ingenious conjectures and amusing fables." By the mid–nineteenth century, no figure in American history was becoming more enshrined in myth and idealization—including tales of a cherry tree–chopping—than George Washington. Women played a crucial early role in preserving his legacy, spearheading efforts to protect Mount Vernon, Washington's Virginia home. Alarmed by its rapidly deteriorating condition, Ann Pamela Cunningham led the formation of the Mount Vernon Ladies' Association in 1853. This group launched a national campaign to raise funds to save and maintain the historic estate, founding America's first historic preservation organization and marking the beginning of the country's historic preservation movement.

The United States was not the only young nation looking to its past for identity and inspiration. In the mid–nineteenth century, the Dutch were also rediscovering their history as a newly independent nation-state, having regained independence from France in 1815. As the Kingdom of the Netherlands, they turned to their narrative as the Dutch Republic, drawing on their successful sixteenth-century revolt against Spanish domination as a unifying and inspirational force.

As part of their efforts to take stock of their historic and cultural legacy, the Dutch established historical organizations, including the *Historisch Gezelschap* (now known as the Royal Dutch Historical Society), an association of academic historians, in Amsterdam in 1845. Throughout the mid–nineteenth century, exhibitions showcasing historic objects, including Dutch Delftware, were organized across the country. Newly appointed Dutch archivists, including Jan Soutendam, the first municipal archivist of Delft in 1859, embarked on missions to identify and preserve historical documents scattered across the Netherlands. They combed through damp storage rooms, pried open locked cabinets, and salvaged troves of invaluable materials ranging from notarial records and registers of births, deaths, and marriages to wills and tax registers.

Amid this renewed interest in preserving history, scholars once again turned their attention to the small town of Delft. Largely forgotten since the eighteenth century, by the late nineteenth century, this unassuming town had become culturally world-renowned for two iconic contributions: Johannes Vermeer and Dutch Delftware.

The rediscovery of Dutch cultural treasures was profoundly influenced by two unlikely French art critics living in exile due to their political beliefs. In the 1860s, Théophile Thoré, writing under the pseudonym William Bürger, extolled the virtues of Johannes Vermeer, bringing the artist to newfound prominence. Meanwhile, his compatriot Henry Havard dedicated nearly a decade to the study of Dutch Delftware, culminating in the publication of the first comprehensive history on the subject, *Histoire de la Faïence de Delft*, in 1878.

Sentenced to death for his role in the revolutionary Paris Commune, Havard fled to the Netherlands in the 1870s, where he became an art critic for several French newspapers, including *Le Siècle* and *Le Monde Illustré*. Traveling extensively through the Low Countries, he visited art collections and penned exhibition reviews. At a time when Dutch museums had yet to embrace Delftware as part of their collections and most Delft potteries had long since closed, Havard's introduction to Dutch Delftware came through private collectors such as John F. Loudon in The Hague. Loudon's remarkable collection of over five hundred pieces included everything from black Delftware to a celebrated decorative blue-and-white "Delftware violin." Intrigued

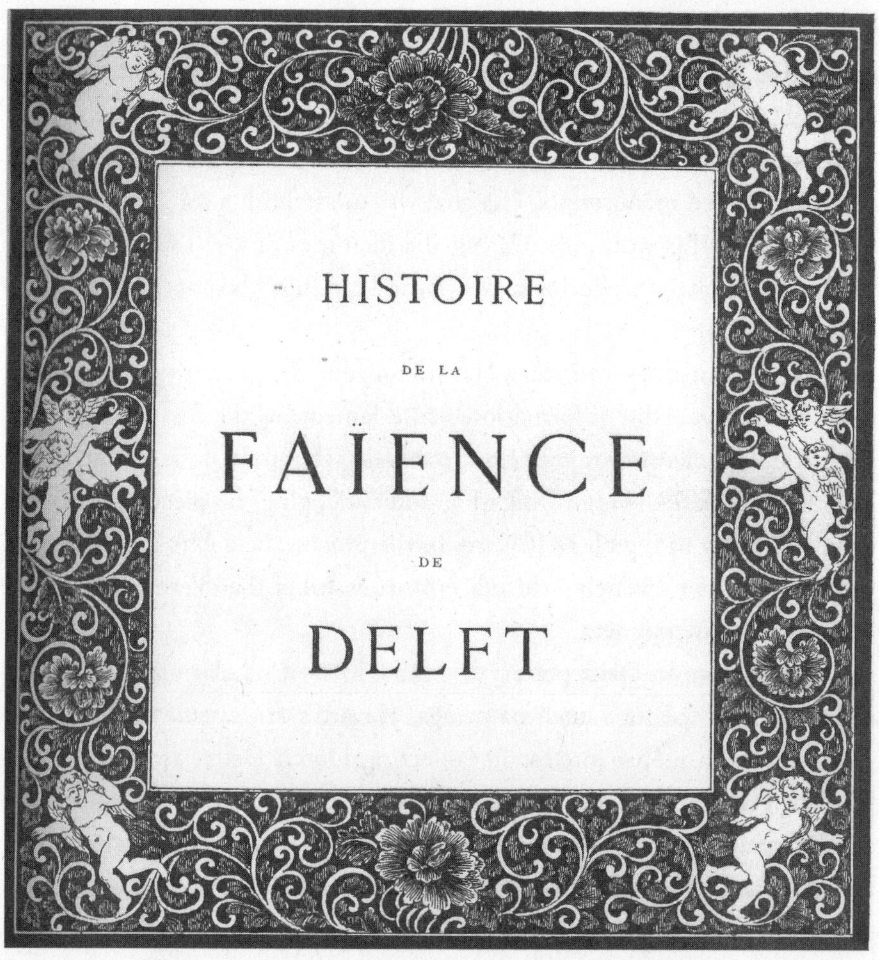

Charles Antoine Goutzwiller's intricate Delftware-inspired illustration frames the title page of Henry Havard's *Histoire de la Faïence de Delft* (1878), echoing the craftsmanship of the ceramics it celebrates. Author's collection.

by the artistry and craftsmanship of Delftware, Havard became determined to unravel its origins and the stories behind its creation.

Havard's quest led him deep into the archives of Delft, where he embarked on what he called his *chasse aux documents*—a hunt for documents. The task was formidable, complicated by what he described as "great difficulties, especially for a foreigner unfamiliar with the Dutch language and its paleography." Nevertheless, he pursued his research with methodical precision, scouring archives and libraries across the Netherlands for overlooked records and unpublished manuscripts. His goal was to establish a solid and credible foundation for his work, uncovering the identities of Delft's potteries and the lives of the artisans, business owners, and families who contributed to the industry.

Over the course of seven years, Havard toiled in damp archival storerooms, uncovering invaluable information while lamenting the loss of countless historical documents to floods, fires, the Delft Thunderclap, and even theft. Through his meticulous investigation and cataloging, he pieced together a detailed history of Dutch Delftware. In the process, he debunked persistent myths, including a widely held but erroneous belief that Vermeer had also been a Delftware painter.

By dedicating to Delft pottery the same level of scholarly attention traditionally reserved for Dutch paintings, Havard's *Histoire de la Faïence de Delft* sparked a global interest in collecting Dutch Delftware throughout the nineteenth and twentieth centuries. His research not only elevated the decorative arts but also opened new avenues for exploring Delft's potteries and their connections to art, culture, and commerce. Havard's work inspired subsequent authors, including Alice Morse Earle, and transformed the creations of Delft potters, or *plateelbackers*, into cultural objects of artistic and historical significance.

The allure of Dutch archives also drew American diplomat and historian John Lothrop Motley to the Netherlands in the 1850s. Inspired by firsthand accounts of Dutch history, Motley introduced American audiences to the dramatic events of the Dutch revolt against Spanish rule in the sixteenth century through his bestseller, *The Rise of the Dutch Republic* (1856). The book, widely embraced by Americans of both Dutch and non-Dutch heritage, sparked a fascination with Dutch culture in the United States. Drawing from archival records, Motley used vivid details to recreate the Dutch sixteenth- and seventeenth-century experience, painting a detailed picture of its heroes that brought the past to life. In the mythic national character of the Dutch Republic, Americans saw reflections of the qualities they aspired to embody in themselves.

By the late 1860s, as the United States began to recover from the Civil War, the nation's focus turned toward its approaching centennial, an occasion to celebrate both its past and its future. Anticipation grew for the planned Centennial Exhibition in Philadelphia in 1876. Officially titled *The United States Centennial International Exhibition*, the event would commemorate the hundredth anniversary of the signing of the Declaration of Independence. As the first major international exhibition held on American soil, it was envisioned as a showcase of the nation's history and its innovative progress.

Arriving by steamships, trains, streetcars, and carriages, nearly ten million visitors flocked to Philadelphia from across the country to attend the Centennial Exhibition. The event offered an experience that was both shocking in its innovations and inspiring in its homage to the past—a place where the Industrial Revolution met the American Revolution. Promoted with flyers and guidebooks adorned with stars and stripes, George Washington's portrait, eagles, and patriotic swag, the Centennial Exhibition featured more than thirty thousand entries from America and twenty foreign countries, showcasing everything from paintings and sculptures to groundbreaking advancements in science and technology.

At a time when the average American wage was $1.21 a day, visitors paid fifty cents for what many considered the experience of a lifetime. They rode the world's first steam-driven monorail, marveled at the Corliss Steam Engine—towering nearly fifty feet high and powering Machinery Hall—and were astonished by the sound of a voice transmitted through Alexander Graham Bell's telephone. Americans also had their first glimpse of the Statue of Liberty, with the recently completed copper right arm and torch on display.

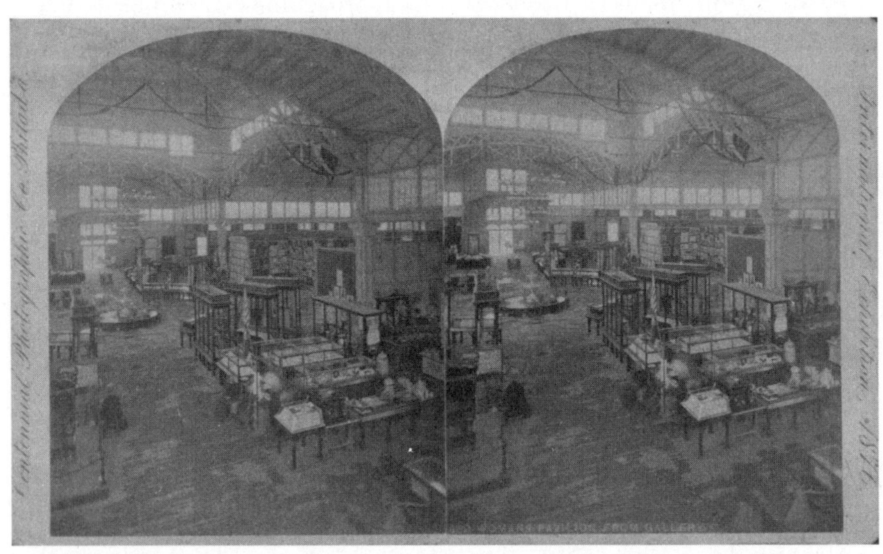

The 1876 stereograph by the Centennial Photographic Co. offers an interior view of the Women's Pavilion from the gallery. The Miriam and Ira D. Wallach Division of Art, Prints and Photographs: Photography Collection, The New York Public Library.

Among the Centennial Exhibition's many firsts was a groundbreaking attraction that celebrated women's contributions to the arts, sciences, education, and industry. It was known as the Women's Pavilion.

Organized and funded by women, the pavilion was described in the *Exposition Guide* as "a handsome structure, devoted entirely to the exhibit of women's work, and is in charge of alternate committees of women." But it was far more than just an exhibition space—it was a bold statement of female innovation and leadership, a testament to what women could achieve when given the opportunity.

At the heart of its creation was Elizabeth Duane Gillespie, one of Philadelphia's most formidable leaders.

The great-granddaughter of Benjamin Franklin, Elizabeth was born in 1821 and raised across from Independence Square in a family that championed female education and self-sufficiency. Privately tutored, she developed an unshakable independence and a lifelong commitment to expanding opportunities for women. A key influence in her life was her grandmother, Sally Franklin Bache, the daughter of Benjamin Franklin. As Elizabeth recalled in her 1901 autobiography, *A Book of Remembrance*, Sally had received advice from her father in a letter written in 1773 while he was in England. As tensions escalated in the Colonies, Franklin urged his daughter to "be extremely circumspect in all your behavior," "go constantly to church," and, most notably, to "acquire those useful accomplishments—arithmetic and bookkeeping." Sally Franklin Bache later demonstrated her own resilience and leadership, raising funds in the streets of Philadelphia to support George Washington's struggling army —a powerful example of female resourcefulness that would shape Elizabeth's own path.

As a young woman, Elizabeth traveled widely throughout Europe. Upon her return to Philadelphia, she married shortly before the Civil War and became a leading organizer of Philadelphia's Great Central, or Sanitary Fair, held in 1864. This national fair, showcasing art, crafts, and historical exhibits, raised funds for the U.S. Sanitary Commission, a Union Army relief organization.

Her ability to organize and rally support did not go unnoticed.

In 1873, when the Centennial Exhibition's all-male Board of Finance faced a funding shortfall, they turned to Elizabeth Gillespie. Appointed president of the newly formed Women's Centennial Executive Committee, Elizabeth was tasked with generating interest in the fair and raising critical funds, including subscriptions for Centennial stock.

But for Elizabeth, this was about more than just fundraising—it was about seizing a historic opportunity. If ever there was a moment to act, this was it. The Centennial Exposition was not just a celebration; it was a national stage, a rare chance for the world to witness women's impact on history, industry, and the arts.

She agreed to take on the challenge, but with one bold condition: there must be a dedicated space honoring women's contributions—a place where their achievements would be displayed, their voices amplified, and their place in history secured.

On May 10, 1876, the Women's Pavilion officially opened with an all-female ceremony led by the Empress of Brazil. The 26,000-square-foot wooden structure, crowned by a central dome rising over ninety feet, showcased the works of women across a range of disciplines, from fine and decorative arts to literature, science, and invention. Among the eighty newly patented inventions on display were a cold handle for hot irons, emergency flares, and model interlocking bricks. The pavilion also featured works of art by female painters, sculptors, and artisans, including contributions from Maria Longworth Nichols Storer, founder of the Rookwood Pottery in Cincinnati, Ohio. Even Queen Victoria lent her support, sending "Two table napkins spun by Her Majesty and etchings" to the exhibit.

For six months, the Women's Pavilion was not only a celebration of women's achievements but also an acknowledgement of the challenges they faced as they fought for recognition and equality in the arts, sciences, and society at large.

Entering the Women's Pavilion, visitors were greeted by one of its most popular attractions: Emma Allison, the "Lady Engineer," dressed in formal attire, tending a steam engine that powered several machines, including the press used to print *The New Century of Woman*, the official newsletter of the Women's Centennial Executive Committee. This pro-feminist weekly newspaper, "written, edited, and printed by women," featured editorials that challenged cultural and institutional barriers. Although stopping short of taking a stand on suffrage, it called for change on issues for women ranging from dress reform to reclaiming married women's legal status and property rights with the abolition of *femme couverte*.

The success of the Women's Pavilion was a shared accomplishment for Elizabeth Gillespie. This achievement, from the construction of the pavilion to the securing of objects for display, was possible only through the collective efforts of committees of countless members, comprising some of the most influential and effective women across the United States, including Elizabeth Hart Jarvis Colt.

In her portrait at the Wadsworth Atheneum in Hartford, Connecticut, Elizabeth Colt is depicted seated comfortably on a gold silk settee, wearing a white silk gown, with her young son Caldwell by her side. It is far from the typical portrayal of an industrialist and it offers little hint of the series of unexpected events that shaped her into one of the most important American businesswomen of the nineteenth century.

The Colt name is synonymous with one of the most recognized weapons of the nineteenth century, the Colt .45 pistol, named after its original designer and producer, Elizabeth's husband, Samuel Colt. However, Samuel Colt died suddenly in 1862, leaving Elizabeth, after fewer than six years of marriage, a widow with controlling interest in the Colt Patent Firearms Manufacturing Company, located in Hartford, Connecticut, the largest private armament factory in the world. With Samuel's premature death, Elizabeth, at the age of forty-seven, also became one of the wealthiest women in the United States.

Elizabeth led the Colt Patent Firearms Manufacturing Company through the Civil War and beyond. Shortly after her husband's death, she suffered a miscarriage and subsequently lost two of her three children to illness. Despite her immense grief, Elizabeth oversaw the company with remarkable skill, ensuring that every U.S. Army order for Colt weapons was fulfilled. In 1864, when the Colt factory burned to the ground, she not only rebuilt but expanded production. Defying expectations, she retained ownership of the company for another forty-two years, while simultaneously advancing social and civic causes and developing her own art collection.

By the end of her life, with guidance from artist Frederic Edwin Church, her collection had grown to over six hundred American and European paintings, including works by Thomas Cole, John Kensett, Albert Bierstadt, and William-Adolphe Bouguereau. In her will, Elizabeth bequeathed more than one thousand pieces of fine and decorative arts to the Wadsworth Atheneum Museum of Art in Hartford. She also donated more than $50,000 to the museum, enabling the construction of a new wing that opened to the public in November 1910, making the Wadsworth the first American municipal museum wing to bear the name of a female patron.

The Colt Patent Firearms Manufacturing Company, a leading innovator of the nineteenth century, made a striking impression at the 1876 Centennial Exhibition with its "wheel" display in the Manufactories Hall, featuring nickel- and gold-plated arms that highlighted its craftsmanship. Across Fairmount Park in the Women's Pavilion, Elizabeth Colt presented a personal contribution to the women's exhibition: "three colored photographs" of the Church of the Good Shepherd, which she commissioned in Hartford, Connecticut in 1867. Overseeing every detail, from the stained-glass windows to the church silver, Elizabeth considered it one of her greatest accomplishments, a lasting tribute to her late husband and their children.

When the Centennial Exhibition closed its gates in November 1876, exhibitors packed up their displays and crates were shipped back across the globe. The Women's Pavilion was disassembled, but the women who had brought it to life emerged invigorated. Reflecting on the experience, Elizabeth Gillespie observed, "the women of the whole country were working not only for patriotic motives, but with the hope that through this Exhibition their own abilities would be recognized, and their works carried beyond needles and thread." Organized and funded entirely by women under Elizabeth's leadership, the Women's Pavilion proved women could not only succeed but excel in the public arena.

The legacy of the Women's Pavilion as a catalyst for women's progress had begun, but Elizabeth Gillespie remained vigilant, determined to ensure its momentum continued.

The Centennial Exhibition's Fine Arts Pavilion, which had showcased paintings and sculptures, remained and became the foundation of the Pennsylvania Museum and School of Industrial Art, known today as the Philadelphia Museum of Art. However, as Elizabeth reviewed the drafted charter and by-laws of the city's new institution, she was surprised to discover:

> . . . there was not the slightest allusion to the work the women of the whole country had done for the Exhibition. The compilers had even decreed that the Trustees of the proposed institution should be males. To this I sent an earnest remonstrance, claiming that our women had gladly given time, money, and energy to the cause, and that they should not be quietly put aside. The remonstrance had the desired effect.

At Elizabeth's insistence, the position of Trustee at the Philadelphia Museum of Art was opened to any woman nominated and elected by the corporators at their annual meeting.

Although the Women's Pavilion and the Centennial Exhibition stood for only six months in 1876, its impact was both considerable and lasting, especially for women. The year 1877 proved pivotal, as many who had visited the Women's Pavilion began creating new opportunities for women's education and advancement. Recognizing the potential for women's careers in design, Candace Wheeler founded the Society of Decorative Art in New York in 1877. That same year, Helen Adelia Rowe Metcalf established the Rhode Island School of Design, and the Hartford School for Decorative Arts was cofounded in Connecticut by a group of prominent women, including Olivia Langdon Clemens (Mrs. Samuel Clemens), Harriet Beecher Stowe, as well as Elizabeth Colt.

Elizabeth Gillespie had set the precedent at Philadelphia's Centennial Exhibition in 1876 for an effective and expertly run event through her leadership in organizing the Women's Pavilion. This model would later be replicated with the formation of a new women's committee for what became known as the Women's Building at the 1893 Chicago World's Fair or the World's Columbian Exposition.

In the meantime, Elizabeth, affectionately described by a fellow Centennial Committee member as the tireless "imperial wizard, the arch-tycoon," was ready to embark on a new endeavor. On April 8, 1891, a group of women gathered at the Philadelphia home of her former Women's Centennial Executive Committee colleague, Fanny Hollingsworth Arnold. Their experience with the Women's Pavilion had given them firsthand insight into what women could accomplish in the public sphere, while the patriotic spirit of the Centennial had deepened their connection to the nation's history. Together with Elizabeth Gillespie, and armed with both inspiration and organizational expertise, they laid the foundation for a new women's organization—not one meant to last a season, but a lasting vehicle for female agency, ensuring that women's contributions to history and society would endure for generations, connecting women across lifetimes. They called it The National Society of Colonial Dames of America.

The term *dame*, though archaic even in the nineteenth century, carried layers of meaning that would have deeply resonated with these women. Originating from the Latin *domina*, meaning lady or mistress, the word also evoked the tradition of early educational institutions run by women, known as *dame schools*. These small, privately operated schools, common across England and America from the seventeenth through the nineteenth centuries, highlighted the role of women as educators and custodians of knowledge. For Elizabeth Gillespie and her peers, this connection held significance.

As *dames*, or teachers, they embraced their role in fostering and facilitating learning about the American past, seeking to narrate the history of the United States from a distinctly female perspective. Once established in Philadelphia, their organization quickly expanded nationally, forming a network of state societies. Membership in each state society was based on lineage and a shared mission to uphold:

> patriotic, historic, and educational purposes to perpetuate the memory and the spirit of the men and women who, in the colonial period, by their rectitude, courage, and self-denial, prepared the way for success in that struggle which gained for the country its liberty and Constitution.

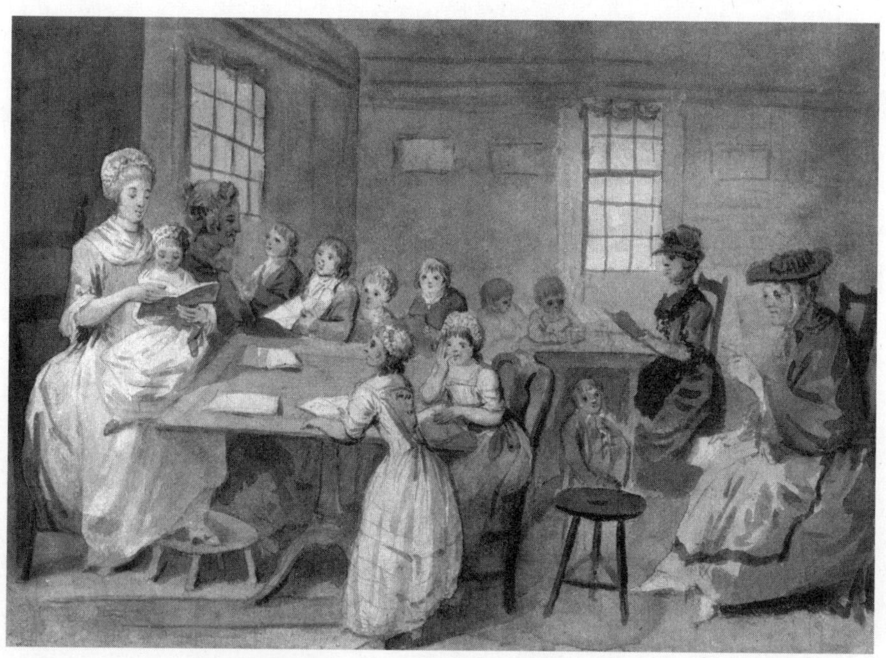

Reading Lesson at a Dame School by Elias Martin (1739–1818), rendered in graphite, pen, and ink, and watercolor, depicts girls and boys learning under the guidance of female teachers. Yale Center for British Art, Paul Mellon Collection.

This mission fueled their pioneering, female-led efforts in collecting and curating fine and decorative arts while preserving historic architecture, ultimately illuminating America's diverse past. Their work soon expanded beyond the colonial era, embracing the nation's evolving identity. Over time, their preservation efforts spanned from George Washington's sixteenth-century ancestral home, Sulgrave Manor in England, to seventeenth-, eighteenth-, and nineteenth-century homes lining America's East Coast. They safeguarded frontier log cabins and homesteads in the Midwest, then moved westward to protect Gold Rush–era structures, weaving a layered, ever-expanding narrative of American history.

As Americans danced to John Philip Sousa's 1896 "The Colonial Dames Waltzes," published by *The Ladies' Home Journal*, this woman's organization's growing popularity became a national focus.

Prominent women from across the country joined Elizabeth Gillespie's latest successful endeavor. From Elizabeth Colt in Connecticut to Emily Warren Roebling in New Jersey—the engineer and overseer of the Brooklyn Bridge—women in the North lent their influence. In the South, Juliette Gordon Low, founder of the Girl Scouts, became a key supporter. Meanwhile, on the West Coast, Jane Lathrop Stanford, cofounder of Stanford University, brought prominence to the movement. Even First Lady Helen "Nellie" Taft, wife of President William Howard Taft, joined its ranks, underscoring the organization's widespread appeal among accomplished American women.

In 1895, Alice Morse Earle was invited to become one of the earliest members of The National Society of Colonial Dames in the State of New York. This inaugural group, based in New York City, included women who would come to define the Gilded Age such as Alice Claypoole Gwynne Vanderbilt (Mrs. Cornelius Vanderbilt II), Frances Tracy Morgan (Mrs. J. Pierpont Morgan), and Louise Whitfield Carnegie (Mrs. Andrew Carnegie).

The group expanded rapidly, drawing women from a wide range of fields and passions including writers, collectors, social activists, educators, philanthropists, suffragists, and historians. Starting with just 168 members in 1895,

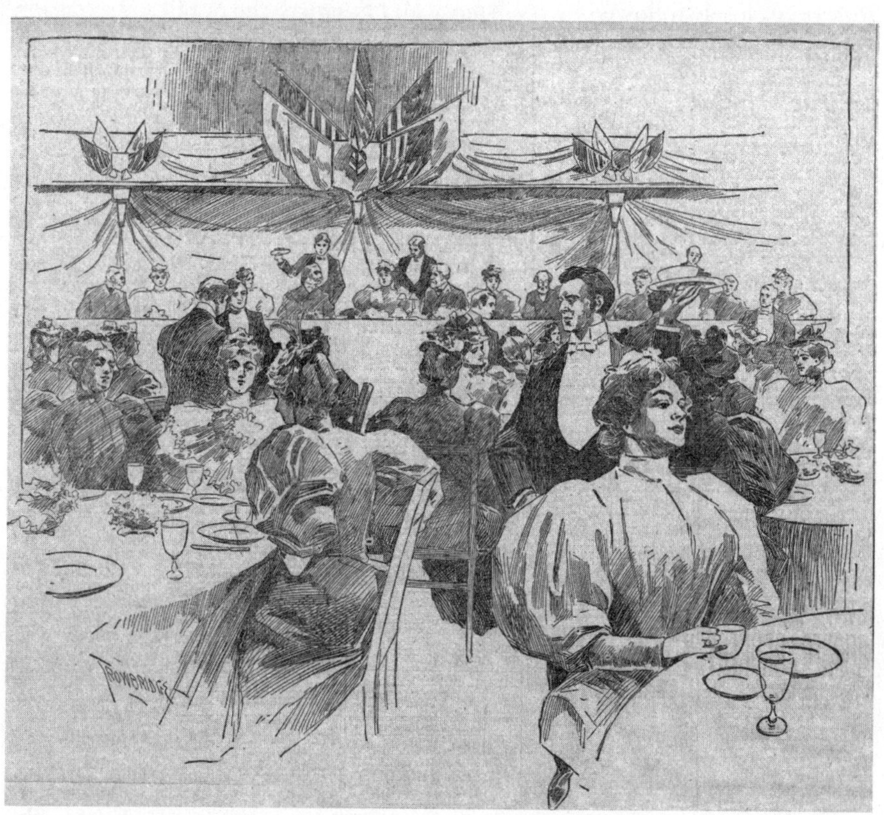

The Journal captured the ladies of the National Society of Colonial Dames in the State of New York breakfasting at Sherry's on March 12, 1896, a premier New York venue known for its grand ballrooms and fashionable gatherings. Library of Congress, Washington, D.C.

its ranks more than doubled to 348 by 1897, as New York's most connected and influential women clamored to join what had quickly become the city's newest and most exclusive organization.

Described by the press as "the crème de la crème of New York society," the women of The National Society of Colonial Dames in the State of New York were closely followed by reporters eager to satisfy the public's fascination with their activities. From private breakfasts at Sherry's—New York's latest and most fashionable restaurant—where they "turned its calendar back to ye olde times . . . and feasted in true Dutch fashion," to educational pursuits including "a course of five lectures to be given by the women" in the spring of 1895, held in the grand ballroom of the newly opened Waldorf Hotel, their endeavors captured widespread attention. On March 5, 1895, Alice Morse Earle attended one of these lectures on "Colonial Architecture" alongside her fellow Dames, Mrs. J. Pierpont Morgan and Mrs. Stanford White.

In the curtained darkness of the Waldorf Hotel's ballroom, the women followed "lantern pictures" as William R. Ware, art historian and founder of the School of Architecture at Columbia University, delivered his lecture. He explored "the most ancient houses in the Atlantic coast states from Massachusetts to South Carolina," emphasizing "the architectural beauties of their construction, external and internal."

But unknown by the press, and hidden from public view, these women were quietly preparing for an architectural project of their own.

Ten miles from Manhattan—an hour's ride by carriage or a quick trip by train—stood an eighteenth-century, two-story house constructed of dressed gray fieldstone. Nestled in the southwestern corner of a sprawling tract of more than one thousand acres in the Bronx, the house was surrounded by swamps, broad open fields, and seemingly timeless woodlands. The land had recently been sold to the City of New York, adding to its growing footprint.

Its wooden front *stoop* remained intact, but the broad steps had rotted. Paint peeled gently from the front door and shards of glass from broken windowpanes, now boarded, lay scattered in the overgrown grass. The house stood deteriorated, empty, and abandoned. Yet this group of women knew its history, its stories, and its significance. They understood the vital role both the house and its former inhabitants had played in the history of New Amsterdam and New York. They had been watching it closely since before 1893—and they had a plan.

The building was a shadow of its former self, once a commanding eighteenth-century manor house at the center of a large working farm surrounded by acres of wheat, buckwheat, rye, and corn. Despite its decline, many of its unique architectural details remained, including the brownstone corbels above its windows in the form of grotesque masks—carved faces, some with mischievous expressions to ward away evil spirits—that gazed southward toward the Spuyten Duyvil Creek and Manhattan.

Much of the land surrounding the house had been acquired by the Dutch West India Company from the Weckquaesgeek people in 1639. Native Americans had long inhabited various sections of the area. In 1889, excavations beneath the fields on the north side of the house unearthed finely honed arrow points and fragments of unglazed, dark reddish-brown clay pots, offering a glimpse into the land's earlier history.

The property was purchased around 1646 by Adriaen Cornelissen van der Donck, a Dutch-born settler who arrived in New Amsterdam in 1641 as a young man, having recently studied law and philosophy at Leiden University. Known as a Dutch *jonkheer*, or "young lordship," his title later inspired the present-day name of Yonkers. Drawn to the area's diverse landscape—its meadow swamps, open flats, dense woodlands, and steep ridges—he set about building a home and establishing his *bowerie*, or farm.

Van der Donck had accepted a commission in New Netherlands from the Dutch West India Company, and he attempted to make his mark on the fledgling settlement. He would become embroiled in the politics of New Amsterdam and was often at odds with Director-General Peter Stuyvesant, as he was an activist for Dutch-style republican government in the Dutch West India Company–run trading post. In 1656 he wrote *Description of New Netherland*, an early testament to his vision for his adopted homeland. In New Netherland van der Donck saw richness and possibility while walking through forests, noting trees and geology and, as a Dutchman, even its clay:

> Some mountains consist solely of fuller's earth, and several of other kinds of fine earth or clay, some white, others red, yellow, blue, gray, and black, all very greasy and sticky, and probably suitable for making such articles as dishes, pots, platters, and tobacco pipes. Good earth for brick and tile is also found, as I know from experience. It is a pity, therefore, that not more people in those trades move there, because they could undoubtably do good business and the country would also benefit.

Adriaen van der Donck would not live to see the realization of his many dreams for his new country. He died in 1655 at the age of thirty-five under mysterious circumstances, with both the nature of his death and the exact location of the structure that served as his home remaining unknown. After van der Donck's death, his widow sold the property, and the house gradually fell into disrepair, with any remnants eventually disappearing into the surrounding fields. Centuries later, in the 1900s, archaeologists uncovered fragments of Delftware and clay pipes near the gray fieldstone house, possibly marking the foundation of his former home.

In 1694 Jacobus van Cortlandt, a wealthy merchant and future mayor of the city with the new name of New York, purchased a small central portion of the previous van der Donck property and over a thirty-year period bought back much of the original footprint. Jacobus was the youngest son of Oloff van Cortlandt, who had arrived in 1638 from the Dutch Republic as an officer of the Dutch West India Company and went on to become one of the wealthiest men in New Netherland. When New Netherland was captured by the English, it was six-year-old Jacobus's father Oloff who was appointed by Director-General Peter Stuyvesant to negotiate the terms of surrender.

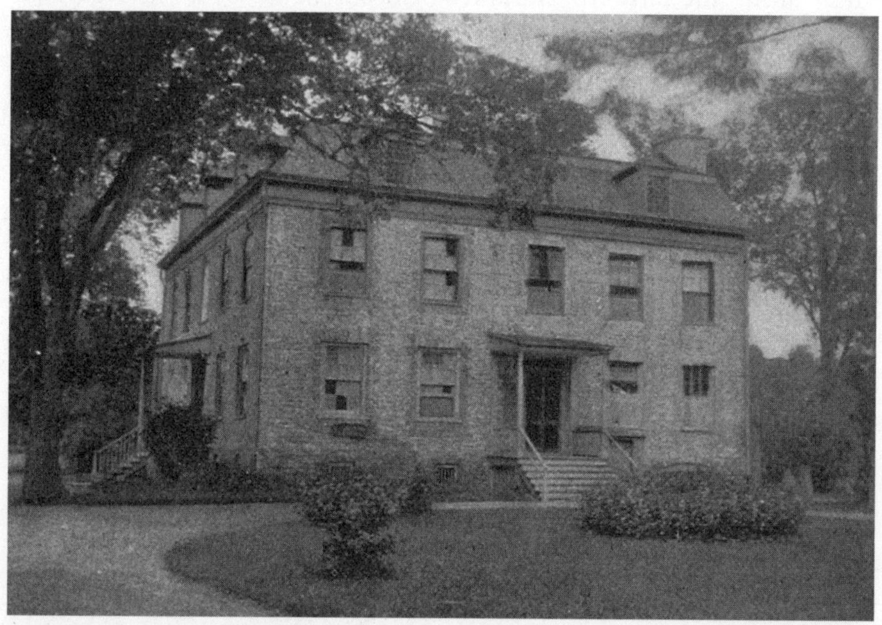

A ca. 1896 view of the Van Cortlandt Mansion, with partially boarded windows before its restoration, as featured in Mrs. Morris Patterson Ferris's *Van Cortlandt Mansion: Erected 1748*. National Society of Colonial Dames in the State of New York.

The gray fieldstone mansion was built in 1748 by Jacobus van Cortlandt's son, Frederick van Cortlandt, and his wife, Françoise "Frances" Jay van Cortlandt. Frances was the daughter of Augustus Jay, who fled France with fellow Protestants following the revocation of the Edict of Nantes in 1685. Constructed from materials quarried nearby, the house blended Georgian and Dutch architectural styles. It served as a rural retreat, spacious and comfortably furnished, situated at the heart of a prosperous wheat farm. The farm's operations relied on the labor of enslaved men and women, who were responsible for maintaining both the house and the agricultural enterprise.

During the American Revolution, the van Cortlandt's home played a notable role in pivotal moments of New York history. With the British threatening New York City, Augustus van Cortlandt, Frederick's son and the city clerk, hid the city's most valuable records in the family burial vault northeast of the house, where they remained for the duration of the war.

In October 1776, as George Washington retreated from the lost city of New York, he stayed several nights at the van Cortlandt house en route to the ill-fated Battle of White Plains. Seven years later, in November 1783, he returned to the house, lodging there before his triumphant reentry into New York as a victorious general.

After the American Revolution, Augustus van Cortlandt's descendants retained ownership of the property, living in the house through the nineteenth century. By 1888, however, the family sold the land and house to the City of New York, marking the start of a new chapter in its history. Over one thousand acres of the estate were transformed into Van Cortlandt Park, now New York City's third-largest public park.

Van Cortlandt Park quickly took shape as the land was dramatically altered. Marshes were drained, earth was moved, and trees were felled to make way for new facilities and uses. Parts of the former farmland became the Parade Ground or drilling fields for New York's regiments, while other areas hosted the first municipal golf course in the United States. For a time, the park even served as a temporary pasture for a herd of endangered American bison—a gift to the city that was later relocated to the Bronx Zoo.

Amid the dust and construction, the stone house, then known as the Van Cortlandt Mansion, stood abandoned and largely overlooked.

While the City ignored the once-graceful but now worn structure, Alice Vanderbilt, and her fellow "Dames" were quietly developing a plan—not just to restore the Van Cortlandt Mansion but to transform it into a public museum. However, they soon discovered that bringing their vision to life would require some unexpected hurdles, not just the approval of New York City but the New York State Legislature.

In late April 1895, Justine Van Rensselaer Townsend boarded a train for Albany.

Justine was not only the head of the Mount Vernon Ladies' Association, serving as its third Regent and leading the esteemed group of women who had restored and maintained George Washington's Mount Vernon in Virginia, but also the president of the newly formed National Society of Colonial Dames in the State of New York. Her dual leadership roles underscored her commitment to preserving early American history.

When the ceiling of Washington's dining room at Mount Vernon collapsed in 1885, Justine had personally funded its reconstruction. Now, as president of the Colonial Dames, she was equally determined to prevent another significant piece of early American architecture—one tied to the histories of both New York and New Amsterdam—from falling into disrepair.

Arriving in Albany at the close of the legislative session, Justine lobbied throughout the new limestone state capitol on behalf of the women in New York. Hurriedly canvasing its halls and offices, she approached the governor of New York and members of the Senate and the Assembly, attempting to convince them to allow the group of women to take custody of this historic building in the Bronx to create a museum. Time was short and the concept she proposed was a new one with little or no precedent. The Van Cortlandt Mansion would be only the fourth historic building in the United States to be used in this public capacity and it was requested by a group of women. The future of the house was seemingly up in the air.

But late in the afternoon on April 29, 1896, during the second-to-last day of the legislative session, a landmark decision was made. The New York State Legislature passed:

> An act authorizing the board of park commissioners of the city of New York to transfer the custody of the Van Cortlandt mansion in Van Cortlandt park to the Society of Colonial Dames of the State of New York for the establishment of a museum for historical relics (No. 2769, Rec. No. 941).

The act was approved with a unanimous affirmative vote, with a majority of all elected Senators in favor "and three-fifths present." In an era when women had not yet gained the right to vote, this decision was groundbreaking. The State of New York entrusted the custodianship of the Van Cortlandt Mansion to a group of women, empowering them to preserve its history and establish a museum. This act was both a recognition of their capabilities and an acknowledgment of their role as stewards of cultural heritage.

Shortly after formalizing their role as stewards of the Van Cortlandt Mansion, Alice Morse Earle reflected on the subject of female capability. Writing in the March 1898 issue of the new American magazine, *The House Beautiful*, she drew on her research and through the lens of Delftware she connected the industrious women of early America to the entrepreneurial spirit of the female pottery owners of Delft. She observed:

> The general aptitude for trading and business, shown so wonderfully and universally two centuries ago by Dutch Dames in America and Holland, did not desert them when they entered into the manufacture of Delft Ware. A large number of women directed factories but were not admitted to the guild as faience-makers, only as faience-sellers, winkelhousteren. Beautiful specimens exist of the production of these women, notably the splendid pieces from the factories of Barbara Rottenel . . .

Alice viewed this aptitude as a timeless and inherent characteristic of women, whether in seventeenth-century Delft, New Amsterdam, or perhaps even nineteenth-century New York.

Now, Alice and a group of determined women found themselves in an unlikely position: stewards of an abandoned fieldstone and brick mansion surrounded by swamp, empty and deteriorated. Yet, to them, this shell of a house was not a lost cause—it was a blank slate, an opportunity for a group of women to tell the shared story of Dutch and American history.

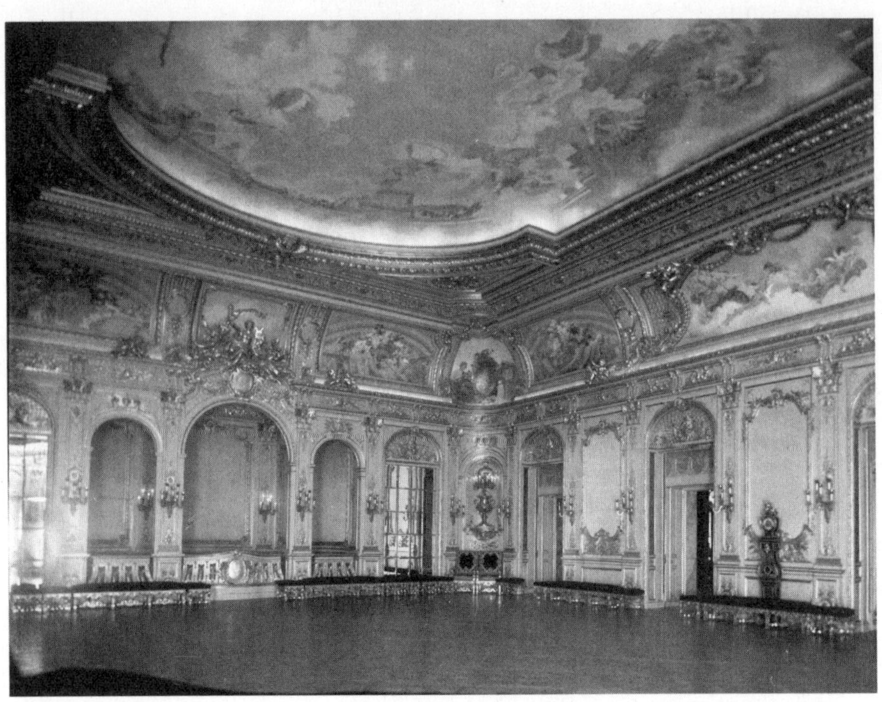

ABOVE: The opulent ballroom of Alice and Cornelius Vanderbilt II, designed by Parisian decorator Gilbert Cuel (1892–1894), epitomizes Gilded Age grandeur, as captured in a photograph taken between 1892 and 1926. Archives of American Art, Smithsonian Institution. OPPOSITE: Burton Frederick Welles's photograph, *West 57th St.—Mrs. Cornelius Vanderbilt—Hotel Plaza—West 59th St.*, from his book *Fifth Avenue New York from Start to Finish,* 1911. Irma and Paul Milstein Division of United States History, Local History and Genealogy, The New York Public Library.

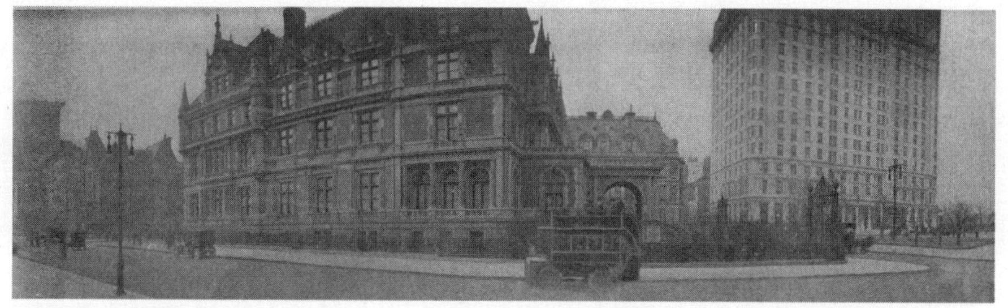

8

Met Wives

"Think of it, ye millionaires of many markets, what glory may yet be yours if you only listen to our advice, to convert pork into porcelain, grain and produce into priceless pottery . . ."

—Joseph H. Choate, Vice President and Trustee, at the public opening of the Metropolitan Museum on Fifth Avenue, March 30, 1880

On the late winter afternoon of March 2, 1897, Alice Claypoole Gwynne Vanderbilt, the wife of Cornelius Vanderbilt II, dressed in her boudoir on the second floor overlooking Fifth Avenue and awaited her afternoon guests.

More than two hundred ladies would shortly arrive at her six-storied residence at 1 West 57th Street. With its turreted windows and Gothic tracery, the recently enlarged red brick and limestone home resembled a French Renaissance château. Protected by a towering wrought iron fence encircling the property, it boasted 130 rooms, including Louis XV– and Louis XVI–style salons, a dining room adorned with works of art, and a Moorish-inspired smoking room. At the heart of this urban palace was the most magnificent room of all—the seventy-five-by-fifty-foot Louis XV–style ballroom, resplendent with glittering mirrors, giltwood *boiserie*, and mural paintings. Stretching an entire city block, it was the largest private home ever built in New York City.

From the housekeeper, butler, and chef to parlor maids, housemen, and footmen, the more than thirty members of staff required to run the Vanderbilt's urban palace were engaged in a well-orchestrated preparation. Chairs were being placed in the grand ballroom, hundreds of porcelain cups, saucers, silver teaspoons, and linen napkins were carefully arranged, and an "elaborate collation" of sweets and savories was crafted—standard fare for a home designed for entertaining. However, on this day, there was an additional, unique task at hand.

Staff carefully opened the variety of boxes and bundles sent by guests in the days leading up to the event, revealing an assortment of items that included "quantities of rare china and old silver." These objects, as described in *The New York Times*'s enthusiastic two-day coverage of the occasion, were artfully arranged to create a private exhibition of the prized "relics" of New York's elite. These treasured items were displayed around Mrs. Vanderbilt's own venerable silver teapot, situated on a brass-mounted mahogany table, forming an evocative tableau of "New Netherland Days."

Above the flurry of activity on the main level, the upper floors of the mansion, with their bedrooms, dressing rooms, sitting rooms, nurseries, and guest chambers, remained notably still. Alice was the only Vanderbilt family member in residence. The corridors were hushed, absent even the sounds of her nine-year-old daughter, Gladys, their youngest child. Alice had returned to New York from Washington, D.C. without her family.

Widely reported in the press, her husband, Cornelius Vanderbilt II—one of America's foremost railroad magnates—had recently suffered a series of debilitating strokes beginning in the summer of 1896. Distressed by the noise of the city, he had ordered the streets surrounding their home to be covered with a layer of shredded tanbark to muffle the clamor of traffic. Eventually, the Vanderbilts temporarily traded the din of New York for the quieter environs of the nation's capital, renting a house in Washington D.C. near the White House for Cornelius's recuperation during the winter season of 1897.

Unwilling to miss her engagement in New York and optimistic about her husband's recovery, the tireless matriarch rushed back to Manhattan for her planned social event. Petite yet commanding, Alice was a dignified and tenacious leader of the Vanderbilt family. Born the daughter of a prominent lawyer, she transformed herself into the reigning empress of Fifth Avenue, orchestrating a successful campaign to elevate her husband's family into the upper echelons of New York and Newport society, a position she maintained with unwavering resolve.

Cornelius, as well as being one of New York's most powerful businessmen, was one of its most prominent philanthropists, supporting organizations and fulfilling his duty as a member of several boards including one of the most elite institutions of New York and vessels of the world's finest art—the Metropolitan Museum of Art, known as "The Met."

The Met had grown exponentially since its founding in 1870, having moved from several more modest temporary quarters to its latest incarnation on Fifth Avenue in 1880—a massive neoclassical edifice in New York's Central Park near 80th Street. By 1897, with its burgeoning collection of masterpieces, from a Roman sarcophagus and Cypriot sculptures to French porcelain and its (and America's) first Vermeer, the Met Board was populated by Alice's husband Cornelius as well as his fellow New York cultural leaders, including the financier J. Pierpont Morgan. Although the Metropolitan Museum of Art had received financial contributions, donations, and loans of art from many women since its founding, it did not elect its first female trustee until 1939. In 1941, Gertrude Vanderbilt Whitney—Alice's eldest daughter—was invited to join this exclusive group. However, committed to her own institution, the Whitney Museum of American Art, Gertrude declined the offer.

Now, nearly fifty years earlier, young Gertrude Vanderbilt joined her mother Alice as the liveried footmen of the Vanderbilt residence swung open its massive twenty-foot-high wrought iron gates to welcome a group of women. Together with Alice, they were founding a public museum. Alice had been invited to join one of New York's newest and most exclusive organizations, The National Society of Colonial Dames in the State of New York, formed in 1893.

Even in the late 1880s, before the society's official founding, these women envisioned a restored historic mansion that would feature exhibitions illustrating and exploring early American and New York history, including its Dutch beginnings. They imagined a museum that would be financed, managed, and curated entirely by women. At a time when women couldn't vote and were excluded from most institutional boards, including the Metropolitan Museum of Art, they created their own "Historical Museum"—a space where they could lead, have their contributions valued, and learn from one another.

Taking no credit for themselves, they named the museum in honor of the Dutch family that had lived there for nearly two centuries. The Van Cortlandt Mansion was reborn as the Van Cortlandt House Museum.

The horse-drawn carriages, manned by grooms and footmen, paused beneath the limestone porte cochère to discharge their elegantly dressed female passengers. Alice's guest list included not only formidable members of New York's social elite, fluent in the nuances of polite etiquette, but also women well-versed in the art of collecting and museum curation. Along with their shared membership in the Colonial Dames, many of these women were also united by another common connection: The Metropolitan Museum of Art.

Among the guests were wives and daughters of the Metropolitan Museum of Art's most influential trustees, including Mrs. J. Pierpont Morgan (Frances Tracy Morgan) and her daughter, Louisa Pierpont Morgan. Others were married to prominent donors, such as Emma Baker Kennedy, whose husband, John Stewart Kennedy, had recently gifted Emanuel Leutze's *Washington Crossing the Delaware* (1851)—now one of America's most iconic historical paintings—and Mary Stillman Harkness, whose husband, Edward Stephen Harkness, a major benefactor of the Met's Egyptian collection, would later provide the museum with the turquoise-blue Egyptian ceramic hippopotamus, affectionately known as "William" and considered the Met's unofficial mascot.

Several women were silent partners in collecting, such as Olivia James Hoe, a bibliophile whom *The New York Times* described as the "intimate advisor" to her husband Robert Hoe, a founder of the Met and a leading figure in America's preeminent books and manuscripts society, the Grolier Club. Others, however, were bold collectors in their own right, making their mark by leaving legacies under their own names. One such figure was Mary Elizabeth Adams Brown, wife of Met Board Treasurer John Crosby Brown, who stunned the Board in 1889 by announcing the donation of her collection, which would eventually include more than 3,600 musical instruments.

As the guests progressed from the entryway, they were greeted by Alice in the Grand Salon before continuing to the Ballroom—one of the most opulent rooms ever created in New York. Reflecting the current fashion for historicist décors among her peers, the Ballroom's design by the Paris decorator Gilbert Cuel was directly inspired by the eighteenth-century Parisian interior of the Galerie Dorée (The Golden Gallery) of the Hôtel de Toulouse. Beneath its painted ceiling with giltwood *boiseries*, however, a very different kind of historic recreation awaited: a table set in the style of seventeenth-century New Amsterdam, adorned with silver, glass, pewter, and the striking blue and white of Chinese porcelain and Dutch Delftware.

Standing before the distinguished group, fellow society member Harriet Mumford Campbell delivered a lecture on "table furnishings and customs" in seventeenth-century New Amsterdam, illustrated by the meticulously arranged table before them. Harriet's father, Douglas Campbell, was the author of *The Puritan in Holland, England, and America*, published in 1892. Hailed by *The New York Times* as "An Epoch-Making Work," it explored the Dutch influence on America's development.

Transporting her audience to a seventeenth-century home at the southern tip of Manhattan, Harriet painted a picture of the customs and decorative arts that shaped New York's early history. She quoted Adriaen van der Donck's 1656 account of New Netherland, where "the colonist found a fruitful country" abundant with "plenty of game," "waters full of fish and oysters," and where "some persons prepare delicate dishes from the water terrapins." She also underscored the prominence of ceramics—both porcelain and earthenware—frequently listed in the household inventories of New Amsterdam, revealing the material culture that defined everyday life in the Dutch colony.

With newly available primary documents—including the 1896 Colonial Dames' commissioned translations of over three thousand Dutch wills and the recently uncovered *Minutes of the Orphan Court of New Amsterdam* in the State Library of Albany—Harriet and other American historians had an abundance of fresh research material. These records enabled them to make more accurate inferences about a past that had often been distorted by legend and assumption.

Harriet concluded her talk with a vivid depiction of how objects played a role in the celebrations, teas, and weddings of early New Amsterdam. She painted a scene of tables laden with "apple pies, preserved peaches and pears, always olekocks," accompanied by tea served in delicate porcelain cups and festive drinks poured from ornately decorated punch bowls. To Harriet, the early residents of New Amsterdam, much like the wealthy women gathered before her in the opulent grandeur of Gilded Age New York, had a shared appreciation for "the good things of life."

The women gathered in the ballroom were in high spirits. The unveiling of the Van Cortlandt House Museum, scheduled for May 27, 1897, to coincide with the 250th anniversary of Director-General Peter Stuyvesant's arrival in New Amsterdam, was fast approaching. However, the preparations had been anything but easy, and with just three months remaining, the completion of the work was coming down to the wire.

For the past year, the women had persevered in "what seemed an almost hopeless task of getting the mansion renovated, swept, and garnished." The three-story fieldstone mansion, which they received in 1896, had suffered years of neglect. Among its unlikely most recent tenants was the City's Engineer of Construction, who transformed its stately rooms into an office for the Engineer Corps during the development of the park's Parade Ground. Even the New York National Guard had laid claim to the mansion, requesting the use of its chambers as makeshift dressing rooms for their cavalry. The once-grand eighteenth-century house had been repeatedly commandeered and its elegant salons and chambers repurposed, leaving it "standing gaunt, bare, despoiled, for some years."

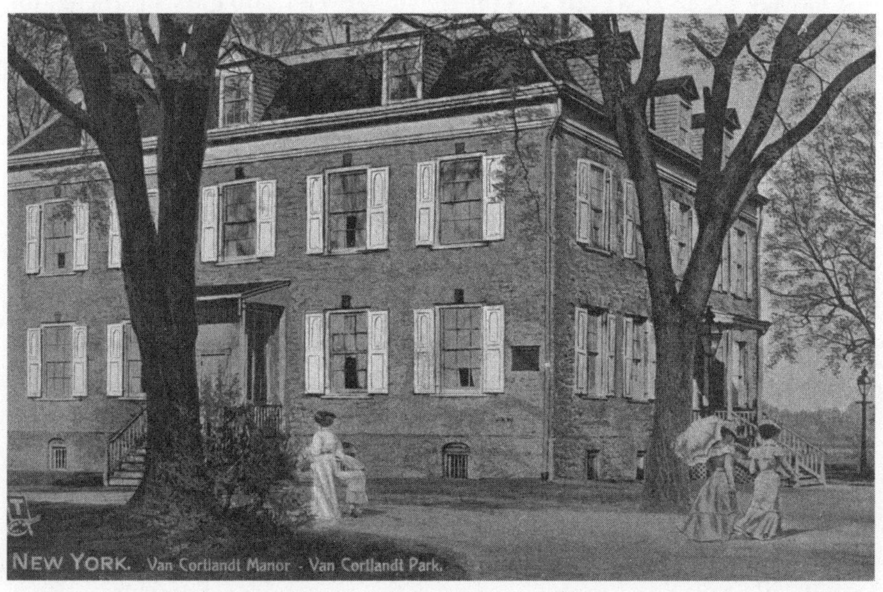

Photomechanical print, ca. 1908, *Van Cortlandt Manor, Van Cortlandt Park, N.Y.*, by Raphael Tuck & Sons, showcases the newly restored mansion with female visitors. Author's collection.

Reclaiming the building and its surrounding land, as well as preparing for their first public exhibition, the women oversaw everything from clearing brush and tree limbs to hiring custodians and security guards, all while procuring gifts and loans of objects for display. Despite the challenges and with little time to spare, the work was completed. The long journey—from an initial vision, lobbying the state legislature, and restoring the house to curating their first exhibition—was finally coming to fruition. Their newly installed Dutch door, donated by the New York Parks Commission, was ready "to be flung wide in welcome."

On May 27, 1897, a "fair and breezy" day, over 1,200 guests gathered for the official opening of New York City's newest destination, the Van Cortlandt House Museum. Flags and banners adorned the covered doorway, and the Seventh Regiment Band filled the air with lively brass arrangements. Among the attendees who arrived in private railroad cars was New York City Mayor William L. Strong. Standing on the top front step with the president of the Board of Park Commissioners Samuel McMillan, the mayor ceremonially handed the keys to Justine Townsend.

The moment was witnessed by Alice Morse Earle and her fellow members, including seventy-six-year-old Elizabeth Gillespie, who had traveled from Philadelphia to stand by Justine's side. Together, they listened as New York State Lieutenant Governor Timothy Lester Woodruff addressed the gathered crowd, marking the triumphant debut of the city's newest museum.

Newspapers from New York to Los Angeles celebrated the launch of the Van Cortlandt House Museum, a "historic museum" nestled in the far reaches of the Bronx, and applauded the women's remarkable efforts. "Although the smallest free museum in the city, it is by far one of the most interesting," proclaimed *The New York Times*.

There was something in the air that spring in New York. In a seemingly inspirational confluence, sisters Eleanor and Sarah Hewitt officially inaugurated their museum of decorative arts, the Cooper Union Museum for the Arts of Decoration (now the Cooper Hewitt Museum), just six days earlier on Friday, May 21, 1897.

At opposite ends of the city—one in a small house in the upper Bronx, the other in the Cooper Union building on the Lower East Side—these

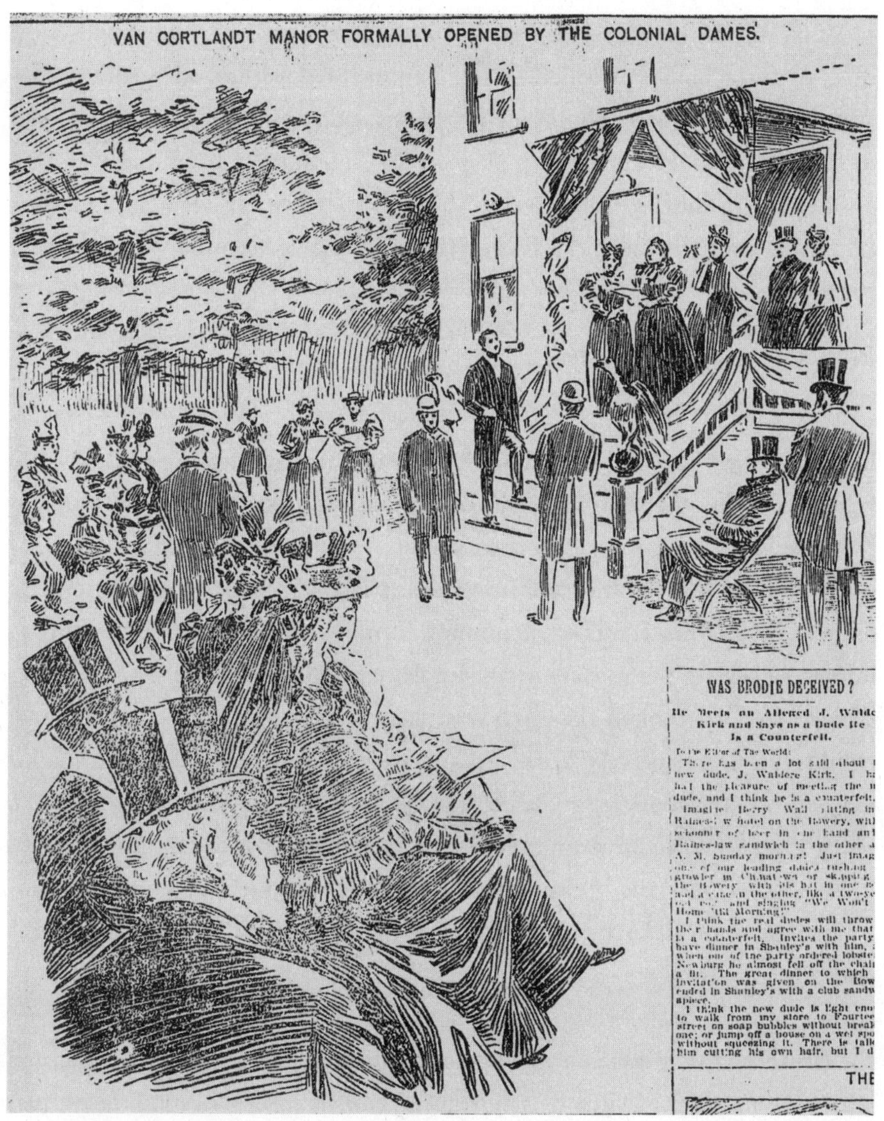

VAN CORTLANDT MANOR FORMALLY OPENED BY THE COLONIAL DAMES.

WAS BRODIE DECEIVED?

He Meets an Alleged J. Walde
Kirk and Says as a Dude He
Is a Counterfeit.

To the Editor of The World:
There has been a lot said about
new dude, J. Waldere Kirk. I h
had the pleasure of meeting the
dude, and I think he is a counterfeit.
Imagine Berry Wall sitting in
Raines-law hotel on the Bowery, wit
schooner of beer in one hand an
Raines-law sandwich in the other
A. M. Sunday morning! Just imag
one of our leading dudes [illegible]
growler in Chinatown or skipping
the Bowery with his hat in one
and a [illegible] in the other, like a two-ye
[illegible] and singing "We Won't
Home 'till Morning!"
I think the real dudes will throw
their hands and agree with me that
is a counterfeit. Invites the party
have dinner in Shanley's with him,
when one of the party ordered lobste
Newburg he almost fell off the chai
a fit. The great dinner to which
invitation was given on the Bow
ended in Shanley's with a club sandw
apiece.
I think the new dude is light eno
to walk from my store to Fourtee
street on soap bubbles without break
one; or jump off a house on a wet sp
without squeezing it. There is tal
him cutting his own hair, but I d

THE

Justine Townsend delivers the opening address from the mansion's south entrance at the Van Cortlandt House Museum's public debut on May 27, 1897, as captured by *The World* newspaper illustrator.

two institutions became the first female-led museums in the United States, reshaping the cultural landscape for generations to come.

What would the public find to view at the Van Cortlandt House Museum, this "treasure house" extolled by the lieutenant governor on opening day? While the press eagerly highlighted objects such as "Aaron Burr's pistols used to shoot Alexander Hamilton," "a piece of Martha Washington's wedding dress," and "a snuffbox of Peter Stuyvesant" displayed in wooden and glass exhibition cases, the most captivating relic might have been the Van Cortlandt Mansion itself.

Stepping through the Dutch door into the spacious entrance hall, visitors were greeted by the soaring height of a broad staircase, brightly illuminated by large windows spanning all three floors. A testament to the family's social status and wealth, the staircase stood as a striking architectural feature to be enjoyed by its inhabitants—uncommon in more modest eighteenth-century homes, where staircases were often simple, practical conduits.

Two parlors flanked the entryway, each representing the dual cultural influences in early New York. To the east, the formal salon showcased exceptional Georgian design, featuring an elaborately carved rococo fireplace and a finely detailed overmantel circa 1760, attributed to two anonymous New York carvers, likely trained as apprentices or journeymen in London. This room would have hosted the family's most festive and significant gatherings.

Across the hall, the west parlor presented a less formal contrast, showcasing the family's Dutch heritage. At the heart of the room was a fireplace framed with blue-and-white Dutch tiles illustrating biblical scenes. Beyond their visual appeal, these tiles also served as a source of moral instruction for the family as they gathered by the fire.

The Van Cortlandt House Museum comprised seven rooms open to the public, including bedrooms and a former dining room repurposed as a space for temporary exhibitions. In its early days, the fledgling museum heavily relied on temporary displays curated by what the women referred to as their "Relic and Loan Committee." Drawing inspiration from practices such as those used by Elizabeth Gillespie and the Philadelphia Centennial's Women's Executive Committee in 1876, they sent out appeals to society members, requesting "loans of furniture, pictures, curios of all kinds, illustrative of the Colonial period."

Coordinating the museum's exhibitions from their elegant city residences, the committee gathered tables, chairs, silver, and Delftware "brought forth from many an old attic and secret storeroom." These items were carefully transported by carriage to the Van Cortlandt House Museum, where they were artfully arranged for display. However, as each season passed and the loaned items were returned to their owners, the urgent need for new objects to exhibit arose once again.

The Relic and Loan Committee devised an approach that was both irresistible and timely, satisfying the demand for fresh objects while appealing to the conscience of Gilded Age donors. In an era when many women of society hastily departed their New York mansions by spring for Europe or summer retreats—including Alice Vanderbilt, who had recently completed The Breakers in Newport, Rhode Island, in 1895—the committee issued a compelling appeal. They suggested,

> It could be wished that works might occasionally be loaned for a season when the owners are absent. Such paintings would be as safe hung at Van Cortlandt as in the usual storage places, and would prove invaluable object lessons to the crowds of sightseers . . .

The approach proved effective. Soon, "almost every member's household has contributed something from its treasured heirlooms," including "specimens of beautiful old china." By aligning the museum's needs with the practicality and prestige of showcasing heirlooms during the owners' absence, the Committee ensured a steady stream of artifacts for public display.

From the Van Cortlandt House Museum's opening day, "eager and curious" New Yorkers flocked to explore the city's newest museum. Arriving by train

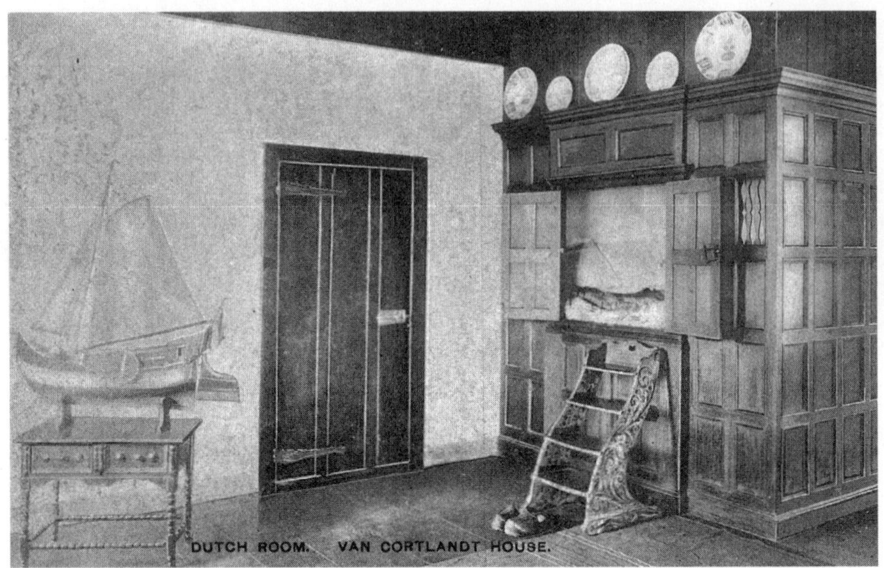

Photomechanical print, ca. 1918, *Dutch Room, Van Cortlandt House Museum*, depicts a former second-floor bedchamber transformed to evoke a seventeenth-century New Amsterdam dwelling. Author's collection.

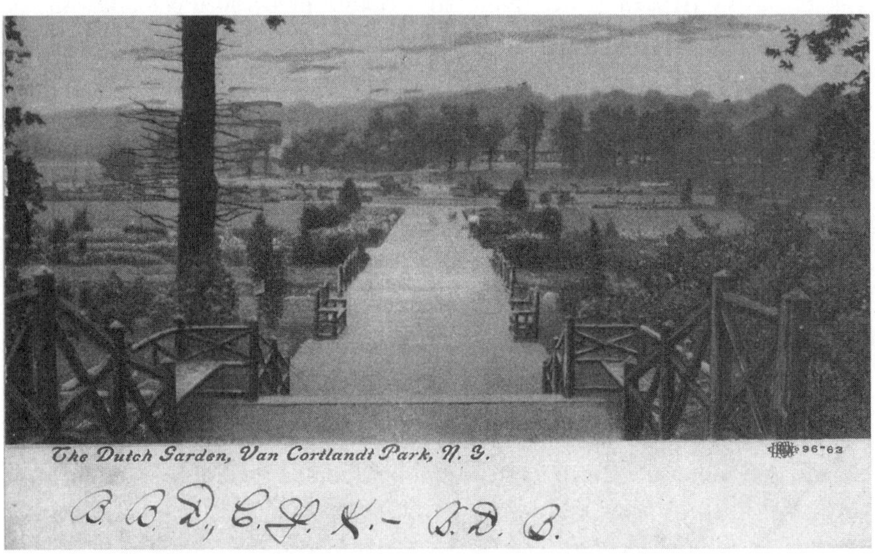

Photomechanical print, 1909, *The Dutch Garden, Van Cortlandt Park, N.Y.*, captures the expansive view from the terraced steps beside the Van Cortlandt House Museum, showcasing Samuel Parsons Jr.'s Baroque-inspired design with symmetrical parterres and long gravel paths. Author's collection.

and the newly popular bicycle, as many as five thousand visitors came daily during the first summer of 1897, overwhelming the fledgling operation. The demand was so great that it became, as one account described, "so difficult was it for the one police officer and the Society's custodian to watch the throngs and see that no damage was done." By July, the constant crush of visitors necessitated the installation of iron barriers at the doorways to all the rooms.

The Van Cortlandt House Museum quickly evolved into a significant public destination. By 1903, the women proudly reported, "The hopes of the Society, seven years ago, when they accepted the charge, have come to fruition, for we are supporting a public museum, in its way truly a place of education and relaxation for the public, as the Metropolitan Museum or that of Natural History."

By 1903, visitors to the Van Cortlandt House Museum could experience a newly added feature adjacent to the grounds—a picturesque retreat where they could relax on rustic benches near newly dug canals or stroll along freshly laid gravel paths. This serene setting, accessed via a terraced brick staircase, was known as the Dutch Garden.

Far from a small or informal planting, the garden spanned five acres of Van Cortlandt Park. Created from drained marshland, its formal axial design was centered around a large fountain, with radiating gravel paths and grass-filled parterres framed by narrow borders showcasing topiary cones, annuals, and bulbs, including over one hundred thousand tulips planted each spring.

The Dutch Garden was designed by Samuel Parsons Jr., a horticulturalist and the city's newly appointed landscape architect, who served the New York Department of Parks for thirty years alongside Calvert Vaux. Progress had been slow, but the "Gardens and Park Committee," led by figures such as Justine Van Rensselaer, Frances Tracy Morgan, and Alice Morse Earle, together with the popular gardening writer Helena Rutherfurd Ely, had tirelessly advocated for its completion since 1896.

Their vision was a nostalgic homage to the Dutch heritage of New York, evoking romanticized images of the past: "Loitering over the bridges, we can see in our mind's eye, the pretty Juffrouw and the young Mynheer may see themselves or each other reflected in the clear waters."

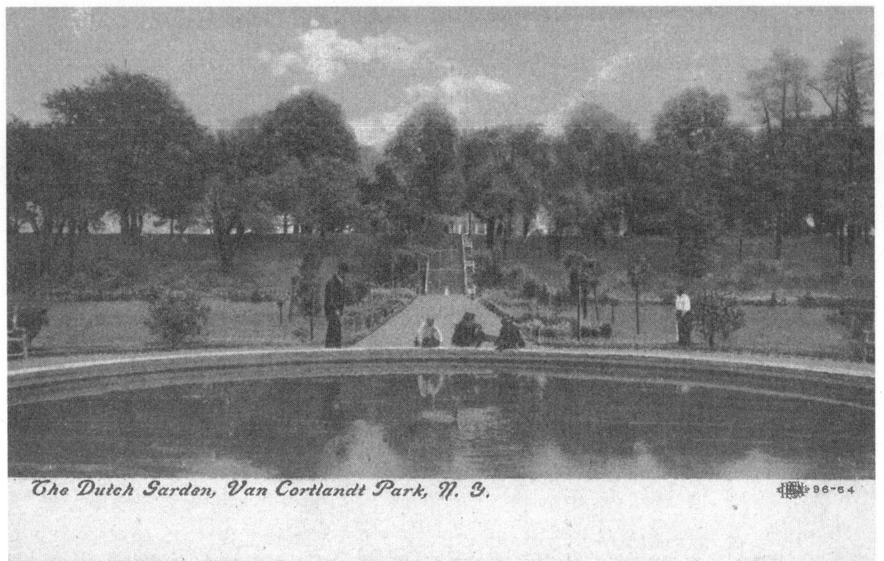

Photomechanical print, circa 1910, *The Dutch Garden, Van Cortlandt Park, N.Y.*, highlights the central fountain, reflecting the formal seventeenth-century Dutch aesthetic in contrast to Central Park's naturalistic design. Author's collection.

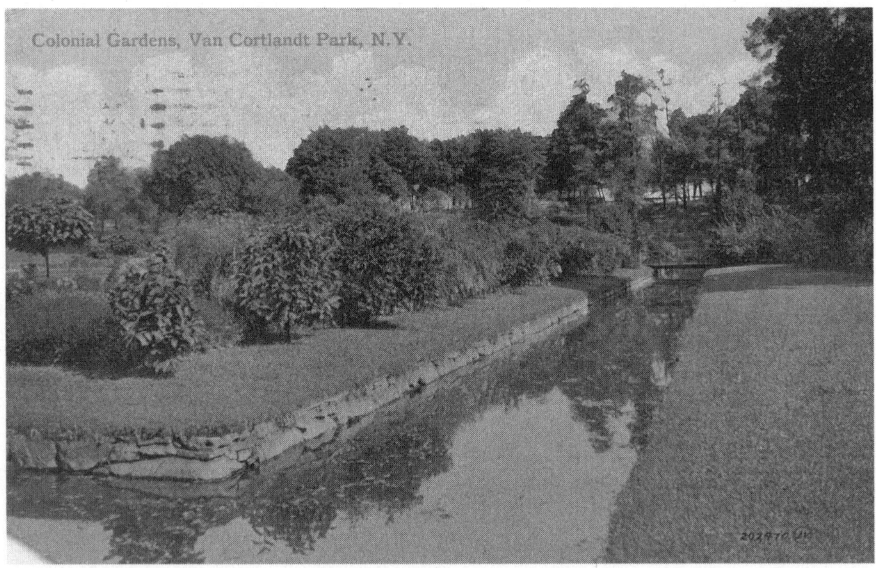

Photomechanical print, ca. 1916, *Colonial Gardens, Van Cortlandt Park, N.Y.*, features the garden's extensive Dutch-inspired stone-lined canals and rustic bridges. Author's collection.

A romanticized fascination with Dutch culture was not confined to New Yorkers. Across the United States, even Americans with no Dutch ancestry were swept up in a "Holland Mania," a revisionist history movement that flourished from 1880 to 1920. Dutch influence could be found permeating nearly every aspect of American life, from popular culture and literature to fashion, design, and architecture.

As New York's *The Journal* observed in 1896, "the Dutch fad has been largely circulated in the fashionable world by collections of windmill china and Delftware by the closetful, resurrections of pewter mugs and tankards from family garrets, and the giving of Dutch luncheons." This enthusiasm extended beyond décor, influencing consumer goods as brands like Old Dutch Cleanser (introduced in 1905) and Dutch Boy Paints (appearing by 1907) capitalized on the craze. Architecture, too, reflected this nostalgia, with the "Dutch-Colonial style"—characterized by distinctive gambrel roofs and overhanging eaves—growing in popularity in American home design between 1910 and 1930.

At the same time, Gilded Age collectors eagerly pursued Dutch Old Master paintings, particularly the works of Delft artist Johannes Vermeer, whose work was experiencing a resurgence in appreciation. This widespread admiration for all things Dutch was more than just an aesthetic preference; it reflected a deeper American interest in exploring and defining its own national identity. As visitors strolled along the newly built canals of Van Cortlandt Park, *The Ladies' Home Journal* editor Edward Bok boldly challenged America's long-standing English influences, declaring in his 1903 article that the Netherlands was "The Mother of America."

Riding the wave of America's fascination with all things Dutch and eager to assert its position as the preeminent United States city, New York City began preparations in 1905 for an event on a scale its citizens had never experienced: The Hudson–Fulton Celebration. Scheduled for 1909, it would commemorate two significant anniversaries—the tercentennial of Henry Hudson's historic voyage for the Dutch East India Company, which paved the way for the founding of New Amsterdam, and the centennial of Robert Fulton's successful application of the steamboat on the Hudson River.

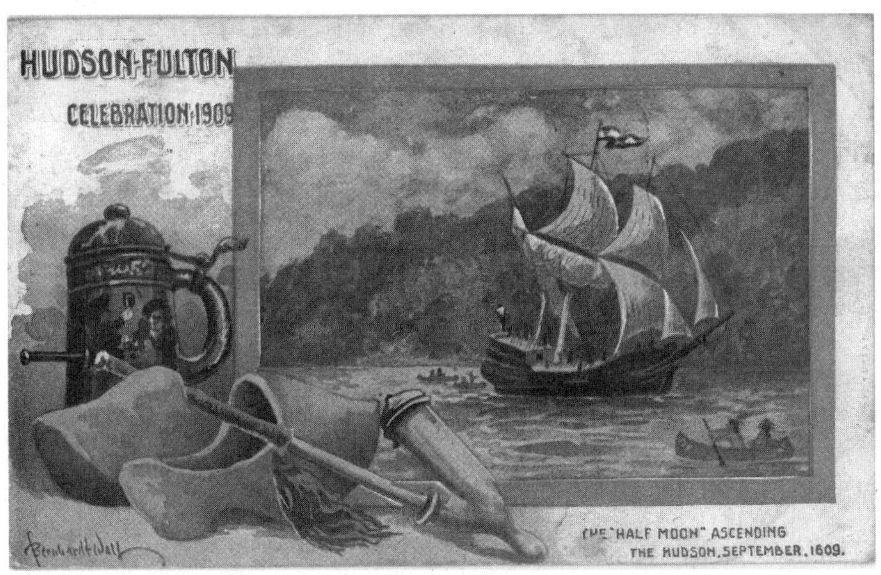

Hudson-Fulton Celebration 1909, a photomechanical print, depicts "The Half Moon" ascending the Hudson River in 1609, with popular references to Dutch culture, including clay pipes, wooden shoes, and Delftware. Author's collection.

Inspired by the era's grand international expositions, such as the 1893 Chicago World's Fair, the Hudson–Fulton Celebration was designed to entertain, awe, and educate on an impressive scale. Over two weeks, a nonstop schedule of festivities and events stretched from New York City up the Hudson River, covering more than 150 miles from Staten Island to Troy. Orchestrated by a committee of prominent New Yorkers, including J. Pierpont Morgan and Andrew Carnegie—husbands of Colonial Dames—the celebration featured free exhibitions at the city's leading museums, institutions, and societies, including the Metropolitan Museum of Art, the New-York Historical Society, and the Museum of Natural History.

Not wanting to be left out of the Hudson–Fulton extravaganza, the women of the Van Cortlandt House Museum submitted an application in 1908 to participate as one of the exhibiting organizations. With less than a year to prepare, they quickly devised a strategy to amass loaned objects, meeting at the residence of Mary Clark Thompson, chairman of the Van Cortlandt House Museum.

Mary Clark Thompson, a philanthropist and collector, was the daughter of a New York governor and the widow of Frederick F. Thompson, cofounder of the First National Bank of New York. Her opulent Madison Avenue home housed her extensive collection of Chinese ceramics, which she would later donate to the Metropolitan Museum of Art. More recently, in 1903, she had provided the funds for the Met to acquire over one hundred Roman sculptures, the "Giustiniani Marbles," in their pursuit to expand their Greek and Roman galleries.

Preparing for their exhibition at the Van Cortlandt House Museum, the Committee initially considered displays that would include "Costumes of the Colonial Period—early Dutch preferred—these to be shown on manikins; a Collection of Colonial Pewter; portraits or old prints of Colonial Governors of New York dating from 1623; and China, especially Dutch Delft." However, their ambitions extended beyond curating their own exhibition in the Bronx. The Committee also sought to collaborate with and assist other museums in organizing their displays, contributing to a broader celebration of American heritage and culture.

It is unclear when or how the women of the Van Cortlandt House Museum approached the Metropolitan Museum of Art to propose a loan of paintings and silver for its exhibition of early American fine and decorative arts, *The Hudson–Fulton Exhibition of American Industrial Arts*. However, shortly after the initial meeting at Mary Thompson's home, they began securing "portraits of distinguished painters, illustrating the Colonial Period and of great historical value; also a collection of Colonial silver fully representing the work of English and American Colonial silversmiths of the seventeenth and eighteenth centuries" for the Met's curators.

This exhibition, the first of its kind in America, positioned American decorative arts as a serious field of study, with the Met establishing itself as the leader in the movement. It also marked a turning point for the nascent Van Cortlandt House Museum, influencing its trajectory and elevating its role both in the curatorial communities as well as the public eye.

When the Hudson–Fulton Celebration officially began on September 9, 1909, the two weeks of jaw-dropping spectacles, monumental constructions, parades, and parties exceeded all expectations. The skies over New York blazed with nightly firework displays, and glittering electric lights illuminated bridges and skyscrapers. New Yorkers were awestruck as they witnessed their first airplane flight, with Wilbur Wright piloting a biplane around the Statue of Liberty and up the Hudson River to Grant's Tomb.

Marine parades filled the Hudson and East rivers, showcasing vessels ranging from a reproduction of Henry Hudson's *Halve Maen* (*Half Moon*) to the ill-fated RMS *Lusitania*. On land, spectators thronged the streets to marvel at a six-mile-long parade of "moving tableaux"—a carnival of pageant floats depicting everything from folk tales to pivotal moments in the city's and state's history. Among these papier-mâché confections were scenes such as Peter Minuit's "purchase" of Manhattan, a gabled Dutch house complete with a vegetable garden and a family milking a cow, and a vignette of New Amsterdam residents smoking pipes as they gathered on Bowling Green beneath a towering twenty-foot-high windmill.

Meanwhile, crowds streamed up to the Bronx via trains, trolleys, and the newly constructed elevated subway to visit the Van Cortlandt House Museum.

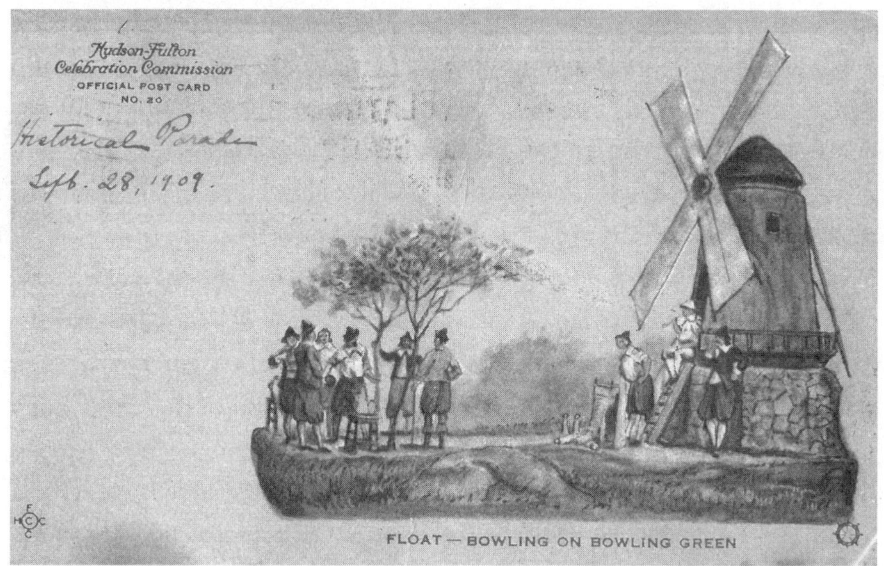

Hudson-Fulton Celebration Commission post card No. 20, 1909, showcases the "Bowling on Bowling Green" float, a highlight of the Historical Parade, which traveled through Manhattan and Brooklyn. Author's collection.

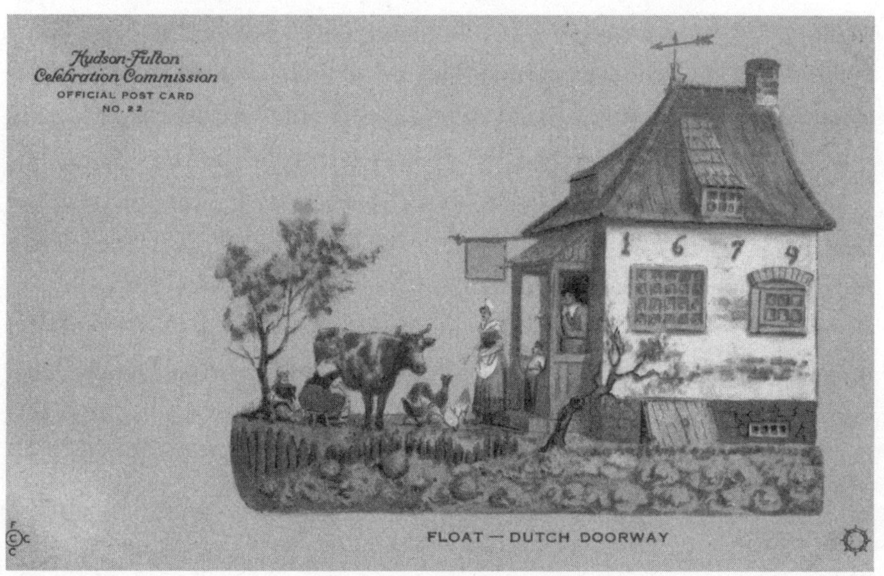

Hudson-Fulton Celebration Commission post card No. 22, 1909, illustrates a float featuring a seventeenth-century home in New Amsterdam, including its "Dutch Doorway." Author's collection.

Each day from 10:00 A.M. to 5:00 P.M., visitors formed long, winding queues down the park's paths. The waiting times grew lengthy as thousands arrived daily to view over six hundred objects displayed in the museum's intimate quarters of less than three thousand square feet. Packed tightly into the small, seven-room space, visitors marveled at exhibitions detailed in the accompanying catalog, which showcased a wide array of fine and decorative arts, from "Colonial Maps" and "Colonial Governors, Mayors, Autographs and Letters" to "The Pewterer's Crafte" and displays on the evolution of "The Chair and the Mirror." Despite the challenging conditions, the museum's popularity soared, with over 300,000 visitors passing through its Dutch door by the end of 1909.

In a grainy photograph in the 1909 exhibition catalog, a small Dutch cabinet is seen, including a first small selection of loaned Dutch Delftware. The image isn't clear but what appears to be a selection of Delftware plates, bowls, and figures of men on horseback sit behind the glass doors of this small wall-mounted case. From this modest beginning, a Dutch Delftware collection would grow.

At the turn of the nineteenth century, America's perception of decorative arts was evolving, as evidenced by the Metropolitan Museum of Art's highly popular Hudson–Fulton exhibition. Meanwhile, in the Netherlands, attitudes toward Dutch decorative arts, including Delftware, were also beginning to shift. Although Delftware had been featured in exhibitions including the *Internationale Koloniale en Uitvoerhandel Tentoonstelling* (The International Colonial and Export Exhibition) held in Amsterdam in 1883, its presence in the nation's most prominent cultural institutions lagged behind.

By 1909, visitors to the Rijksmuseum in Amsterdam—the national museum of the Netherlands—would have found little or no Dutch Delftware on display amid its grand Gothic and Renaissance-style galleries. While Delftware was widely collected privately throughout the nineteenth century, and the *Gemeentemuseum* (Municipal Museum) in The Hague had recently acquired the Van der Burgh collection of Delftware in 1904, curators at the Rijksmuseum remained unconvinced of its significance.

This began to change in 1916 with the acceptance of the first major donation of Dutch Delftware to the Rijksmuseum: approximately 530 pieces from the collection of John F. Loudon, gifted by his descendants. Now displayed under the same roof as masterpieces including Rembrandt's *The Night Watch* (1642), the blue-and-white ceramics were elevated to the status of works of art. Dutch Delftware had finally arrived as a celebrated national cultural treasure.

Although the Hudson–Fulton Celebration lasted just fourteen days, its cultural impact on New York City was profound, solidifying its status as a major metropolis. The celebration's influence was particularly significant for the nascent Van Cortlandt House Museum, inspiring its members to expand their ambitions. Energized by their success, the women declared: "Let us not forget that we are now upon the list of Museums and must sustain the position we have gained."

When the exhibition concluded and the loaned artworks were returned, the connections forged between the Van Cortlandt House Museum and the Metropolitan Museum of Art deepened. These relationships proved pivotal in shaping the future of the museum. Over the next fifteen years, as Robert de Forest, Henry Watson Kent, and curator R. T. Haines Halsey developed the Met's collection of American decorative arts—culminating in the 1924 opening of its American Wing—they also served on the Van Cortlandt House Museum's newly appointed Advisory Committee. The committee expanded to include notable figures such as Luke Vincent Lockwood, the pioneering furniture scholar and former Metropolitan Museum of Art adviser; Grosvenor Atterbury, the prominent architect; Emily Chadbourne, the distinguished collector who later bequeathed over two thousand works to the Art Institute of Chicago; and Henry Sleeper, the influential interior decorator. The Met's influence extended beyond expertise. From a set of wood-mounted vitrines to "artistic and appropriate labels for exhibits, specially designed by Merrymount Press," provided by Henry Kent, the Met supported the Van Cortlandt House Museum's exhibitions materially and curatorially. By 1912, the wives of the Met American Wing founders and notable collectors themselves Emily Lockwood de Forest, Effie Underhill Halsey, and Alice Burrell Lockwood all joined the Van Cortlandt House Museum's efforts, further enhancing its scope.

By 1910, the women of the Van Cortlandt House Museum recognized the need for a more deliberate approach to building their collection. "The Relic and

Loan Committee feel that the past year has been most valuable and instructive," they stated. "Its best asset has been a lesson in the need of a definite and intelligent line of action for the furnishing of Van Cortlandt House Museum . . . towards which all loans, gifts, and purchases shall tend."

This new direction was championed by Alice Lockwood, who took the reins as "Chair of Relics and Loans" following the Hudson–Fulton Exhibition. Best known as one of America's premier garden historians and author of *Gardens of Colony and State* (1931), Alice was an astute collector of American native plants but also of its decorative arts. Alice shaped the collection of the Van Cortlandt House Museum with a scientific approach, characterized by classifying styles and periods, adopting a systematic plan in the arrangement of the various rooms. Eschewing relics and temporary loans, she, as also urged by her husband, Luke Vincent Lockwood, stressed the need to seize every opportunity for meaningful acquisitions. As she explained, "Van Cortlandt, he assures us, can now be made a unique museum. Other museums began before classifying was understood . . ."

With growth, however, came the pressing need for funding. "From the small beginnings and the large conceptions of twenty-one years ago, the work has increased so steadily and rapidly that at last it has outstripped the means to carry on." In 1914, three prominent philanthropists—Mary Clark Thompson, Margaret Olivia Slocum Sage (Mrs. Russell Sage), and Helen Deming Sherman Pratt (Mrs. George D. Pratt)—responded to this challenge by creating an endowment to secure the Van Cortlandt House Museum's future.

These women were not only advocates for the arts but also champions of social progress, including women's rights and suffrage. Helen Pratt, in particular, exemplified this commitment. On October 23, 1915, she joined over 25,000 women marching down Fifth Avenue in New York City to demand the right to vote, embodying the determination and progress of the era.

As women across America fought for equality—lecturing, writing, marching, lobbying, and even practicing civil disobedience—the women of the Van Cortlandt House Museum recognized their own contributions to a larger movement. In 1898, shortly after the museum's founding, they reflected on their importance as equal participants in the museum community. One address to the society articulated this sentiment:

> The work of this society, which offers to the public a museum . . . and expert knowledge in many branches, is considered on par with professional work. Van Cortlandt is accepted as a sister museum to the Metropolitan, the Historical Museum, and so on, and the advice or the backing of this Society is asked for daily. We are asked to use our influence in many public ways, too numerous to mention. This means that the standard of our work is recognized as high, and it is the duty of its members to keep it so.

By 1917, New York State granted women the right to vote, becoming one of the first states to do so. This milestone set the stage for the ratification of the Nineteenth Amendment to the United States Constitution in 1920, securing the right to vote for women across the United States. While opportunities for women were growing in the early twentieth century, the art world remained far from inclusive. The field of art dealing, in particular, continued to be a male-dominated domain, where women faced persistent barriers to entry, recognition, and influence.

Yet, behind the scenes, some women quietly made their mark.

Following the Hudson–Fulton Exhibition, the Van Cortlandt House Museum continued to produce thematic exhibitions that were widely promoted in the press to ensure the public's continued interest in returning to the Bronx. Displays ranged from *Huguenot Memorials and Colonial Tea Sets*, 1911 to *Fashions in Pottery Turning in the Colonies of the seventeenth and eighteenth Centuries,* 1912. In 1913 the museum hosted *Portraits, Miniatures, and Silhouettes.* The exhibition, as well as its accompanying newspaper coverage, was organized by Alice Leffingwell Buell Creelman —a woman who would soon prove that the art world's greatest barriers did not always exist where they were most expected.

Described as "pretty and spritely," Alice had once been an artist in Europe, moving in elite cultural circles before marrying the renowned journalist and war correspondent James Creelman. As a member of the Van Cortlandt House Museum Committee, she was recognized for her keen eye for art and seemingly boundless knowledge of American and European collections—a surprising depth of expertise for a stay-at-home mother of three. But what her fellow committee members may not have known was that Alice Creelman was more than an art historian—she was an art dealer operating behind closed doors.

At a time when Roland Knoedler and Joseph Duveen commanded Manhattan's art scene with grand offices and vast inventories, Alice worked discreetly from her duplex apartment on East 66th Street. She entered trade out of necessity after the death of her husband in 1915 to support herself and her children. What began as survival quickly became something more—she became an indispensable conduit for the transatlantic sale of European masterpieces to America's wealthiest collectors.

Alice tirelessly lobbied the nation's most powerful collectors, offering them works by Donatello, Fragonard, Giorgione, Rubens, Tiepolo, and Vigée-Lebrun. She worked outside the established channels, using her knowledge, connections, and discretion to broker major deals.

In 1915, after a deal with Charles Lang Freer fell through—where Alice had offered him paintings, silver gilt plates, and "blue vases" from James McNeill Whistler's *Peacock Room*—she pivoted to sell Henry Clay Frick several significant pieces. These included Whistler's *Symphony in Flesh Color and Pink: Portrait of Mrs. Frances Leyland* (1871–74), Titian's *Portrait of a Man in a Red Cap* (c. 1510), and Hans Holbein the Younger's *Thomas Cromwell* (1532–33), sourced from Sir Hugh Lane. The transaction earned Alice a substantial commission of $26,000.

Yet, despite her successes, Alice's role as an art dealer remained largely invisible—perhaps by her own design. Her correspondence lay tucked away in museum archives, her involvement in transactions left unacknowledged by the prominent dealers of the day. But while Alice Creelman remained in the shadows of the art market, her influence extended beyond it. Throughout the 1930s, she dedicated her spare time to curating exhibitions at the Van Cortlandt House Museum. She may not have had a gallery bearing her name, but through the masterpieces she placed in Frick's collection and the exhibitions she curated, she quietly shaped the cultural landscape of twentieth-century New York.

By the late 1920s, the remnants of New York's Gilded Age were vanishing. The city razed Fifth Avenue palaces, including Alice Vanderbilt's home in 1927. A commercial structure, including the new department store Bergdorf Goodman, was quickly built in its place.

Facing their own changes, the women of the Van Cortlandt House Museum acknowledged the shifting landscape: "We have grown so large that we can no longer meet in the drawing rooms of our members. The drawing rooms themselves are disappearing."

Determined to establish a lasting presence, The National Society of Colonial Dames in the State of New York commissioned architect Richard Henry Dana Jr. to design a four-story headquarters on East 71st Street modeled after an eighteenth-century townhouse. When the cornerstone was laid in 1930, the nation was grappling with the Great Depression, yet this economic crisis paradoxically became a period of significant cultural creation.

As the Colonial Dames' headquarters took shape, its members' female-led initiatives flourished. Abby Aldrich Rockefeller cofounded the Museum of Modern Art in 1929 and, alongside her husband John D. Rockefeller Jr., established Colonial Williamsburg in 1932. Meanwhile, Mildred Barnes Bliss laid the groundwork for Dumbarton Oaks, her museum and library in Washington, D.C., in 1936.

At the same time, Gertrude Vanderbilt Whitney, daughter of Alice Vanderbilt, sought to expand opportunities for American artists. In 1929, she offered her collection of American art to the Metropolitan Museum of Art, but her proposal was rejected by its director, Edward Robinson. Undeterred, she founded the Whitney Museum of American Art in 1930, cementing her legacy as a pioneering patron of modern American art.

Elizabeth Gould Robinson, the wife of Edward Robinson, spent much of her life deeply engaged in the museum world. She accompanied her husband on his illustrious career, from his archaeological digs in Athens—where she gave birth to their son—to his leadership roles at the Museum of Fine Arts in Boston and the Metropolitan Museum of Art, where he served as its third director for over twenty years. During his tenure, Edward made significant contributions to the Met, including the development of the Pompeii Court and the establishment of The Cloisters. When Edward passed away in 1931, Elizabeth stepped into an unexpected leadership role: Chairman of the Van Cortlandt House Museum.

In 1934, one of her earliest initiatives stemmed from her observation of the growing prominence of Dutch Delftware in the museum's collection. Recognizing the need for a proper display solution, Elizabeth remarked, "As the balance was now so large, it would be better for the museum to own its own cases and no longer be a borrower." Drawing on her experience as the wife of a classical archaeologist, Elizabeth meticulously designed new display cases. She prepared detailed specifications and cost estimates, choosing bronze for its strength, durability and the beautiful patina it develops over time, along with thick plate glass shelves, and locks to ensure the safety of the museum's treasured Delftware. Once the new cases were installed, Elizabeth requested that the Van Cortlandt House Museum's old wood-mounted vitrines be "returned to the Metropolitan Museum and a letter of thanks to be written."

Eager to fill the newly acquired cases with an expanded collection of Dutch Delftware was Exhibition Committee Chairman Florence Bates Carter (Mrs. Russell S. Carter). Florence possessed a remarkable talent for acquiring exceptional pieces of seventeenth- and eighteenth-century ceramics. Her passion for English ceramics would lead to her donation of over 145 pieces to the Metropolitan Museum of Art in 1941, a collection she frequently revisited with pride in the museum's galleries as a testament to her contributions and curatorial achievements.

Described as "a keen and discriminating collector and indefatigable hunter" by the Met, Florence thrived on the thrill of pursuing new ceramic challenges. In her new role at the Van Cortlandt House Museum, she saw an opportunity to refine and elevate the Dutch Delftware collection. Her new goal became curating a selection of seventeenth- and eighteenth-century Delftware distinguished by unique forms, exceptional quality, and pristine condition, with examples from a variety of well-known makers. Casting a wide net, she tapped into an array of sources, including fellow collectors, dealers, and auction houses, to source outstanding pieces.

In early 1941, Florence's ambitions aligned with a monumental opportunity: the dispersal of the vast art collection of William Randolph Hearst.

An American businessman, newspaper publisher, and politician known for creating the nation's largest media company, Hearst Communications, William Randolph Hearst had amassed a vast and sometimes eccentric collection of decorative and fine arts during the 1920s. From Hearst Castle in San Simeon, California, to his Riverside Drive apartment in New York, he filled his numerous residences with treasures ranging from medieval Italian armor and ancient Egyptian stone reliefs to Tiffany lamps and Spanish sixteenth-century reliquaries.

However, the Great Depression forced Hearst into a financial reckoning. On the verge of bankruptcy by 1940, Hearst began liquidating his assets, which included over ten thousand accrued objects. Homes were emptied and his four-story storage warehouse, occupying an entire city block in the Bronx, was cleared. In a marathon sale held at Gimbels department store in Manhattan in 1941, crowds flocked to view and purchase Hearst's vast collection, from Chinese porcelain, silver, furniture, Egyptian antiquities, and Roman objects to guns, frescoes, swords, jewelry, rugs, and flags. Displayed across 80,000 square feet of space, objects were hung on walls, crammed into display cases, and arranged on aisles of tables. The accompanying catalog, nearly an inch thick, became the guide to this overwhelming bazaar.

Among this sea of treasures, Exhibition Committee Chairman Florence Carter spotted the Dutch Delftware. Reflecting Hearst's eclectic taste, the selection included unusual pieces such as a "Persian Blue" jug, a figure of a standing woman and a pair of birdcages. However, Florence's eye was drawn to the fine painting and soft curves of a puzzle jug, simply listed in the catalog as "A Puzzle Blue and White Jug 57-31." Recognizing its craftsmanship, she quickly negotiated the purchase and brought this and other Delftware treasures to the Van Cortlandt House Museum. Opening the bronze cases in the Exhibition Room, she delicately placed the new acquisitions side by side in their new home, adding depth to the museum's growing collection.

But 1941 brought new challenges. With the attack on Pearl Harbor and America's entry into World War II, the third-floor gallery at the new headquarters was transformed into a workspace for preparing bandages for soldiers. The war also brought new threats closer to home. In September 1942, the War Department's Civilian Protection School staged mock air raids and bombings at the Polo Grounds in the Bronx, just a few miles from the Van Cortlandt House Museum. Crowds of over thirty thousand watched as model structures were bombed, burned, and exploded to demonstrate the effects of incendiaries. Alarmed by the potential risks to the delicate ceramics, Florence suggested storing the Delftware safely "away for the air raids."

Despite her concerns, Florence Carter was committed to making art accessible to the public. Her generosity was well documented; in 1941, she donated nearly two hundred works of seventeenth- and eighteenth-century English ceramics, including rare teapots, to the Metropolitan Museum of Art. Yet one exceptional piece—a rare "Persian Blue" Dutch Delftware teapot and cover, c. 1700, by *De Paauw* (The Peacock)—was reserved for the Van Cortlandt House Museum. With its delicate white decoration against a striking blue ground, the teapot stood out as an extraordinarily rare and technically challenging example. Its base bore her collector's label, "Carter," alongside another label from the dealer, M. Keezer & Fils, Amsterdam—a family of antiquarians who had been sourcing fine decorative arts since the nineteenth century.

As New York prepared for war, Florence may not have been aware that, across the Atlantic, another struggle was already unfolding. The Keezer gallery had been seized during the German invasion of the Netherlands in 1940, and the family's property was confiscated. Forced to flee Amsterdam, the gallery's owner, Benjamin Keezer, left behind a lifetime of work. His son, Marcellus B.

Keezer, joined the Dutch resistance and later played a key role in postwar efforts to recover looted cultural treasures. Serving as an officer in the Netherlands Liaison Office for Restitution, he became part of the Monuments, Fine Arts, and Archives program—the Monuments Men and Women—dedicated to safeguarding and restoring Europe's artistic heritage. His work stands as a powerful testament to the enduring importance of cultural preservation, even in the face of global conflict.

Following World War II, the Van Cortlandt House Museum reopened its doors, welcoming back crowds eager to see its now well-developed collection of American and European decorative and fine arts. With treasures ranging from a portrait by Gilbert Stuart to a rare painted *kast* crafted in the Hudson Valley, c. 1700, the museum had firmly established itself as a significant cultural institution. In 1949, *The Magazine ANTIQUES* praised its holdings, describing the museum as home to "a splendid collection of Dutch Delftware."

In September 1959, New York City experienced a renewed wave of Holland Mania with the visit of Princess Beatrix, the future Queen of the Netherlands. Invited to commemorate the 350th anniversary of Henry Hudson's discovery of the Hudson River, the young princess was the centerpiece of a weeklong celebration. The city came to a standstill for her visit, which featured a ticker-tape parade up Broadway, jet flyovers, twenty-one-gun salutes, and a series of luncheons and dinners hosted by city leaders and society members. Among the events was a reception at the Colonial Dames' East 71st Street headquarters, where the princess was honored before embarking on a ceremonial journey retracing Hudson's voyage up the river that bears his name.

Shortly after the princess's visit, a new chapter began for the Van Cortlandt House Museum. In 1960, Julia Parker Wightman stepped into the role of chairing the Art Committee of the Colonial Dames. A self-described "bibliomaniac," Wightman was celebrated for her collection of rare books, which included incunabula, miniature books, and illuminated manuscripts. Though unfamiliar with Dutch Delftware when she assumed her role, she

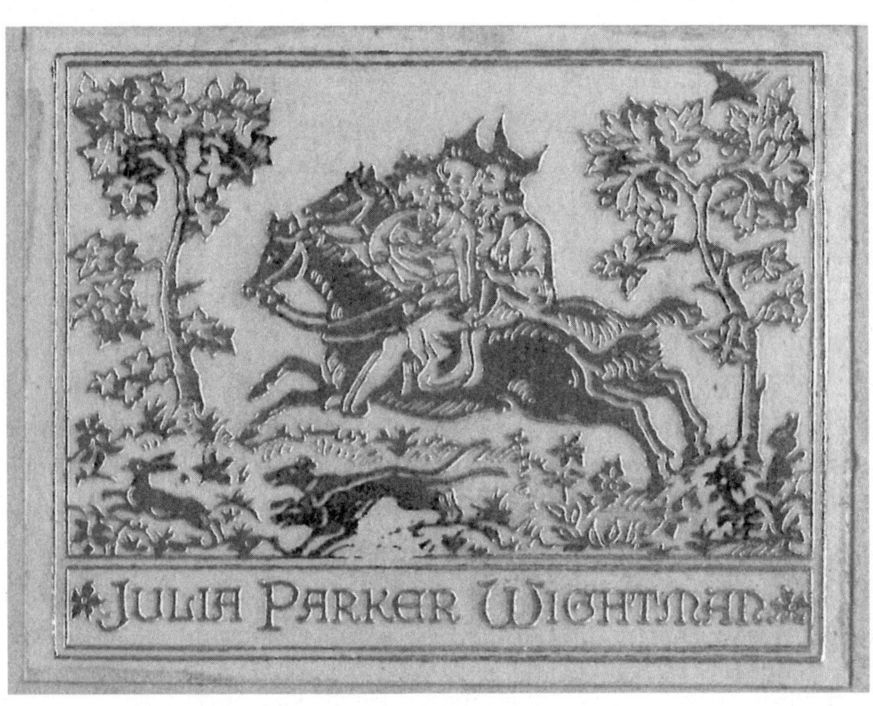

Julia Parker Wightman's bookplate, ca. 1945, an engraving in metallic gold ink, captures her passion for book collecting with hunters on horseback pursuing a rabbit—a fitting tribute to a literary "hunter." Author's collection.

brought with her a collector's sharp eye, a network of deep connections in the art market, and an unparalleled skill for identifying rare and exceptional works of art.

Julia was a member of the elite Hroswitha Club, a prestigious female group in the world of rare books founded in 1944 by collectors and scholars, including Belle da Costa Greene, the first director of the Pierpont Morgan Library. Julia not only later served as the Hroswitha Club's president for two decades but also as a trustee of the Morgan Library for over twenty years. In 1976, she became one of the first female members of the exclusive Grolier Club, the private literary society dedicated to book collecting. Although she never attended college, Julia was driven by a passion for learning. She maintained a bookbindery in her home, where she learned to craft bindings and cases for some of the volumes in her library—a collection she would later bequeath to the Morgan Library.

Under the guidance of Van Cortlandt House Museum's curator Olga Dahlgren, Julia developed a keen interest in Dutch Delftware and became proficient in ceramic studies. When the museum temporarily closed in 1962 for an extensive restoration overseen by Abbott Lowell Cummings, Julia embarked on her own Delftware hunt. Working with auction houses and dealers, she acquired significant pieces, including an eighteenth-century sugar caster from the Parke-Bernet Galleries and a circular butter tub with a cover and stand depicting a child with a birdcage, crafted by The White Star pottery.

When the museum reopened in 1963, the house had been carefully restored, and its collections were more dynamic than ever. Yet Julia faced an increasingly urgent dilemma—one that reflected the broader struggles gripping New York City.

Although the early 1960s were marked by ambitious urban renewal projects, such as Robert Moses's transformation of Lincoln Center and the city's focus on the futuristic 1964 New York World's Fair, symbolized by the gleaming Unisphere, an undercurrent of decline was spreading throughout the boroughs. As the city faced mounting economic challenges, crime incidents began to rise as early as the late 1950s. By 1964, FBI director J. Edgar Hoover famously condemned Central Park as a "hoodlum haven," declaring that "no one dares walk in the daytime."

Van Cortlandt Park, once known for its open meadows, freshwater marshes, and stone-walled forests, was also falling deeper into neglect. Playground equipment sat in disrepair, golf course fairways turned patchy and worn, and once-manicured gardens grew untended. By the late 1960s, the Dutch Garden, with its canals and parterres, would be replaced under Robert Moses's plans to make way for a swimming pool. In the meantime, its flower beds were left overgrown, paths faded into disuse, and its fountain—a remnant of the original design—lay dismantled.

Committee members at the Van Cortlandt House Museum witnessed firsthand New York's worsening conditions, noting that "the lights east of the mansion all the way to the Major Deegan Thruway have not been functioning at night since early spring, and Broadway Maintenance has no plans at present to correct the matter." Streetlights remained unlit for months, leaving the neighborhood in darkness after dusk. As the city edged closer to financial collapse, municipal services, including sanitation and policing, were cut to the bare minimum, further deepening the sense of neglect. By the spring of 1964, the Van Cortlandt House Museum had been vandalized "within and without the house," despite the iron fencing installed around its perimeter in the 1950s under Robert Moses's direction—using repurposed municipal materials from construction on Delancey Street.

Then, on the evening of November 9, 1965, as evening settled over New York City, an abrupt and silent crisis unfolded. The Great Northeast Blackout plunged New York, parts of seven states, and eastern Canada into complete darkness. Commuters were stranded in subway cars and tunnels deep beneath the city, elevators froze mid-floor in towering skyscrapers, and the city came to a dangerous halt. At the Metropolitan Museum of Art, director James Rorimer—a former Monuments Man—spent the night patrolling the galleries, pistol in hand, determined to protect the treasures under his care.

From her townhouse, Julia gazed out at the darkened city, the only illumination coming from streams of car headlights cutting through the streets below. As she lit candles, her thoughts turned to the Van Cortlandt House, sitting in its shadowed fields, surrounded by seemingly timeless woodlands. The Delftware rested in their cases, their delicate surfaces exposed to the uncertainty of the darkness. She was the steward of a collection built by generations of women, and now she faced the possibility of losing what had taken lifetimes to preserve. Julia deliberated on what she had long considered only a last resort—removing the Delftware from Van Cortlandt for safekeeping.

A decision needed to be made quickly.

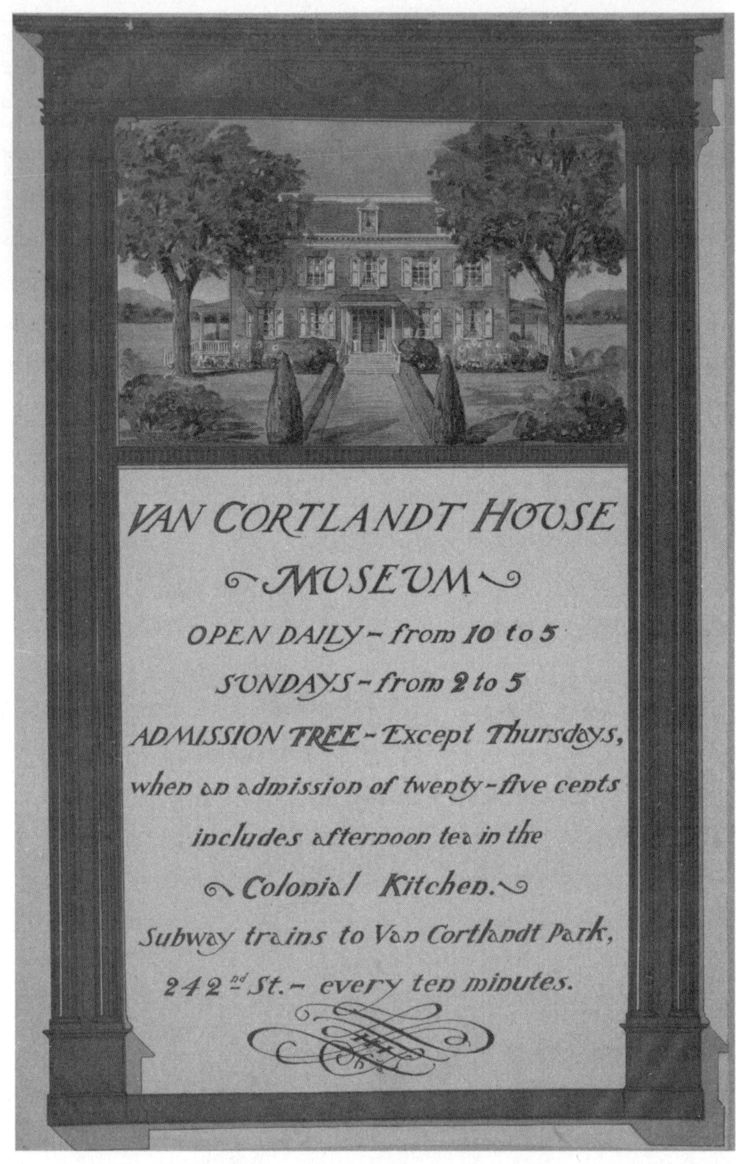

ABOVE: Van Cortlandt House Museum poster, ca. 1911, a commercial color lithograph by architect and painter Francis L. V. Hoppin, co-designer of Edith Wharton's Lenox estate, *The Mount*. The Miriam and Ira D. Wallach Division of Art, Prints and Photographs: Art & Architecture Collection, The New York Public Library. OPPOSITE: A photographic reproduction of an exhibition case of Dutch Delftware at the Van Cortlandt House Museum, as illustrated in a museum guide from 1955. National Society of Colonial Dames in the State of New York.

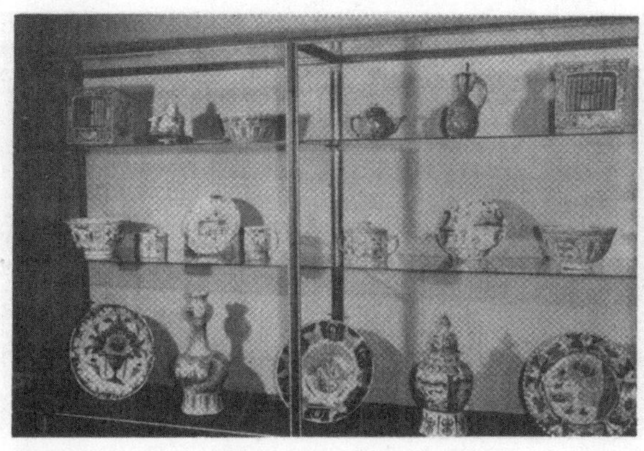

9

Vessels

VE'SSEL. n.s. [vasselle, Fr. vas, Lat.]

1. Any thing in which liquids, or other things, are put.

For Banquo's issue have I fill'd my mind; Put rancours in the vessel of my peace, Only for them. Shakesp. Macbeth. . . .

3. Any vehicle in which men or goods are carried on the water.

Now secure the painted vessel glides;
The sun-beams trembling on the floating tides. Pope.

4. Any capacity; any thing containing.

I have my fill
Of knowledge, what this vessel can contain. Milton.

—Samuel Johnson, *A Dictionary of the English Language*, 1755

Julia Wightman navigated her car up the Henry Hudson Parkway on a cool fall morning in 1965. The winding route hugged the Hudson River along Manhattan's West Side before crossing the Spuyten Duyvil Creek on a steel bridge into the Bronx. The early hour allowed her a smooth journey, with only a handful of cars sharing the road. However, the numerous potholes—steadily increasing in number for New York City drivers lately—demanded her attention.

As she approached Van Cortlandt Park, the towering pin oaks lining Broadway created a canopy over the roadway. Beyond them, she caught glimpses of the park's playing fields, their green expanse littered with leaves and windblown debris—crumpled paper bags and fluttering sheets of newspaper scattered by shifting breezes. Nearby, what had been the Dutch Garden was overgrown with tall grasses, encroaching shrubs, and young trees. The central fountain was now filled with a mass of bottles and cans.

Julia pulled into a parking spot near the entrance of the Van Cortlandt House Museum. Hours remained before the first visitors would arrive at the museum's door. Inside the silent space, she was greeted by stacks of empty cardboard boxes, reams of tissue, rolls of brown paper, and tape. Today's task would be long and meticulous: carefully wrapping and packing the museum's collection of Dutch Delftware.

Following a dark, narrow hallway away from the museum's richly paneled salons with their rare examples of eighteenth-century furniture and portraits, Julia walked as the floorboards creaked softly beneath her feet. She soon arrived at a more modestly appointed space—the Exhibition Room.

Despite its name, which suggested a grand gallery densely hung with artwork, the Exhibition Room of the Van Cortlandt House Museum was modest in scale and understated in its architectural details. Sunlight streamed through generous multipaned windows set deep within thick brick and fieldstone walls. The room featured worn pine floors and a simple wooden mantelpiece set with blue-and-white Dutch tiles.

It was a space that didn't overtly reveal its original purpose. But outside its windows under the lawn in the strata of silty loams and earth lay the evidence of its past when it served as the house's dining room for more than two centuries. Tens of thousands of excavated ceramic sherds found by archaeologists spoke of generations of gatherings and meals, of former colorful table landscapes filled with blue-and-white ceramics—countless Chinese porcelain cups, Delftware dishes, and English transferware bowls.

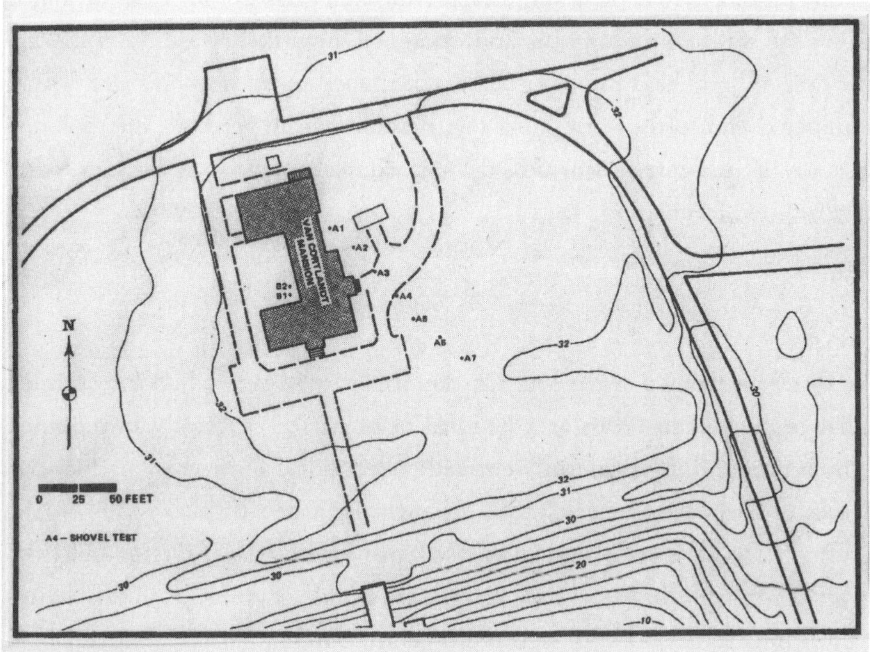

Archaeological diagram, *Location of Shovel Tests at Van Cortlandt Mansion, Bronx, New York*, 1987, mapping excavation points. The New York City Landmarks Preservation Commission.

Some of these breakfasts, lunches, and dinners had included illustrious guests during the Revolutionary War when both sides of the conflict had used the house as a resting place between battles over the control of New York. General George Washington, the Comte de Rochambeau, the Marquis de Lafayette, John Adams, and even the future King William IV of England—who served in New York during the American War of Independence—all dined under the roof of the "van Cortlandt Mansion."

She paused before the seven bronze-mounted glass display cases arranged along the walls containing the collection of Dutch Delftware. Julia studied the nest of brass keys in her hands. Each shaped metal bow was tied with a numbered and softly worn paper tag. Before starting her task, she took one last view of the carefully arranged Delftware, admiring it in the home that had inspired its creation.

By 1965, the women of the Van Cortlandt House Museum had transformed what began in the 1890s as a handful of objects in a small wall-mounted Dutch cabinet into a carefully curated collection of more than seventy-five pieces of Delftware, necessitating its own dedicated display room on the ground floor. The collection showcased a diverse range of Delftware, from seventeenth-century *kraak*-style pieces with Buddhist emblems to the technically sophisticated works of eighteenth-century master potters, featuring bold Imari designs or rococo-inspired forms with elegantly curved *rocaille* scrolls.

Since its opening to the public in 1897, more than a million visitors had stepped through its Dutch door, climbed the light-filled staircase, and explored the rooms of the Van Cortlandt House Museum. These "eager and curious crowds" came from around the world, across the country, or simply the five boroughs of New York, venturing out for the afternoon by train, elevated subway, or trolley to see this unique exercise of curation not replicated in any other American museum. There were thousands of schoolchildren with their teachers, brought in buses that regularly lined the street by the entrance to Van Cortlandt Park.

For many it was their first time seeing Dutch Delftware but for others, for whom ceramics was their passion, the Van Cortlandt House Museum was a Delftware destination. In the 1960s it was one of the few museums in the United States with a developed collection of Dutch Delftware. Ceramic enthusiasts, magazine editors, collectors, and museum curators, including the former director of the Rijksmuseum in Amsterdam, Dr. David Röell, all ventured to the Bronx to review the Delftware and the collection of Dutch decorative arts.

Julia realized that lining the shelves that surrounded her was Delftware in every form. There were easily recognizable objects—dishes, bowls, lidded vases, and teapots in a myriad of shapes and sizes. But there were also less familiar objects made for habits, customs, and traditions long since forgotten, including "pipe stands" for Dutch clay tobacco pipes with their long delicate stems; a scalloped "barber's bowl" with an oval depression on the rim that allowed a gentleman to be shaved with the bowl flush with the neck; and a large footed cauldron-shaped vessel with a protruding spout, called a "posset pot," for serving a hot drink made of milk curdled with wine or other liquor.

While some pieces were functional, such as covered butter dishes and salt cellars, others were purely decorative and sculptural, showcasing refined and nuanced craftsmanship. These pieces depicted animals and people engaged in various actions. Among them was a Laughing Buddha, or *Budai Heshang,* characterized by a large belly and a wide grin. In this unique Dutch Delftware interpretation, however, the Buddha sat holding a Dutch pipe and a cup of tea. Another striking piece featured was a figure of a Dutch woman wearing a hat and long petticoat, standing proudly with her hands on her hips. Although only six inches tall and crafted in tin-glazed earthenware, her presence is unapologetically commanding, her gaze confronting the viewer with quiet authority.

Many pieces on display were signed or marked examples of ceramic artistry, showcasing the exceptional skill of specific Delft potters. Among them was a sculptural covered dish from The Greek A, cleverly shaped like a mother plover. The piece featured a naturalistically painted head, beak, and feathers, as though the bird were quietly tending her nest of meticulously rendered twigs and grass. A butter tub by The White Star depicted a seated boy in a blue coat, playing with his pet yellow bird in a tiny birdcage.

Unsigned pieces, crafted by anonymous hands, were no less opulent or masterfully made. A particularly remarkable example was a pair of gilt Delftware birdcages, circa 1730. Intricate in design, they told a story of the Dutch Republic's global reach: alongside spices such as pepper, nutmeg, and cinnamon, luxurious silks, and alluring porcelain, the VOC also transported countless exotic animals from East Asia to Holland in the seventeenth century. Among them were Indian birds, ranging from large, vibrant parrots to diminutive parakeets. These exotic creatures commanded high prices, gracing both royal palaces and the homes of the wealthy as prized pets.

The Delftware birdcages of the Van Cortlandt House Museum were rectangular with slanting roofs and front openings adorned with delicate metal bars and functioning doors. Painted in soft hues of pink and green with scrolling peonies against an iron-red ground, the cages were exquisitely detailed. Their pierced sides featured scenes in moss green, pink, black, and gold: a bird in flight above another perched on a fence beneath peonies growing from a rock. Inside, earthenware feeding troughs and small fitted food drawers completed the design, and the tops were pierced for suspension.

Would something so fragile have been hung and used for actual birds? Likely not. These birdcages exemplified the technical prowess of eighteenth-century Delft potters, who pushed the earthenware, challenging the soft material to perform in ways that seemed impossible.

For Julia, the Exhibition Room was an experience in color. Not limited to every shade of blue—from pale sky tones to saturated indigos, deep cobalts, and "Persian Blue"—the display also included bursts of iron reds, rose pinks, blacks, oranges, greens, browns, violet, manganese purples, deep yellows, and glints of lustrous gold. As Julia observed, Delftware was far more than just blue and white; its chromatic possibilities were, in fact, endless.

Although the Dutch Delftware collection of the Van Cortlandt House Museum was not as extensive as those in major European institutions or filled with pieces of royal provenance, it held a unique history—one shaped over a century through the cumulative and collaborative efforts of women. Wrapping up this Dutch Delftware exhibition was not just about safeguarding objects of beauty, technical artistry, or historical significance. To Julia, these pieces were deeply personal. They embodied the female experience—the lives of the women whose efforts had brought them here—and perhaps, in many ways, her own.

Over the past century since its founding, many of the women of the Van Cortlandt House Museum were not only art collectors and ceramic enthusiasts but also suffragists, philanthropists, bibliophiles, botanists, historians, socialites, authors, art dealers, and preservationists. They ranged from young to old, and while some came from modest means, others were among the wealthiest and most influential women in American history. Using their varied talents, experiences, and expertise, they created a collective masterpiece, transforming the museum from a historic structure and a place where art is displayed into a work of art in its own right.

Far from a static assemblage, their Dutch Delftware collection was a living, evolving entity that grew organically as its legacy passed from one generation of women to the next. Once established, each succeeding group of women brought their unique skills, abilities, and influence to expand the collection and add new pieces to its shelves.

These vessels held not only memories of individual contributions but also the shared experiences of collaborative efforts. The women collected not merely for acquisition but as a means of exploration, expression, shared inquiry, and connection. Together, they created a collective work of art while making space for future generations of women to continue the collecting tradition, united by the common thread of Delftware.

By building a collection that looked to the future, they also preserved the legacies of countless women who had come before them, ensuring their contributions would endure. Some of these women were pottery owners in Delft who, as young girls in the seventeenth and eighteenth centuries, were trained alongside their mothers to eventually take over the family potteries. Many, like Johanna van der Heul, were widowed and continued to run the potteries after their husbands' deaths. Not only did they manage these businesses successfully, they also contributed to the innovation and refinement of

Delftware techniques, including the development of ceramic gilding as seen in the Imari style or the use of challenging color palettes, such as those found in the elusive black Delftware.

As patrons, women provided more than just financial support to Delftware factories. They also offered encouragement that inspired the creation of pieces of the highest quality. Queen Mary II, Delftware's greatest patron, significantly shaped the development of new designs and elevated levels of artistry through her commissions. Her love of Delftware influenced the marketplace, driving its popularity across Europe and beyond.

Many women were active sellers of Delftware. Whether peddling dishes door-to-door, handling transactions in pottery salesrooms, or facilitating mass orders of thousands of pieces with foreign merchants, they served as vital conduits for the blue-and-white market. By establishing networks of buyers both domestically and internationally, they contributed to the popularity and commercial success of Dutch Delftware while supporting their families.

Countless women became avid collectors of Delftware, embarking on their own ceramic hunts. They stepped out of their homes to explore their cities in search of blue-and-white treasures, and some, like Mary Prime, even traveled the world to build their collections. Whether scouring Europe or the dusty back roads of New England, they embraced the thrill of the "chasse." Driven by passion and creativity, these women found both joy and personal expression through their collections.

As historians and authors, women including Alice Morse Earle captured the public's interest in ceramics, crafting novels, ceramic guides, and histories. Their work, investigating and celebrating blue-and-white, supported and contributed to the growing appreciation of Dutch Delftware, which in turn fueled collecting. As a result of their efforts, they too would be lauded for their work and their creations on the page.

Finally, women played a critical role in founding museums. Those who established institutions like the Van Cortlandt House Museum shaped scholarship, curated exhibitions, and stewarded works of art for future generations. Through collections like this Dutch Delftware, they preserved history, shared knowledge, and ensured the legacy of Delft's artistry would endure.

Looking at the shelves of Delftware and the legacy they represented, Julia reflected on all that was at stake. Beyond the display cases, through the window, she could see the changing environment surrounding the small museum. In 1964, security reports from the Van Cortlandt House Museum guards warned Julia and the Art Committee that "incidents of vandalism both within and outside the house" were likely to escalate. The guards admitted they could no longer guarantee the safety of the artwork. Julia knew she couldn't take that risk.

Julia carefully inserted the key to unlock the first display case. Turning it gently, she felt the mechanism release, and the glass front swung open smoothly on its hinge as she pushed it aside. One by one, she lifted each piece of Delftware, inspected its condition, wrapped it carefully in paper, and nestled it into a box resting on the wide pine floorboards.

Her approach was as organized and methodical as her work with the collection of books and manuscripts that lined the shelves of her English oak–paneled library in Manhattan. With her typed inventory of the Delftware collection in hand, she meticulously checked off each piece as it was placed into the awaiting boxes.

She finally reached the blue-and-white puzzle jug crafted by the pottery of Geertruij Verstelle. As she held its body, she noticed the neck was pierced with trelliswork framed within oval panels, while the painter had applied color to the entire surface with rocaille scrolls and a central cartouche depicting a fisherman and a female figure. For the first time, she noticed the woman—a contemplative figure in a Grecian gown, seated on a rock. Like the other pieces, it was in near-perfect condition. Carefully wrapping the puzzle jug in a sheet of brown paper, she placed it securely in a box. She closed the lid, applied a length of tape to the cardboard seam, and ran her fingertips across the surface to ensure the seal. Julia returned to the last display case, now empty, and closed it. Sliding the key into the lock, she turned it with a soft click, securing it one final time before slipping the key into her pocket.

Her task at the Van Cortlandt House Museum was complete, and the Delftware was ready for its next journey. Outside the fieldstone house, a truck idled, waiting. At Julia's signal, the movers stepped inside, carefully lifting the packed boxes and empty display cases with practiced care. Each case was wrapped in thick blankets, padded for protection before being loaded alongside the Delftware, bound for the Upper East Side, where its new home awaited.

At headquarters, the movers carried the boxes and cases through the Dutch door and up the wide staircases to the third-floor gallery—a light-filled space where the Delftware was unpacked and arranged once more.

There, settled in its aerie overlooking 71st Street, the Delftware remains, preserved to this day.

Dutch Delftware is fragile and yet, as a ceramic, one of the most enduring artifacts throughout history, as countless fine-pointed fragments in archaeological sites attest. Although the fledging colony of New Netherland only lasted a short time, beneath the surface from Delaware through Connecticut, evidence of Dutch lives in the form of small pieces of tin-glazed earthenware are scattered up and down America's East Coast. It has been a witness to the economic ascendency of nations, celebrated in royal courts, and withstood transport across oceans, catastrophic explosions, and revolutions. Tin-glazed earthenware like this should not have survived intact and yet remarkably it exists, unscathed.

Women's identities and the attributes of ceramics have often been intertwined. Throughout centuries of literature, "china" has been closely associated with women. Like a piece of clay, a young girl is "shaped" or "molded" into an idealized female figure. As a "weaker vessel," she is portrayed as fragile, easily broken or chipped. Her skin is described as "like porcelain." She becomes a "china doll" to be handled with special care or placed "on her pedestal" in unattainable perfection.

These metaphors, associating women with the refined nature of ceramics and porcelain, emphasize delicacy and fragility. Yet the stories of these women, as told through their relation to Dutch Delftware, illustrate that women are anything but easily broken.

Delftware is more than a fragile, delicate form of art.

It is a moment frozen in time, captured by fire. Its glazed colors remain as bright, vibrant, and alluring as they were the day they were created. When placed in kilns and exposed to intense heat, the clay undergoes physical and chemical transformations, fusing together into a work of art that is both durable and stable.

Unlike materials such as canvas, paper, or wood, ceramics like Delftware are less sensitive to environmental extremes or fluctuations. They do not expand or contract with atmospheric changes, nor do they warp. Unlike most metals, they won't tarnish or oxidize. Made from inorganic materials such as clay, minerals, and oxides, ceramics are inherently stable and resistant to chemical reactions caused by light, heat, or moisture. Unlike organic materials like dyes or pigments, which degrade over time, the chemical structure of ceramics remains relatively unchanged. Its shiny surface retains its clarity, and the brilliance of its cobalt blue continues to glisten as vividly as ever.

As a result, when we view Delftware today, we are transported through time, seeing it just as it appeared in the 1960s—or even the 1660s.

Dutch Delftware, its vases, plates, bowls, and figures, have been touched by women over three centuries, from shop daughters and potter's widows to Queens and American heiresses. The women who made, collected, and preserved them were all responding to unique opportunities, challenges, and pivotal change. Their lives are intertwined with these vessels; this blue-and-white holds their stories.

Epilogue

I return to the townhouse on East 71st Street. We are getting ready to pack up the Dutch Delftware for the restoration of the display cases. Although the Delftware remains as vibrant, bright, and colorful as the day it was removed from the kiln, the rest of the world around it has evolved, changed, and aged. The ivory velvet-covered cabinet panels have grown dusty and warped. They will be removed for cleaning and repair. The cabinets have been opened and the Delftware is being carefully removed for temporary storage.

I'm drawn once again to the puzzle jug. Holding it carefully in my hands, I review its glistening decoration and intricate construction one last time before nestling it into a flat plastic storage container between cushioning layers of packing paper. I admire the delicate spouts, the painting across its body of the man fishing as well as a reclining woman within rococo cartouches that wrap the rounded body. But a detail I hadn't noticed before catches my eye. Hidden within scrolling foliage on the body are four numerals. It is the date 1769. What did this date signify? A celebration? A birth? A wedding?

This would have been Geertruij's last year as owner of the pottery. She died in 1773 and is buried in the *Nieuwe Kerk*, joining other auspicious members of *Delft's* pottery families as well as the Dutch royal family. It was the same church where Barbara Rotteveel was christened and where Johanna van der Heul laid her husband to rest before starting on her own to oversee one of Dutch Delftware's greatest potteries. Within the next two decades the Dutch Republic would be invaded, and the era of Dutch Delftware would end by 1850.

But before it did, sometime in 1769, Geertruij Verstelle, whose initials the puzzle jug bears, held this object proudly.

Geertruij is a Dutch variation for Gertrude, meaning "spear of strength," derived from the old Germanic elements "*ger*" for "spear" and "*thrud*" for "strength." Possibly she was named in honor of St. Gertrude the Great, a German thirteenth-century nun, who was fluent in three languages and became a renowned and influential mystic writer. It was certainly a name to inspire a young, strong Dutch girl.

The puzzle jug could have been gently placed in a small wood box tightly stuffed with loose hay or wrapped in straw sewn mats, then packed into lidded baskets. Was a boat awaiting her on the Delft canal outside her door ready for the delivery to her buyer? She would have made a good profit on a piece such as a puzzle jug, commissioned for a special occasion. Who would it belong to? Where did it go?

Heading off on a journey that would take it around the world, more than two centuries have passed as it has been through countless hands, changing nature as a commodity, going to places and cultural realms unimaginable to its original Delftware makers and users. It would travel by carriage or boat across Europe then possibly later by train or steamship.

Upon leaving a pottery, Delftware could symbolize many things: a source of income, a utilitarian object, a luxurious decoration, a gift of affection, a marker of wealth, or even a political signifier. Over the centuries, it has assumed new identities—as an object of desire, a decorative piece, a means of personal expression, an aesthetic symbol, a historic relic, or a work of art.

Perhaps today, Delftware can take on an additional role: as a medium for telling the stories of women.

In this story I have only mentioned a few of the women who have touched these objects or were a part of the story of Delftware. Names in archival documents can sometimes stand out like the shining ceramic fragments that begin to be revealed under the surface. Many glittering stories poked out from the layers of earth catching the light. The sheer abundance of dynamic accounts of women's lives in Delftware was an encouraging presence.

Sometimes from a very narrow perspective, such as the blue-and-white of Dutch Delftware, there is an expansive view, one that can reveal hidden lives, giving women equal historical representation and changing our perception.

These are stories that have been hidden in plain sight. Today, when seen collectively and reassembled, they enable us to further understand women before us—and reveal what we, too, can achieve within our own unique confines.

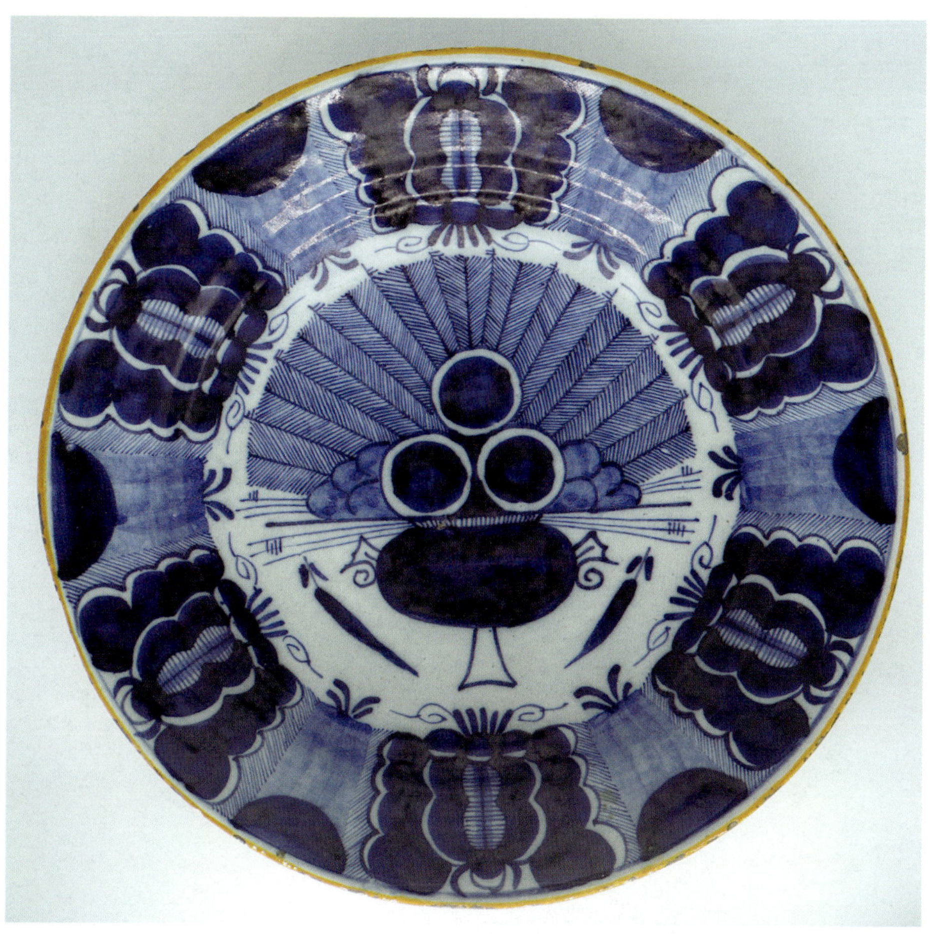

Figure 20. A Dutch Delft Blue and White Large Dish. De Drie Klokken (The Three Bells) Factory, ca. 1775. Boldly painted in the center with a stylized vase of flowers and foliage within a border of stylized butterflies alternating with panels of hemispheres and hatchwork on the ochre-edged rim. The National Society of Colonial Dames in the State of New York. This popular Delftware pattern features a fan-shaped bouquet in a vase, often described as resembling peacock feathers.

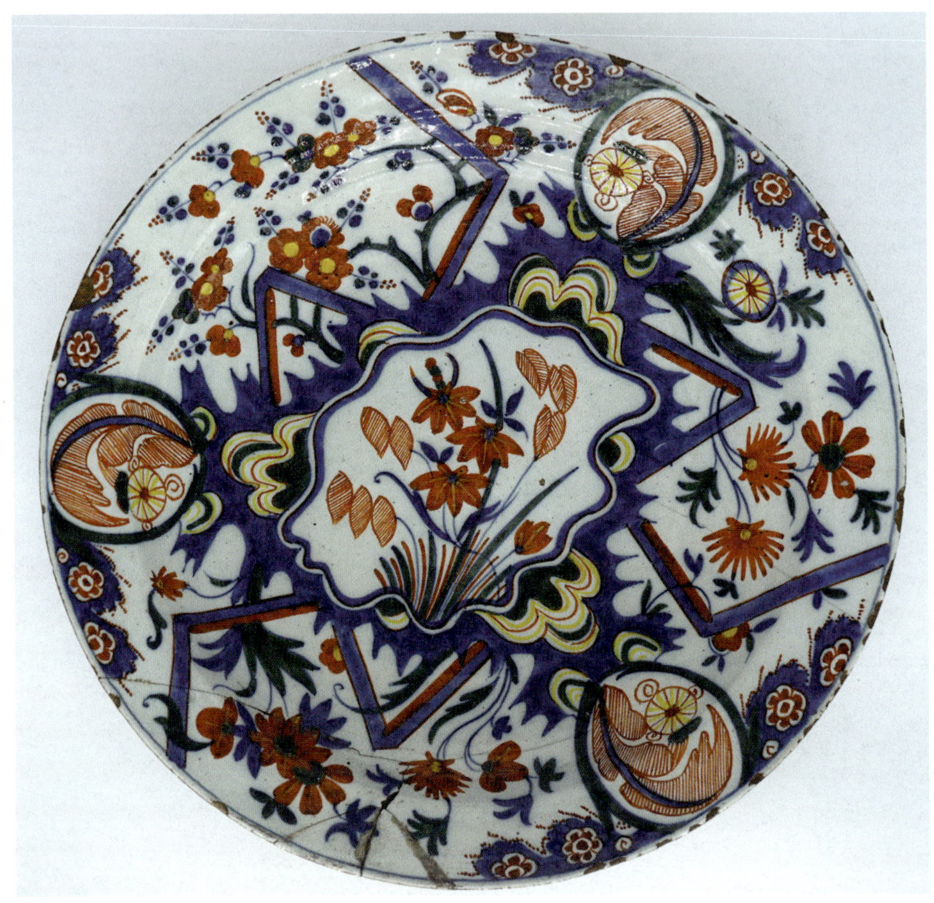

Figure 21. A Dutch Delft Polychrome *Bliksem* (Lightning) Plate. De Paauw (The Peacock) Factory, ca. 1720. Painted in the Imari style in iron-red, green, yellow, and blue with flowering plants and zigzags of lightning. The National Society of Colonial Dames in the State of New York. The much-sought-after *bliksem* (lightning) style may have been inspired by Imari depictions of winding twigs or, as suggested by H. P. Bremmer, footbridges from Japanese water gardens. Its popularity led to numerous modern copies, including those produced by the French factory Samson & Cie in the nineteenth and early twentieth centuries.

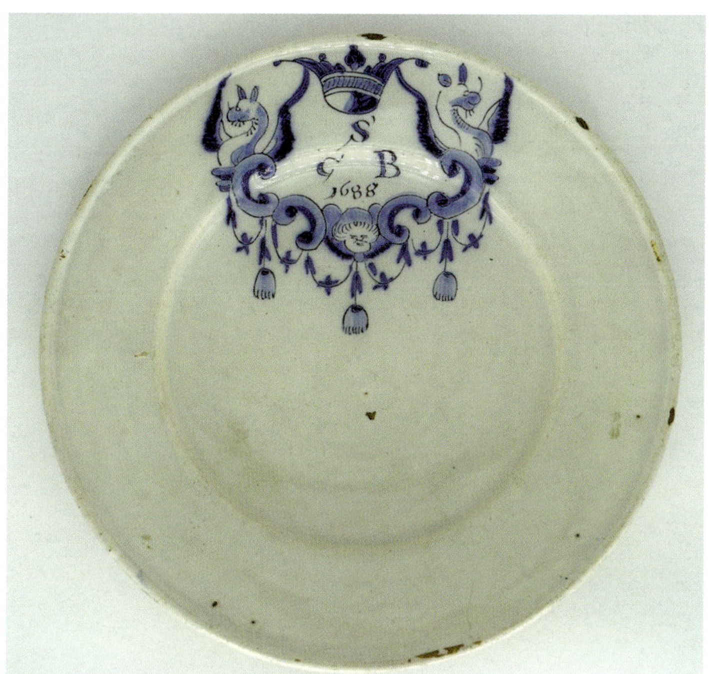

Figure 22 (above). A Blue and White Dutch Delft "Marriage" Plate, 1688. Painted with a scrollwork cartouche surmounted by a stylized crown, flanked by demi-griffins and an angel head and tassels, reserving the initials SCB over the date 1688. The National Society of Colonial Dames in the State of New York. Commemorative plates of this type, produced in Holland for export, were exceptionally popular in the late seventeenth century.

Figure 23 (right). A Dutch Delft Blue and White Large Dish, ca. 1790. Painted with a flower-filled neoclassical urn between two floral sprigs within a stylized floral and foliate border around the rim. The National Society of Colonial Dames in the State of New York.

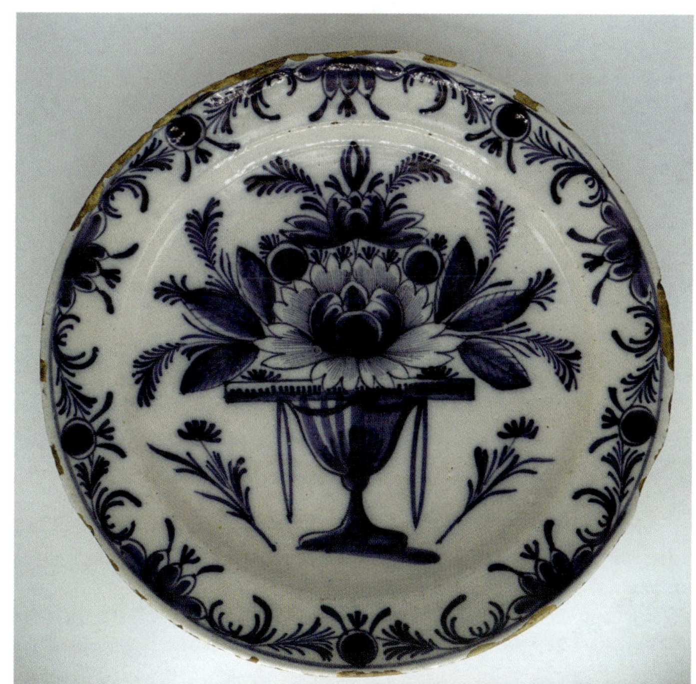

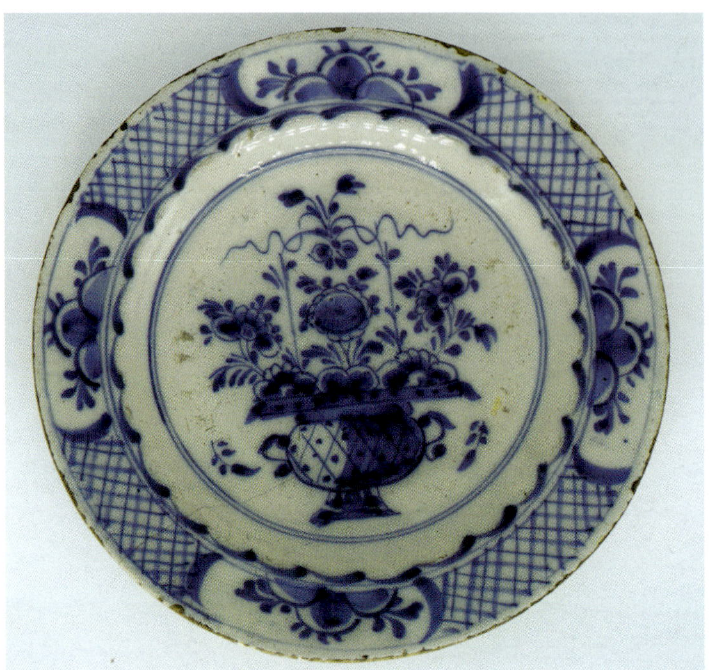

Figure 24 (above). A Dutch Delft Blue and White Small Plate, ca. 1740–50. Painted in the center with a beribboned basket of flowers, the rim with a hatchwork border interrupted with four panels of demiflowerheads. The National Society of Colonial Dames in the State of New York.

Figure 25 (right). A Dutch Delft Blue and White Large Plate. De Dubbelde Schenkkan (The Double Jug) Factory, ca. 1765. Painted in the center with a bird in flight amid large blossoms above a pair of swimming ducks, and on the rim with five stylized blossoms in grass-edged panels alternating with "rock"-edged panels within a "piecrust" edge. The National Society of Colonial Dames in the State of New York.

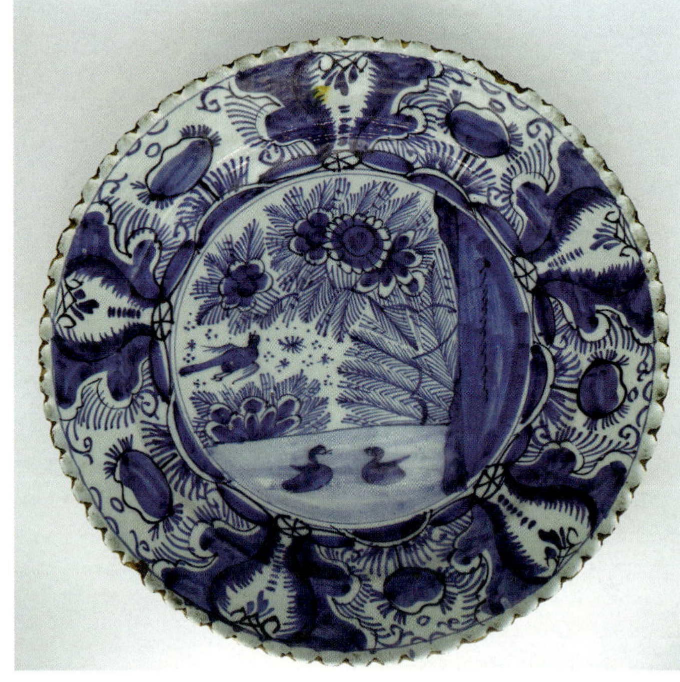

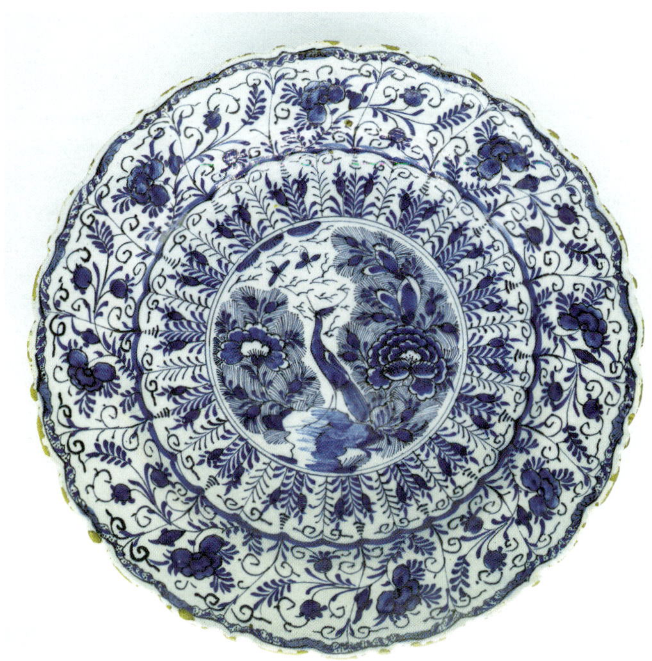

Figure 26 (right). A Dutch Delftware Blue and White Large Plate. De Klaauw, (The Claw) Factory, ca. 1725–40. Painted in the center with an exotic bird perched on a rock amid peonies and eyeing two insects within a roundel encircled by scallop-edged panels of floral sprigs, the rim with further floral panels within a narrow dotted and dashed band at the scalloped and barbed edge. The National Society of Colonial Dames in the State of New York.

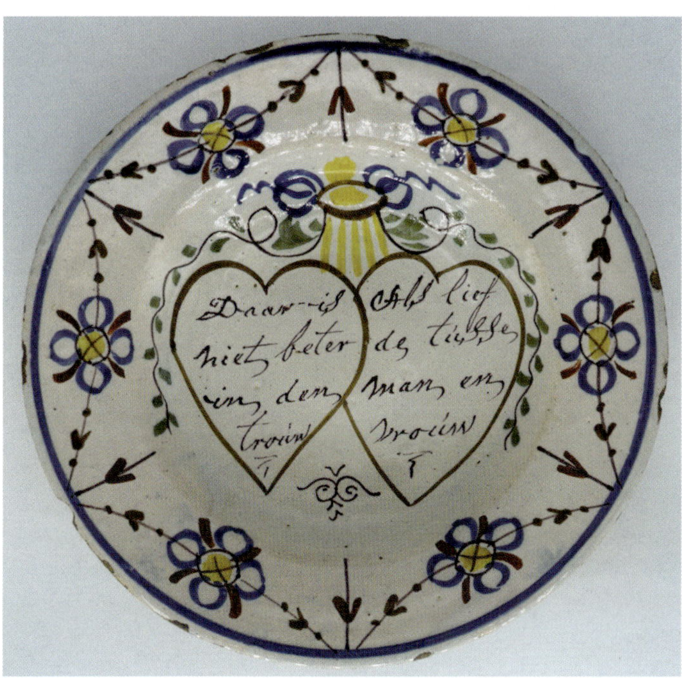

Figure 27 (above). A Dutch Delft Polychrome Plate, ca. 1790. The center painted with two brown hearts suspended from a blue and yellow bowknot issuing leafy vines and inscribed in manganese *Daar is Niet beter in den trouw, Als lief de tusse man en vrouw* (There is nothing better in marriage, than love between man and woman). The National Society of Colonial Dames in the State of New York.

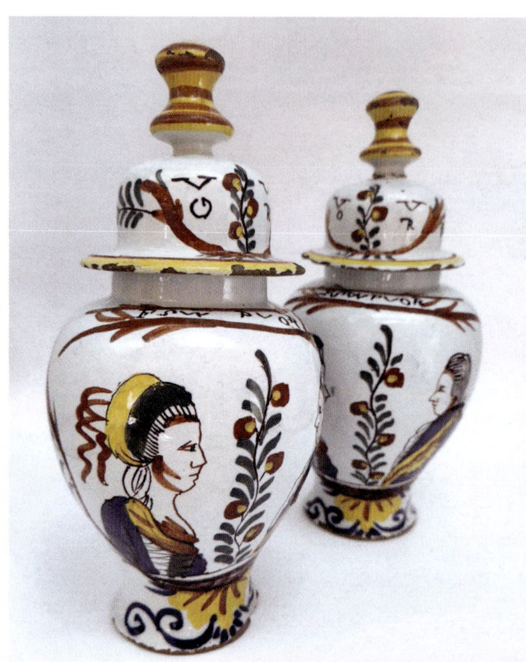

Figure 28. Two Dutch Delft Polychrome Orangist Vases and Covers, ca. 1785–95. Each of baluster form and painted in blue, iron-red, yellow, green, and manganese on the front with half-length profile portraits of Princess Frederika Sophia Wilhelmina and Prince William V of Orange flanking an orange tree beneath the inscription FSW PVOR. The National Society of Colonial Dames in the State of New York.

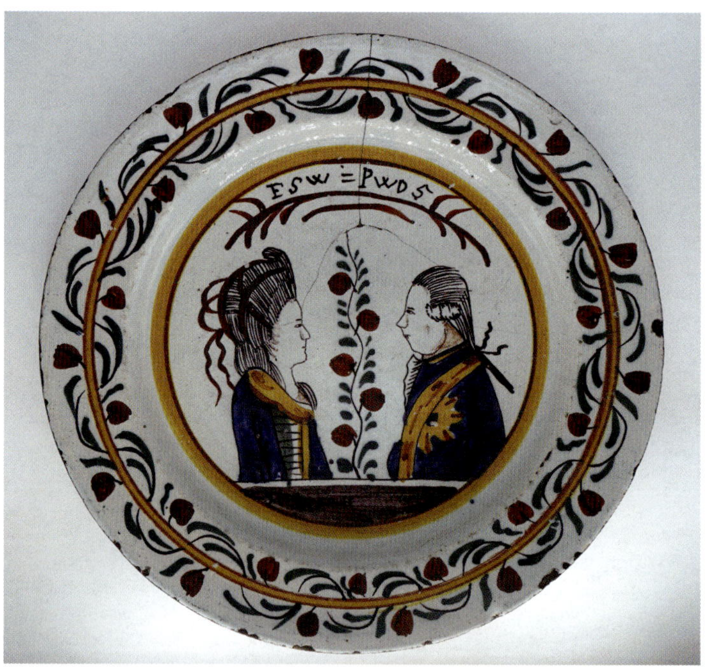

Figure 29. A Dutch Delft Polychrome Orangist Large Plate, ca. 1789. Painted in blue, manganese, iron-red, yellow, and green with half-length portraits of Frederika Sophia Wilhelmina and Prince William V of Orange facing each other and flanking an orange tree beneath the Inscription "FSW=PWD5" within an iron-red and yellow roundel, the rim with a similar roundel entwined with an orange vine. The National Society of Colonial Dames in the State of New York.

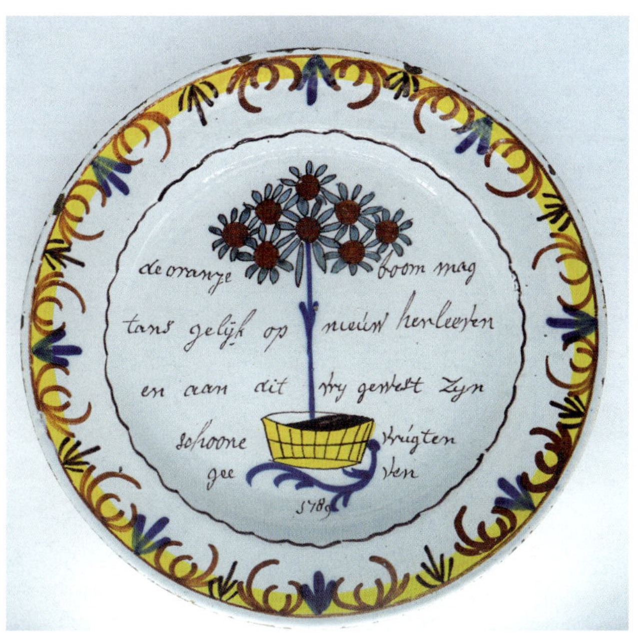

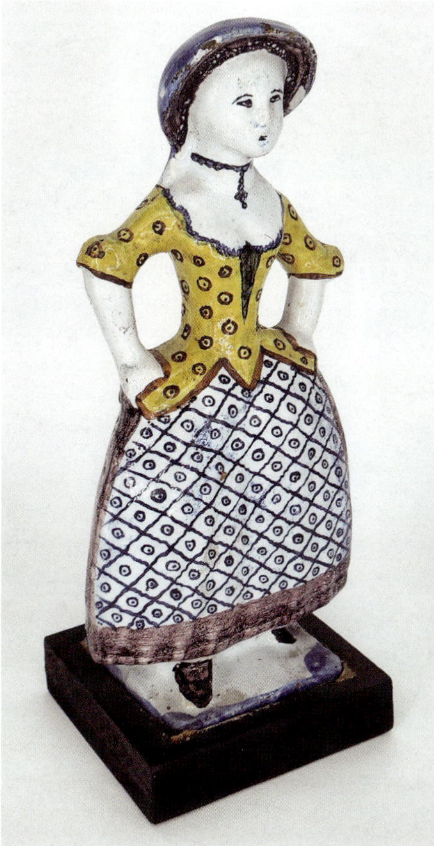

Figure 30 (above). A Dutch Delft Orangist Large Plate, ca. 1789. Painted in iron-red, green, blue, yellow, and manganese with an orange tree in a tub surrounded by the inscription "*de oranje boom mag tans gelyk op nieuw herleeven en aan dit vry gewest Zyn schoone vrigten gee ven 1789*" (the orange tree may now revive again and give this free region its beautiful fruits 1789) in manganese. The National Society of Colonial Dames in the State of New York.

Figure 31 (left). A Dutch Delft Polychrome Figure of a Woman, ca. 1760. Modeled wearing a blue hat with a manganese inner brim, a blue necklace, a yellow bodice patterned with iron-red circlets and with a green stomacher over a manganese skirt and a blue trellis-patterned white apron, standing with her arms akimbo on a blue-edged rectangular mound base. Provenance: The William Randolph Hearst Collection. The National Society of Colonial Dames in the State of New York.

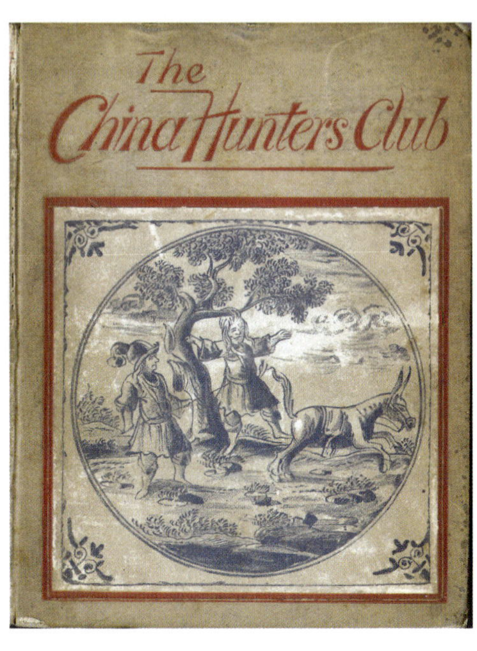

Figure 32 (right). Cover, *The China Hunters Club* by Annie Trumbull Slosson (New York: Harper & Brothers, 1878), author's collection. Author and collector Annie Trumbull Slosson selected a vibrant blue and white Dutch tile for the cover of *The China Hunters Club*, a captivating work which quickly became an American bestseller.

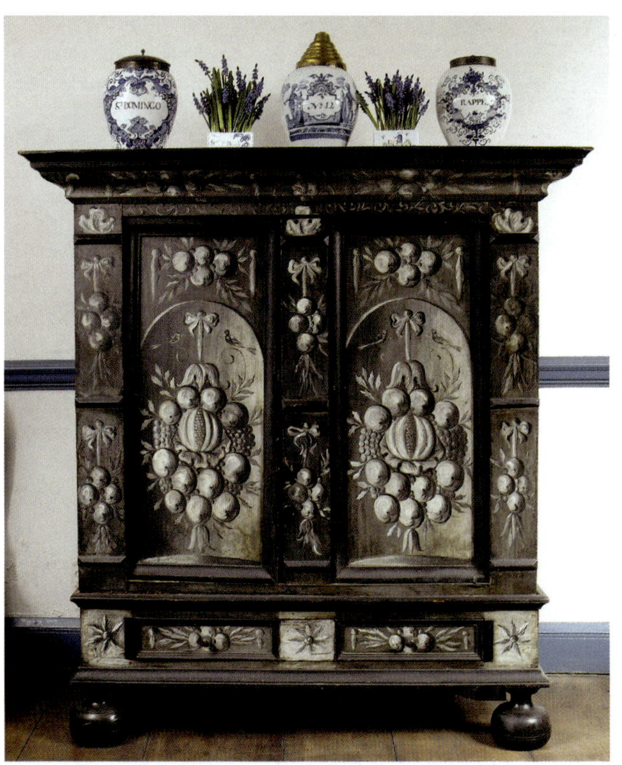

Figure 33 (left). An American Grisaille-Painted Kast, Hudson River Valley, ca. 1700. Topped with three eighteenth-century Dutch Delft blue and white tobacco jars with brass lids, this kast embodies both a traditional cupboard form and a decorative style inspired by Dutch prototypes. Its ornamentation, featuring large pendants of fruit in niches, is rendered in blue-gray, black, and white using the grisaille technique. The Van Cortlandt House Museum, New York. The National Society of Colonial Dames in the State of New York. (Photo: Laura J. Carpenter Myers)

Acknowledgements

Beyond Blue and White began as a personal curiosity and evolved into a journey—one that crisscrossed continents and centuries. But it could never have taken shape without the extraordinary people who opened doors, sparked ideas, shared expertise, and offered encouragement at every turn across America, England, and the Netherlands.

My heartfelt thanks go first to Ann Leslie Tuttle at Dystel, Goderich & Bourret LLC, whose guidance and steady support were indispensable. At Pegasus Books, Jessica Case brought not only adept leadership but also creative enthusiasm to the process. I'm also grateful to Josh Krigman for his deft and thoughtful assistance throughout.

To the institutions that provided resources, inspiration, and sanctuary, I owe immense gratitude: the New York Society Library; the Frick Art Reference Library; the Thomas J. Watson Library at the Metropolitan Museum of Art in New York; the Oliver Wolcott Library in Litchfield, CT; the Gunn Memorial Library in Washington, CT; The London Library; and the Rijksmuseum Research Library in Amsterdam—all places where past and present intersected in the most illuminating ways.

To the members and staff of the National Society of Colonial Dames of America and the National Society of Colonial Dames in the State of New York, who so generously shared not only exquisite works of decorative art and archival records but also their time, knowledge, and enthusiasm—including Anna Duff, Katherine Taylor Cammack, Edith H. Stickney, Isabel T. Wallop,

Susan Walker, Marguerite Morrison, Lee Potter, Valerie Westcott, Laura Correa Carpenter, Hilory Wolden, and Clint Allen—thank you.

I am also deeply grateful to Robert Aronson, Femke Haitsma Mulier, Léon-Paul van Geenen, and Suzanne Lambooy for their expertise and generosity, which added richness and dimension to the narrative. Thanks as well to Helen Allen, Cheryl Hurley, and Lindsey Bednar for their thoughtful support along the way.

To the friends and family who offered steady encouragement, insightful feedback, and inspired countless ideas and conversations—Karen Tompkins, Karen Glover, Karla Harwich, Nathalie Kaplan, Virginia Tracy, Paula Hornbostel, Mary Stobaugh, Melissa Gibbons, Sophie Muir Rothschild, Pilar O'Leary, Lisa Foster, Louise Dye, Muffy Flouret, Margret Frame, Elizabeth Belfer, Leslie Banker, Nell Kleinschmidt, Naomi Novik and Charles Ardai, Peri and David Clark, Elizabeth Wheeler, Jennifer Wheeler, and George Y. Wheeler IV— thank you for accompanying me on this journey.

In memory of Susanne Earls Carr, who first invited me down this blue-and-white path—I'm so glad I accepted.

And finally, to my husband and "the companion of my china hunts"—Peter Chase Hayden Brown—your companionship makes every detour worthwhile.

Illustration Credits

Front Endpapers: Anon. engraving, etching and letterpress, *Plattegrond van Delft* (Map of Delft), Amsterdam, 1652. Rijksmuseum, Amsterdam.

Back Endpapers: Anon. *Historical Sketch Map of Kings Bridge, 1645–1783,* compiled by Thomas Henry Edsall (1887). Lionel Pincus and Princess Firyal Map Division, The New York Public Library.

Frontispiece: Charles Antoine Goutzwiller, lithograph, "Planche XII. Bouquetiers à Jacinthes décorés en Camaïeu bleu" from Henry Havard, *Histoire de la Faïence de Delft* (Paris: E. Plon et Cie, 1878). Author's collection.

p. xx: Henry Beford Lemere (photographer), *The Peacock Room, 49 Princes Gate, London* (1892). Victoria and Albert Museum, London.

p. 1: George Hayward, lithograph with tint stone, *New York & City Banks and the McEvers Mansion, Wall Street in 1800.* From *Manual of the Corporation of the City of New York* (known as *Valentine's Manual*) (New York, 1856). The Miriam and Ira D. Wallach Division of Art, Prints and Photographs: Picture Collection, The New York Public Library.

p. 8: Ignaz Schiffermueller, color plate. *Versuch eines Farbensystems.* From Johann Wolfgang von Goethe, *Zur Farbenlehre* (Tübingen, 1810). British Library Board.

p. 10: Illustration, *That Dreadful Kobold Swooping Down Upon Them* from Lucy Rider Meyer, *Real Fairy Folks, or Fairy Land of Chemistry: Explorations in the World of Atoms* (Boston, Lothrop Publishing Company, 1887). Courtesy of Science History Institute.

p. 14: Charles Antoine Goutzwiller, lithograph, *Planche XXIV Pot à Surprise (Décor en camaïeu blue)* from Henry Havard, *Histoire de la Faïence de Delft* (Paris: E. Plon et Cie, 1878). Author's collection.

p. 18: Charles Antoine Goutzwiller, *La boutique de la Marchande de faïences, (d'après J. Kilian.)* from Henry Havard, *La Céramique Hollandaise: Histoire des faïences de Delft, Haarlem, Rotterdam, Arnhem, Utrecht, etc.; et des porcelaines de Weesp, Loosdrecht, Amsterdam et La Haye* (Amsterdam, 1909). Courtesy of the Getty Research Institute.

p. 19: Charles Antoine Goutzwiller, illustration of the sign of The Porceleyn Fles (The Porcelain Bottle) pottery. From Henry Havard, *Histoire de la Faïence de Delft* (Paris: E. Plon et Cie, 1878). Author's collection.

p. 22: Jan Caspar Philips, etching and engraving, title page for *Nederlands water-nood van den jaare MDCCXL en MDCCXLI* (*Dutch Water Emergency of the Year MDCCXL and MDCCXLI*), (Amsterdam, 1741). Rijksmuseum, Amsterdam.

p. 26: Caspar Luyken and Jan Luyken, etching, "De Tichgellaar," (The Brick maker) from *Het Menselyk Bedrof* (Amsterdam, 1694). Rijksmuseum, Amsterdam.

p. 28: Jan Gerritsz. Visser, etching, *Gezicht op Delft* (*View of Delft*) (Amsterdam, 1792). Rijksmuseum, Amsterdam.

p. 30: Leonard Schenk after a drawing by Abraham Rademaker, etching, *Gezicht van de Groote Markt te Delft* (*View of the Grote Markt in Delft*) (1706–1767). Rijksmuseum, Amsterdam.

p. 33: "Experiens Sillemans, engraving, 'Maeghde-wapen'" (The Maiden's Coat of Arms) from Jacob Cats, Houwelyck (Marriage), (Amsterdam, 1642). Rijksmuseum, Amsterdam.

p. 36: Anon. engraving after a print by Abraham Bosse, *Gereformeerde school, ca. 1650* (*Reformed school, ca. 1650*), (1642–1665). Rijksmuseum, Amsterdam.

p. 40: Leonaert Bramer, pen and ink drawing, *Straatverkoopster aardewerk*: "*Aerde Plateelen*" (*pottery street vendor*), 17th century. Universitaire Bibliotheken Leiden.

p. 43: Attributed to Robert de Baudous, engraving, *Een vloot van negen schepen vertrekkend van Amsterdam voor een reis naar Oost-Indië, 1603* (*Fleet of nine ships leaving Amsterdam for the East Indies, 1603*) (1603). Rijksmuseum, Amsterdam.

p. 46: Charles Antoine Goutzwiller, illustration, "Figure 46–Grand plat creux, décoré en camaïeu bleu foncé" from Henry Havard, *Histoire de la Faïence de Delft* (Paris: E. Plon et Cie, 1878). Author's collection.

p. 52: Casper Luyken, etching, *Ontploffing van de kruittoren te Delft, 1654* (*Explosion of the gunpowder tower in Delft, 1654*), from Johann Ludwig Gottfried, *Joh. Lodew. Gottfrieds Historische kronyck*, vol. II., (Leiden, 1698). Amsterdam, Rijksmuseum.

p. 53: Simon Fokke after a painting by Egbert Lievensz. van der Poel, etching, *Verwoesting in Delft na de ontploffing van het buskruitmagazijn op 12 oktober 1654* (*Destruction in Delft after the explosion of the gunpowder magazine on October 12, 1654*), (Amsterdam, 1654). Rijksmuseum, Amsterdam.

p. 56: Notarial deed, signed by Barbara Cornelisdochter Rotteveel, June 25, 1655, 161.2091, Folio 33, Old Notarial Archive Delft. Stadsarchief Delft (Delft City Archives).

p. 58: Carel Fabritius, *A View of Delft, with a Musical Instrument Seller's Stall*, 1652, oil on canvas. National Gallery, London.

p. 62: Johannes de Ram, engraving and etching, *Plattegrond van de Kaart Figuratief van Delft, deel rechtsonder* (*Map of the Figurative Map of Delft, part bottom right*) (Amsterdam, 1703–1752). Rijksmuseum, Amsterdam.

p. 65: Leonardus Schenk, engraving, *Gesigt van het St. Lucas Gilde-huys, Vue de la Maison de S. Luc,* (*View of the St. Luke Guildhouse*). From Abraham Rademaker and Leonardus Schenk, *Alle de voornaamste Gesigten van de Wydberoemde Steeden Alkmaar, Delft en Dordregt (. . .)*, (Amsterdam, 1736). Universiteitsbibliotheek Leiden.

p. 69: Gerrit Paape, engraving, illustration of a thrower and tools in *De Plateelbakker of Delftsch Aardewerkmaaker, from Volledige beschrijving van alle konsten, ambachten, handwerken, fabrieken, trafieken, derzelver* *werkhuizen, gereedschappen, enz . . .* (Dordrecht: A. Blussé en zoon, 1794). Universiteitsbibliotheek Utrecht.

p. 71: Gerrit Paape, engraving, illustration of the kwaarten technique in *De Plateelbakker of Delftsch Aardewerkmaaker, from Volledige beschrijving van alle konsten, ambachten, handwerken, fabrieken, trafieken, derzelver werkhuizen, gereedschappen, enz . . .* (Dordrecht: A. Blussé en zoon, 1794). Universiteitsbibliotheek Utrecht.

p. 73: Gerrit Paape, engraving, illustration of a kiln in *De Plateelbakker of Delftsch Aardewerkmaaker, from Volledige beschrijving van alle konsten, ambachten, handwerken, fabrieken, trafieken, derzelver werkhuizen, gereedschappen, enz . . .* (Dordrecht: A. Blussé en zoon, 1794). Universiteitsbibliotheek Utrecht.

p. 77: Jan Luyken, engraving, *Het Porselyn: 't Is maar een Vertooning* from *Het Leerzaam Huisraad, vertoond in vyftig konstige figuuren, met godlyke spreuken en stichtelyke verzen* (Amsterdam, Pieter Arentsz. II (wed.) en Cornelis van der Sys, 1711). Rijksmuseum, Amsterdam.

p. 80: Simon Fokke, etching, *Funeral of Anna of Hannover in the New Church in Delft, 1759,* (Amsterdam, 1760). Rijksmuseum, Amsterdam.

p. 81: Charles Antoine Goutzwiller, "Planche XVIII.- Garniture de cinq pieces polychromes sur fond noir" illustration, from Henry Havard, *Histoire de la Faïence de Delft* (Paris: E. Plon et Cie, 1878). Author's collection.

p. 84: Anon. drawing, *Plattegrond van de Nieuwe Kerk te Delft met de ligging van de graven, 1751* (*Map of the New Church in Delft with the location of the graves, 1751*). Rijksmuseum, Amsterdam.

p. 85: Attributed to Coenraet Decker, etching, *Interieur van de Nieuwe Kerk te Delft* (*Interior of the Nieuwe Kerk in Delft*), 1680. Rijksmuseum, Amsterdam.

p. 87: Attributed to Coenraet Decker, etching, *Gezicht op het stadhuis te Delft* (*View of the town hall in Delft*), (Amsterdam, 1678–1703). Rijksmuseum, Amsterdam.

p. 91: Pieter Jansz. Post, pen drawing, "*stant op sijn lanckte van Binnen vant Pack ende Cuyp huys*" (*standing on its length from the inside of the Pack and Kuyp house*). From Grond-, *stant en Profilteickeningen van's Lands*

Magasijn ofte Kruit-Huis buijten de Stadt Delft (*Ground, position and profile drawings of the State Warehouse or Gunpowder House outside the City of Delft*), 1659. Stadsarchief Delft (Delft City Archives).

p. 91: Pieter Jansz. Post, pen drawing, "*stant op sijn Eynde van Binnen vant Pack ende Kuyp huys*" ("*standing at the end of the inside of the Pack and Kuyp house*"). From Grond-, *stant en Profilteickeningen van's Lands Magasijn ofte Kruit-Huis buijten de Stadt Delf* (*Ground, position and profile drawings of the State Warehouse or Gunpowder House outside the City of Delft*), 1659. Stadsarchief Delft (Delft City Archives).

p. 96: Charles Antoine Goutzwiller, illustration of the sandstone sculpture of a swag from Henry Havard, *Histoire de la Faïence de Delft* (Paris: E. Plon et Cie, 1878). Author's collection.

p. 99: Charles Antoine Goutzwiller, illustration of cashmere style Delftware from Henry Havard, *Histoire de la Faïence de Delft* (Paris: E. Plon et Cie, 1878). Author's collection.

p. 102: Charles Antoine Goutzwiller, illustration of a black Delftware plate from Henry Havard, *Histoire de la Faïence de Delft* (Paris: E. Plon et Cie, 1878). Author's collection.

p. 106: Initials of the Widow of Charles Antoine Goutzwiller, illustration of the WVDB mark from Henry Havard, *Histoire de la Faïence de Delft* (Paris: E. Plon et Cie, 1878). Author's collection.

p. 108: Pieter van Gunst, engraving, *Portrait of Mary II Stuart*, 1694, after a painting by Jan Hendrik Brandon. Rijksmuseum, Amsterdam.

p. 109: Photomechanical print, *Hampton Court Palace West Front* (London: John Swain & Son Ltd., ca. 1910). Author's collection.

p. 111: Gesina ter Borch, *Vrouw te paard in een landschap*, pen and ink, 1660. Rijksmuseum, Amsterdam.

p. 118: Daniel Marot, etching and engraving, *Design for a Chimney Wall with Laquered Panels and Porcelain*, 1673–in or before 1703. Rijksmuseum, Amsterdam.

p. 120: Bastiaen Stopendael, etching and engraving, *Gezicht op Paleis Het Loo* (View of Het Loo Palace), (Gerard Valck, Amsterdam, 1689–1693). Rijksmuseum, Amsterdam.

p. 122: Daniel Marot (possibly), etching, *Paviljoen tus.sen twee hoge heggen* (*Garden pavilion between two Hedges*) 1703–1712. Rijksmuseum, Amsterdam.

p. 124: Anon. etching, after design by Daniel Marot (I) *L'Escallier de la Maison Royalle de Loo, Invente par D. Marot* (*Staircase of the Palais Het Loo, Designed by D. Marot*), after 1703–before 1800. Rijksmuseum, Amsterdam.

p. 126: Anon. engraving and letter press, title page *from De verstandige kock, of sorghvuldige huyshoudter . . .* (*The Sensible Cook or Careful Housekeeper . . .*), (Amsterdam: M. de Groot, 1683). General Research Division, The New York Public Library.

p. 128: Anna Maria Vaiani, engraving, from Giovanni Battista Ferrari, *De florum cultura* (Rome: Stephanus Paulinus, 1633). Dumbarton Oaks Research Library and Collection, Trustees for Harvard University, Washington, D.C.

p. 131: Jan Luyken, etching, *Kroning van Willem III en Maria II, 1689* (Amsterdam: Jurriaen van Poolsum, Utrecht: 1689). Rijksmuseum, Amsterdam.

p. 133: James Basire (1730–1802), engraving after an unknown artist, *A View of the Old Palace at Hampton Court from the Thames.* Yale Center for British Art, Paul Mellon Collection.

p. 135: Nicolas Bazin, etching, *Femme de qualité déshabillée pour le bain* (*A woman of quality undressed for bathing*), 1683. Musée Carnavalet–Histoire de Paris.

p. 138: Jacques Rigaud, *Prospect of Hampton Court from the Garden Side*, 1736, engraving, Yale Center for British Art, Paul Mellon Collection.

p. 141: Anon. engraving, *Queen Mary II Lying in State* (London: John Overton, 1695). Wellcome Collection, London.

p. 144: Etching and engraving, *Trade card of china-woman Jane Taylor & Son, china & glass sellers, at the Feathers in Pall Mall, London*, ca. 1750–1770. © The Trustees of the British Museum.

p. 145: Anon. etching, "*Stand Coachman, or the haughty lady well fitted*" (J. Wakelin, 1750). ©The Trustees of the British Museum. All rights reserved.

p. 154: Engraving, "Chimney in the China Room" from Horace Walpole, *A description of the villa of Mr. Horace Walpole : youngest son of Sir Robert Walpole Earl of Orford at Strawberry-Hill at Twickenham, Middlesex. With an inventory of the furniture, pictures, curiosities, &c* . . . (London: Thomas Kirgate, 1784). Yale University, Lewis Walpole Library.

p. 158: Barent de Bakker, after a drawing by Antoni Zürcher, etching, *Portret van Prinses Frederica Sophia Wilhelmina te paard* (*Portrait of Princess Frederica Sophia Wilhelmina on horseback*), (Amsterdam, 1789–1804). Rijksmuseum, Amsterdam.

p. 162: Walter Crane, color wood engraving, "My Lady's Chamber," frontispiece from Clarence Cook, *The House Beautiful, Essays on Beds and Tables, Stools and Candlesticks* (New York: Scribner, Armstrong and Company, 1878). Author's collection.

p. 165: Samson & Cie, pen, ink and watercolor, original design for a Delft *bliksem* (lightning) dish, ca. 1845 or later. Author's collection.

p. 168: Frontispiece, "China Hunting at Daisy Farm," from Annie Trumbull Slosson, *The China Hunter's Club*, (New York, Harper & Brothers, 1878). Author's collection.

p. 172: Illustration, "Philadelphia, Pa.—Headquarters of the Women's Centennial Executive Committee, 903 Walnut St.—Mrs. E. D. Gillespie receiving reports from sub-committees." From Frank H. Norton, ed., *Frank Leslie's Historical Register of the United States Centennial Exposition, 1876* (New York: Frank Leslie's Publishing House, 1877). Courtesy of the Free Library of Philadelphia, Print and Picture Collection.

p. 173: Illustration, "The Women's Pavilion", from Frank H. Norton, ed., *Frank Leslie's Historical Register of the United States Centennial Exposition, 1876 (*New York: Frank Leslie's Publishing House, 1877). Author's collection.

p. 175: Cover, from Alice Morse Earle, *China Collecting in America* (Charles Scribner's Sons, 1892). Author's collection.

p. 181: Charles Antoine Goutzwiller, title page from Henry Havard, *Histoire de la Faïence de Delft* (Paris: E. Plon et Cie, 1878). Author's collection.

p. 184: Stereograph, *Woman's Pavilion from Gallery*, The Centennial Photographic Co., 1876. The Miriam and Ira D. Wallach Division of Art, Prints and Photographs: Photography Collection, The New York Public Library.

p. 191: Elias Martin (1739–1818*), Reading Lesson at a Dame School*, undated, graphite, pen and ink, and watercolor. Yale Center for British Art, Paul Mellon Collection.

p. 193: Illustration from "Colonial Dames of New York State Give Their Friends a Breakfast at Sherry's," *The Journal* (New York), March 13, 1896. Library of Congress, Washington, D.C.

p. 197: Photographic illustration, "The van Cortlandt Mansion" from *Van Cortlandt mansion : erected 1748, now in the custody of the Colonial Dames of the State of New York / [prepared by Mrs. Morris Patterson Ferris]*. 1897. National Society of Colonial Dames in the State of New York.

p. 202: Anon. photograph, *Ballroom, Mr. and Mrs. Cornelius Vanderbilt II residence, New York*, 1892–1926. Archives of American Art, Smithsonian Institution.

p. 203: Burton Frederick Welles, photograph, *West 57th St.–Mrs. Cornelius Vanderbilt–Hotel Plaza–West 59th St., from his book Fifth Avenue New York from Start to Finish*, (New York: Welles & Co., 1911). Irma and Paul Milstein Division of United States History, Local History, and Genealogy, The New York Public Library.

p. 209: Photomechanical print, *New York. Van Cortlandt Manor–Van Cortlandt Park*, Raphael Tuck & Sons, ca. 1908. Author's collection.

p. 211: Illustration from "Van Cortlandt Manor Formally Opened by the Colonial Dames." *The World* (New York), May 28, 1897, 9. https://newscomwc.newspapers.com/image/3161944/.

p. 214: Photomechanical print, *Dutch Room, Van Cortlandt House*, (The Albertype Co., Brooklyn, NY, ca. 1918). Author's collection.

p. 214: Photomechanical print, *The Dutch Garden, Van Cortlandt Park, N.Y.*, 1909. Author's collection.

p. 216: Photomechanical print. *The Dutch Garden, Van Cortlandt Park, N.Y.*, ca. 1910. Author's collection.

p. 216: Photomechanical print, *Colonial Gardens, Van Cortlandt Park, N.Y.*, ca. 1916. Author's collection.

p. 218: Photomechanical print, *Hudson-Fulton Celebration, 1909* (Valentine & Sons Pub. Co., 1909). Author's collection.

p. 221: Photomechanical print, *Hudson-Fulton Celebration Commission Official post card no. 20, Float-Bowling on Bowling Green (*Redfield Brothers, Inc., 1909). Author's collection.

p. 221: Photomechanical print, *Hudson-Fulton Celebration Commission Official post card no. 22, Float-Dutch Doorway*, 1909. Author's collection.

p. 232: Anon. engraving, *Julia Parker Wightman* bookplate, ca. 1945. Author's collection.

p. 236: Francis L. V. Hoppin, *Van Cortlandt House Museum*, ca. 1911, commercial color lithograph. The Miriam and Ira D. Wallach Division of Art, Prints and Photographs: Art & Architecture Collection, The New York Public Library.

p. 237: Photographic reproduction "Collection of Dutch Delft" from *Van Cortlandt House Museum, Van Cortlandt Park, City of New York,* 1955. The National Society of Colonial Dames in the State of New York.

p. 239: Louis Berger & Associates, diagram, "Location of Shovel Tests at Van Cortlandt Mansion, Bronx. New York" from *Phase I Archaeological Investigation Of Proposed Sewage/Plumbing Lines And Seepage Basin At Van Cortlandt Mansion . . . ,* 1987. The New York City Landmarks Preservation Commission.

Color Illustrations

Figure 1: A Dutch Tile Panel Depicting a Tile and Pottery Factory in Bolsward, painted decoration attributed to Dirk Danser (1698–1763), Bolsward, ca. 1745–1765. Rijksmuseum, Amsterdam.

Figure 2: A Pair of Dutch Delft Blue and White Bloempiramides (Flower Pyramids), attributed to De Metaale Pot (The Metal Pot) Factory (Lambertus van Eenhoorn), ca. 1692–1700, three segments and top executed by Tichelaar, Makkum, 2004, glazed earthenware. Rijksmuseum, Amsterdam.

Figure 3: Disassembled View of a Dutch Delft Blue and White Bloempiramide (Flower Pyramid), attributed to De Metaale Pot (The Metal Pot) Factory (Lambertus van Eenhoorn), ca. 1692–1700, three segments and top executed by Tichelaar, Makkum, 2004, glazed earthenware. Rijksmuseum, Amsterdam.

Figure 4: A Dutch Delft Blue and White Large Tile with a Bust of William III, De Grieksche A (The Greek A) Factory, period of Adrianus Kocx, ca. 1694. The Metropolitan Museum of Art, New York.

Figure 5: A Dutch Delft Blue and White Large Tile with a Birdcage and Putti, De Grieksche A (The Greek A) Factory, period of Adrianus Kocx, ca. 1690. Rijksmuseum, Amsterdam. Loan from the Royal Antiquarian Society.

Figure 6: A Dutch Delft blue and white large tile with a covered urn flanked by two female warriors, De Grieksche A (The Greek A) Factory, period of Adrianus Kocx, ca. 1690. Rijksmuseum, Amsterdam, loan from the Royal Antiquarian Society.

Figures 7A and 7B: A Dutch Delft Blue and White Puzzle Jug, Het Oude Moriaanshooft (The Old Moor's Head) Factory, marks G.VS for Geertruij Verstelle, ca. 1769. The National Society of Colonial Dames in the State of New York.

Figures 8A and 8B: A Dutch Delft Blue and White "Wanli" Style Deep Bowl, 1677. The National Society of Colonial Dames in the State of New York.

Figure 9: A Dutch Delft Blue and White Seated Figure of Budai Heshang, ca. 1720. The National Society of Colonial Dames in the State of New York.

Figure 10: Two Dutch Delft Polychrome Groups of Birds Perched in Trees, ca. 1760. The National Society of Colonial Dames in the State of New York.

Figures 11A and 11B: A Pair of Dutch Delft Doré Birdcages, ca. 1730. The National Society of Colonial Dames in the State of New York.

Figure 12: A Dutch Delft Polychrome Circular Butter Tub, Cover and Stand Depicting a Child with Birdcage, De Witte Ster (The White Star) Factory, ca. 1764. The National Society of Colonial Dames in the State of New York.

Figures 13A and 13B: A Dutch Delft Doré Circular Scalloped Barber's Bowl, ca. 1720–30. The National Society of Colonial Dames in the State of New York.

Figures 14A and 14B: A Dutch Delft Doré Butter Tub and Cover, ca. 1740. The National Society of Colonial Dames in the State of New York.

Figures 15A and 15B: A Dutch Delft Doré Plate, De Grieksche A (The Greek A) Factory, ca. 1710, marked PAK in iron-red for Pieter Adriaensz. Kocx, the owner of The Greek A from 1701 to 1703, or his widow Johanna van der Heul, the owner of the factory from 1703 to 1722. The National Society of Colonial Dames in the State of New York.

Figure 16: A Dutch Delft Polychrome Oval Butter Tub and Cover, De Grieksche A (The Greek A) Factory, ca. 1758–64. The National Society of Colonial Dames in the State of New York.

Figure 17: A Pair of Dutch Delft Blue and White Models of Sleighs, ca. 1740. The National Society of Colonial Dames in the State of New York.

Figure 18: A Dutch Delft 'Persian Blue' Pewter-Mounted Ewer, De Paauw (The Peacock) Factory, ca. 1690–1710. The National Society of Colonial Dames in the State of New York.

Figures 19A and 19B: A Dutch Delft 'Persian Blue' Teapot and Cover, De Paauw (The Peacock) Factory, ca. 1690–1710. The National Society of Colonial Dames in the State of New York.

Figure 20: A Dutch Delft Blue and White Large Dish, De Drie Klokken (The Three Bells) Factory, ca. 1775. The National Society of Colonial Dames in the State of New York.

Figure 21: A Dutch Delft Polychrome Bliksem (Lightning) Plate, De Paauw (The Peacock) Factory, ca. 1720. The National Society of Colonial Dames in the State of New York.

Figure 22: A Blue and White Dutch Delft "Marriage" Plate, 1688. The National Society of Colonial Dames in the State of New York.

Figure 23: A Dutch Delft Blue and White Large Dish, ca. 1790. The National Society of Colonial Dames in the State of New York.

Figure 24: A Dutch Delft Blue and White Small Plate, ca. 1740–50. The National Society of Colonial Dames in the State of New York.

Figure 25: A Dutch Delft Blue and White Large Plate, De Dubbelde Schenkkan (The Double Jug) Factory, ca. 1765. The National Society of Colonial Dames in the State of New York.

Figure 26: A Dutch Delftware Blue and White Large Plate, De Klaauw (The Claw) Factory, ca. 1725–40. The National Society of Colonial Dames in the State of New York.

Figure 27: A Dutch Delft Polychrome Plate, ca. 1790. The National Society of Colonial Dames in the State of New York.

Figure 28: Two Dutch Delft Polychrome Orangist Vases and Covers, ca. 1785–95. The National Society of Colonial Dames in the State of New York.

Figure 29: A Dutch Delft Polychrome Orangist Large Plate, ca. 1789. The National Society of Colonial Dames in the State of New York.

Figure 30: A Dutch Delft Orangist Large Plate, ca. 1789. The National Society of Colonial Dames in the State of New York.

Figure 31: A Dutch Delft Polychrome Figure of a Woman, ca. 1760. The National Society of Colonial Dames in the State of New York.

Figure 32: Cover, *The China Hunters Club* by Annie Trumbull Slosson (New York: Harper & Brothers, 1878). Author's collection.

Figure 33: An American Grisaille-Painted Kast, Hudson River Valley, ca. 1700, with three Dutch Delft blue and white tobacco jars with brass lids, 18th century. The Van Cortlandt House Museum, New York. The National Society of Colonial Dames in the State of New York. (Photo, Laura J. Carpenter Myers).

Bibliography

Archives and Document Collections

The Frick Collection and Frick Art Research Library Archives, New York: Henry Clay Frick Papers, Correspondence.

Koninklijke Bibliotheek (KB), National Library of the Netherlands, The Hague, Netherlands.

The Metropolitan Museum of Art Archives, New York: Annual Reports.

The National Museum of Asian Art Archives, Smithsonian Institution, Washington, D.C.: Charles Lang Freer Papers, Correspondence.

The National Society of Colonial Dames in the State of New York, New York: Archives, Annual Reports, Committee Minutes, Registers.

The National Society of Colonial Dames of America, Dumbarton House, Washington, D.C.: Archives, NSCDA Historic Roster.

Stadsarchief Delft (Delft City Archives), Den Hoorn, South Holland, Netherlands: Doop, Trouw en Begrafenisregister (DTB); Oud Notarieel Archief (ONA).

The Van Cortlandt House Museum, Bronx, New York: Archives.

Books, Periodicals, and Miscellaneous Sources

General Reference

Aken-Fehmers, Marion S. van, Loet A. Schledorn, A. G. Hesselink, and Titus M. Eliëns. *Delfts Aardewerk: Geschiedenis van een Nationaal Product*. Vol. I. Waanders Uitgevers; Gemeentemuseum Den Haag, 1999.

Aken-Fehmers, Marion S. van, Loet A. Schledorn, and Titus M. Eliëns. *Delfts Aardewerk: Geschiedenis van een Nationaal Product*. Vol. II. Waanders Uitgevers; Gemeentemuseum Den Haag, 2001.

Aken-Fehmers, Marion S. van, Loet A. Schledorn, and Titus M. Eliëns. *Delftware: History of a National Product, De Porceleyne Fles*. Vol. III. Waanders Uitgevers, 2003.

Aken-Fehmers, Marion S. van, Titus M. Eliëns, and Suzanne M. R. Lambooy. *DelftWare WonderWare: Het Wonder van Delfts Blauw*. Waanders Uitgevers; Gemeentemuseum Den Haag, 2012.

Aken-Fehmers, Marion S. van, Frederike Burghout, Nina Linde Jaspers, Suzanne M. R. Lambooy, Luc Megens, Sebastiaan Ostkamp, and Gus Verhaar. *Delfts Wit, Het is niet alles blauw dat in Delft blinkt/ White Delft, Not just blue*. Vol. V. Waanders Uitgevers; Gemeentemuseum Den Haag, 2013.

Alayrac-Fielding, Vanessa. "'Frailty, Thy Name Is China': Women, Chinoiserie, and the Threat of Low Culture in Eighteenth-Century England." *Women's History Review* 18, no. 4 (2009): 659–668.

Aronson, Robert D., Celine Ariaans, and Sacha Serra. *Below the Glaze: A Family Affair, Delftware Facts and Figures*. Aronson Antiquairs, 2019.

Ayers, John, Olivier Impey, and J.V.G. Mallet. *Porcelain for Palaces: The Fashion for Japan in Europe 1650–1750*. Philip Wilson, 1990.

Bischoff, Cordula. "Women collectors and the rise of the porcelain cabinet," in *Chinese and Japanese porcelain for the Dutch Golden Age*, ed. Jan van Campen and Titus Eliëens (Waanders, 2014), 171–189.

Bleyswijck, Dirck van. *Beschryvinge der Stadt Delft*. Arnold Bon, 1667.

Chen, Jennifer, Julie Emerson, and Mimi Gates, eds. *Porcelain Stories: From China to Europe*. University of Washington Press, 2000.

Dam, Jan Daniël van. *Delffse Porceleyne/Dutch Delftware 1620–1850*. Rijksmuseum; Waanders Uitgevers, 2004.

Dekker, Rudolf Michel, and Marybeth Carlson. "Women in the Medieval and Early Modern Netherlands." *Journal of Women's History* 10, no. 2 (Summer 1998): 165–188.

De Jonge, Caroline H., and Marie Christine Hellin. *Delft Ceramics*. Praeger Publishers, 1970.

Emerson, Julie, et al. *Porcelain Stories from China to Europe*. Seattle Art Museum/ University of Washington Press, 2000.

Havard, Henry. *Histoire de la Faïence de Delft*. E. Plon et Cie, 1878.

Havard, Henry. *Histoire de la Faïence de Delft, Seconde Partie*. E. Plon et Cie, 1878.

Helmers, Helmer J., and Geert H. Janssen, eds. *The Cambridge Companion to the Dutch Golden Age*. Cambridge Companions to Culture. Cambridge University Press, 2018.

Heuvel, Danielle van den. *Women and Entrepreneurship: Female Traders in the Northern Netherlands c. 1580–1815*. Aksant, 2007.

Hoekstra-Klein, Wik. *De Griekse A, 1657–1818: Geschiedenis van de Delftse Plateelbakkerijen, Deel 9*. Projectgroep Delfts Aardewerk, Stedelijk Museum Het Prinsenhof Delft, 2003.

Hoekstra-Klein, Wik. *De Porceleyne Clauw: Geschiedenis van de Delftse Plateelbakkerijen, Deel 2*. Projectgroep Delfts Aardewerk, Stedelijk Museum Het Prinsenhof Delft, 1999.

Hufton, Owen. *The Prospect Before Her: A History of Women in Western Europe.* HarperCollins, 1995.

Hufton, Olwen. *Signs* 14, no. 1 (1988): 223–228. http://www.jstor.org/stable/3174674.

Impey, Oliver, and Arthur MacGregor, eds. *The Origins of Museums: The Cabinet of Curiosities in Sixteenth- and Seventeenth-Century Europe.* Clarendon, 1985.

Israel, Jonathan. *The Dutch Republic: Its Rise, Greatness, and Fall, 1477–1806.* Oxford University Press, 1995.

Lahaussois, Christine. *Faïences de Delft.* Musée Sèvres; Réunion des Musées Nationaux, 1998.

Macleod, Dianne Sachko. *Enchanted Lives, Enchanted Objects: American Women Collectors and the Making of Culture, 1800–1940.* University of California Press, 2008.

Montias, John Michael. *Artists and Artisans in Delft: A Socio-Economic Study of the Seventeenth Century.* Princeton University Press, 1982.

Montias, John Michael. "The Guild of St. Luke in 17th-Century Delft and the Economic Status of Artists and Artisans." *Simiolus: Netherlands Quarterly for the History of Art* 9, no. 2 (1977): 93–105. https://doi.org/10.2307/3780327.

Moore, N. Hudson. *Delftware, Dutch and English.* Frederick A. Stokes Company, 1908.

Munger, Jeffrey H., and Elizabeth L. Sullivan. *European Porcelain in The Metropolitan Museum of Art.* Metropolitan Museum of Art, 2018.

Neurdenburg, Elisabeth. *Old Dutch Pottery and Tiles.* Translated by Bernard Rackham. Benn Brothers Ltd., 1923.

Odell, Dawn. "Delftware and the Domestication of Chinese Porcelain." In *EurAsian Matters: China, Europe, and the Transcultural Object, 1600–1800,* edited by Anna Grasskamp and Monica Juneja. Springer, 2018.

Paape, Gerrit. *De Plateelbakker of Delftsch Aardewerkmaaker.* A. Blussé en Zoon, 1794. Reprint. B. V. Buijten & Schipperheijn/Repro Holland, 1978.

Pierson, Stacey. *Collectors, Collections and Museums: The Field of Chinese Ceramics in Britain, 1560–1960.* Peter Lang, 2007.

Sabben, Arno van, Johan ten Broeke, and Richard Oudenberg. *Antieke Tegels, Antique Tiles, Carreaux Anciens.* Van Sabben Kunst en Antiquiteiten, 2000.

Schama, Simon. *The Embarrassment of Riches: An Interpretation of Dutch Culture in the Golden Age.* Alfred A. Knopf, 1987.

Schmidt, Ariadne. "Women and Guilds: Corporations and Female Labour Market Participation in Early Modern Holland." *Gender & History* 21, no. 1 (April 2009): 170–189.

Shorto, Russell. *The Island at the Center of the World: The Epic Story of Dutch Manhattan and the Forgotten Colony That Shaped America.* Vintage Books, 2005.

Sloboda, Stacey. "Porcelain Bodies: Gender, Acquisitiveness and Taste in 18th-century England." In *Material Cultures 1740–1920: The Meanings and Pleasures of Collecting,* edited by Alla Myzelev and John Potvin. Ashgate, 2009.

Spaander, I. and R. A. Leeuw, eds. *De stad Delft: Cultuur en maatschappij van 1572 tot 1667.* 2 vols. Stedelijk Museum Het Prinsenhof, 1981.

Temple, William. *Observations upon the United Provinces of the Netherlands.* A. Maxwell for Sa. Gellibrand, 1673.

Wheeler, Walter. "'Once Adorned with Quaint Dutch Tiles . . .': A Preliminary Analysis of Delft Tiles Found in Archaeological Contexts and Historical Collections in the Upper Hudson Valley." In *Soldiers, Cities, and Landscapes: Papers in Honor of Charles L. Fisher,* edited by Penelope B. Drooker, John P. Hart, and Charles Fisher. University of the State of New York, State Education Department, 2010.

Wiel, Kees van der. "A Look Inside the Homes of Rich and Poor in 18th century Delft." Posted October 7, 2019. https://www.achterdegevelsvandelft.nl/achtergrondverhalen/thera%20wijsenbeek-olthuis/Kijkje-binnenshuis.html.

A blue-and-white *woordenlijst*

Ten Broeke, Johan, Arno van Sabben, and Richard Woudenberg. *Antieke Tegels/Antique Tiles/Carreaux Anciens.* Van Sabben Art and Antiques, 2000.

Washburn, E. W., H. Ries, and A. L. Day. "Report of the Committee on Definition of the Term 'Ceramics.'" *Journal of the American Ceramic Society* 3, no. 7 (1920): 526–536. https://doi.org/10.1111/j.1151-2916.1920.tb17297.x.

Introduction

Earle, Alice Morse. *China Collecting in America.* Charles Scribner's Sons, 1892.

Stott, Annette. *Holland Mania: The Unknown Dutch Period in American Art & Culture.* Overlook Press, 1998.

Vincentelli, Moira. *Women and Ceramics: Gendered Vessels.* Manchester University Press; St. Martin's Press, 2000.

Chapter One: *Delven*

Abellan, C. Arias. "'Albus-Candidus, Ater-Niger and Ruber-Rutilus' in Ovid's 'Metamorphoses' A Structural Research." *Latomus* 43, no. 1 (1984): 111–117. http://www.jstor.org/stable/41533888.

Banta, Andaleeb Badiee, and Alexa Greist, with Theresa Kutasz Christensen. *Making Her Mark.* Goose Lane Editions, in association with the Art Gallery of Ontario and the Baltimore Museum of Art, 2023.

City of New York, Landmarks Preservation Commission. Marianne S. Percival. *National Society of Colonial Dames in the State of New York Headquarters Designation Report.* Landmarks Preservation Commission, 2019. https://s-media.nyc.gov/agencies/lpc/lp/2605.pdf.

Erickson, Michelle. "How Was It Made? A Puzzle Jug by Michelle Erickson." Video. Posted September 30, 2015, by Victoria and Albert Museum. YouTube, 6:26. https://youtu.be/s7gXmra-i7M.

Goethe, Johann Wolfgang von. *Theory of Colours*. Translated from the German with notes by Charles Lock Eastlake. John Murray, 1840.

Griffith, R. Drew. "Gods' Blue Hair in Homer and in Eighteenth-Dynasty Egypt." *The Classical Quarterly,* 55, no. 2 (2005): 329–34. http://www.jstor.org/stable/4493341.

Grimm, Jacob. *Teutonic Mythology*. Vol. 2. Translated by James Steven Stallybrass. George Bell & Sons, 1883.

Grimm, Jacob, and Wilhelm Grimm. *Deutsches Wörterbuch*. Contributions by Moriz Heyne, Rudolf Hildebrand, Friedrich Ludwig Karl Weigand, and Matthias von Lexer. Verlag von S. Hirzel, 1868.

Merrill, Linda. *The Peacock Room: A Cultural Biography*. Freer Gallery of Art, Smithsonian Institution; Yale University Press, 1998.

Newton, Isaac. "A Letter of Mr. Isaac Newton . . . Containing His New Theory about Light and Colors." *Philosophical Transactions of the Royal Society*, no. 80 (February 19, 1672): 3083. Published online January 2003. https://www.newtonproject.ox.ac.uk/view/texts/normalized/NATP00006.

Orsel, Edwin. "Brickwork in Leiden: A Survey of Sixteenth and Seventeenth Century Characteristics." Paper presented at Proceedings of The Second International Congress on Construction History, Queens' College, Cambridge University, March 29–April 2, 2006.

Pastoureau, Michel. *Blue: The History of a Color*. Princeton University Press, 2001.

Rosenzweig, Roy, and Elizabeth Blackmar. *The Park and the People: A History of Central Park*. Cornell University Press, 1992.

Saarinen, Aline B. *The Proud Possessors: The Lives, Times and Taste of Some Adventurous American Art Collectors*. Random House, 1958.

The Welikia Project. "Manahaata Map 1609." Wildlife Conservation Society, Bronx, New York. 2010–2013. https://welikia.org/explore/mannahatta-map/.

Winter, John, and Elisabeth West FitzHugh. "Some Technical Notes on Whistler's 'Peacock Room.'" *Studies in Conservation* 30, no. 4 (1985): 149–154. https://doi.org/10.2307/1506035.

Chapter Two: Shop Daughter

Bakker, R. *Den opkomst, bloei, verval en tegenwoordigen toestand der stad Delft, in derzelver fabryken en trafyken*. [n.p.], c. 1800.

Berkhey, Johannes le Francq van. *Natuurlyke Historie van Holland*. Vol. 2. Yntema and Tieboel, 1769.

Berkhey, Johannes le Francq van. *Natuurlyke Historie van Holland*. Vol. 3. Yntema and Tieboel, 1772.

Borschberg, Peter. "The Seizure of the Sta. Catarina Revisited: The Portuguese Empire in Asia, VOC Politics and the Origins of the Dutch-Johor Alliance

(1602–c. 1616)." *Journal of Southeast Asian Studies* 33, no. 1 (2002): 31–62. http://www.jstor.org/stable/20072387.

Brook, Timothy. "Trading places: the Santa Catarina brought the first large shipment of porcelain from the Far East to Europe, creating a demand for new luxury goods, which feature in paintings of the Dutch Golden Age." *Apollo*, November 2015, 70–74.

Cats, Jacob. *Houwelyck, dat is, De gansche gelegtheydt des Echten staets.* Inde druckerye van Jan Pietersz van de Venne, 1625.

Child, Josiah. *Brief Observations Concerning Trade and Interest of Money.* Printed for Elizabeth Calvert at the Black-Spread Eagle in Barbican, and Henry Mortlock at the Sign of the White-Heart in Westminster Hall, 1668.

Coutis, Howard. *The Art of Ceramics: European Ceramic Design 1500–1830.* Yale University Press, 2001.

Dobson, C. G. "Two Thousand Years of Slating and Tiling." *Official Architecture and Planning* 23, no. 9 (1960): 397–406. http://www.jstor.org/stable/44128777.

Dubelaar, C. W., P.J.M. Kisters, and J. W. Stroucken. "A Natural-Stone City Walk Through Maastricht, the Netherlands." *Netherlands Journal of Geosciences—Geologie en Mijnbouw* 90, no. 2/3 (2011): 197–208.

Frijhoff, Willem. "Calvinism, Literacy, and Reading Culture in the Early Modern Northern Netherlands: Towards a Reassessment." *Archiv für Reformationsgeschichte—Archive for Reformation History* 95, no. 1 (2004): 252–265. https://doi.org/10.14315/arg-2004-0111.

Gabbard, D. Christopher. "The Dutch Wives' Good Husbandry: Defoe's Roxana and Financial Literacy." *Eighteenth-Century Studies* 37, no. 2 (2004): 237–251. https://dx.doi.org/10.1353/ecs.2004.0006.

Groen, Karin. *Earth Matters: Paintings in the Laboratory: Scientific Examination for Art History and Conservation.* Archetype Publications, 2014.

Guicciardini, Lodovico. *Descrittione di tutti Paesi Bassi, The Description of the Low Countreys and of the Prouinces Thereof, Gathered into an Epitome out of the Historie of Lodouico Guicchardini.* Peter Short for Thomas Chard, 1593.

"History of Clay Science: A Young Discipline." In *Developments in Clay Science*, edited by Faïza Bergaya, Benny K. G. Theng, and Gerhard Lagaly, vol. 1, 1163–1181. Elsevier, 2006.

Houston, Rab. "Literacy and Society in the West, 1500–1850." *Social History* 8, no. 3 (1983): 269–293. http://www.jstor.org/stable/4285275.

Ittersum, Martine Julia van. "Hugo Grotius in Context: Van Heemskerck's Capture of the 'Santa Catarina' and Its Justification in 'De Jure Praedae' (1604–1606)." *Asian Journal of Social Science* 31, no. 3 (2003): 511–548. http://www.jstor.org/stable/23654730.

Kaestle, Carl F. "The History of Literacy and the History of Readers." *Review of Research in Education* 12 (1985): 11–53. https://www.jstor.org/stable/1167145.

Kuijpers, Erika. "Lezen en Schrijven: Onderzoek naar het Alfabetiseringsniveau in de Zeventiende-Eeuws Amsterdam." *Tijdschrift voor Sociale Geschiedenis*, no. 4 (1997): 490–522.

Letwin, William. *Sir Josiah Child, Merchant Economist*. Baker Library, Harvard Business School, 1959.

Lucassen, Jan. "A Multinational and Its Labor Force: The Dutch East India Company, 1595–1795." *International Labor and Working-Class History*, no. 66 (2004): 12–39. http://www.jstor.org/stable/27672956.

Miert, Dirk van. "Education." In *The Cambridge Companion to the Dutch Golden Age*, edited by H. J. Helmers and G. H. Janssen, Cambridge Companions to Culture. Cambridge University Press, 2018.

Montague, William. *The delights of Holland: or, A three months travel about that and the other provinces With observations and reflections on their trade, wealth, strength, beauty, policy, &c. together with a catalogue of the rarities in the anatomical school at Leyden*. Printed for John Sturton and A. Bosvile, 1696.

Moryson, Fynes. *An Itinerary Written by Fynes Moryson Gent. First in the Latine Tongue, and Then Translated by Him into English: Containing His Ten Yeeres Travell Through the Twelve Dominions of Germany, Bohmerland, Sweitzerland, Netherland, Denmarke, Poland, Jtaly, Turky, France, England, Scotland, and Ireland. Divided into III Parts.* John Beale, 1617.

Orsel, Edwin. "Brickwork in Leiden: A Survey of Sixteenth- and Seventeenth-Century Characteristics." In *Second International Congress on Construction History*, Queens' College, Cambridge University, March 29–April 2, 2006, 2379–2394.

Riemens, Kornelis Jacobus. *Esquisse Historique de l'Enseignement du Français en Hollande du XVIe au XIXe Siècle*. Société d'Éditions A. W. Sijthoff, 1919.

Schurman, Anna Maria van. *The Learned Maid, or, Whether a Maid May Be a Scholar*. Printed by John Redmayne, 1659.

Sewel, Willem. *Groot Woordenboek der Nederduytsche en Engelsche*. De Weduwe van Steven Swart by de Beurs, 1708.

Shulsky, Linda R. "Kensington and de Voorst: Two Porcelain Collections." *Journal of the History of Collections*. 2, no. 1 (1990): 47–62.

Smith, Terence Paul. "On 'Small Yellow Bricks . . . from Holland.'" *Construction History* 17 (2001): 31–42. http://www.jstor.org/stable/41613829.

Staubach, Suzanne. *Clay: The History and Evolutions of Humankind's Relationship with Earth's Most Primal Element*. Berkley Books, 2005.

TeBrake, William H. "Taming the Waterwolf: Hydraulic Engineering and Water Management in the Netherlands during the Middle Ages." *Technology and Culture* 43, no. 3, Water Technology in the Netherlands (July 2002): 475–499.

Technische Adviescommissie voor de Waterkeringen (Technical Advisory Committee for Flood Defense in The Netherlands). *Technical Report: Clay for Dikes*. The Road and Hydraulic Engineering Institute (DWW) of the Directorate-General of Transport, Public Works and Water Management (Rijkswaterstaat), May 1996.

Temple, William. *Observations upon the United Provinces of the Netherlands.* A. Maxwell for Sa. Gellibrand, 1673.

Tilburg, Marja van. "Becoming a Woman in the Dutch Republic: Advice Literature for Young Adult Women of the Seventeenth and Eighteenth Centuries." In *The Youth of Early Modern Women*, edited by Elizabeth S. Cohen and Margaret Reeves, 255–274. Amsterdam University Press, 2018. https://doi.org/10.2307/j.ctv8pzd5z.15.

Van Beek, Pieta. *The First Female University Student: Anna Maria van Schurman (1636).* Translated by Anna-Mart Bonthuys and Dineke Ehlers. Igitur, Utrecht Publishing & Archiving Services, 2010.

Vries, Annette de. "Toonbeelden van huiselijkheid of arbeidzaamheid? De iconografie van de spinster in relatie tot de verbeelding van arbeid en beroep in de vroegmoderne Nederlanden." *Tijdschrift voor Sociale en Economische Geschiedenis* 2, no. 3 (2005): 103–125. https://doi.org/10.18352/tseg.764.

Chapter Three: The Delft Thunderclap

Drees, M. M. "'Providential Discourse' Reconsidered: The Case of the Delft Thunderclap (1654)." *Dutch Crossing* 40, no. 2 (2016): 108–121.

Hoekstra-Klein, Wik. *De Drie Klokken: Geschiedenis van de Delftse Plateelbakkerijen, Deel 4.* Projectgroep Delfts Aardewerk, Stedelijk Museum Het Prinsenhof Delft, 2000.

Marck, Liesbeth van der, and Marianne Eisma, eds. *De Notaris in Woord en Beeld: De Cultuurhistorische Collectie van de Stichting tot Bevordering der Notariële Wetenschap / The Notary in Words and Images: The Cultural-Historical Collection of the Foundation for the Promotion of Notarial Science.* Waanders Publishers, 2013.

Obreen, F.D.O. *Archief voor Nederlandsche Kunstgeschiedenis.* 7 vols. Rotterdam, 1877–1890.

Rintjus, Hendrick. *Klioos stall. Part 1.* Leeuwarden, 1656.

Wheelock, Arthur K., Jr. *The Public and the Private in the Age of Vermeer.* Exh. cat. Osaka Municipal Museum of Art, 2000.

Chapter Four: *Weduwes*

Aken-Fehmers, Marion S. van. "'Ik dank Sinjeur voor zijne gunst, wij sullen het gedenken': De plateelbakkerij 'de Grieksche A' te Delft." *Jaarboek Haags Gemeentemuseum (1997).* The Hague, 1998, 52–63.

Bhattacharyya, Rituparna, and Suman Singh. "Exclusion (and Seclusion): Geographies of Disowned Widows of India." *GeoJournal* 83, no. 4 (2018): 757–774. http://www.jstor.org/stable/45117527.

Heuvel, Danielle van den, and Elise van Nederveen Meerkerk. "Introduction: Partners in Business? Spousal Cooperation in Trades in Early Modern England and the

Dutch Republic." *Continuity and Change* 23, no. 2 (2008): 209–216. https://doi.org/10.1017/S0268416008006838.

Houbraken, Arnold. *De Groote Schouburgh der Nederlantsche Konstschilders en Schilderessen (The Great Theatre of Netherlandish Painters and Paintresses), 1718–1721.* Translated by Hein Horn and Rieke van Leeuwen. RKD Nederlands Instituut voor Kunstgeschiedenis, 2021. https://houbraken-translated.rkdstudies.nl/.

Johnson, Samuel. *A Dictionary of the English Language*, 1755, 1773, edited by Beth Rapp Young, Jack Lynch, William Dorner, Amy Larner Giroux, Carmen Faye Mathes, and Abigail Moreshead. 2021. https://johnsonsdictionaryonline.com.

Jouwe, Nancy, Gerrit Verhoeven, and Ingrid van der Vlis, with the assistance of Marion Claessens and Bas van der Wulp. *Rapport Slavernijverleden van Delft.* Stadsarchief Delft, June 2023.

Schmidt, Ariadne. "Generous Provisions or Legitimate Shares? Widows and the Transfer of Property in 17th-Century Holland." *The History of the Family* 15, no. 1 (2010): 13–24.

Schmidt, Ariadne. "The Profits of Unpaid Work: 'Assisting Labour' of Women in the Early Modern Urban Dutch Economy." *The History of the Family* 19, no. 3 (2014): 301–322. https://doi.org/10.1080/1081602X.2014.884509.

Schmidt, Ariadne, and Manon van der Heijden. "Women Alone in Early Modern Dutch Towns: Opportunities and Strategies to Survive." *Journal of Urban History* 42, no. 1 (2016): 21–38. https://doi.org/10.1177/0096144215610771.

Wyntjes, Sherrin Marshall. "Survivors and Status: Widowhood and Family in the Early Modern Netherlands." *Journal of Family History* 7, no. 4 (Winter 1982): 396–405.

Zuidervaart, H. J. "A New Theory on the Origin of Two Paintings by Johannes Vermeer (1632–1675) of Delft." English translation of "Een nieuwe theorie over twee schilderijen van Johannes Vermeer (1632–1675)," in *Jaarboek Delfia Batavorum* 28 (2018): 9–34. Published May 23, 2019.

Zumthor, Paul. *Daily Life in Rembrandt's Holland.* Stanford University Press, 1994.

Chapter Five: Queen of Blue-and-White

Aken-Fehmers, Marion van, Sarah A. Bosmans, Claire Dumortier, Wies Erkelens, Ben Groen, and Christine Lahaussois. *Delfts Aardewerk, Geschiedenis van een Nationaal Product: Vazen met Tuiten, 300 Jaar Pronkstukken.* Deel iv / *Dutch Delftware, History of a National Product: Vases with Spouts, Three Centuries of Splendour.* Vol. IV. Gemeentemuseum Den Haag; Waanders Uitgevers, 2007.

Anonymous. *The Royal Diary: containing, I. King William's secret devotion. II. His practice of self-examination. III. His performance of relative duties . . . VIII. The private minutes relating to his last sikness.* The second ed. Printed for S. Malthus, c. 1702.

Archer, Michael. "Delft at Dyrham." *National Trust Yearbook 1975–76*, (1976): 12–18.

Archer, Michael. "Pyramids and Pagodas for Flowers." *Country Life*, January 22, 1976.

Archer, Michael. "Dutch Delft at the Court of William and Mary." *The International Ceramic Fair and Seminar Handbook*. London, 1984, 15–20.

Chapman, Hester W. *Mary II Queen of England*. Jonathan Cape, 1953.

Colvin, H. M., J. Mordaunt Crook, Kerry Downes, and John Newman. *The History of The King's Works, Vol. V, 1660–1782*. Her Majesty's Stationery Office, 1976.

Cowen, Pamela. "The Trianon de Porcelaine at Versailles." *The Magazine Antiques*, January 1993, 136–143.

Defoe, Daniel. *A Tour through the Whole Island of Great Britain*. Abridged and edited by P. N. Furbank and W. R. Owens, picture research by A. J. Coulson. Yale University Press, 1991.

Fiennes, Celia. *Through England on Side Saddle in the Time of William and Mary, Being the Diary of Celia Fiennes*. Field & Tuer; The Leadenhall Press; Simpkin, Marshall & Co.; Hamilton, Adams & Co.; Scribner & Welford, 1888.

Hamilton, Elizabeth. *William's Mary: A Biography of Mary II*. Taplinger Publishing Company, 1972.

Huygens Jr., Constantijn. *The Diary of Constantijn Huygens Jr: Secretary to Stadholder-King William of Orange*. Selected and translated by Rudolf Dekker. Panchaud, 2015.

Impey, Oliver, and Johanna Marshner. "'China Mania': A Reconstruction of Queen Mary II's Display of East Asian Artefacts in Kensington Palace in 1693." *Orientations* 29, no. 10 (November 1998): 60–61.

Keates, Jonathan, *William III and Mary II: Partners in Revolution*. Allen Lane, 2015.

Lambooy, Suzanne M. R. ed., *Koninklijk Blauw: Het Mooiste Delfts Aardewerk van Willem en Mary/ Delfts Aardewerk. Geschiedenis van een Nationaal Product,* Deel VI. Waanders Uitgevers; Kunstmuseum Den Haag; Paleis Het Loo, 2020.

Lipski, Louis L., and Michael Archer. *Dated English Delftware: Tin-Glazed Earthenware, 1600–1800*. Sotheby Publications, 1984.

Martin, Meredith. "Interiors and Interiority in the Ornamental Dairy Tradition." *Eighteenth Century Fiction* 20, no. 3 (2008): 357–384. https://dx.doi.org/10.1353/ecf.0.0002.

Martin, Meredith. *Dairy Queens: The Politics of Pastoral Architecture from Catherine de' Medici to Marie-Antoinette*. Harvard University Press, 2011.

Memoirs of Mary, Queen of England (1689–1693), Together with Her Letters and Those of King James II and William III to the Electress, Sophia of Hanover. Ed. Dr. R. Doebner. Veit & Comp.; D. Nutt, 1886.

Pomper, Linda. "Kensington and de Voorst: Two Porcelain Collections." *Journal of the History of Collections* 2, no. 1 (1990): 47–62.

Ronnes, Hanneke, and Merel Haverman. "A Reappraisal of the Architectural Legacy of King-Stadholder William III and Queen Mary II: Taste, Passion and Frenzy." *The Court Historian* 25, no. 2 (2020): 158–177.

Rose, Peter G. *The Sensible Cook: Dutch Foodways in the Old and the New World.* Translation of *De Verstandige Kok.* Syracuse University Press, 1989.

Shulsky, Linda Rosenfeld. "Queen Mary's Collection of Porcelain and Delft and Its Display at Kensington Palace: Based upon an Analysis of an Inventory Taken in 1697." *American Ceramic Circle Journal* 7 (1989): 51–74.

"The Archaeology of Hampton Court." *Current Archaeology*, September 14, 1994. https://archaeology.co.uk/articles/features/the-archaeology-of-hampton-court.htm.

Thurley, Simon. *Hampton Court: A Social and Architectural History.* Yale University Press, 2003.

Thurley, Simon. "William and Mary: The Court Divided." Lecture, Gresham College, London, June 10, 2020.

Treanor, Virginia. "'Une Abondance Extra Ordinaire': The Porcelain Collection of Amalia van Solms." *Early Modern Women* 9, no. 1 (2014): 141–154. http://www.jstor.org/stable/26431288.

Van der Kiste, John. *William and Mary: Heroes of the Glorious Revolution.* The History Press, 2008.

Wilson, Joan. "A Phenomenon of Taste: The China Ware of Queen Mary II." *Apollo Magazine* XCVI, no. 126 (New Series) (August 1972): 166–123.

Chapter Six: China-Women to China Hunters

Adams, Elizabeth. "Women in the Eighteenth Century Ceramic Trade and Some Detailed Prices of That Time." *Northern Ceramic Society Journal* 16 (1999): 1–2.

Almeroth-Williams, Thomas. *City of Beasts: How Animals Shaped Georgian London.* 1st ed. Manchester University Press, 2019.

Anderson, Anne. "'Fearful Consequences . . . of Living up to One's Teapot': Men, Women, and 'Cultchah' in the English Aesthetic Movement c. 1870–1900." *Victorian Literature and Culture* 37, no. 1 (2009): 219–254. http://www.jstor.org/stable/40347222.

Anderson, Anne. "Let Us Live up to It! Or Wilde about Teapots." *The Wildean*, no. 30 (2007): 13–35. http://www.jstor.org/stable/45269060.

Artan, Tülay. "Eighteenth-Century Ottoman Princesses as Collectors: Chinese and European Porcelains in the Topkapı Palace Museum." *Ars Orientalis* 39 (2010): 113–147.

Berry, Helen. "Polite Consumption: Shopping in Eighteenth-Century England." *Transactions of the Royal Historical Society* 12 (2002): 375–394.

Bolger, Doreen (Contributor). *In Pursuit of Beauty: Americans and the Aesthetic Movement.* The Metropolitan Museum of Art. Rizzoli, 1986.

Cocks, Anna Somers. "The Nonfunctional Use of Ceramics in the English Country House During the Eighteenth Century." *Studies in the History of Art* 25 (1989): 195–215. http://www.jstor.org/stable/42620696.

Coutts, Howard, with contributions from Patricia F. Ferguson. "Setting the Table at Gibside: The Bowes Family of County Durham and Their Ceramic Acquisitions in the 18th Century." *Transactions of the English Ceramic Circle* 27 (2016): 161–199.

Demaria, Robert, and Gwin J. Kolb. "Johnson's 'Dictionary' and Dictionary Johnson." *The Yearbook of English Studies* 28 (1998): 19–43. https://doi.org/10.2307/3508754.

Earle, Alice Morse. "A China Hunter in New England." *Scribner's Magazine*, September 1891.

Earle, Alice Morse. "Delft Ware." *The House Beautiful* 3, no. 4 (March 1898): 110—114.

Garachon, Isabelle. "Old Repairs of China and Glass." *The Rijksmuseum Bulletin* 58, no. 1 (2010): 35–54.

Gelber, Steven M. *Hobbies Leisure and the Culture of Work in America*. Columbia University Press, 1999.

Grosley, Pierre Jean. *A Tour to London, Or, New Observations on England and Its Inhabitants*. Vol. 1. Translated by Thomas Nugent. Lockyer Davis, 1772.

Hamilton, Walter. *The Aesthetic Movement in England*. Reeves and Turner, 1882.

Hildyard, Robin, comp. "Dealers: A List of 'China-men,' Their Customers and Associates in 17th, 18th and 19th Century Britain and Abroad." *Northern Ceramic Society*, November 2023.

Hitchcock, Tim, Robert Shoemaker, Clive Emsley, Sharon Howard, and Jamie McLaughlin, et al. *The Old Bailey Proceedings Online, 1674–1913*. Version 9.0. Autumn 2023. www.oldbaileyonline.org.

Janssen, Door Mirjam. "De Sterke Vrouw Achter Willem V." *Historisch Nieuwsblad*, July/August 2013, 68–76.

Jonge, C. H. de. "Hollandse Tegelkamers in Duitse en Franse Kastelen: Uit de Eerste Helft van de 18e Eeuw." *Nederlands Kunsthistorisch Jaarboek (NKJ) / Netherlands Yearbook for History of Art* 10 (1959): 125–209.

Kowaleski-Wallace, Beth. "Women, China, and Consumer Culture in Eighteenth-Century England." *Eighteenth-Century Studies* 29, no. 2 (1995): 153–167.

Marryat, Joseph. *Collections Towards a History of Pottery and Porcelain, in the 15th, 16th, 17th, and 18th Centuries*. John Murray, 1850.

McLoud, Bet. "Horace Walpole's Ceramics at Strawberry Hill." *International Ceramics Fair and Seminar Handbook*. London, 1995, 28–35.

The Metropolitan Museum of Art. *Pottery and Porcelain: Handbook for the Use of Visitors Examining Pottery and Porcelain in the Metropolitan Museum of Art*. 1875.

Oczko, Piotr and Jan Pluis. "Dutch Tiles in Poland: A Short Survey." *CODARTfeatures*. September 2016. https://www.codart.nl/feature/curators-project/dutch-tiles-in-poland-a-short-survey/.

Outcalt, Leela. "Elizabeth Robins Pennell's Cookery Book: A Symphony in the Gender Politics of Nineteenth-Century Dining." *Nineteenth Century* 40, no. 2 (Fall 2020): 3–11.

Palliser, Mrs. Bury. *The China Collector's Pocket Companion*. S. Low, Marston, Low & Searle, 1874.

Pennell, Elizabeth Robins. *The Feasts of Autolycus: The Diary of a Greedy Woman*. J. Lane; The Merriam Co., 1896.

Pierson, Stacey. *Collectors, Collections and Museums: The Field of Chinese Ceramics in Britain, 1560–1960*. Peter Lang, 2007.

Pol, Lotte van de. *Wilhelmina of Prussia*, in: *Digital Women's Lexicon of the Netherlands*. Accessed January 13, 2014. https://resources.huygens.knaw.nl/vrouwenlexicon/lemmata/data/WilhelminavanPruisen.

Prime, William Cowper. *Pottery and Porcelain of All Times and All Nations, With tables of factory and artist's marks for the use of collectors*. Harper & Brothers, 1878.

Richards, Sarah. *Eighteenth-Century Ceramics: Products for a Civilised Society*. Manchester University Press; St. Martin's Press, 1999.

Schreiber, Charlotte, Lady. *Lady Charlotte Schreiber's Journals: Confidences of a Collector of Ceramics and Antiques Throughout Britain, France, Holland, Belgium, Spain, Portugal, Turkey, Austria and Germany from the Year 1869–1885*. John Lane, 1911.

Sloboda, Stacey. "Displaying Materials: Porcelain and Natural History in the Duchess of Portland's Museum." *Eighteenth-Century Studies* 43, no. 4 (2010): 455–472. http://www.jstor.org/stable/40864418.

Slosson, Annie Trumbull. *The China Hunters Club*. Harper & Brothers, 1878.

Steele, Richard. *The Spectator*, no. 336, Wednesday, March 26, 1712.

Tleunissen, Hans. "Dutch Tiles in the 18th Century Ottoman Baroque-Rococo Interiors: Hünkâr Sofası and Hünkâr Hamamı." *Sanat Tarihi Dergisi* 18, no. 2 (October 2009): 71–135.

Toppin, Aubrey J. "The China Trade and Some London Chinamen." *English Ceramic Circle Transactions* 1, no. 3 (1935): 37–56.

Tufan, Ömür. "Topkapi Sarayi Avrupa Porselenleri Koleksiyonu." *Milli Saraylar Sanat Tarih Mimarlık Dergisi*, sy. 23 (Aralık 2022): 128–159.

Vignon, Charlotte, et al. *Duveen Brothers and the Market for Decorative Arts, 1880–1940*. The Frick Collection, in association with GILES, an imprint of D Giles Limited, 2019.

Walpole, Horace. *A Description of the Villa of Horace Walpole, Youngest Son of Sir Robert Walpole, Earl of Orford, at Strawberry-Hill, near Twickenham: With an Inventory of the Furniture, Pictures, Curiosities, &C*. Strawberry-Hill. Thomas Kirgate, 1774.

Walsh, Claire. "Shop Design and the Display of Goods in Eighteenth-Century London." *Journal of Design History* 8, no. 3 (1995): 157–176. http://www.jstor.org/stable/1316030.

Westgarth, Mark. *SOLD! The Great British Antiques Story*. CreateSpace Independent Publishing Platform, 2019.

Weston, Rachel. "Old Blue China." *Boston Cooking-School Magazine* 13, no. 6 (January 1909): 259–264.

Wheeler, Walter. "'Once Adorned With Quaint Dutch Tiles . . .': A Preliminary Analysis of Delft Tiles Found in Archaeological Contexts and Historical Collections in the Upper Hudson Valley." In *Soldiers, Cities, and Landscapes: Papers in Honor of Charles L. Fisher*, edited by Penelope Ballard Drooker and John P. Hart. The University of the State of New York, The State Education Department, 2010.

Wills, Geoffrey. "Ceramic Causerie: Women China Dealers." *Apollo Magazine* LXV, no. 385 (March, 1957): 103.

Young, Jennie J. *The Ceramic Art: A Compendium of the History and Manufacture of Pottery and Porcelain.* Harper & Brothers, 1878.

Chapter Seven: Dames

Bankoff, H. A., C. A. Winter, and C. Ricciardi. "Excavations at the Van Cortlandt Mansion 1990–1992." archeology report, New York Landmark Preservation Commission, 1992.

Cadou, Carol Borchert, et al. *The Mount Vernon Ladies' Association: 150 Years of Restoring George Washington's Home.* Edited by Stephen A. McLeod. Foreword by Cokie Roberts. Mount Vernon Ladies' Association, 2010.

Centennial Exhibition. *First[-second] Annual Report of the Women's Centennial Executive Committee.* J.P. Lippincott & Co., 1874–75.

Cooper, Carolyn C., and Robert B. Gordon. Review of *"Sam and Elizabeth: Legend and Legacy of Colt's Empire": An Exhibition Review*, by William Hosley. *Winterthur Portfolio* 32, no. 4 (1997): 275–284. http://www.jstor.org/stable/1215194.

Cordato, Mary Frances. "Toward a New Century: Women and the Philadelphia Centennial Exhibition, 1876." *The Pennsylvania Magazine of History and Biography* 107, no. 1 (1983): 113–135. http://www.jstor.org/stable/20091742.

Curinier, C. E. *Dictionnaire national des contemporains: contenant les notices des membres de l'Institut de France, du gouvernement et du Parlement français, de l'Académie de médecine, et de toutes les personnalités vivantes, françaises ou demeurant en France, qui se sont fait connaitre par leur action dans les lettres, les sciences, les arts, la politique, l'armée, les cultes, l'industrie, l'administration, etc.* Vol. V. Office général d'édition, 1899–1905.

Daalen, A.P.A. van. *Van Stadhuistoren naar het wapen van savoye, Lotgevallen van het archief van Delft.* Gemeentelijke Archiefdienst Delft, 1984.

de Forest, L. E. *The Van Cortlandt Family.* Historical Publication Society, 1930.

Donck, Adriaen van der. *A Description of New Netherland.* Ed. Charles T. Gehring and William A. Starna. Translated by Diederik Willem Goedhuys. Foreword by Russell Shorto. University of Nebraska Press, 2008.

Ferris, Mary Lanman (Mrs. Morris Patterson Ferris). *Van Cortlandt Mansion: Erected 1748 Now in the custody of the Colonial Dames of the State of New York.* De Vinne Press, 1897.

Gillespie, Mrs. E. D. *A Book of Remembrance.* J.B. Lippincott Company, 1901.

Granston III, David W. "Memory, Materiality, and Meaning: Hartford's Church of the Good Shepherd." *Nineteenth Century* 40, no. 1 (Spring 2020): 2–13.

Haan, David de, and Femke Diercks. "Leonaert Bramer and Delftware: Additions and Missing Links." *The Rijksmuseum Bulletin* 71, no. 2 (2023): 127–135. https://www.jstor.org/stable/27223408.

Higginson, J. H. "Dame Schools." *British Journal of Educational Studies* 22, no. 2 (1974): 166–181.

Hosley, William. *Colt: The Making of an American Legend.* University of Massachusetts Press; Wadsworth Atheneum, 1996.

Matthews, Catharine Van Cortlandt. *Historical Sketch of the Van Cortlandt House: Prepared for the Society of Colonial Dames of the State of New York.* National Society of Colonial Dames in the State of New York, 1903.

Nash, Gary B. *First City: Philadelphia and the Forging of Historical Memory.* University of Pennsylvania Press, 2006.

National Society of the Colonial Dames of America. *The National Society of the Colonial Dames of America: Its Beginnings, Its Purpose and a Record of Its Work, 1891–1913.* New York, 1913.

Oldschool, Oliver. "New-York Historical Society." *The Port Folio.* New Series 3, no. 1 (January 1810): 245–247.

Ricciardi, C. *From Private to Public: The Changing Landscape of Van Cortlandt Park; Bronx, New York in the Nineteenth Century.* MA Thesis, Syracuse University, 1997.

Stillman, P. Gordon. *One Hundred Years in New York: The Story of the First Century of The National Society of Colonial Dames in the State of New York.* The National Society of Colonial Dames in the State of New York, 1996.

United States Centennial Commission. *International Exposition: Official Catalogue.* Vols. 1–4. J.R. Nagle and Company, 1876.

Wheaton, Robert. "Motley and the Dutch Historians." *The New England Quarterly* 35, no. 3 (1962): 318–336. https://doi.org/10.2307/363823.

Williams, Susan Reynolds. *Alice Morse Earle and the Domestic History of Early America.* University of Massachusetts Press, 2013.

Wyman, Andrea. "The Earliest Early Childhood Teachers: Women Teachers of America's Dame Schools." *Young Children* 50, no. 2 (1995): 29–32.

Chapter Eight: Met Wives

Ashby, Anna Lou. "Julia Parker Wightman." In *Grolier 2000: A Further Grolier Club Biographical Retrospective in Celebration of the Millennium 2000.* The Grolier Club, 2000.

Avery, C. Louise. "English Earthenwares: The Carter Collection." *The Metropolitan Museum of Art Bulletin*, New Series 4, no. 3 (November 1945): 84–86.

Berman, Avis. *Rebels on Eighth Street: Juliana Force and the Whitney Museum of American Art.* Atheneum, 1990.

Biornbaum, Charles A., and Stephanie S. Foell, eds. *Shaping the American Landscape: New Profiles from the Pioneers of American Landscape Design Project.* Charlottesville: University of Virginia Press, 2009.

Brown, Sally B. "A Gift of Sound: The Crosby Brown Collection of Musical Instruments." *Metropolitan Museum of Art Bulletin* 76, no. 1 (Summer 2018): 4–47.

Diercks, Femke. "Decorative Arts in the Rijksmuseum: The Collections and Their Collectors." *CODARTfeatures*, October 2013. https://www.codart.nl/feature/curators-collection/decorative-arts-in-the-rijksmuseum-the-collections-and-their-collectors/.

Hall, Edward Hagaman. *The Hudson-Fulton Celebration, 1909, the Fourth Annual Report of the Hudson-Fulton Celebration Commission to the Legislature of the State of New York.* 2 vols. J.B. Lyon Company for the State of New York, 1910.

Hammer Galleries, New York. *Art Objects and Furnishings from the William Randolph Hearst Collection, Catalogue Raisonné Comprising Illustrations of Representative Works Together with Comprehensive Descriptions of Books, Autographs and Manuscripts and Complete Index.* Hammer Galleries, 1941.

Howe, Winifred E. *A History of The Metropolitan Museum of Art, with a Chapter on the Early Institutions of Art in New York.* The Metropolitan Museum of Art, 1913.

Hudson-Fulton Celebration Commission. *Hudson-Fulton Celebration A Collection of the Catalogues issued by the Museums and Institutions in New York City and Vicinity.* The Trow Press, 1910.

Kathrens, Michael C. *Great Houses of New York, 1880–1930.* Acanthus Press, 2005.

Lockwood, Alice. *Gardens of Colony and State. Gardens and Gardeners of the American Colonies and of the Republic Before 1840.* 2 vol. Scribner's, 1931 & 1934.

Manas, Arnaud. *La galerie dorée de la Banque de France: quatre siècles d'art, d'histoire et de pouvoir.* Réunion des Musées Nationaux, 2018.

Mayor, A. Hyatt. "The Gifts That Made the Museum." *The Metropolitan Museum of Art Bulletin* 16, no. 3 (1957): 85–107. https://doi.org/10.2307/3257714.

Ozment, Kate. *The Hroswitha Club and the Impact of Women Book Collectors.* Cambridge University Press, 2023.

Parke-Bernet Galleries Inc., New York. *XVII & XVIII Century American Furniture and Paintings: The Celebrated Collection Formed by the Late Mr & Mrs Luke Vincent Lockwood May 13, 14, 15, 1954.* Parke-Bernet Galleries Inc., 1954. Auction catalogue.

Parsons, Samuel Jr. *The Art of Landscape Architecture.* Reprint of the 1915 edition, with a new introduction by Francis R. Kowsky. ASLA Centennial Reprint Series. University of Massachusetts Press in association with Library of American Landscape History, 2009.

Peck, Amelia. "Robert de Forest and the Founding of the American Wing." *The Magazine ANTIQUES* 157, no. 1 (January 2000): 176–181.

Ricciardi, C. *From Private to Public: The Changing Landscape of Van Cortlandt Park; Bronx, New York in the Nineteenth Century*. MA Thesis, Syracuse University, 1997.

Ryskamp, Charles. "The Ladies God Bless Them." The Grolier Club, 2007.

U.S. Congress. House Committee on Banking and Financial Services. *Restitution of Holocaust Assets: Hearings before the Committee on Banking and Financial Services, U.S. House of Representatives, One Hundred Sixth Congress, Second Session, February 9, 10, 2000*. Statement of Charlotte E. van Rappard-Boon, Chief Inspector for Cultural Heritage, Ministry of Education, Culture and Science of the Netherlands. Serial no. 106-44. U.S. Government Printing Office, 2000.

Van Cortlandt, C. M. *Historical Sketch of the Van Cortlandt House*. Society of Colonial Dames in the State of New York, 1903.

Vanderbilt, Arthur T., II. *Fortune's Children: The Fall of the House of Vanderbilt*. William Morrow and Company, Inc., 1989.

Yarnall, James L. "Souvenirs of Splendor: John La Farge and the Patronage of Cornelius Vanderbilt II." *American Art Journal* 26, no. 1/2 (1994): 67–105. https://doi.org/10.2307/1594594.

Chapter Nine: Vessels

Bankoff, H. Arthur, Frederick A. Winter, and Christophe Ricciardi. "Archaeological Excavations at Van Cortlandt Park, The Bronx, 1990–1992." New York City Landmarks Preservation Commission, 1992.

Van Cortlandt House Museum, Van Cortlandt Park, City of New York. The National Society of Colonial Dames in the State of New York, 1973.

Notes

A blue-and-white *woordenlijst*

"It will be necessary as we proceed . . ." Young, *The Ceramic Art: A Compendium of the History and Manufacture of Pottery and Porcelain*, 48.

"Delft porcelyne" van Aken-Fehmers, et al., *Delfts Aardewerk, Geschiedenis van een Nationaal Product: Vazen met Tuiten, 300 Jaar Pronkstukken*, 9.

"Between 1602–1682, at least 3.2 million pieces of Chinese and Japanese porcelain were imported . . ." Shulsky, "Kensington and de Voorst: Two Porcelain Collections," 47.

"vases with spouts" van Aken-Fehmers, et al., *Delfts Aardewerk, Geschiedenis van een Nationaal Product: Vazen met Tuiten, 300 Jaar Pronkstukken*, 9.

Introduction

"and the enthusiasm of Holland Mania . . ." Stott, *Holland Mania*, 11.

Chapter One: *Delven*

"delven" Instituut voor de Nederlandse Taal, *Woordenboek der Nederlandsche Taal*, accessed March 1, 2024, https://ivdnt.org/woordenboeken/zoeken-in-woordenboeken/?w=delven.

". . . cofounder of the Washington Antiques Show . . ." Jean M. White, "Antiques Show: In the Midst of Temptation," *The Washington Post*, January 10, 1977.

". . . was a modernist . . ." Adam Berstein, "Jane Suydam; D.C. Socialite, Founder of Spiritual Group," *The Washington Post*, April 29, 2008.

". . . in a former fire station by the water's edge . . ." "Designs Art Center in R.I.," *The Gettysburg Times*, July 3, 1959.

". . . we love to contemplate blue . . ." Johann Wolfgang von Goethe, *Theory of Colours*, trans. Charles Lock Eastlake (John Murray, 1840), 311.

". . . a colour noble, beautiful, and perfect beyond all other colours." Cennino Cennini, *The Book of the Art of Cennino Cennini: A Contemporary Practical Treatise of Quattrocento Painting*, trans. C. Jane Powell Herringham (G. Allen, 1899), 47.

"Kobold" Jacob Grimm and Wilhelm Grimm, *Deutsches Wörterbuch*, Contributions by Moriz Heyne, Rudolf Hildebrand, Friedrich Ludwig Karl Weigand, and Matthias von Lexer. (Leipzig: Verlag von S. Hirzel, 1868) s.v. "kobold."

"The Old English word *hwit* . . ." *Oxford English Dictionary*, s.v. "white (adj. & n.), Etymology," accessed May 11, 2024, https://doi.org/10.1093/OED/6030926928.

"whiteness is the usual color of light." Isaac Newton, "A Letter of Mr. Isaac Newton . . . Containing His New Theory about Light and Colors," *Philosophical Transactions of the Royal Society*, no. 80 (February 19, 1672): 3083, https://www.newtonproject.ox.ac.uk/view/texts/normalized/NATP00006.

"For those colours which you mean should appear beautiful" John Francis Rigaud, "Leonardo Da Vinci," in *A Treatise on Painting, by Leonardo Da Vinci. Faithfully Translated from the Original Italian, and Now First Digested Under Proper Heads* (J.B. Nichols and Son, 1835), 131.

". . . not objective spectators." Saarinen, *The Proud Possessors,* xix.

Chapter Two: Shop Daughter

"The women of Holland are verie faire" Guicciardini, *Descrittione di tutti Paesi Bassi*, [n.p.].

"Winkeldochter (f)" Willem Sewel, *Groot Woordenboek der Nederduytsche en Engelsche*, (De Weduwe van Steven Swart by de Beurs, 1708), s.v. "Winkeldochter."

"schryf pen" Willem Sewel, *Groot Woordenboek der Nederduytsche en Engelsche* (De Weduwe van Steven Swart by de Beurs, 1708), s.v. "schryf pen."

"rightly called a low country . . ." van Berkhey, *Natural History of Holland, Part 2*, 2.

"Our enemy the sea never rests . . ." Paul Wagret, *Polderlands* (Methuen, 1968), 82.

"Various ideas, and not infrequently completely unfounded opinions . . ." van Berkhey, *Natural History of Holland, Part 2*, 241.

"exceptionally good at repelling the damp exhalation of the soil . . ." van Berkhey, *Natural History of Holland, Part 2*, 241–242.

"a goodly large town wel built thrughout . . ." Guicciardini, *Descrittione di tutti Paesi Bassi*, 64.

"a most sweet town . . ." Pepys, Samuel, *The Diary of Samuel Pepys: Daily Entries from the 17th Century London Diary*, Dev. Phil Gyford, https://www.pepysdiary.com/diary/1660/05/18/.

"Tis very observable here, more Women are in the Shops . . ." Montague, *The Delights of Holland,* 183.

"The Women governe all . . ." Guicciardini, *Descrittione di tutti Paesi Bassi,* [n.p.].

"Nothing is more frequent than for little girls . . ." Moryson, *An Itinerary Written by Fynes Moryson Gent.*, 288.

"Upon the Mothers death the children may compel their father . . ." Moryson, *An Itinerary Written by Fynes Moryson Gent.*, 288.

"Not too sweet, not too sour" Jacob Cats, *Houwelyck* (1625), [n.p].

"De man moet op de straet on sijnen handel gaen . . ." Martha Moffitt Peacock, "Early Modern Dutch Women in the City: The Imaging of Economic Agency and Power," in *Urban Space in the Middle Ages and the Early Modern Age*, ed. Albrecht Classen (Walter de Gruyter, 2009), 668.

"Between 1700 and 1794, of the 8,340 seamen departing from Delft" Jan Lucassen, "A Multinational and Its Labor Force: The Dutch East India Company, 1595–1795," *International Labor and Working-Class History*, no. 66 (2004): 15, http://www.jstor.org/stable/2767295.

"thus enabling them to earn an honest living . . ." van Berkhey, *Natuurlyke Historie van Holland*, vol. 3, 1321.

". . . place their daughters in a merchant's shop . . ." van Berkhey, *Natuurlyke Historie van Holland*, vol. 3, 1321.

"born and bred in Holland . . ." Benjamin Franklin, *Autobiography of Benjamin Franklin*, ed. by John Bigelow (J. B. Lippincott & Co.; Trübner & Co., 1868), 238–239.

"some Maids are ingenious . . ." Anna Maria van Schurman, *The Learned Maid, or, Whether a Maid May Be a Scholar*, (London: Printed by John Redmayne, 1659), 2.

"By 1650, approximately 70 percent of Amsterdam bridegrooms and 50 percent of brides were able to sign their names in marriage records . . ." Erika Kuijpers, "Lezen en Schrijven: Onderzoek naar het Alfabetiseringsniveau in de Zeventiende-Eeuws Amsterdam," *Tijdschrift voor Sociale Geschiedenis*, no. 4 (1997): 507.

"the *Carryers of the World*." Daniel Defoe, *Plan of the English Commerce: Being a Compleat Prospect of the Trade of this Nation, as well the Home Trade as the Foreign. In Three Parts*, (Printed for Charles Rivington, 1728), 192.

"of every sort and kind." Peter Borschberg, "The Seizure of the Sta. Catarina Revisited: The Portuguese Empire in Asia, VOC Politics and the Origins of the Dutch-Johor Alliance (1602–c.1616)," *Journal of Southeast Asian Studies* 33, no. 1 (2002): 38.

"the great mortality among the porcelain makers." Stephen Little, "Economic Change in Seventeenth-Century China and Innovations at the

Jingdezhen Kilns," *Ars Orientalis* 26 (1996): 47–54, http://www.jstor.org/stable/4629498.

"Envy of some, the Fear of others . . ." William Temple, *Observations upon the United Provinces of the Netherlands* (A. Maxwell for Sa. Gellibrand, 1673), [page unnumbered].

"Finally, a shop of Delft earthenware is visited . . ." G. J. Hoogewerff, *De Twee Reizen van Cosimo de' Medici, Prins van Toscane, Door de Nederlanden, 1667–1669* (Amsterdam: Johannes Müller, 1919), 177.

"Si vedono con amirazione le majoliche . . ." G. J. Hoogewerff, *De Twee Reizen van Cosimo de' Medici, Prins van Toscane, Door de Nederlanden, 1667–1669* (Johannes Müller, 1919), 236.

"Seventhly, The education of their Children . . ." Josiah Child, *Brief Observations Concerning Trade and Interest of Money* (Printed for Elizabeth Calvert at the Black-Spread Eagle in Barbican, and Henry Mortlock at the Sign of the White-Heart in Westminster Hall, 1668), 4.

Chapter Three: The Delft Thunderclap

"One spark, one moment destroys a city . . ." Hendrick Rintjus, *Klioos stall, 1*, (1656), 57, https://www.dbnl.org/tekst/_kli001klio01_01/_kli001klio01_01_0023.php.

"It is the feet of clay . . ." Oscar Wilde, *The Picture of Dorian Gray* (Vintage Books, 2011), 158.

"Baptized in Delft . . ." DTB, inv. nr. 55, doopboeken Nieuwe Kerk, 3-12-1627.

"behind the Nieuwe Kerk . . ." DTB, inv. nr. 2574, 28-09-1650.

"By December 29, 1670, the property, known as De Drie Klokken . . ." ONA 1956, fol. 96, 29-12-1670 (Not. J. J. van Ophoven).

"September 28, 1650, at the age of twenty-five, Barbara was married . . ." DTB, inv. nr. 2574, 28-09-1650.

"highly esteemed . . ." Havard, *Histoire de la Faïence de Delft, Seconde Partie*, 262.

"compensation for those whose homes had been damaged . . ." Stadsarchief Delft (1654), *Lijsten van personen die schade hebben geleden, per kwartier, met totaallijst*, In *Archieven van het stadsbestuur van Delft,* (1222) 1246–1813 (1853) (Inventory number 2065). Accessed on May 5, 2023, from https://zoeken.stadsarchiefdelft.nl/detail.php?nav_id=35-3&id=10344417.

"On October 10, 1707, nearly a half century after the Delft Thunderclap struck their city . . ." ONA, inv. nr. 2541, fol. 168 (not. C. Gravesande) 10-10-1707.

"As For the art off Painting . . ." *The Travels of Peter Mundy in Europe and Asia, 1608–1667*, vol. 4, ed. R. C. Temple and L. M. Anstey (London: The Hakluyt Society, 1925), 70.

Chapter Four: *Weduwes*

"Their was not Widdow, Wife, or Maid . . ." *Hogan-Moganides: or, the Dutch Hudibras*, (Printed for William Cademan [etc.], 1674), 27.

"Yet, just two years after . . ." DTB, inv. nr. 14.46, fol. 303v., begraafboek Oude en Nieuwe Kerk, 7-5-1703, https://hdl.handle.net/21.12115/NL-DtAD21849859.

"weduwe" Willem Sewel, *Groot Woordenboek der Nederduytsche en Engelsche*, (De Weduwe van Steven Swart by de Beurs, 1708), s.v. "Weduwe."

"very large and airy room . . ." Bleyswijck, *Beschryvinge der Stadt Delft*, 646.

"Johanna was one of four children" DTB, inv.nr. 14.11, doopboek Oude en Nieuwe Kerk, 25-4-1668.

"she died at the age of seventy years old . . ." DTB, inv.nr. 14.49, begraafboek Oude en Nieuwe Kerk, 15-6-1736.

"all those earning their living here . . ." Montias, *Artists and Artisans in Delft*, 350.

"fines and punishments." Montias, *Artists and Artisans in Delft*, 350.

"With the exception and on the understanding . . ." Montias, *Artists and Artisans in Delft*, 363.

"*Chineejche manier van verlakkin*" Simon Witgeest, *Het Natuurlyk Tover-boek, of 't Nieuw Speel-toneel der Konsten* (Jan Claesz ten Hoorn, 1686), 493.

"doth incourage their Husbands to hold on in their Trades" Josiah Child, *Brief Observations Concerning Trade and Interest of Money* (Printed for Elizabeth Calvert at the Black-Spread Eagle in Barbican, and Henry Mortlock at the Sign of the White-Heart in Westminster Hall, 1668), 5.

Chapter Five: Queen of Blue-and-White

"She strikes the Rock . . ." Thomas Rymer, *A Poem on the Arrival of Queen Mary, February the 12th, 1689* (Awnsham Churchill, 1689), 3.

"The Queen brought in the custom or humour . . ." Daniel Defoe, *A Tour Through the Whole Island of Great Britain*, abridged and edited by P. N. Furbank and W. R. Owens, picture research by A. J. Coulson (Yale University Press, 1991), 65.

"looks Like a little town ye buildings runn so great a Length on ye ground . . ." Celia Fiennes, *Through England on Side Saddle in the Time of William and Mary, Being the Diary of Celia Fiennes*, (Field & Tuer; The Leadenhall Press; Simpkin, Marshall & Co.; Hamilton, Adams & Co.; Scribner & Welford, 1888), 47.

"very nice thing, in the parterres" Constantijn Huygens Jr., *The Diary of Constantijn Huygens Jr: Secretary to Stadholder-King William of Orange*, selected and translated by Rudolf Dekker (Panchaud, 2015), 229.

"the pleasantest little Thing within Doors that could possibly be made" Daniel Defoe, *A Tour Through the Whole Island of Great Britain*, abridged and edited by P. N. Furbank and W. R. Owens, picture research by A. J. Coulson (Yale University Press, 1991), 72.

"with great pleasure play[ing] with his little girle . . ." Samuel Pepys, *The Diary of Samuel Pepys: Daily Entries from the 17th Century London Diary*, dev. Phil Gyford, https://www.pepysdiary.com/diary/1664/09/12/.

"October 21st, 1677—The Duke of York din'd at Whitehall . . ." *Diary of Dr. Edward Lake, Archdeacon and Prebendary of Exeter, Chaplain and Tutor to the Princesses Mary and Anne, Daughters of the Duke of York, Afterwards James the Second, in the Years 1677—1678*, edited by George Percy Elliot (The Camden Society, 1847), 5.

"a small cool room very pleasant in summer where there is an abundance of china;" Lambooy, ed., *Koninklijk Blauw: Het Mooiste Delfts Aardewerk van Willem en Mary/ Delfts Aardewerk. Geschiedenis van een Nationaal Product,* 60.

"To preserve the fruit-marrow of Cherries, Plums, Apricots . . ." Rose, *The Sensible Cook* (Syracuse University Press, 1989), 103.

"was so far from being fond of great Dainties . . ." Anonymous, *The Royal Diary: The Third Edition*, (Printed for John Marshall, 1705), 3.

"fill'd with this china and every other place, where it could be plac'd, with advantage." Daniel Defoe, *A Tour Through the Whole Island of Great Britain*, abridged and edited by P. N. Furbank and W. R. Owens, picture research by A. J. Coulson (Yale University Press, 1991), 72.

"I do certify there is due unto Adrianus Koex . . ." Michael Archer, "Dutch Delft at the Court of William and Mary," *The International Ceramic Fair and Seminar Handbook* (1984), 19.

"where I had led "a life so suitable to my humour . . ." *Memoirs of Mary, Queen of England (1689–1693), Together with Her Letters and Those of King James II and William III to the Electress, Sophia of Hanover,* edited by Dr. R. Doebner (Veit & Comp.; D. Nutt, 1886), 4.

Chapter Six: China-Women to China Hunters

"*China's the passion of her soul . . .*" *John Gay, To a Lady on Her Passion for Old China, 1725* (Clarendon Press, 1925), 19.

"A true china hunter will drive for days through the country . . ." Alice Morse Earle, "A China Hunter in New England," *Scribner's Magazine* 10 (1891): 357.

"This morning an over-drove bullock rushed into the China shop of Miss Powell . . ." *Lloyd's Evening Post* (London, England), issue 2453, part I, March 19–22, 1773.

"Chi'na, n.s." *A Dictionary of the English Language*, by Samuel Johnson, 1755, accessed March 1, 2024, https://johnsonsdictionaryonline.com/1755/china_ns.

"Delf. Delfe. n.s." *A Dictionary of the English Language*, by Samuel Johnson, 1755, accessed March 1, 2024, https://johnsonsdictionaryonline.com/1755/delf_ns.

"Their business is altogether shopkeeping . . ." Robin Hildyard, comp., "Dealers: A List of 'China-men,' Their Customers and Associates in 17th, 18th and 19th Century Britain and Abroad," *Northern Ceramic Society*, November 2023, 1.

"rich China-woman, that the courtiers visited so often" Ben Jonson, *The Workes of Benjamin Jonson* 1 (Will[iam] Stansby, 1616), 537.

"the custom or humour, as I may call it, of furnishing houses with china-ware . . ." Daniel Defoe, *A Tour Through the Whole Island of Great Britain*, abridged and edited by P. N. Furbank and W. R. Owens, picture research by A. J. Coulson (Yale University Press, 1991), 65.

"contagion of china-fancy" Samuel Johnson, *The Letters of Samuel Johnson*, ed. Bruce Redford, vol. 3 (Princeton University Press, 1992), 70–71.

"generally deal in Tea, Coffee and Chocolate." Robin Hildyard, comp., "Dealers: A List of 'China-men,' Their Customers and Associates in 17th, 18th and 19th Century Britain and Abroad," *Northern Ceramic Society*, November 2023, 1.

"I am, dear Sir, one of the top China-Women about Town" *The Spectator*, no. 336, March 26, 1712.

". . . several Houses in England, from Holland" Robin Hildyard, comp., "Dealers: A List of 'China-men,' Their Customers and Associates in 17th, 18th and 19th Century Britain and Abroad," *Northern Ceramic Society*, November 2023, 1.

"the Prisoner at the Bar came into my Shop, and asked for some enamelled China Plates . . ." *Old Bailey Proceedings,* April 1743, Alice Burk (t17430413-6).

". . . Eleanor Hine was apprehended for shoplifting several items, including a group of 'Delft plates.'" *Old Bailey Proceedings*, Eleanor, wife of Samuel Hine otherwise Eleanor Long (t17540530-30).

"From your own garden gather a bunch of late tulips . . ." Elizabeth Robins Pennell, *The Feasts of Autolycus: The Diary of a Greedy Woman* (J. Lane; The Merriam Co., 1896), 29.

"A popular speaker . . ." *The Illustrated London News*, May 31, 1884, vol. 84, no. 2354.

"We had some sport in our chasse among the shops." Lady Charlotte Schreiber, *Lady Charlotte Schreiber's Journals: Confidences of a Collector of Ceramics and Antiques Throughout Britain, France, Holland, Belgium, Spain,*

Portugal, Turkey, Austria and Germany from the Year 1869–1885 (John Lane, 1911), 81.

"went to Gouda, where we had a charming chasse . . ." Lady Charlotte Schreiber, *Lady Charlotte Schreiber's Journals: Confidences of a Collector of Ceramics and Antiques Throughout Britain, France, Holland, Belgium, Spain, Portugal, Turkey, Austria and Germany from the Year 1869–1885* (John Lane, 1911), 133–134.

"Ten years ago there were probably not ten collectors of pottery . . ." William Cowper Prime, *Pottery and Porcelain of All Times and Nations: With Tables of Factory and Artists' Marks for the Use of Collectors* (Harper and Bros., 1878), [n.p.].

"it is cheaper to buy from country homes . . ." Rachel Weston, "Old Blue China," *The Boston Cooking-School Magazine* 13 (1909): 264.

"The day was a hot one in August, but our road was full of shade and beauty . . ." Annie Trumbull Slosson, *The China Hunters Club* (Harper & Brothers, 1878), 119.

"Here in Hartford . . . the China Craze . . ." *The Hartford Daily Times*, October 17, 1877.

"It may appear to scoffing outsiders . . ." Alice Morse Earle, "A China Hunter in New England," *Scribner's Magazine*, September 1891, 357.

Chapter Seven: Dames

"The common-sense of Americans has long ago perceived . . ." *Exposition Volume, The New Century for Woman, Philadelphia, May 13th–November 11th, 1876* (Women's Centennial Committee, 1876), 4.

"In the early morning hours of January 23, 1909 . . ." "Some of Those in the Wreck," *The Sun* (New York, NY), January 24, 1909.

"Known as the "Millionaires' Ship . . ." Paul O'Brien, "Irish connections with the doomed 'Millionaires' Ship', the RMS Republic," *Irish Heritage News*, May 29, 2023.

"Speeding through the darkness on its journey from New York to the Mediterranean . . ." "Blame on Florida," *The Citizen* (Honesdale, Wayne Co., PA), January 27, 1909.

"The Companion of My China Hunts" Earle, *China Collecting in America*, dedication page.

"The SS *Florida* had departed Naples . . ." "Blame on Florida," *The Citizen* (Honesdale, Wayne Co. PA), January 27, 1909.

"Passengers were thrown from their berths . . ." "Baltic Brings Full Details of Fog Crash," *New York Times*, January 26, 1909.

"According to a local Massachusetts newspaper . . ." *The Worcester Magazine*, January–December 1909 Vol. XII, The Board of Trade Worcester, MA, 47.

"The identity of the Italian sailor . . ." "Blame on Florida," *The Citizen* (Honesdale, Penn.), January 27, 1909.

"Taken aboard the smaller SS *Florida*, its prow buckled . . ." "Florida Here; Has Three Dead," *New York Times*, January 26, 1909.

"More than five thousand New Yorkers gathered to welcome the returning ship . . ." "Rescuing Ships Safe in Port," *The Sun* (New York), January 26, 1909.

"many still dressed in nightclothes . . ." "In Scant Attire Survivors Land," *New York Times*, January 26, 1909.

"Without the aid of original records . . ." Oliver Oldschool, "New-York Historical Society," *The Port Folio*, New Series, vol. 3, no. 1 (January 1810): 246.

". . . great difficulties, especially for a foreigner unfamiliar with the Dutch language . . ." ". . .grandes difficultés, surtout pour un étranger peu familiarisé avec la langue néerlandaise et sa paléographie," Havard, *Histoire de la Faïence de Delft*, 34.

"a handsome structure, devoted entirely to the exhibit of women's work, and is in charge of alternate committees of women . . ." *Visitors' Guide to the Centennial Exhibition and Philadelphia* (J.B. Lippincott & Co., ca. 1875), 21.

"be extremely circumspect in all your behavior . . ." Gillespie, *A Book of Remembrance*, 18–19.

"Two table napkins spun by Her Majesty and etchings" United States Centennial Commission, *International Exposition: Official Catalogue, 1–4* (J.R. Nagle and Company, 1876), 98.

"three colored photographs . . ." *Souvenir of the Centennial Exhibition: or, Connecticut's Representation at Philadelphia, 1876* (George D. Curtis, 1877), 132.

"the women of the whole country were working not only for patriotic motives . . ." Gillespie, *A Book of Remembrance,* 313.

". . . there was not the slightest allusion to the work the women . . ." Gillespie, *A Book of Remembrance,* 372.

"imperial wizard, the arch-tycoon," Gary B. Nash, *First City: Philadelphia and the Forging of Historical Memory* (University of Pennsylvania Press, 2006), 272.

"patriotic, historic, and educational purposes to perpetuate the memory and the spirit of the men and women . . ." "Congressional Record-House, May 18, 1896," *Congressional Record: The Proceedings and Debates, Fifty-Fourth Congress, First Session*, vol. 28 (Washington, D.C.: Government Printing Office, 1896), 5366.

"The Colonial Dames Waltzes," *The Ladies' Home Journal* 13, no. 5 (April 1896), 12–13.

"From private breakfasts at Sherry's . . ." "Colonial Dames Give a Breakfast: Olden Days Revived by the Descendants of the Early Dutch Settlers," *The Journal* (New York), March 13, 1896.

"the crème de la crème of New York society," "Get Out Your Blue China: Here is a Find that Makes it Very Valuable, 3,000 Dutch Wills Unearthed," *The Journal* (New York), March 8, 1896.

"lectures on "Colonial Architecture . . ." "About Colonial Architecture: Prof. Ware Gives a Lecture Before the Colonial Dames," *New York Times*, March 5, 1895.

"Some mountains consist solely of fuller's earth . . ." Adriaen van der Donck, *A Description of New Netherland*, ed. Charles T. Gehring and William A. Starna, trans. Diederik Willem Goedhuys, foreword by Russell Shorto (University of Nebraska Press, 2008), 41.

"In late April 1895, Justine Van Rensselaer Townsend boarded a train . . ." "Work of the Colonial Dames: Conversion of the Van Cortlandt Mansion into a Museum of Colonial History," *New York Times*, April 4, 1897.

"An act authorizing the board of park commissioners of the city of New York to transfer the custody of the Van Cortlandt mansion" Journal of the Senate of the State of New York at Their One Hundred and Nineteenth Session, vol. 2 (Albany and New York: Wynkoop Hallenbeck Crawford Co., 1896), 2031.

"The general aptitude for trading and business . . ." Alice Morse Earle, "Delft Ware," *The House Beautiful* 3, no. 4 (March 1898): 114.

Chapter Eight: Met Wives

"Think of it . . ." Howe, *A History of The Metropolitan Museum of Art*, 200.

"More than two hundred ladies . . ." "elaborate collation" "Mrs. Vanderbilt's Guests: A Delightful Afternoon for 200 Colonial Dames," *The New-York Tribune*, March 3, 1897.

"quantities of rare china and old silver." "Mrs. Vanderbilt's Guests: A Delightful Afternoon for 200 Colonial Dames," *The New-York Tribune*, March 3, 1897.

". . . Mrs. Vanderbilt's own venerable silver teapot" "Mrs. Vanderbilt's Guests: The Colonial Dames Saw Some Rare Colonial Relics," *New York Times*, March 3, 1897.

"New Netherland Days." "In New Netherland Days," *New York Times*, March 7, 1897.

"Alice had returned to New York . . ." "Mrs. Vanderbilt's Guests: The New York Chapter of Colonial Dames to be Entertained Tuesday," *The Topeka State Journal* (Topeka, Kan.), March 5, 1897.

"renting a house in Washington, D.C." "Vanderbilts Going Away: The Head of the Family Benefited by the Washington Climate," *The Washington Post,* April 21, 1897.

". . . declined the invitation." Berman, *Rebels on Eighth Street*, 432.

"Historical Museum" "The Van Cortlandt House Committee's Report for the Year Ending April 4th, 1897," *Van Cortlandt Museum Committee Minute Book No. 1*, 1.

"Taking no credit for themselves . . ." "It's a Public Museum Now," *New York Times*, May 28, 1897.

"Among the guests were wives and daughters . . ." "Mrs. Vanderbilt's Guests: A Delightful Afternoon for 200 Colonial Dames," *The New-York Tribune*, March 3, 1897.

"Emma Baker Kennedy, whose husband, John Stewart Kennedy . . ." "Memorial Resolutions: In Memoriam: John Stewart Kennedy, William Mackay Laffan, Charles Stewart Smith," *The Metropolitan Museum of Art Bulletin* 5, no. 1 (1910): 2–4. http://www.jstor.org/stable/3253083.

"intimate advisor" "Mrs. Robert Hoe 3d Dead at Age of 98," *New York Times*, August 4, 1935.

". . . sisters Eleanor and Sarah Hewitt officially inaugurated their museum" "The New Cooper Union Museum," *New-York Tribune*, May 27, 1897.

". . . Harriet Mumford Campbell delivered a lecture on "table furnishings and customs" "In New Netherland Days: Table Furnishings and Customs of the Dutch," *New York Times,* March 7, 1897.

"the colonist found a fruitful country . . ." "plenty of game," "waters full of fish and oysters," "In New Netherland Days: Table Furnishings and Customs of the Dutch," *New York Times,* March 7, 1897.

"apple pies, preserved peaches and pears, always olekocks," "liked the good things of life." "In New Netherland Days: Table Furnishings and Customs of the Dutch," *New York Times,* March 7, 1897.

"over 3,000 Dutch wills and the Minutes of the Orphan Court of New Amsterdam discovered in the State Library of Albany" "Get Out Your Blue China: Here is a Find that Makes it Very Valuable, 3,000 Dutch Wills Unearthed," *The Journal* (New York*),* March 8, 1896.

"what seemed an almost hopeless task of getting the mansion renovated, swept, and garnished." "Van Cortlandt House Committee's Report for Year Ending April 4th, 1898," *Reports of Officers of The Colonial Dames of the State of New York at the Annual Meeting, April Fourth 1898, New York City* (1898), 36.

"standing gaunt, bare, despoiled, for some years." "Van Cortlandt House Committee's Report for Year Ending April 4th, 1898," *Reports of Officers* *of The Colonial Dames of the State of New York at the Annual Meeting, April Fourth 1898, New York City* (1898), 35.

"to be flung wide in welcome." "Van Cortlandt House Committee's Report for Year Ending April 4th, 1898," *Reports of Officers of The Colonial Dames of the State of New York at the Annual Meeting, April Fourth 1898, New York City* (1898), 36.

"On May 27, 1897, a "fair and breezy" day . . ." "Van Cortlandt House Committee's Report for Year Ending April 4th, 1898," *Reports of Officers of The Colonial Dames of the State of New York at the Annual Meeting, April Fourth 1898, New York City* (1898), 40.

"Although the smallest free museum in the city . . ." "New Colonial Garden," *New York Times*, August 22, 1897.

"this "treasure house"" "Colonial Dames Receive: Van Cortlandt Mansion, Now the Home of the Dames Thrown Open to Visitors," *New-York Tribune*, May 28, 1897.

"loans of furniture, pictures, curios of all kinds, illustrative of the Colonial period." "Van Cortlandt House Committee's Report for Year Ending April 4th, 1898," *Reports of Officers of The Colonial Dames of the State of New York at the Annual Meeting, April Fourth 1898, New York City* (1898), 37.

"brought forth from many an old attic and secret storeroom." "Van Cortlandt House Committee's Report for Year Ending April 4th, 1898," *Reports of Officers of The Colonial Dames of the State of New York at the Annual Meeting, April Fourth 1898, New York City* (1898), 37.

"It could be wished that works might occasionally be loaned for a season when the owners are absent" "Van Cortlandt House Committee's Report for Year Ending April 4th, 1898," *Reports of Officers of The Colonial Dames of the State of New York at the Annual Meeting, April Fourth 1898, New York City* (1898), 38–39.

"almost every member's household has contributed something from its treasured heirlooms," "Van Cortlandt House Committee's Report for Year Ending April 4th, 1898," *Reports of Officers of The Colonial Dames of the State of New York at the Annual Meeting, April Fourth 1898, New York City* (1898), 38.

"eager and curious" "Van Cortlandt House Committee's Report for Year Ending April 4th, 1898," *Reports of Officers of The Colonial Dames of the State of New York at the Annual Meeting, April Fourth 1898, New York City* (1898), 40.

". . . so difficult was it for the one police officer . . ." "Van Cortlandt House Committee's Report for Year Ending April 4th, 1898," *Reports of Officers* *of The Colonial Dames of the State of New York at the Annual Meeting, April Fourth 1898, New York City* (1898), 40.

"The hopes of the Society . . ." "Report of the Van Cortlandt House Committee," *Annual Report of the Colonial Dames of the State of New York, 1903* (1903), 31.

"the Dutch fad has been largely circulated in the fashionable world by collections of windmill china and Delftware . . ." "Get Out Your Blue China," *The Journal,* March 8, 1896.

"Loitering over the bridges . . ." "Report of the Garden and Grounds Committee, April 1903," *Annual Report of the Colonial Dames of the State of New York, 1903* (1903), 36.

"The Mother of America" Edward Bok, "The Mother of America," *The Ladies' Home Journal* 20, no. 11 (October 1903): 16.

"she had provided the funds for the Met to acquire over 100 Roman sculptures, "The Giustiniani Marbles," . . ." Edward Robinson, "The Giustiniani Marbles," *The Metropolitan Museum of Art Bulletin* 1, no. 6 (May 1906): 80–82.

"Costumes of the Colonial Period—early Dutch preferred . . ." *Minutes of the Van Cortlandt Committee, January 29, 1909.* The National Society of Colonial Dames in the State of New York. [n.p.].

"portraits of distinguished painters . . ." The Hudson-Fulton Celebration Commission, *Catalogue, Van Cortlandt House Museum for the Hudson-Fulton Celebration, September, 1909* (Irving Press, 1909), 60.

"Let us not forget . . ." "Report of the Van Cortlandt Committee," *The Colonial Dames of the State of New York Annual Report 1911, Reports of Officers and Standing Committees 1910–191* (Irving Press, 1911), 39.

"artistic and appropriate labels for exhibits . . ." "Report of the Van Cortlandt Committee," *The Colonial Dames of the State of New York Annual Report 1913, Reports of Officers and Standing Committees 1912–1913* (1913), 42.

"Its best asset has been a lesson . . ." "Report of the Van Cortlandt Committee," *The Colonial Dames of the State of New York Annual Report 1911, Reports of Officers and Standing Committees 1910–1911* (Irving Press, 1911), 37.

"Van Cortlandt, he assures us, can now be made a unique museum. Other museums began before classifying was understood . . ." "Report of the Van Cortlandt Committee," *The Colonial Dames of the State of New York Annual Report 1913, Reports of Officers and Standing Committees 1912–1913* (1913), 57.

"From the small beginnings . . ." "Preliminary Report of the Committee Appointed to Raise an Endowment Fund," *The Colonial Dames of the*

State of New York Annual Report 1914, Reports of Officers and Standing Committees 1913–1914 (1914), 78.

"The work of this society, which offers to the public a museum . . ." "Report of the Recording Secretary," *The Colonial Dames of the State of New York Annual Report 1911, Reports of Officers and Standing Committees 1910–1911* (Irving Press, 1911), 12.

"In 1913 the museum hosted *Portraits, Miniatures, and Silhouettes* . . ." "Heirlooms Exposed For First Time To Public Gaze," *New York Times,* November 16, 1913.

"pretty and spritely," "Types of Fair Women," *Munsey's Magazine* 15, no. 1 (April 1896): 170–171.

"In 1915, after a deal with Charles Lang Freer fell through . . ." "Letter from Alice B. Creelman to Charles Lang Freer, 26 June 1916," and "Letter from Charles Lang Freer to Alice B. Creelman, 27 June 1916," Charles Lang Freer Papers, correspondence.

". . . she pivoted to sell Henry Clay Frick several significant pieces." "Letter from Alice Creelman to Henry Clay Frick, 15 May 1915," "Letter from [Henry Clay Frick] to Alice Creelman, 13 April 1915," "Letter from Alice Creelman to Henry Clay Frick, 15 May 1915," Henry Clay Frick Papers, correspondence.

"We have grown so large . . ." Stillman, *One Hundred Years in New York*, 58.

"As the balance was now so large . . ." *Minutes of the Van Cortlandt Committee November 21, 1934*, The National Society of Colonial Dames in the State of New York Archives, [n.p.].

"returned to the Metropolitan Museum . . ." *Minutes of the Van Cortlandt Committee November 21, 1934*, The National Society of Colonial Dames in the State of New York Archives, [n.p.].

"a keen and discriminating collector and indefatigable hunter" C. Louise Avery, "English Earthenwares: The Carter Collection," *The Metropolitan Museum of Art Bulletin*, New Series 4, no. 3 (November 1945): 84.

"In September 1942, the War Department's Civilian Protection School staged mock air raids . . ." "Army Plans Realistic Raid Show to Instruct Eastern Cities," *Salt Lake Telegram* (Salt Lake City), September 8, 1942.

"Forced to flee Amsterdam, the gallery's owner . . ." "Marcellus B. Keezer," Monuments Men and Women Foundation, https://www.monumentsmenandwomenfnd.org/keezer-marcel-b.

"a splendid collection of Dutch Delftware." *The Magazine ANTIQUES* 56, no. 2 (August 1949), [n.p.].

"bibliomaniac" Ozment, *The Hroswitha Club and the Impact of Women Book Collectors*, 66.

"hoodlum haven" John Sibley, "Hoover Draws Angry Response for Comment on Central Park," *New York Times*, November 20, 1964.

"the lights east of the mansion all the way to the Major Deegan Thruway have not been functioning at night . . ." *Nancy H. Walker, Chairman, to the Van Cortlandt House Museum Committee, September 27, 1964*, The National Society of Colonial Dames in the State of New York Archives, [n.p.].

Chapter Nine: Vessels

"VE'SSEL" *A Dictionary of the English Language*, by Samuel Johnson, 1755, accessed 2024/03/01, https://johnsonsdictionaryonline.com/1755/china_ns.

"Some of these breakfasts, lunches, and dinners . . ." "New Colonial Garden," *New York Times,* August 22, 1897.

Epilogue

"St. Gertrude the Great" H. C. Graef, "St. Gertrude, The Mystic of the Sacred Heart," *The Life of the Spirit (1944–1946)* 2, no. 16 (1945): 66–70, http://www.jstor.org/stable/43702595.

Index

E

W

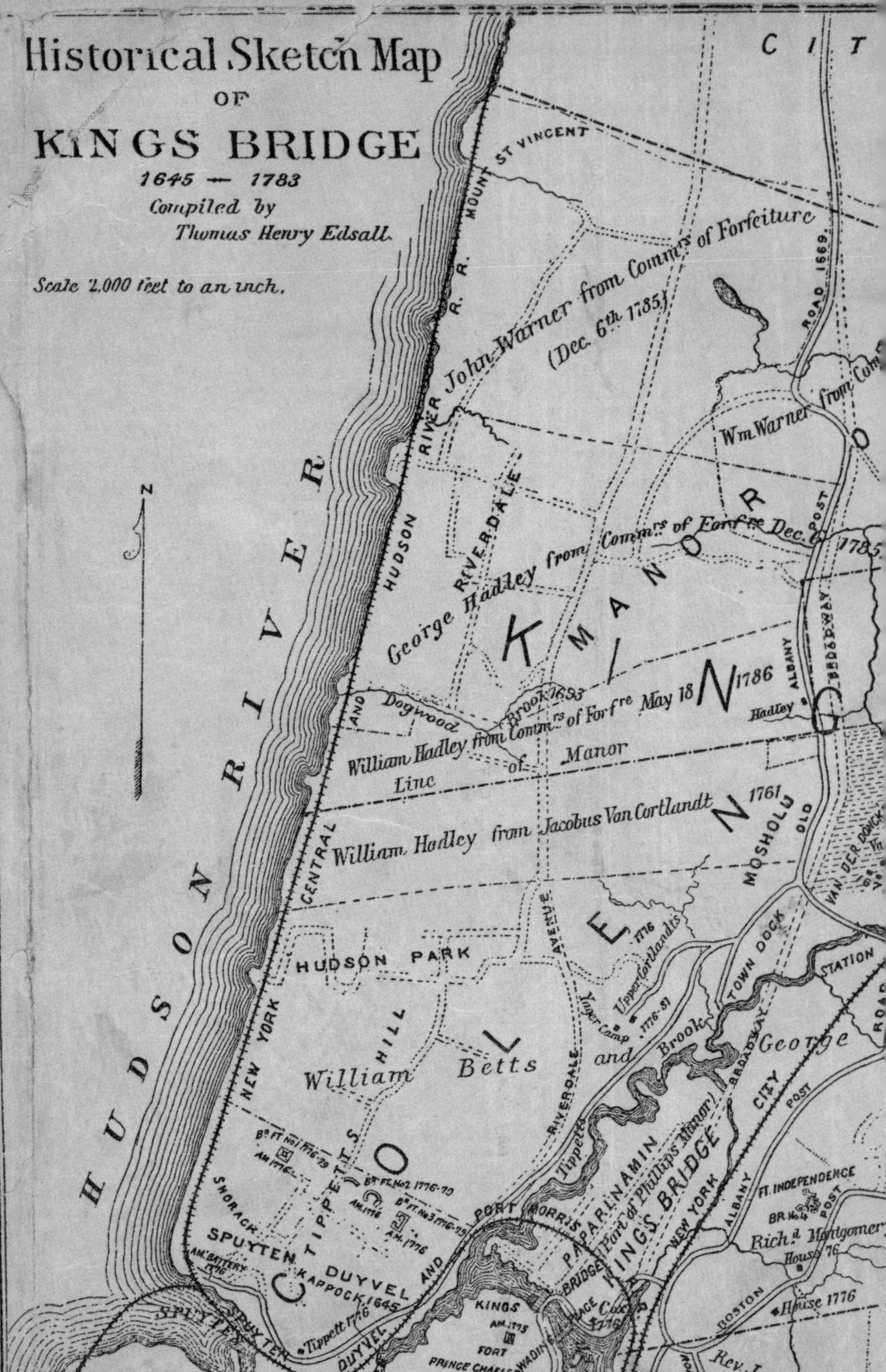

Historical Sketch Map
OF
KINGS BRIDGE
1645 — 1783
Compiled by
Thomas Henry Edsall.
Scale 2,000 feet to an inch.
N
CIT
MOUNT ST VINCENT
R. R.
John Warner from Comm.rs of Forfeiture
(Dec. 6th 1785)
ROAD 1669
Wm. Warner from Com
HUDSON RIVER
RIVERDALE
HUDSON
George Hadley from Comm.rs of Forf.re Dec. 6 1785
MANOR
POST
ALBANY
BROADWAY
K
I
N
1786
Dogwood Brook 1693
AND
William Hadley from Comm.rs of Forf.re May 18
Hadley
Line of Manor
CENTRAL
William Hadley from Jacobus Van Cortlandt
N 1761
MOSHOLU
OLD
VAN DER DONCK
AVENUE
E
1776
Upper Cortlandts
HUDSON PARK
TOWN DOCK
STATION
ROAD
Yager Camp 1776-81
NEW YORK
HILL
L
William Betts and Brook
George
BROADWAY
CITY
POST
RIVERDALE
Tippetts
TIPPETTS
O
PAPARINAMIN
(Part of Phillips Manor)
KINGS BRIDGE
NEW YORK
ALBANY
FT. INDEPENDENCE
Br. Ft. No 1 1776-79
Am. 1776
Br. Ft. No 2 1776-79
Br. Ft. No 3 1776-79
Am. 1776
Am. 1776
SHORACK
SPUYTEN DUYVEL
AND
PORT MORRIS
BR. No 4
POST
Rich.d Montgomery
House 76
Am. Battery 1776
KAPPOCK 1645
C
BRIDGE
Cox
1776
BOSTON
House 1776
SPUYTEN
SPUYTEN
Tippett 1776
DUYVEL
KINGS
Am. 1776
FORT
PRINCE CHARLES
WADING PLACE
Rev. J.